Mack, McGraw and
the 1913 Baseball Season

Library of Congress Cataloguing-in-Publication Data

Adler, Rich.
    Mack, McGraw and the 1913 baseball season / Richard Adler.
        p.   cm.
    Includes bibliographical references and index.

    ISBN 978-0-7864-3675-0
    softcover : 50# alkaline paper

    1. World Series (Baseball) (1913)   2. Philadelphia Athletics
(Baseball team) — History.   3. New York Giants (Baseball team) —
History.   I. Title.
GV878.4.A325   2008
796.357'646 — dc22   2008017258

British Library cataloguing data are available

On the cover: *top inset* Connie Mack (Library of Congress); *bottom, left
to right* Philadephia team captain Danny Murphy; umpires Cy Rigler, Bill
Klem, Rip Egan and Tom Connolly; and New York manager John McGraw
before Game One of the 1913 World Series (National Baseball Hall of Fame
Library, Cooperstown, New York)

Manufactured in the United States of America

McFarland & Company, Inc., Publishers
    Box 611, Jefferson, North Carolina 28640
    www.mcfarlandpub.com

Table of Contents

Preface   1

One.   "The Tall Tactician"   5
Two.   "The Old Oriole"   39
Three.   The American League Race   92
Four.   The National League Race   149
Five.   Athletics vs. Giants: Analysis of the Opponents   194
Six.   Game One   208
Seven.   Game Two   222
Eight.   Game Three   234
Nine.   Game Four   247
Ten.   Game Five   257

Epilogue   265
Appendix: World's Series Team Totals   297
Chapter Notes   299
Bibliography   309
Index   311

Preface

Certainly more transpired in the world of 1913, the last year of relative "peace" before the conflagration of a world war, than Philadelphia defeating New York in the World's Series.[1] The Balkans were a tinderbox, as they have continued to be to our day. The First Balkan War resulted in the expulsion of the Turks from much of Europe in 1912, only to be followed by a second regional war over the territories in 1913. Ultimately, alliances that formed set the stage for a far greater conflict that began in 1914. In the United States, the Seventeenth Amendment was adopted, resulting in the popular election of members of the Senate. As I put the finishing touches on this introduction, I am also reminded of other work that must be finished, the result of the adoption of the Sixteenth Amendment in 1913 — the creation of an income tax. While exemptions and other adjustments would affect the amount any person would pay, the adopted rate was 1 percent of net income above $3,000 for an individual, $4,000 if married. Average wages varied with the level of education — generally little more than post-elementary for most people — and with the type of job skills. But for most people, $2 to $3 per day was the norm. Henry Ford's offer of $5 per day to work in his factories was considered phenomenal. The cost of living for the times makes it difficult to compare the early 1910s with ours — a stamp cost 2 cents, as an example — but the point is that few earned anywhere close to $3,000 per year.

On the American political front, New Jersey governor Thomas Woodrow Wilson took the oath of office to become the 28th president of the United States. Women had little say in the matter; the suffrage movement still had a long way to go. A women's suffrage parade took place just prior to the inauguration, only to be attacked by a mob. The Twentieth Amendment would not become law until 1920.

So why is the subject here 1913 and not 1905, the first post-season meeting between Connie Mack and John McGraw, or 1911, their second meeting? Why Mack versus McGraw, and not the Giants versus the Athletics — the dynasties of the early and late 1920s? I had several reasons, some personal and some simply because of my interest in the sport. On the personal level, my interest in the 1913 season originated with a baseball I possess, likely used during the

1913 Series, and signed by Eddie Plank and Christy Mathewson. I also believe one can argue that the Giants and Athletics teams of the first two decades of the new century peaked with the 1913 World's Series. The 1905 series was noted for five shutouts, including three by Mathewson. But neither New York nor Philadelphia dominated the opposition to the extent they did a half-decade later. In the three-year period ending in 1913, the Giants won a total of 303 games, lost 153 and finished a composite 30 games ahead of the runner-up. Philadelphia, from 1910 to 1914, excluding the 1912 season when Boston won the pennant, won 398, lost 208, and finished a composite 43 games in front. Not only did they have McGraw, the 1913 Giants included future Hall of Famers Christy Mathewson and Rube Marquard. Both the offense and defense were solid if not spectacular, and included such "name" players as Larry Doyle, George Burns and Fred Merkle. The Athletics featured Eddie Plank, Chief Bender, Eddie Collins and Frank "Home Run" Baker, all future Hall of Famers, the latter two part of "the $100,000 infield." The 1920s Giants and Athletics certainly were on a par with these teams, and included more than their share of Hall of Famers, but to use the cliché, both had "been there, done that."

As they did for most of that four-year period (1910–1914), the Giants and Athletics won their respective 1913 races with relative ease, despite the fact several of their name players had passed their peaks: Mathewson, Bender, Frank Baker, and even Jack Coombs, who spent most of the season recovering from a near-fatal battle with typhoid. Others, among them Burns and Collins, were approaching their peaks as major leaguers.

I have no pretensions that this book breaks any new ground in the study of that era in major league baseball, though few books or articles deal specifically with 1913. To me, the primary importance of the work was that it was fun. I have also included excerpts from newspapers and other print media to provide the "flavor" of the period, when sports photography was in its infancy, and the public followed the nascent color commentary of the sportswriter secondhand. While name writers could be found in the offices of the major newspapers in New York, Washington and Chicago, most newspapers were dependent on the Associated Press for stories out of the large cities. Hugh Fullerton, Grantland Rice and I.E. Sanborn may have been known to those who followed sport, but in most cases stories were written anonymously for the reader. Perhaps the extensive use of print sources sets the work apart from others.

As noted in the text, the primary source of data was *Total Baseball*.[2] Hopefully this explains why such specific data as batting averages and pitching records may differ from that referenced in other works.

There are some people I would like to acknowledge or thank for their patience or help. In my family, my wife SaraJane (Sally) puts up with my frustrations and mood swings, while my daughter Rose helps me surf the Internet — her advice ranges from "just punch this key" to extended periods figuring out what I deleted by accident. Employees of the National Baseball Hall of Fame and Museum were wonderful at searching for information and photographs, both online and in person, as when my daughter Ruth and I visited Cooperstown last summer. Likewise, employees of the Library of Congress were patient in helping me locate relevant information and photographs. SABR member Norman Macht took time out from finishing his upcoming definitive work on Connie Mack to read and correct portions of the manuscript. Peter Morris and William Hickman, SABR members as well, patiently addressed my questions.

CHAPTER ONE

"The Tall Tactician"

"We waste too much of our youth growing old."[1] Cornelius McGillicuddy, or, as he is universally known among baseball followers, Connie Mack, was born during the administration of our 16th president, Abraham Lincoln, and died during the administration of our 34th president, Dwight David Eisenhower. He observed the expansion of the continental United States until it stretched coast to coast, and from Canada to Mexico. And while they had not yet become states, both Alaska and Hawaii became American territories during these years.

Mack was born just before midnight on December 22, 1862, the second son and third child of Irish immigrants Michael McGillicuddy from County Kerry, and Mary McKillop, who came to America in the late 1840s to escape starvation and British rule during the years of the potato famine. By 1854, Michael and his wife Mary had settled in East Brookfield, Massachusetts, one of a "family" of four villages with the Brookfield name. Whether in the name of patriotism for his adopted country, or simply one of the tens of thousands of Irish who joined the Union army during the Civil War, Michael McGillicuddy was off at war serving as a private in Company B, 51st Massachusetts infantry, when Connie was born. With the end of the war, Michael came home to work in an East Brookfield mill. Connie noted in his autobiography that his father supported six children — a seventh died in infancy — on a salary of about ten dollars a week. Among Connie's friends associated with the Brookfield area was entertainer and composer George M. Cohan, the "Yankee Doodle Boy" (who actually was born July 3, not the Fourth of July as the myth surrounding Cohan liked to profess). Cohan's grandparents lived in North Brookfield during Mack's early years in the American League, and the entertainer often went there for visits.

Mack's boyhood years were typical of that time and place. At the age of nine, he worked summers in a local cotton mill, earning approximately six dollars per month for running errands or operating the elevator.[2] Money earned was contributed to the family coffers, including the few cents he was paid by neighbors for helping with farm chores. And, of course, there was time for sports, particularly a game called four-o-cat, which consisted of hitting a rag ball and running between two positions drawn thirty feet apart in the dirt. Any ball caught on the fly was an out, as well as being hit by a thrown ball. Tall and thin even as a boy, Connie soon acquired the nickname "Slats." (His surname was soon abbreviated by friends to Mack; the name stuck, though legally he would remain a McGillicuddy.)

As he aged through his teen years, Mack became more adept at the increasingly popular game of baseball. During the latter quarter of the nineteenth century, it became commonplace for town teams to be established, with honors conferred on those who could assist in defeating opponents from other towns or villages. East Brookfield was no exception, and Mack became a catcher for the team. Mack recalled that in his last year with the team, 1883, they defeated the North Brookfield team, 2–1, and earned a silver bat and the championship of Central Massachusetts.[3]

Among the players on the East Brookfield team was a pitcher named William Hogan. Mack's interest in Hogan was both personal and professional. Hogan had a sister named Margaret, who on November 2, 1887, became Mack's wife. Hogan also had signed with a professional team in the town of Meriden in the Connecticut State League. Both Meriden and the CSL drifted in and out of organized baseball during these last decades of the nineteenth century, but it was professional baseball nevertheless.[4] Mack's source of income, used in part to help support his family, consisted of his salary at a local shoe manufacturer. Mack had applied for a tryout with Meriden, but the team turned him down. However, a spot opened on the team, and upon Hogan's recommendation, the Meriden club signed Mack at a salary of ninety dollars a month for the 1884 season. When Mack received the news, he immediately left his job as a cutter to join the club and caught Hogan the same day he reported.

Now 6'2 or 2½", and 150 pounds, Mack played one season with Meriden. There was no reserve clause in the league, and when Meriden did not immediately sign Mack for the 1885 season, he joined Hartford of the Southern New England League, playing in both the 1885 and 1886 seasons with the club. This was followed by a brief appearance with the New York Metropolitans of the American Baseball Association. On September 8, 1886, the Washington Nationals, then in the National League, purchased from Hartford the contracts of Mack, pitchers Frank Gilmore and John Henry, catcher Bill Krieg and outfielder George Shoch for $3,500 and two players to be determined.[5] Three days later in their major league debuts, the battery of Gilmore and Mack led the Nationals to a 4–3 victory over Philadelphia. Gilmore struck out ten, and Mack, "catching in the most approved style,"[6] contributed one hit, scored a run, and handled 11 putouts.[7] Mack caught ten games with the Nationals during the last month of the season, batting .361 with 13 hits in 36 at-bats. Washington finished in the cellar with a record of 28–92, sixty games behind the champion Chicago White Stockings. There was one discordant note at season's end. On October 9, manager John Gaffney received three telegrams from St. Louis informing him that something crooked was afoot with the pitching battery of Gilmore and Mack scheduled to face the Kansas City Cowboys that day. Suspecting that the sender had bet heavily on Kansas City, Gaffney remained firm with his original decision. For the record, Washington was victorious as Gilmore shut Kansas City down, 3–0.[8] With a record of 30–91, Kansas City barely finished in front of Washington, so why anybody would bet on this particular game must remain in the realm of conjecture. As for Mack, he resided in the highest rung of professional baseball, where he would remain until he retired as manager more than 60 years later.

It is only in recent years that players undergo year-around conditioning. In the past, players often worked other jobs during the winter months or participated in "behaviors" not conducive to remaining in ball playing shape. If a player wished to maintain a proper physical condition, they generally did so on their own. In 1888, Washington manager Ted Sullivan decided if he could get the players into shape early, they might start the season ahead of the competition. Consequently, he arranged for the team to travel to Jacksonville, Florida for early training. Mack continued to travel to Florida most winters for 65 years. Despite the best of intentions, Sullivan's attempt proved unsuccessful as the team still finished the 1888 season in the National League basement, with a record of 48–86.

Mack played three full seasons in Washington. He served primarily as a catcher, though he did appear from time to time in the outfield and at all infield positions except shortstop. He was not a strong hitter, batting .220 or lower for two of the three years.

Relations between the players and owners were tested from the beginning of the National League's formation in 1876. Issues centered on money. Contentions included the existence of a reserve clause in player contracts that effectively bound a player as long as the owner wished him to play on his team, severance of a player from the team, and in the late 1880s, the institution of a classification system that limited salaries. Led by John Montgomery Ward, a player and lawyer, the players formed a new league in 1890 called the Brotherhood of Professional Baseball Players. The circuit eliminated the reserve clause, and in theory profits were shared between players and backers of the league. Connie Mack was among the leaders of the "rebellion," investing $500 in the Buffalo Bisons and becoming one of the seven backers of the team. Mack played in 123 games that season, 112 behind the plate, and batted .266. Once again he played for a team destined for the basement, as Buffalo managed only 36 victories against 96 losses. While the Players League managed to hold its own in attendance against the two other major leagues, the National League and the American Association, the hemorrhaging of money resulted in the backers giving up after the one season. The league was dissolved, and players rejoined the other leagues.

Following the 1890 season, Mack agreed to a "personal services" contract with the Boston Reds, then still in the Players League. Reds owner Charles Prince had been elected president of the PL in November 1890 succeeding Edwin McAlpin. Mack also signed with Pittsburgh in the National League. Manager Ed Hanlon of Pittsburgh had even advanced Mack $250 for signing. The issue was which team had priority. Prince, also a lawyer, assured Mack the contract with Boston was binding, but that Mack was obliged to return his advance to Hanlon.[9]

In February 1891 the Board of Control made their ruling. Mack had signed his agreement with Boston three weeks before a franchise from that city had been admitted to the American Association. Consequently, the board "held the agreement had no value because the Boston association club with which it [agreement] was made did not exist at the time the agreement was signed. The Pittsburg [sic] contract was drawn up in regular form and the player was awarded to the Smoky [sic] City."[10]

Mack spent six seasons with Pittsburgh, primarily playing in a part-time role as catcher, though occasionally appearing in the outfield as well as several games at first. His batting was modest, to say the least, ranging from .214 to .306 in 14 games in 1895. Mack's playing time was limited in 1893 after he suffered a broken leg midway through the season. Worse, tragedy struck his family prior to the start of the season. On December 15, 1892, his wife died from tuberculosis, leaving Mack with three babies: daughter Marguerite, and sons Roy and Earle.

Mack's well-deserved reputation was that of a calm, dignified individual, almost a "father figure" to his players. When he left East Brookfield, Mack made a promise to his mother that he would never develop the bad habits, particularly drinking, found among many of his contemporaries on the diamond. He kept his promise; even his two wives were religious. But this was not to say that as a player he did not on occasion lose his temper. He was once fined by umpire Bob Emslie for being "offensive" during a game in Brooklyn.[11] Nor was Mack above plying some of the "tricks of the trade." He was known, for example, to occasionally tip the bat of an opposing player, "and give you a look of injured innocence that would make you think you had robbed your mother ... Connie's long suit was in getting an umpire to commit himself upon a certain play before making it. I understand he did it to [umpire Tom] Lynch in the fourth of July game at Pittsburg, and learning that Tom would call the batsman out and allow the runner to advance on interference with the catcher's throw hugged [John] Peltz until [Lou] Bierbauer was on second. That's headwork. The decision was not good, but having given it against the home club Lynch could not reverse himself."[12]

With its finances damaged fatally during the tenure of the Players-league, the American Association went out of business following the 1891 season, with four teams being absorbed into the National League. The Pittsburgh Pirates first managed in these years by future Hall of Famer Ed (Ned) Hanlon and then under Al Buckenberger when Hanlon attempted to reign in some of the players' wild behaviors, finished second in the twelve-team "big league" in 1893. The team began to fall on hard times by the following season, and on September 3, Buckenberger was fired and replaced by Connie Mack. The firing apparently came as a surprise. However, "the owners of the club ... have been dissatisfied with Buckenberger for some time, but the latter claims that the poor showing of the club is the cause of his release, and that this poor showing is due in a large measure to interference by some of the owners with his management. Buckenberger was also in bad odor with stockholders Temple and Auten for other reasons which have not been made public."[13] After the completion of the season, Pittsburgh owner William Kerr offered the job once again to Ned Hanlon, now the manager of the Baltimore Orioles. When Hanlon turned the Pirates down, Mack was asked to continue to serve as manager. Connie Mack would continue to manage throughout the remainder of his baseball career, until he retired in 1950.

Serving as a part-time player as well as manager, Mack led the team to a seventh-place finish for the remainder of the season as well as the next before climbing one position to sixth in 1896. On September 21, however, Mack resigned from the Pirates, and announced he had accepted a managerial job with Milwaukee of the Western League. The reasons for Mack's departure remain vague — he never stated a reason in his autobiography. It is possible management considered him as being too "easy" on the players.[14]

Mack was now manager and part-owner of the Milwaukee Creams/Brewers of what was then a minor league. The Western League had been formed in November 1893 with newspaper reporter Ban Johnson being named president. During the next six years, sixteen different cities had franchises in the new league. At the end of the 1890s, with the league fielding teams in Minneapolis, St. Paul, Milwaukee, Columbus, Detroit, Indianapolis, Buffalo and Kansas City, Johnson decided the circuit was ready to be "upgraded" to major league status. During the next two seasons, the league underwent significant rearrangements, including the addition of Chicago (replacing St. Paul) and Cleveland for 1900, and in 1901, replacing Buffalo, Indianapolis, Kansas City and Minneapolis with teams in Boston, Baltimore (later replaced by New York), Philadelphia and Washington. In 1902, Milwaukee transferred to St. Louis. The Western League was renamed the American League for the 1900 season; that same year, President Johnson announced the league would have major league status. During the 1900 season, the newly named American League still consisted primarily of teams from the original Western League, with Chicago the only city in which there was competition with the National League. That would change with the rearrangements being readied for the 1901 season. As a friend of Johnson's, Mack was awarded the new Philadelphia franchise, one goal of which was to compete with the National League Phillies for fans from that city. In 1901, while renouncing the National Agreement, the American League began raiding players from National League teams, in effect creating a war between the two leagues.

Mack may have been manager of a franchise, but the team's success was dependent on a source of cash, a stock of players and a park in which the team could play. An immediate influx of money was provide by millionaire Cleveland industrialist Charles Somers. Somers was an example of what was sometimes called "syndicate baseball," the ownership of multiple franchises in the same league by the same syndicate of investors. But Somers was willing to invest significant capital for several franchises in what might prove to be a competitive league.

Mack later recalled walking the streets of the city, looking at vacant lots where a stadium might be placed, even suggested a city playground.[15] With the help of two local sportswriters, Sam Jones and Frank Hough, Mack finally found a site in North Philadelphia at 29th and Columbia. After a ten-year lease was signed, and with the start of the season only five weeks away, stands and fences were hurriedly put in place. The location became known as Columbia Park.

The writers also put Mack in touch with local entrepreneur Ben Shibe, who had also been recommended by Ban Johnson. The thirty-seven-year-old Shibe was from the Kensington area of east Philadelphia, knew the city well, and had become wealthy after aligning his financial interests with Al Reach, a manufacturer and seller of baseball equipment. Among Shibe's inventions was a machine to wind baseballs. Shibe eventually became a partner in the company, first named Shibe and Reach, then renamed A.J. Reach & Company to differentiate the name from Shibe's old company.

Mack suggested to Shibe that he might be interested in investing in the new franchise, now named the Athletics. Mack also offered to designate the Reach baseball as the "official baseballs of the American League." Initially hesitant — the venture, after all, did possess some risk — Shibe became convinced that the franchise could be a success. Shibe agreed to purchase 50 percent of the stock, while Mack held 25 percent, and the two sportswriters, Hough and Jones, would hold the other 25 percent. Mack, however, held the voting rights for the writers' portion, so in effect Mack and Shibe had equal ownership of the team. In the fall of 1912, Mack purchased the shares from Hough, then seriously ill, and Jones, to become an equal owner with Shibe.

The partnership of Mack and Shibe was exemplary in their working relationship. Shibe was primarily a businessman; the team provided an additional measure of social standing for a man, and family, who lived the American dream — starting poor and working their way to wealth. Mack was a baseball man. And as long as Mack represented the best in sports, a clean and quiet life, the two were a perfect match.

Having a place to play and money to invest solved two of Mack's immediate problems. The third, players for the team, required some underhanded dealings involving the signing of available players and raiding the existing franchises in the National League. For Mack, the most obvious source was the cross-town Phillies. Fortunately for Mack, the penny-pinching policies of Phillies majority owner John Rogers had alienated many of the players. The most prominent player Mack raided from the Phillies' roster was second baseman Nap Lajoie, whom he signed for $4,000. Lajoie, then in his fifth season with the Phillies, was already considered one of the outstanding players in the National League. Lajoie would have one of the greatest seasons ever put together in twentieth century baseball in 1901 with Mack, batting .426 with 232 base hits, including 14 home runs and 125 RBIs. Others "hired" off the Phillies' roster prior to the season included pitchers Chick Fraser, Bill Bernhard and Wiley Piatt.[16] Fraser went 22–16 that season, his second twenty-victory total in three years. Mack also signed Eddie Plank, a left-hander who had pitched for Gettysburg College and who would win 17 games that year to begin a career that would take him to the Baseball Hall of Fame. Catcher Michael "Doc" Powers was signed from Indianapolis. Mack also added first baseman Harry Davis, who had previous professional experience with Providence of the Eastern League, outfielder Socks Seybold from Indianapolis, and thirty-five-year-old veteran third baseman Lave Cross. Though frequently injured, Cross still played a serviceable third base, batting .328 in 100 games that season. The Athletics finished fourth during their initial season in the league with a record of 74–62.

While the team was competitive in its initial season, Mack knew he would have to strengthen his squad if it hoped to have a realistic chance at a pennant. Among the players he signed during the off-season were outfielders "Topsy" Hartsell, shortstop Monte Cross and pitcher Bill Duggleby and from the Phillies again, future Hall of Famer Elmer Flick. "One can use field glasses on that Philadelphia team and find few flaws."[17]

Flick played only 11 games with the Athletics. The Phillies appealed for an injunction from the courts as a result of the Athletic signings. While a lower court ignored the request, an injunction from the Pennsylvania Supreme Court on April 21, 1902, resulted in a ruling that Lajoie, Fraser, Bernhard, Flick and Duggleby could not play for the Athletics. An appeal in May was denied. Fraser and Duggleby, who had one victory for Mack in the young season, returned to the Phillies. The injunction by the supreme court, however, only applied to Pennsylvania; Lajoie, Flick and Bernhard joined the Cleveland Blues (referred to by the newspapers in the future as the Naps, in honor of Lajoie). As a result of the injunction, none of the new Cleveland players could play in Philadelphia. Only when peace was declared between the leagues in 1903 could the players safely play in the state.

With the season already underway, Mack had to scramble to replace the players. Several players were obtained from other teams: Fred Mitchell and Pete Husting from the Red Sox, and catcher and utilityman Ossee Schrecongost (Schreck), who had recently been released from Cleveland. From the Norwich Reds in the Connecticut League, Mack purchased the contract of second base-

Harry Davis (1910), played 22 seasons in the major leagues, primarily with Mack's Athletics. For nearly a decade between 1901 and 1910, he was the regular first baseman. He was replaced by Stuffy McInnis in 1911. From 1904 through 1907, Davis led the league in home runs. Davis was reduced to only sporadic appearances in the lineup by 1913, but remained one of Mack's most popular players (Library of Congress, Bain Collection).

man Danny Murphy in July. Murphy had been hitting over .460 in the Class D league, but showed he was no fluke by producing six hits in his first game with the Athletics and finished at .313 in 76 games. With the likelihood of a major league career, Murphy married the following month.

It was a signing in mid–June, however, that was the key factor in the success Mack found that season. Left-hander Rube Waddell could qualify as the most eccentric character to ever play major league baseball. Waddell had previously played with Mack at Milwaukee, and the Athletics' manager was well aware of what he could do on the mound when in the mood. Waddell had been pitching for Los Angeles in the independent California League when he agreed to join Philadelphia. Mack sent a $200 advance and Pinkerton detectives to bring him to Philadelphia. Even then there was no guarantee he would appear.

"Waddell agreed to go back to Connie Mack's team a week ago, but manager [James] Morley got wind of his departure and made such a strong plea that Rube took his belongings from the sleeping-car, and, as a guarantee that he would not listen to the tempter again, turned over the ticket sent him to Morley, who still has it. But it appears there were more tickets, and Mack was so sorely in need of pitching talent that he sent an agent all the way from Chicago to bring in the pitcher, 'dead or alive.' The agent talked Waddell over, today, and loss of the game that he pitched in the afternoon did the rest."[18]

Waddell's debut with the Athletics was not one to remember. Allowing seven hits while hitting two batters against Baltimore, he was beaten by a score of 7–3. Waddell settled down after his debut, striking out 39 in his first five games, on his way to a league-leading 210 for the season. He finished with a record of 24–7 for the season. The youngster Eddie Plank produced his first 20-victory season. Socks Seybold hit a then-record 16 home runs, a total not surpassed until Babe Ruth came along, and batted .316, one of six regulars to hit over .300. Mack finished the season with a record of 83–53, acquiring the first of his ten pennants.

Mack credited the entire team for the successful showing, but singled out one person in particular: Rube Waddell. "The acquisition of Waddell was a ten-strike. It was due to the 'Rube' more than to any one man that we fly the pennant. He not only pitched phenomenal ball and batted hard and timely, but his presence was an inspiration to his teammates."[19] "This is Connie Mack's story of how the Athletics won the American League pennant.... Long live the White Elephant."[20]

White elephant? What became the symbol of the Philadelphia Athletics, and continues today with its Oakland descendent, started as a pejorative phrase spit from the mouth of one of Ban Johnson and the American League's strongest detractors: John McGraw. Midway through the season, McGraw, then managing the Baltimore franchise in the American League, jumped to the National League New York Giants. When asked to discuss his feelings towards his former league, McGraw made plain his wrath. "The policy of the American League is everything for Boston, Chicago and Philadelphia, the remainder of the organization to take what they can.... The Philadelphia club is not making any money. It has a big white elephant on its hands."[21] The press immediately grabbed onto the white elephant as a catch phrase to characterize the team. Rather than object to the phrase, Mack endorsed it. "'Boys,' Mack said, 'we accept McGraw's appellation. We will name our Philadelphia A's the White Elephants.' Inasmuch as these were the days when the Republican Party was winning elections with the elephant, I was thankful that John McGraw's quick wit had not called us donkeys."[22]

Whether or not Mack and the Athletics were profitable at the time is unknown — certainly the problem was neither the attendance nor the product on the field. The Athletics drew over 420,000 patrons during the 1902 season, double that of the previous year, and nearly four times that of the cross-town Phillies. Even the Giants, the team to which McGraw jumped, drew only some 302,000 for the season. Several years later, it was revealed that Mack's salary by 1906 was $15,000.[23] By 1913, the Shibes had turned a tidy profit of more than $350,000.[24]

The 1903 team was improved with the addition of a nineteen-year-old rookie from the Carlisle Indian School in Pennsylvania. Chief Bender made his debut on April 20, pitching five innings in relief, and a week later tossed a four-hit shutout against Clark Griffith and the New York Highlanders. Bender put the fear of God in Highlander minds, or at least the fear of Bender, when he hit first baseman John Ganzel in the back with a pitch in the second inning. Bender went 17–14 in the first season of a Hall of Fame career.

Yet, the best news for the Athletics and baseball in general was the peace agreement signed in January to end the "war" between the two leagues. Contracts of disputed players were sorted out — American League teams received eight players, including future Hall of Famers Ed Delahanty, Sam Crawford and Willie Keeler. The National League received seven, including Christy Mathewson and Vic Willis. Playing rules were sorted out, including the foul-strike rule in which foul balls would constitute a first or second strike. The rule had previously been in effect only in the National League. A logical outcome was also discussion of possible post-season play between the pennant winners from the two leagues. With peace declared, the Athletics and Phillies also played a pre-season series; the National League Phillies won four of the five games.

The season began on April 20, with the split of a doubleheader between Boston and the Athletics. Waddell started for Mack, striking out the first four batters. But with five runs in the fifth, Boston went on to a 9–4 victory. Boston's strategy was simple: bunt on Waddell. The eccentric pitcher had apparently been out partying much of the night, and his fielding showed it.[25] The pennant race remained close through the first months of the season, with six teams owning 17 or more wins by the end of May. But Boston gradually pulled away, finishing on top by 14½ games over the second-place Athletics, before defeating the Pirates in the first modern World Series. Eddie Plank surpassed twenty-victories (23–16) for the second season in a row, and Waddell, despite his frequent problems with the bottle and lack of discipline during the season, likewise broke the twenty-victory level (21–16).

The lineup for the Athletics was largely unchanged for the next two seasons, 1904 and 1905, though with very different results. In 1904 they finished fifth. In 1905, however, everything, particularly pitching, came together. Plank had the finest season in his career to date, going 24–12 with 210 strikeouts and an ERA of 2.26. Bender won 18. Waddell reported to spring training in shape, and produced a record of 27–10, the highest victory total of his career. His 287 strikeouts led the league for the fourth consecutive season to go along with a league-leading 1.48 ERA. Waddell made his first start of the season on May 4 against a surprisingly strong first-place Washington Nationals team. The left-hander held them to two hits, striking out five and winning easily, 6–0. This is not to say Waddell did not continue to have his "moments." While the Athletics were in Washington, a fire broke out at a nearby livery stable. The team walked over to watch, only to observe Waddell on the second floor helping fight the fire —fireman's hat and all.[26] During August and September, Waddell pitched 44 consecutive scoreless innings to help the Athletics take over first. His contribution was critical, as the race remained close throughout the season. But in September, Waddell injured his shoulder while horsing around on a railroad platform in Providence. The injury initially seemed to be minor, requiring about a week's rest. Meanwhile, the second-place White Sox moved from four games behind to a half-game on September 26. Mack tried Waddell in relief against Detroit a day later, when it became clear the injury was more serious than initially thought. With excellent pitching from Plank and Bender, Mack held on to the small lead, winning the pennant by two games over the White Sox.

The 1905 World's Series represented the first match-up between two managers already considered among the best in the game. While the press highlighted the possible meeting of Mathewson and Waddell, Mack's tall southpaw remained doubtful. According to Rube, his arm had been fine ever since he felt a "click" in the shoulder while shaving.[27] But on October 6, Mack brought Waddell in to pitch in relief of Andy Coakley against Washington. Rube walked five and had two wild pitches in a 10–4 loss. All was not lost, though, as Chicago lost to St. Louis, clinching the pennant for Mack that day. But Waddell's arm was clearly having problems. Rumors swelled that the gamblers were controlling Waddell's arm and not an injury. But his performance had been questionable even before the season ended, and the Athletics were certainly not guaranteed a pennant until the last few days. In the end it was an injury that disabled Mack's ace.

Even without Waddell, Mack still had a formidable staff to throw against McGraw. In addition to Plank and Bender, there was the twenty-two-year-old collegian from Holy Cross, Andy Coakley, winner of 18 games that season. Waddell was key, however, as the Giants had trouble with left-handers during the season. There was still Plank, and he would have to do for Mack.

On the Giants' side, there was "Iron Man" Joe McGinnity and Christy Mathewson. Both had a fabulous season, Mathewson producing a 31–9 record, the third consecutive year in which he won more than thirty games. He led the league with eight shutouts, including a no-hitter, 206 strikeouts and an ERA of 1.28. McGinnity contributed 21 victories, a decrease compared to his two consecutive thirty-victory seasons the past two years. Nor were these the only hurlers McGraw could call upon. Red Ames had a 22–8 record, and Hooks Wiltse went 15–6.

The series began October 9 in Philadelphia, with Plank facing Mathewson. Columbia Park's seating was limited, but 17,955 still managed to squeeze into the site. Both Mack and McGraw demonstrated that despite the animosity which may have existed in their respective pasts, each still had a sense of humor. Just prior to the start of the game, while Athletics captain Lave Cross was standing at the plate with umpires Hank O'Day and Jack Sheridan, McGraw walked out to participate in the conference. Upon McGraw's arrival, Cross presented the Giants' manager with a white elephant sitting on a green pedestal. McGraw took the gift, bowed, and posed for a photograph while holding the elephant. He then walked off to the cheers of the crowd.[28]

The pre-game ceremony was not the only time McGraw enjoyed himself. Plank's "slant ball" had its usual speed, but the Giants were ready and hit him when needed. In the end, he gave up ten hits and three runs. Mathewson, on the other hand, was superb, scattering four hits, striking out five and throwing a 3–0 shutout. McGraw may have won more than the match, reportedly having bet $400 on the outcome of the game.[29]

The teams traveled back to New York for the next game, with Bender scheduled to face McGinnity. This time, nearly 25,000 patrons watched the Athletics battle back, tying the series with their own four-hit, 3–0 shutout victory. As pointed out by the newspaper writers, the Giants had an easy time during the season, practically winning the pennant by mid–April. The Athletics, conversely, had to fight hard all the way, and the strain showed. Coakley lost fifteen pounds during the last weeks of the season. Plank pitched poorly in the series' opener. But now Bender had tied the series with his own shutout. "If Coakley is in anything like his proper form, the Giants should not make a runaway job of the big end of the purse."[30]

Coakley never had the chance to demonstrate whether he had "anything like his proper form." The next day's game was scheduled for Philadelphia. But the rains came, and Umpire Sheridan announced just before the start that it would be postponed. Mathewson had been scheduled to pitch for the Giants on two days rest, but the postponement allowed another day for his arm to recover. As Giant shortstop Bill Dahlen walked back to the clubhouse with outfielder George Browne, Browne turned to Dahlen and asked, "Say, what do you think of this American League baseball?" Dahlen's reply, "Don't know what to think. Haven't hit one yet."[31]

October 12 in Philadelphia was another damp, cold day, but the teams still attempted to play. Mathewson facing the youngster Andy Coakley, returned to the slab looking to duplicate his work from three days earlier. The Athletics were more successful in hitting Mathewson this time, but the Giant fielders played brilliantly, holding their opponents scoreless. In contrast, the Giants managed nine hits, and combined with five Athletic errors, easily won, 9–0. The game was over in the first inning. Coakley hit leadoff batter Roger Bresnahan in the back with a pitch "with sufficient force to melt the marrow in his spinal column."[32] After an out, Mike Donlin singled Bresnahan to third, then

Dan McGann scored him with a single. Danny Murphy fumbled Sam Mertes' grounder, scoring Donlin, and Mathewson had all the run support he would need. The Giants were now ahead two games to one.

The teams returned to New York to continue the series. Mack sent Waddell out to warm up, but it quickly became apparent to all that his arm was not capable of pitching his best. One of his warm-up pitches even flew into the stands, hitting a fan.[33] Waddell sat down, and Plank was once sent out to try to even the series again. Facing him was the "Iron Man," Joe McGinnity. The Giants scored the only run of the game in the fourth. Outfielder Sam Mertes reached base on an error by shortstop Monte Cross, went to second on a sacrifice, then scored on a single by second baseman Billy Gilbert. McGinnity scattered five hits in the 1–0 shutout.

McGraw sent Mathewson out once again to finish the job. The Athletics managed six hits, with only Doc Powers reaching second as he led off the fifth inning with a double. But Powers was quickly erased from the base paths when he was caught between second and third on a grounder by Bender. The Giants were more effective against Bender than they had been in his first appearance, managing only five hits but still pushing across two runs. In what was arguably one of the most unusual World Series, each of the five games resulted in a shutout. Mathewson pitched three of them, posting 27 consecutive scoreless innings against the American League's best. The Athletics batted an anemic .196.

The defending American League champions changed little in 1906. Lave Cross went to Washington, and youngster Bris "the Human Eyeball" Lord was ready to play regularly in the outfield. Probably most important aspect for a close pennant race was the fact that, the pitching staff was once again intact. Plank and Bender were ready, and Rube Waddell pronounced his shoulder healthy for the new season. Mack took the team to Montgomery, Alabama, for training at the beginning of March. True to form Rube demonstrated how he was still capable of driving Connie to drink had the man so chosen. One evening a fire broke out near the training site. Rube heard the alarm, ran to the scene, and after borrowing a helmet, helped fight the fire.[34]

At the beginning of April, Mack and his team returned to Philadelphia for what had become an annual intra-city series. This time, the Athletics won three of the four games versus the Phillies, including one by Waddell, who struck out eleven. Bender then won the opener on the road against Washington. The following day, Athletics pitcher Jimmy Dygert gave up two fast runs and was relieved by Waddell, who pitched eight strong innings. By mid–May, the Athletics were 17–7, four games ahead of second-place Cleveland. But several days later, Waddell was injured in a freak accident, breaking the thumb on his pitching hand while jumping out of a carriage. The thumb continued to bother him for the remainder of the season, and Waddell's record slipped to 15–17, though his 196 strikeouts still led the league. A portion of the slack was taken up by

Jack Coombs (1911). Signed off the campus of Colby College in Maine, Coombs won 31 games for the Athletics in 1910, finishing the season with three more victories in the World Series against the Cubs. In the subsequent two seasons, Coombs won 28 and 21 games. A life-threatening typhoid infection limited his work in 1913 to two appearances (Library of Congress, Bain Collection).

Jack Coombs, a young chemistry student signed out of Colby College in Maine by Connie's brother Tom. (It may have actually been Connie who signed Coombs.) Coombs made his debut for Mack on July 5, shutting down Washington, 3–0, giving up seven hits while striking out six. Though much was expected from the twenty-three-year-old rookie, such expectations were unrealistic. Though he had pitched (and hit) Colby to the college championship of Maine that spring, 1906 was his first season at a purely professional level. He did win 10 games for the season, losing the same number. But one afternoon in particular stood out.

On September 1, Coombs hooked up in a duel with Joe Harris and Boston that lasted 24 innings. The game, which took nearly five hours to complete, was finally decided on consecutive triples by Seybold and Murphy. Coombs allowed fifteen hits, but only a single run. Coombs pitched two additional complete games in the next two weeks, and perhaps to no surprise, was bothered by arm trouble towards the end of the season. In the end the Athletics came close to repeating, but Chicago, the "hitless wonders," overcame a season full of injuries, and buoyed by a nineteen-game winning streak during August, won the pennant by three games over New York. The Athletics fell to fourth, twelve games behind.

For spring training in 1907, Mack decided to take the team to Dallas, Texas. The region had several advantages—far from the temptations of a large city, and also approximately 100 miles from Marlin where McGraw and the Giants were training. The two managers scheduled several practice games between the two teams to help the players work themselves into playing condition as well as hopefully generate some revenue. It was also close enough to Dallas that the Athletics could play exhibitions with local teams. Once again, Waddell was not one to let any opportunity for fun slide by. While the team was in Dallas, Rube turned up missing for several days. Mack finally found him when, standing in front of the team hotel, he watched a fire truck go by on a practice run. Mack had to look twice to be sure the man who was driving, wearing a metal hat, boots and red flannel shirt, was actually his missing pitcher.[35]

While playing exhibition games with the Giants as well as local teams, the Athletics worked their way to New Orleans and headed north. Despite the addition of a few new pitchers, the Athletic roster was not significantly better than the fourth-place team from the year before. Even the writers picked Mack for a second-division finish.[36] The city series with the Phillies certainly did nothing to change their minds, as the National League team swept the four games.

The Athletics started well, beating the Highlanders in New York by a score of 9–6 behind Dygert, with Bender in relief. Waddell, however, pitched poorly in his first appearances. Finally having had enough of the big lefty's shenanigans, on April 26, Mack suspended Waddell for thirty days. Waddell protested, claiming he was not out carousing, but had been spending time at a Turkish bath; he even provided an affidavit as proof.[37] Mack had difficulty believing it, but nevertheless reinstated the man who was still critical to the team's success. Mack saved face with the reporters by explaining the suspension had "not been due to dissipation, but because he was not getting himself into condition as quickly as he [Mack] thought he should."[38]

Despite the pessimism associated with the Athletics' chances, Mack had the team playing well as the first month of the season came to a close. "As a handler of a ballclub, Mack has not an equal in the business. With teams that do not look to have more than a look in, he has pulled away with two pennants, and has been in every fight that the American League has had.... Being in a 25-cent town, Mack has never been able to cope with some of the other clubs in the matter of paying salaries, and as he cannot afford to carry a player unless his salary suits the conditions, he has been forced to allow many a good man slip through his fingers. But this fact has never prevented him from being in the hunt on all occasions."[39]

As the season moved into September, the pennant race evolved into one of the closest on record. Detroit, Philadelphia, Chicago and even Cleveland were all within striking distance of one another. As late as September 26, the

Athletics were in first place, a half-game behind Detroit, which had played more games. Mack had made the decision not to reschedule several games that had been rained out and now resided in front by but percentage points. By taking two of three from the White Sox, the Athletics dropped the Chicago team in the standings. On the September 27, Detroit came into town. By this time, Mack's staff was simply worn out. Bender and Plank were tired, and Waddell was out being Rube. With little choice, Mack opened with Plank, pitching for the second time in three days, and facing "Wild Bill" Donovan. Donovan was hit hard, giving up 13 hits, but still managed to pull out a 5–4 victory. The Athletics were out of first place for the first time since the beginning of the month. The Saturday game was rained out, and since baseball was not played in Philadelphia on Sundays, a doubleheader was scheduled for Monday.

A paid crowd of more than 24,000 persons was in the park, with possibly many more having worked their way in. Mack started the first game with Dygert, facing Donovan who had just pitched three days earlier. In the bottom of the first inning, the Tigers reached Donovan quickly, scoring three runs. The pressure was too much for Dygert in the Tigers' half of the second. Two wild throws loaded the bases with one out, and Mack decided to call on Waddell. This time Rube came through, striking out the two batters he faced. By the seventh inning, the Athletics held a 7–1 lead, but two errors and generally poor play on the part of the Athletics allowed Detroit to close the gap to 7–5. In the top of the ninth the score was 8–6. But with Sam Crawford on first with a lead-off single, Ty Cobb smacked the only home run he ever hit off Waddell and tied the game. So stunned was Mack, he fell into the bat rack.[40] Mack replaced Waddell with Plank, and the game went into extra innings.

A riot nearly ensued in the bottom of the 14th inning. Harry Davis led off for Philadelphia, and hit a high fly ball towards center field. The overflow crowd had spilled into the outfield, with only a ring of policemen separating them from play. Davis' hit bounced off the glove of Detroit center fielder Sam Crawford and landed among the fans. Umpire Tom Connolly initially ruled the hit a ground-rule double, and Davis stopped at second. But Crawford claimed the crowd had interfered with the catch, and plate umpire Silk O'Loughlin ruled in his favor, declaring Davis out. As the Athletics began to argue, Detroit first baseman Claude Rossman came to blows with Athletics coach Monte Cross; Cobb had allegedly told Rossman that Cross called him a "Jew-bastard." Rossman was neither, but while using any excuse for a fight, he was eventually tossed from the game. The contest continued for seventeen innings prior to being called because of darkness, leaving Detroit in first place. Mack remained angry with O'Loughlin for years.

A week later, the Athletics and Tigers had 56 losses apiece, but Detroit had 90 wins to Philadelphia's 84. The season came down to the last day, October 5. Even though the Athletics swept a doubleheader with Washington, the second game a five-inning no-hitter by rookie Harry Vickers, Detroit beat St. Louis to

Connie Mack (left) and Ira Thomas in 1914. Thomas was a part-time catcher and long-time coach and scout for Mack. He also served for a time as team captain (Library of Congress).

win the pennant. Mack's Athletics finished 1½ games back in second place. Waddell won 19 of 32 decisions that season and led the league for the sixth consecutive year in strikeouts, with 232. His habits, however, may have cost the Athletics the pennant. Mack had been patient, even facing open revolt on the team as a result of Waddell's behaviors. On February 7, 1908, Mack sold Waddell outright to the St. Louis Browns, the price later believed to have been $5,000.[41] Said Mack, "I think the team will play better without him than with him."[42] Plank won 24 games for the season, Bender won 16, and Dygert posted a career-high of 21. Discounting the strain on the arms of the men who took up the slack, an extra couple victories from Waddell might have been the difference in the close pennant race.

The last week of February, Mack and his team began their southern tour, training in New Orleans for two weeks to work themselves into playing shape, then gradually working their way north through Mobile, Memphis, Nashville, Columbus, Ohio, and back through Pennsylvania, arriving home for the city series in the beginning of April. Waddell was gone, and that in itself would likely improve what today would be called "team chemistry." Mack still had his other regulars for the staff: Plank, Bender, Coombs and the spit-baller Jimmy Dygert. Rube Vickers also had potential. Among the position players, twenty-one-year-old Eddie Collins was ready to handle second base on a regular basis. Outfielder Rube Oldring, likewise, had another year behind him. Generally speaking, the Athletics had undergone fewer changes than other teams, a fact noted by the media.[43] The complaints that circulate among contemporary baseball fans, centered on players rarely remaining with the same team throughout most of their careers, is not unique to our times.

The season opened at home against New York on April 14. Rookie Nick "Connie" Carter, whom Mack had obtained from the Syracuse Stars of the New York State League, pitched twelve innings, only to lose, 1–0. Vickers went down the next day by a 2–1 score. Seybold injured his knee during the spring in New Orleans, and Coombs started in his place in right field. Though not considered a strong hitter, Coombs nevertheless held his own in the early part of the season.

By the end of May, five clubs, including the Athletics, were playing over .500 ball, with each team within one game of the league-leading Highlanders. A month later, the teams began to spread out, with the Athletics simply breaking even. At the beginning of June, St. Louis was in front, with Cleveland, Detroit and Chicago within three games. The Athletics were in fifth, 4½ behind. Little changed as the season progressed, with the race being primarily between the four teams in the first division. Mack simply did not have the pitching necessary to keep up, and the hitting was not sufficient to make up the difference. Dygert was hit hard as often as he was effective and Coombs was bothered by arm trouble. Vickers and Carter did not live up to initial expectations; Vickers managed to post 18 victories to lead the staff, but also had a team-high 19 losses. Bender seemed to lose all effectiveness, finishing 8–9. Only Plank pitches well, even though he was losing as much as he won (14–16). The only change Mack made as the season drew to a close was to sell Schreck to the White Sox. Apparently Schreck had picked up too many habits from his old friend Waddell, and "had too many friends [in Philadelphia] who were willing to entertain him."[44] One signing bode well for the future when Amos Strunk of the Shamokin, Pennsylvania, team in the Atlantic League signed on the recommendation of Lave Cross. Another signing that did not pan out as well, at least for the Athletics, was that of Shoeless Joe Jackson. The close of the season found the Athletics in sixth, twenty-two games back with a record of 68–85.

Mack began an overhaul of the team for the 1909 season. Eddie Collins, who had played nearly every position except pitcher and catcher in 1908, settled in as the regular second baseman. Harry Davis still held down first, but he was clearly aging. John "Stuffy" McInnis was obtained from the New England League. Though still expected to play shortstop, McInnis would eventually replace Davis. For third base, Mack employed Frank Baker, who had been purchased from Reading in September of 1908, and his hitting during those last weeks of the season won him the job. Likewise, Jack Barry was signed out of Holy Cross and given every opportunity to win the job at shortstop. The pitching staff that started the season was largely the same as Mack prepared to head to New Orleans early in March. Only twenty-one-year-old left-hander Harry Krause, signed the previous year in California, was added to the mix. Ira Thomas, Bert Blue and Doc Powers were expected to handle the catching. William "Heinie" Heitmuller, a big (6'2, 215 pounds) outfielder from California, was counted on to contribute. Danny Murphy was expected to spell Collins at second, though he too could play outfield if necessary.

Another significant change affected baseball in Philadelphia that season. Columbia Park, too small for a sport growing in popularity, and as a wooden structure, simply was not safe and had to be replaced. North Philadelphia in the first decade of the twentieth century was largely open land, though still accessible to transportation lines. Shibe chose an area bounded by Twentieth and Twenty-first streets, Somerset Street and Lehigh Avenue. Even the street names were misleading this far north of the main portion of the city. Streets were laid out, but relatively few homes existed. The only noteworthy structures nearby were SPCA kennels and the old "smallpox hospital," Philadelphia's Hospital for Contagious Diseases. Also known as Municipal Hospital, it had become infamous during the decade under the direction of William H. Welch, no relation to the William Welch who was instrumental in the development of Johns Hopkins in Baltimore. Welch's management left much to be desired, and the building was old, dilapidated, and a pest house for disease.[45]

Yet Shibe knew something that others did not. The city was preparing to tear down the building, and the Athletics' ownership began to purchase the surrounding land at a lower price than would be required once the information became available. In June 1909 the structure was demolished. The stadium, named Shibe Park, was ready by Opening Day, becoming the first entirely concrete and steel stadium built for the major leagues. The investment proved worthwhile, as attendance jumped from approximately 455,000 in 1908 to 675,000 in 1909.

The season started off with tragedy. Popular catcher Doc Powers suffered an abdominal injury, possibly the result of a collision with the cement wall around the field. Before the extent of the injury was realized, he developed an intestinal abscess, and died on April 26. Powers had been with Mack since the team had joined the league in 1900. Though a poor hitter, Powers' contribution had been as a coach and stabilizing influence for young players. Powers were buried on April 29, with a crowd of thousands present. Flowers were sent by most teams, including a baseball diamond made from green ferns and carnations. White roses in the infield spelled out the word "Out."[46]

The mixture of youth and veterans paid off for Mack, as the team remained close throughout the season. Bob Ganley was obtained from Washington, and while a weak hitter, he too was a stabilizing influence for the younger players. At the midpoint in July, the two-time American League champion Detroit Tigers were still in first, but the Athletics were holding second place, 6½ games behind. The next weeks, however, saw the Athletics steadily gain on Detroit, and a victory over St. Louis on August 15 sent them ahead of Detroit into first for the season's first time. Even so, the baseball writers still felt the youth and inexperience of key players would prevent Mack from holding the league lead.[47] They proved correct.

On August 26, the Tigers defeated Plank and the Athletics, 4–3, despite an exemplary fielding performance by Barry, and regained the lead. Mack was particularly upset with Tiger outfielder Ty Cobb and expressed an opinion that had become commonplace among American League opponents. "I am going to see to it that the American League puts a stop to Ty Cobb and his style of ball playing. Cobb has vowed to get Baker, Barry and Collins. He got Baker and knocked Collins' feet out from under him sliding yesterday, but failed to drive his spikes home. I am not well enough acquainted with the young man to understand why he should do these things. It looks to me like he gets up with a grouch and tries to take it out on the players of the opposite team." Manager Hughie Jennings defended Cobb, saying "Connie wouldn't have said that if he hadn't been bitterly disappointed by the result of the games which Detroit won by superior gamesmanship.... Connie's worst trouble is found in the fact that he himself knows his team is still sheltering a bunch of the yellow dogs who laid down in the world's series of 1905 and later on to us when it came to a pinch in the pennant race of 1907." Cobb was perfectly capable of defending himself, and did so. "I never spiked a man deliberately, and he knows that the runner is entitled to the line, and if the baseman gets in his way he is taking his chances.... It's a plain case of squeal on the part of Mack, and I'm going to tell him so. Baker tried to block me off on Tuesday, but I dumped him. He did not say a word because he knew that I was right. He goes into the bases the same way that I do, and he has hurt as many men as I have."[48]

The same week, Mack's mother had a close call. While swimming in the ocean at Atlantic City, she was pulled under and out by a breaker. She was rescued unconscious from the surf by lifeguards, who revived her and saved her life.[49]

The strain began to tell on the Athletics as September drew to a close. Mack's team continued to win, but could not gain ground on first-place Detroit. Barry was badly spiked in a game against Detroit, with Cobb once again the culprit. The Tigers were still 2½ games in front when the finishing touch occurred on September 29. Ed Walsh and the White Sox won the first game of a doubleheader, 2–1, in ten innings, as Plank once again pitched a fine game but received little support. The second game was a blowout, with Bender and

Shibe Park, Philadelphia, around 1920. Named for Ben Shibe, one of the team owners, the Athletics played here from 1909 until 1954, when the franchise relocated to
Kansas City. Opened in 1909, the park was the first of the new concrete and steel
structures that replaced the older wooden "firetraps" The National League Phillies
played here until 1970, and the structure was subsequently demolished (Baseball Hall
of Fame and Museum, Cooperstown, New York).

the Athletics defeating the Sox, 10–1, but they lost ground as Detroit won two
from Boston. A doubleheader loss the next day, with Dygert and Krause being
the victims, eliminated the Athletics, as Detroit took its third consecutive pennant. The Athletics ended the season with a doubleheader win over Washington, John Kull a winner in relief in his only major league appearance, and Rube
Vickers winning his second game of the season and last in the majors.

Mack had come close, finishing 3½ games behind Detroit. Plank went
19–10, significantly better than his 14–16 record the year before. Bender won 18
of 26 decisions. Krause was a pleasant surprise, going 18–8 with seven shutouts
and leading the league with a 1.39 ERA. Coombs improved to 12–11. Cy Morgan, acquired/stolen from Boston during the season in a trade for "Biff"
Schlitzer, produced 16 victories. Among regular position players, Eddie Collins
hit .347, his first solid season in a career that took him to the Baseball Hall of
Fame. Frank Baker hit .305 and led the league in triples with 19. Jack Barry hit
only .215, but his fielding helped solidify the infield. With any improvement
on the part of his youngsters, Mack would remain in the thick of the pennant
race for years to come.

As Mack headed south in the winter of 1910, he brought with him one of the strongest pitching staffs he had developed. Eddie Plank and Harry Krause were two of the best southpaws in the league the previous year. Among the right-handers, Jack Coombs had improved, and much was expected if he could stay healthy, while Chief Bender, despite some threats to quit baseball, was coming off a solid 18-victory season. Jimmy Dygert had grown a little heavy, but Mack was hopeful he could work himself into shape. Along with Cy Morgan, the four right-handers produced an effective complement to Plank and Krause. Ira Thomas, Pat Livingston and Jack Lapp, ready after a year of seasoning at Newark, handled the catching. Infielders Baker, Collins and Harry Davis were expected to provide much of the offense, while Jack Barry was quickly developing into one of the best fielding shortstops in the league. Danny Murphy could do his part in the outfield. "Topsy" Hartsel had aged quickly the previous year, and was expected to only play part-time while platooning with Jackson and Heinie Heitmuller.

The American League champion Tigers were coming off their third consecutive pennant, and not surprisingly were the favorites for the 1910 season.

Albert "Chief" Bender, the only Native American member of the Baseball Hall of Fame, in 1911. Bender won six World Series games in his career, including two in 1913. His 21 victories and 13 saves in 1913 demonstrated his role as a "go to" man for Mack (Library of Congress, Bain Collection).

Manager Hughie Jennings praised his team, of course, but picked the White Sox as "dark horses," especially if Ed Walsh remained as effective as he had been in the past. He was skeptical about the Athletics, primarily because Jennings felt that Krause could not repeat his 18-victory season.[50]

The Athletics opened their season in Washington on April 14; Walter Johnson was on the slab for the Nationals, facing Eddie Plank. Johnson was at his best, holding Philadelphia to a single hit — a seventh-inning fly ball by Frank Baker that right fielder Doc Gessler missed when he stumbled over a boy sitting with the crowd in the outfield. The only runs in the game came in the first, as Washington won 3–0, Plank was not at his best, allowing 13 hits, but held Washington when needed. President William Howard Taft started a tradition by attending the game, and the next day sent an autographed ball to Johnson from the White House. It read, "For Walter Johnson, with the hope that he may continue to be as formidable as in yesterday's game."[51]

The next day Bender came back to even the series. Like Plank, Bender was not at his best in the initial stages of the season, giving up ten hits. But the Athletic hitters found their eyes, and won, 8–2. The Nationals defeated Philadelphia in the "rubber" game of the series by a 4–3 score; Washington batters were hitting at a .318 clip at this point. But Mack was confident and showing no concern.

> We have played three games so far this season and lost two of them, yet I will say I have the strongest and most resourceful team that I have ever shaped for a pennant fight, and I don't except the Athletics of 1902 and 1905 which won American League pennants.... My men have simply dazed me by their speed this year. My infield is two years old this season, and they are doing the most phenomenal fielding that I have ever saw done by a team in my career ... Collins is simply a marvel. Baker and Barry share in this improvement. Davis hasn't slowed down one bit and this combination of whirlwind youngsters and a brainy first baseman gives me an infield I never dreamed I would have. In the outfield, Hartsel, Oldring and Murphy are playing rattling ball.[52]

The pitching settled down, and by mid–May, the Athletics were in first place, having won 16 of 20, including eleven straight. New York and Detroit had been on their tail, but the Athletics' streak pulled them ahead in the race. It was not to last, and as June began, the lead passed back and forth. New York passed the Athletics on June 5, but lost the lead on June 13. Two days later New York regained the top position, only to lose it again on June 16. On June 19, the Yankees defeated Cleveland, the Athletics lost to Chicago, and New York was back in first. But in a head-to-head matchup, Mack's team won consecutive doubleheaders against the Yankees, putting them back into the lead once again. And on July 2, they did it again, sweeping two from the Yankees for the fourth time during the season. As the season passed the midpoint of July, the Athletics opened a seven-game lead over Boston, which by then had overtaken New York by half a game for second place. From then until the end of the season, the Athletics would not be caught. Even so, there were still problems that had to be addressed. Hartsel was clearly finished as an everyday player, and Jackson was increasingly homesick and unhappy in Philadelphia. In July, Mack traded Jackson to Cleveland, re-acquiring journeyman outfielder Bris Lord, whom Mack had originally signed back in 1905. Mack was subsequently criticized for trading a man who was among the best in the history of baseball. But Jackson was unhappy and unproductive, and the Athletics were in a pennant race.

As the season reached Labor Day early in September, the Athletics had opened an 11½ game lead over second-place Boston and 12½ over the Yankee team that had briefly provided competition back in July. A week later, the lead was 15½ games, effectively ending the American League pennant race.

In the National League, the Chicago Cubs also were running off with the pennant, making the likely matchup in the October series one between equals. Each team had certain advantages. Pitching was clearly to the advantage of the Athletics. Harry Krause had lost much of the effectiveness he demonstrated the year before due to recurring arm problems and was limited to eleven starts. The veteran of the staff, Eddie Plank, had perfected his side-arm fastball by this, his tenth year with Mack. Few would argue with the opinion that he was now the best left-hander in the business. Bender had developed into one of the best right-handers in the league, and would win twenty games this season for the first time in his career. Jack Coombs was having a phenomenal year and was on his way to a thirty-win season.

The Cubs also had pitching but several of the club's standout hurlers from previous years had shown the effects of age. Mordecai "Three Finger" Brown and Orval Overall were bothered by arm trouble. Ed Reulbach had taken much of the season to recover from tuberculosis suffered in the spring. King Cole and Jack Pfiester, the "Giant killer" of years past, still could be counted on. Experience and hitting may have been to the Cubs' advantage. This would be their fourth series appearance since 1906. The celebrated infield of Tinker, Evers and Chance was probably no better than Barry, Collins and Davis. For hitting and experience, Frank Chance and Harry Davis were equivalent, even allowing for the health problems Chance had encountered. The outfields of Jimmy Sheckard, Frank Schulte and Art Hofman for Chicago, and Philadelphia's Danny Murphy, Rube Oldring and Bris Lord/"Topsy" Hartsel were about equal.

Final standings showed the Athletics easily winning the third of Mack's pennants, as the team finished 14½ games in front of New York; the team's record of 102–48 was its best since joining the American League. Coombs won 31 games against 9 losses, tossing a league-record (which still stands), 13 shutouts, and posted an ERA of 1.30, second only to the White Sox's Ed Walsh. Bender had a career season of 23–5 and an ERA of 1.58, a mark that included a May 12 no-hitter against Cleveland. Krause slumped to 6–6, but Cy Morgan, acquired early in the season from Boston, went 18–12 with an ERA of 1.55.

Plank also faltered, but still finished with 16 victories in 26 decisions and an ERA of 2.01. Jimmy Dygert, at 4–4, was barely missed; this would be his last season in the majors, as Mack would sell him to Baltimore during the off-season.

The series opened at Philadelphia on October 17, with Bender matched against the Cubs' Overall. The Athletics had already suffered a significant loss, as outfielder Rube Oldring had badly twisted his knee while chasing a fly ball during a pre-series exhibition against an American League all-star team, and would not appear in the series. Bris Lord would be his replacement.

Bender provided one of the outstanding performances of his career, allowing only a single hit through the first eight innings while striking out eight. He was helped by the excellent fielding of Baker and Barry. Only in the ninth, when singles by Joe Tinker and Johnny Kling sandwiched by errors on the parts of Thomas and Strunk, allowed the Cubs to score their single run. A ground ball by Hofman to Baker ended it. Baker was the hitting star for Philadelphia, with his two doubles limited by the ground rules and could easily have been triples. His first double in the second inning resulted in a score when Murphy singled him home. Bender knocked in the second and deciding run with a single in the inning.

The second game in the series on the following day matched Brown of the Cubs against 31-game winner Jack Coombs. Coombs was not at his best, giving up eight hits, nine walks and three runs, but the Athletics' defense came through when it had to by making three double plays, including one on a fly ball to Murphy, followed by the right fielder making a perfect throw to Ira Thomas at the plate to nail Brown, who was coming in from third. Eddie Collins and Thomas led the fifteen-hit attack, with each contributing three hits and scoring two runs. Six runs in the seventh inning ended all suspense, the excitement among Philadelphia fans reaching such a level that two young spectators collapsed during the rally.[53]

Two days later Mack returned Coombs to the mound, and the right-hander came through once again. As had been the case earlier, Coombs was not at his best, but the Athletic bats allowed for a performance that was more than sufficient for the 12–5 victory. Coombs produced three hits, including a double, and drove in three runs in his own support. On the slab, he struck out eight and reduced his walk count to four.

Rain postponed the fourth game by one day, allowing for a discussion that would sound familiar to a baseball fan throughout the twentieth century, centering on the nature of the baseball used in play.

As is the case even today, game balls are provided by the home team. Suspicions were raised, however, concerning the liveliness of the baseballs based on the number of hits and runs the series had produced thus far. White Sox president Charles Comiskey first asserted the baseballs were not the same as had been used during the season. "The balls used in that game yesterday were not like the balls batted by the White Sox this season. They were livelier.... They bounded higher than seemed natural and they left the bats of the players differently."[54] Former White Sox manager Fielder Jones chimed in with similar comments. "They are using a different ball than the ones we had when I was in the game."[55] Comiskey and Jones were just a little premature; a new cork center ball would be in use for the next season.

Livelier ball or not (and one must remember both clubs were hitting the same baseballs) the series resumed on October 22, as Bender returned to face King Cole. The Athletics held a 3–2 lead heading into the ninth when Mordecai Brown relieved Cole, who had been lifted for a pinch-hitter. With Frank Schulte on third and one out, Cubs manager Frank Chance hit a fly over Amos Strunk's head that the outfielder initially misjudged. Schulte scored the tying run and Chance had a triple. The Cubs failed to score again in the inning. But in the tenth with two out, the Cubs' Jimmy Sheckard singled home Jimmy Archer from third with the winning run.

Manager Mack picked Jack Coombs to pitch the fifth game and face Brown once again. Three Finger had pitched the day before and was given credit for the victory, yet having only thrown twenty pitches, was again Manager Chance's choice. In the eighth inning, the Athletics held a slim 2–1 lead. Coombs started the Athletics' rally with a solid single to right, and by the time the inning was over, the Athletics held a 7–1 lead. The Cubs managed to score a second run in the bottom of the eighth, but that was it. Jack Barry grabbed a ground ball by Johnny Kling in the bottom of the ninth, stepped on the bag, and Mack had won his first championship. Coombs had accomplished a feat seen only once before in the post-season by winning three games in a best-of-seven series. The Cubs' Johnny Evers may have blamed poor umpiring for their defeat, but the fact was the Athletics had good pitching and defense when they were needed and solid hitting throughout.[56] The team's batting average of .316, including 56 hits, was a record that stood until 1960.

Mack prepared for the 1911 season knowing his team was relatively young, intact, and more experienced. The only major change was at first base. Harry Davis would turn thirty-eight years old during the season, and had shown clear signs of slowing. Ready to step into his position was Stuffy McInnis. McInnis had played a utility role the previous seasons, mostly at shortstop, but given his ability in the field, Mack was ready to start him at first base. The experiment proved successful, and the infield of Frank Baker at third, Jack Barry at shortstop, Eddie Collins at second and McInnis at first would display such prowess that it became known as "the $100,000 infield"—representing a value beyond the ability of any other club to purchase *en masse*. Other possible changes included the addition of Clarence "Lefty" Russell to the pitching staff, and Bill Hogan as competition for Strunk.

Given the future of major league baseball during the decade, comments made by Mack prior to the start of the season in response to gambling on the game seem quite naïve in retrospect.

The average baseball fan is entirely too wise to fall for this latest get-rich-quick scheme. Why a man would be crazy to get into that game. Suppose that you had $100 to bet that the St. Louis Americans would finish first at the odds of 60–1, as quoted in their books. You must turn over your coin in April. How do you know that you're going to get your money from that crowd in October? Suppose these Kentucky fellows receive tons of money from people around the country? A good earnest ballplayer is trying his best. He makes an error at a critical moment.... There would be hundreds of people in hundreds of cities who would figure that he did it purposely.[57]

Unfortunately, the gamblers had no such qualms, and their influence would reach a peak in the 1919 World Series.

But that was eight years in the future. For now, Mack was preparing for the upcoming season as defending world champions. The routine was the same as in previous years: spring training in the south and the intra-league series with the Phillies prior to the start of the season (the Athletics won three of five games). But in the opener against New York, Jim Vaughn of the Yankees out-pitched Bender, holding the Athletics to three hits as the champions lost, 2–1. Hogan and Davis started for the Mackmen. The worst was not over, as the Yankees swept the opening three-game series. Plank finally ended the streak, blanking Boston, 1–0. Mack had his own theory as to the reason behind the poor start. "Too many bridegrooms.... My recently married men get on the field, their brides sit in the grand stand and the men are so anxious to please they just forget what they know of the game." Mack would know. "The worst of it all is that I'm a bridegroom myself [having recently re-married], so what on earth am I going to do about it?"[58] Mack neglected the case of Eddie Collins, also a newlywed. Collins was hitting .556 at the time. Only he and Danny Murphy were hitting over .200 at this stage, certainly among the reasons for the poor start. Whatever the cause, at the end of April, hot-hitting Detroit was the league leader with a 14–2 record; the champion Athletics were 6½ behind with a record of 6–7.

By the end of May, the Athletics had begun to right themselves, winning 23 of 39 decisions, but still resided seven games behind the Tigers. The problem centered on pitching. Waivers were asked on Russell, who had proven to be a bust. Krause still suffered from arm problems and was often day-to-day. The staff came down to Plank, Coombs, Bender and Morgan. Harry Davis had produced only two hits in twenty-eight official at-bats, and was replaced by McInnis at first. McInnis had been filling in for the injured Barry at shortstop, and after hitting .476 in his first fourteen games, had remained in the lineup. The infield started to hit, the pitching remained strong behind the four regulars, and the Athletics had effectively caught Detroit by the end of the month: Detroit, 44–22, with Philadelphia at 42–22. Even Barry had become an offensive plus, beating Detroit with a steal of home on the ninth. Two doubleheader sweeps in two days at the beginning of July against the Yankees put the Athletics on top of the standings, albeit only for a few days.

The end of July saw Detroit visiting Philadelphia for a critical series. On July 28 before a crowd of more than 36,000, the Athletics swept a doubleheader, the first game an eleven-inning 1–0 shutout behind Bender, the second a 6–5 victory behind Coombs. In the excitement, a 33-year-old man died from a heart attack. The following day, Philadelphia won again, 11–3, behind Plank and in front of another crowd estimated at more than 34,000. Detroit won the fourth game of the series, and as July came to a close, the race showed Detroit ahead by one-half game with a record of 61–32, and Philadelphia at 60–32.

In August, the Mackmen began to pull away. With a 17–10 record for the month, coupled with Detroit's 13–16 mark, the Athletics' lead was 4½ by the end of August, stretching to 11 games by the end of September. The Athletics finished the season with a record of 101–50, 13½ over Detroit while breeching the century mark in wins for the second consecutive season. It was a combination of strong defense, especially with McInnis now the regular first baseman, pitching and offense. The infield averaged .323 in hitting, with Collins batting .365 and Baker at .334 with a league-leading 11 home runs. Barry hit only .265, but had developed a reputation as a tough hitter in the clutch and an excellent fielder. In his first full season, McInnis batted .321, though an injury would keep him from anything but a token appearance in the series. Among the pitchers, Plank won 23 against 8 losses and led the league with six shutouts, and Coombs again led the league in wins with a 28–12 record. Bender went 17–5, even though he had to deal with a tragedy — the sudden death of his brother in September. Morgan produced a 15–7 record in his last effective year, and Krause managed an 11–8 season despite arm problems.

Facing the Athletics in the series once again was the Giants. But this was not the Giants team that had defeated Mack six years earlier. Among the pitchers, Mathewson and Wiltse remained two of the mainstays, with a young left-hander named Rube Marquard, who had won 24 games in his first full season. Among position players, only Buck Herzog and Art Fletcher were considered the equals of their counterparts on the Athletics. Philadelphia was strongly favored.

The series opened on October 14 in New York. Mathewson was McGraw's choice. The big right-hander had won 26 games during the season. In the previous encounter between these two teams back in 1905, he had pitched three shutouts. Mathewson started where he had left off, holding Philadelphia scoreless in the first. But in the top of the second, the Athletics broke through. Baker singled and was sacrificed to second. A passed ball by catcher Chief Meyers advanced him to third, from where he scored on a single by Davis, who had replaced the injured McInnis for the series. The Giants tied the game in the fourth, the run scoring with two outs on an error by Eddie Collins, and went ahead in the seventh. Meyers doubled with one out and scored what would be the winning run on a double by Josh Devore. Bender pitched well, striking out eleven. But the Athletics managed only six hits and the one run, and in the end, Mathewson ran his streak against the Mackmen to four straight victories.

Marquard was McGraw's choice for the second game as the teams traveled to Philadelphia. Mack was forced to decide between Coombs and Plank. If Coombs pitched, Lapp would be the catcher. But Marquard, a left-hander, was more likely to be successful facing Lapp as a batter than if Thomas caught for the Athletics. Thomas was Plank's regular catcher, and Mack felt Plank could have a better temperament in dealing with the pressure of a "must win" situation.[59] Mack chose Plank. The Athletics quickly jumped to a one-run lead in the first. Bris Lord singled and advanced to second when Eddie Murray fumbled the ball in center. Following a sacrifice, Lord scored on a wild pitch. The Giants quickly tied the game on a double by Herzog, a grounder by Fletcher and a single by Meyers.

The game remained tied in the sixth. But in the bottom of the inning with two outs, Collins doubled and Baker followed with a hard smash over the right-center field wall. That ended the scoring as Plank held the Giants to five hits. Marquard later admitted that the pitch he threw to Baker, a fastball, was not what Meyers had called. Marquard had retired Baker twice before with curveballs. Baker had one strike already, and Marquard decided to try to fool the Athletics' third baseman. He didn't, and the pitch went over the fence.[60]

Game three on October 17 saw Christy Mathewson return to the slab on three days' rest to face Mack's choice, Jack Coombs. Both pitchers remained undefeated in post-season play, Mathewson working on a four-game win streak, Coombs three. The 37,216 fans at the Polo Grounds saw one of the greatest pitching duels to take place in a World's Series. For eight innings, the Athletics were helpless against the tall right-hander. New York managed only a single run through ten innings. In the bottom of the third, with one out, Meyers bounced a grounder over Baker's head. Mathewson singled him to third, and Meyers scored on a grounder by Devore to Barry. The two hits represented the Giants' total until the eleventh inning.

The big play occurred in the ninth. With one out, Frank Baker came to bat. Matty quickly jumped ahead with two curveballs for strikes. Marquard had been in a similar situation the day before and tried to fool Baker with a fastball. Matty made the same mistake. Thinking that Baker would be looking for a fastball, Mathewson attempted to throw another curve past the Athletics' third baseman. Once again Baker was ready, smashing the ball on a drive over the right-field wall. The score remained tied until the eleventh inning, with both Mathewson and Coombs continuing in the game. In the top of the eleventh, Collins singled with one out, and Baker followed with a hard grounder to Herzog at third. Herzog's throw went wild, and the runners ended up at second and third. An error by Fletcher on Murphy's grounder allowed one run to score, and a single by Davis scored Baker with another. The Giants managed to come close in their half of the inning, but fell short. Mathewson pitched well, allowing only three hits, but ended up on the short end of the score.

Baker confirmed he had been looking for the pitch. "Connie Mack told

Frank Baker, (1912), slugging third baseman for Mack acquired the sobriquet "Home Run" as a result of his hitting in the 1911 World Series against these same Giants (Baseball Hall of Fame and Museum, Cooperstown, New York).

me that when I went to the bat that I would not get a fast one and he was right. I set myself and looked them over against Mathewson and when he tossed me that curve and I saw her starting to break and I busted her." Collins also had his own perspective on the Giant fans. "Say, those Giant fans love to lose, don't they? They pan Marquard for throwing over one that Baker murdered; they roast Matty for throwing one that Baker did the same thing to; they roast Umpire Connolly because they were thrown out five times stealing by Johnny Lapp; they say Snodgrass did not try to hurt Baker at third base [after Baker was spiked in the tenth inning]; they claim Connie Mack wet the grounds here and they claim we have their signals, but they are not claiming the world's championship for 1911 so that any one can notice it."[61]

Then the rain started. Day after day in Philadelphia the rain continued, forcing one postponement after another. Finally on October 24, the field was ready for play. Having waited a week since his last appearance, Mathewson was again the choice for McGraw, now in a position in which another Athletics victory could mean the end. Mack's choice was Bender, producing the same matchup as in the opening game. The Giants struck in the first inning, scoring two runs on Devore's single, a triple by Larry Doyle and a sacrifice fly by Fred Snodgrass. The Athletics went ahead in the fourth inning, when they scored three of their four runs with three consecutive doubles, starting with one by Baker, and a sacrifice fly. Mathewson struck out five, but allowed eleven hits.

Game Five pitted Coombs against Marquard, and once again the New York fans were treated to a real pitchers' duel. In the third, Philadelphia jumped to a three-run lead — the result of two Giant miscues and a three-run home run by Oldring. Marquard was removed for a pinch-hitter in the bottom of the inning and replaced by Red Ames. The Giants chipped away at the lead, scoring once in the seventh and tying the game in the ninth. Coombs lasted through the ninth and was replaced by Plank. The Giants won in the tenth on a sacrifice fly, as Doyle scored on a long fly ball by Fred Merkle. Ironically, Doyle did not actually touch the plate, but since none of the Athletics brought it to the attention of umpire Bill Klem, the run counted.[62] The Giants now trailed Mack three games to two.

The Giants came back with Ames as the series moved back to Philadelphia. Bender was once again the choice for Mack. The game and the series were over quickly. New York jumped to a fast 1–0 lead in the first; the Athletics tied the game in the third on a walk to Thomas and double by Lord. They finished it the following inning. Baker and Murphy singled, and Baker scored on an infield single by Davis. Murphy and Davis scored when a throw by Ames on a Barry bunt hit the batter in the head and Murray's throw went wild, allowing Barry to come around to score. Seven runs in the seventh only added to the total, as Bender pitched a four-hitter in the 13–2 victory. Once again, as was seen the year before, solid pitching and timely hitting made the difference. Baker led all position players with a .375 average, which included nine hits and two home runs. His 9 RBIs tied Harry Davis for the lead in that department. Bender won two of three decisions, striking out 20 in 26 innings pitched and throwing three complete games. The combined ERA for Mack's pitchers was 1.29. Mack was so pleased with Bender's work in particular that after the series, he gave the pitcher a $2,500 check to pay off the mortgage on his home.[63] "The Tall Tactician" also had managed a modicum of revenge for the defeat to McGraw six years earlier.

In February 1912 Mack headed to San Antonio for spring training with the rookies, and Danny Murphy proceeded with the rest of the squad shortly thereafter. Also training in Texas that year were the Giants and White Sox, who were taking advantage of the pleasant weather of late winter. For the first time in the American League, a championship team had repeated the feat for a second consecutive year. There was no reason to think Mack would not continue his success. The youngsters, particularly McInnis, had another year under their respective belts, as well as two years of the pressure associated with post-season play. There would be no barnstorming between the Giants and Athletics this year, as National Commission rules now forbade games between the regulars of major league clubs that had appeared in the World's Series. Mack also had other things on his mind — his mother died in February at age 72.

The writers likewise expected the Athletics to repeat, in no small measure due to Mack's managing ability. "No frills, no seeker of applause, no absorber of the limelight, no stage manager.... He obtains results, as maybe McGraw would testify, or Chance. He is known as the silent man of baseball, but his is an absolute monarchy, as absolute as that of the Czar of Russia and lots more friendly.... He is usually about three steps ahead of his opponents when it comes to that idea thing. Perhaps that is why he is a winner. The man who outguesses Connie Mack, declared a rival manager once, ought to give up the baseball business. What he is, is a clairvoyant."[64]

The 1912 season for the Athletics opened on April 11 in Philadelphia, as Jack Coombs outpitched Washington's Walter Johnson by holding the Nationals to four hits and striking out six in a 4–2 triumph. Coombs aggravated a groin pull from the previous season and missed much of the first month of the season. Johnson gained his revenge a week later in Washington's home opener, outpitching Athletics rookie Boardwalk Brown with a three-hit, 6–0 shutout. Johnson struck out eight. With three victories in four games, Mack was particularly pleased with the play of one of his young men in particular: Eddie Collins. "I have a young man on my team for whom I predict a great future. His name is Edward Trowbridge Collins, and although outside of his hitting, fielding and base running he is now a poor ball player, experience, I expect, will develop him in time. He almost let one ball get by him today [following a 7–0 shutout of the Yankees by Plank], and if he does not get on the job I'll bench him."[65] Nevertheless, the Athletics ended the first month on sour notes, falling to a fourth-place tie with a record of 7–6, 2½ games behind league-leader Chicago for the young season.

Philadelphia continued to play no better than .500 ball through May, ending the month with a 17–16 record, now 7½ behind Chicago, and five games behind second-place Boston. On May 14 in a losing cause against Chicago, Mack replaced his "Iron Man" Jack Coombs with a youngster from a local military academy: Herbert "Jack" Pennock. Pennock walked two and allowed only a single hit in the first professional appearance of a Hall of Fame career. The ineffectiveness of Mack's regulars was further exacerbated when Bender, with a record of 1–1 in the two games he appeared, developed a sore arm.

The Athletics regained momentum in June, winning 22 of 31 decisions, but still remained 5½ games behind the Red Sox, whose play was even better. Bender again was ineffective. Outfielder Danny Murphy injured his knee, and was doubtful for much of the season. However, at least one writer — Hugh Fullerton — remained convinced the Athletics would overtake the Red Sox by August.[66]

Reality was different. By the end of July, Philadelphia had fallen to third, the Athletics' 55–41 record placing them 11 games behind first-place Boston and five games behind a surprising Washington team. Three of the top seven hitters in the league were Athletics; Baker, McInnis and Collins were hitting .335 or higher, behind Cobb, Speaker and Joe Jackson. Among the pitchers, only Plank, at 14–3, and Coombs, 16–5, were showing consistency. Bender was 8–6, Houck stood at 5–4. Even Mack was beginning to accept the possibility that the Red Sox would not be caught.[67] At the beginning of September, he conceded as much. Following a loss to Boston, Mack was quoted as saying he had not realized how strong Jake Stahl's squad actually was, and predicted the Boston lead at the end of the season would be larger than at the present time.[68] Mack's prediction was close. The Athletics were 13½ games behind at the end of August 15 games behind at the end. Mack was also becoming increasingly frustrated with the play of two of his players—Oldring and Bender—going so far as to imply the loss of the pennant was due in part to their erratic play. Reading between the lines, it appeared whiskey was the real problem.[69] On September 6, both were suspended without pay and sent home.[70]

The final standings found the Athletics remaining in third place, a single game behind second-place Washington. Their record of 90–62 was certainly

In his 53 years as manager of Pittsburgh and then of Philadelphia, Connie Mack (shown here in 1911) won more games than any other major league manager (3,731), and lost more games (3,948), while winning nine pennants and five World Series, including two against McGraw (Library of Congress, Bain Collection).

exemplary. Plank produced a fine 26–6 record, though good enough only for fourth among victories in the league. Coombs recovered sufficiently to win 21 games. Bender slipped to 13 triumphs in 21 decisions. Among the hitters, Frank Baker continued to lead the league in home runs, hitting 10, and produced 130 RBIs, also leading the league in that category, while hitting a career-high of .347. McInnis hit .327 with 101 RBIs. Eddie Collins hit .348. Along with Jack Barry, Philadelphia continued to have the best infield in the major leagues. But the Red Sox, winning a then American League record 105 games, were simply too strong and temporarily ended Mack's dominance of the American League.

CHAPTER TWO

"The Old Oriole"

I was talking about the next two pennant races with Judge Kenesaw Mountain Landis, the high commissioner of baseball, when someone handed him a message. When he looked up there were tears in his eyes. "The greatest of all the old Orioles is flying west. John McGraw is dead." Few people can understand what John McGraw meant to baseball. He was one of the greatest natural leaders any sport has ever known. Baseball to him was more than a game. It was a religion and a war combined.... Few can understand how he gave his very soul to the game he loved so well — to the game he followed from a kid of 18 for forty years until ill health removed most of his old fire.... He was emblematic of the fire and dash that belongs to the national game. He knew ballplayers and he knew how to handle them.... The game of baseball missed the old McGraw in his retirement. The game of baseball will miss the McGraw that still took the keenest interest in everything that took place.... He was the kind of manager that every fan secretly or openly admired, and I happen to be still a fan above being a commissioner. No one who loves baseball and understands the spirit of the game can help from knowing what the dead Oriole — the dead Giant — meant to this sport — to the fighting spirit of all sports and all games.

There was no mistaking the deep sincerity of Judge Landis's remarks. For after all, only a few knew the real McGraw — the man who loved victory — the leader with the rasping, cutting voice that so often poured sarcasm and invective upon umpires, the enemy, his own players — and who in turn gave away thousands of dollars every year to old ballplayers, broken down in the service of the game. There were many who hated John McGraw and to many of these he gave a reason. But when they knew him at closer range — the real John McGraw away from the battle line — they usually switched their judgements.... McGraw was a stout believer in showmanship — in color — in anything that would add to baseball interest. He was the most vital spark the bench and the coaching lines have ever known.[1]

Who was this man, this baseball icon? John Joseph McGraw was born at home on April 7, 1873, in Truxton, New York. His father, John William McGrath (McGraw), had emigrated with his brother Michael from Ireland, arriving in the United States about 1850. During the Civil War he either enlisted or was drafted in 1862 —"drawn" according to Charles Alexander, one of John McGraw's biographers— serving primarily with a battalion of engineers, and was honorably discharged in August 1865. McGrath, now McGraw, married a local girl named Ellen Comerfort around 1870. John Joseph, named for his grandfather, was one of eight children in the Catholic household born within a twelve-year period. A maintenance worker with the Elmira, Cortland and Northern Railroad, John William could barely keep his family clothed and fed.

Like most small-town children of the era, the younger John spent much of his early youth fending for himself. He had the reputation of being thoughtful and courteous, and a good ball player. So good, in fact, he had a growing tendency to hit what passed for a base ball (sic), and sometimes simply stones, through local windows, a habit which caused his father endless annoyance given it was he who paid the 15 cents to repair them. Beatings were not rare. The family managed to survive reasonably well — poverty was certainly no stranger to the town — until the winter of 1884–1885, when diphtheria arrived. In its wake, Ellen and three children were dead, a tragedy from which the elder McGraw would never recover.[2, 3] The family moved to a newer house closer to town, and what little patience the father had with the younger John evaporated as he tried to hold his family together. Finally, after the boy broke one too many windows, the father snapped. After enduring a beating once again, young John ran away, never returning to the household.

John McGraw, now about twelve, found refuge in Truxton at the home/ hotel of a young widow — tragedy was a common feature of life — named Mary Goddard. Goddard gave him the attention he had lacked with the death of his mother, a stable home, and a sense of responsibility. In addition to doing chores in the hotel for Goddard, McGraw worked for the railroad, selling magazines, fruit and "what-nots" to passengers, and became a paper boy for the local newspaper — no easy task, especially in winter, given that much of the route was in farm country. With some of the money he earned, McGraw bought real baseballs as well as baseball guides published by A.J. Spalding, among the earliest annual publications by which one could follow the growing sport. Though small even by contemporary standards at less than 5'8" and 105 pounds, McGraw could pitch and field, and had no difficulty playing on local teams. His first big moment on the diamond may have been at age 15 or 16, when the manager of a team in the nearby town of East Homer paid him $5, plus transportation, to pitch.[4] For a few weeks, the young Johnny McGraw was being paid for doing something he loved.

McGraw's chance at a baseball career in came when a hotel owner in Truxton, Bert Kenney, invested in the Olean, New York, team in the newly formed New York–Pennsylvania League. McGraw begged Kenney, named the captain/ manager and center fielder on the team, for a chance to join Olean. Kenney agreed, offering a contract of forty dollars per month if McGraw was good enough to stick. And so on April 1, 1890, John McGraw signed his first professional baseball contract. A month later, McGraw joined the team.

John McGraw had shown a real talent for the game when playing against the competition of local town teams. But the New York–Pennsylvania League represented a significant increase in the quality of play, and McGraw simply was not ready for that level of competition. In his first game, playing third base against Erie on May 16, McGraw's contribution was eight errors in ten chances.[5] After several days in which no improvement was seen, Kenney released McGraw from his contract, lending the boy seventy dollars to try and catch on with another team. McGraw was not the only "victim" of poor play, as at least five other players were dismissed in Kenney's revamping of the team. Eventually even Kenney was dismissed, replaced by Edward Troy.

Following brief stops in Hornellsville and Canisteo, McGraw went as far as Wellsville, a small town east of Olean. McGraw participated in twenty-four games for Wellsville between June and the end of September, earning approximately sixty dollars a month. Still raw on defense, McGraw managed to hit .365 during his four-month stint. Another member of the team was Alfred Lawson, a London-born self-promoter who had some pitching experience in the (then depleted) National League. Lawson was in the process of recruiting a team of "American All-Stars" that would play a series of exhibitions in Florida and Cuba during the winter of 1890–1891, and offered McGraw a position with the team. McGraw joined Lawson in mid–January and played a number of games in isolated communities against local teams. Years later when traveling through Florida, McGraw would recall where playing fields had once existed in those towns.

The "American All-Stars" played about a half-dozen games in Cuba, facing competition that was stronger than they had been led to expect. Lawson's squad won only a single game and barely made enough money to pay their way back to Florida. During February 1891 they worked their way north in what was then a rural state with extensive swampland and few inhabitants. The warm weather in early spring was ideal even then for training, and major league teams often traveled there for conditioning. On March 26, what remained of the "All-Stars" scheduled a game in Gainesville with the Cleveland Spiders who were training in Jacksonville. Unlike the local teams Lawson's squad had beaten up, the Spiders were a legitimate organization, and included such stars as Patsy Tebeau, Big Ed McKean, and a rookie pitcher named Denton "Cy" Young. Scheduled to face Lawson's "All-Stars" was Len Viau. Viau had twice won more than 20 games with Cincinnati of the American Association, but at this point in training he was still working his arm into condition. Cleveland won 9–6. McGraw had three doubles and a single in five at-bats, scoring three runs while playing an errorless game at shortstop. McGraw later recalled the events.

> They were a bit raw, having had only a few days practice, while I was as spry as a kid my age [18] could be. We played the Clevelands one day with Viau in the box, and Viau was a good pitcher in those days. But, of course, he did not have a seasoned arm, so he just lobbed the ball up to the plate. And maybe I didn't soak the horsehide! I got three doubles and a single, and it proved to be the start of my career. The funniest thing was no one ever got on to the fact that the pitcher was just lobbing them over the plate. A few days later I was receiving telegrams from

all over the country. Some offered me $60 a month, and that was still good money to me. I kept putting them off, however, until the Cedar Rapids club wired me an offer of $125.[6]

Manager Jim Plumb of the Cedar Rapids Canaries sent McGraw a $75 advance on his salary. But it appears that despite McGraw's disclaimers, he also had agreed to play with as many as five other clubs, including Fort Wayne, Davenport and Rockford. Eventually the fall-out settled, and by April 1891 McGraw was the property of the Cedar Rapids Canaries.[7]

Experience and maturity had made a ballplayer of McGraw. Only eighteen years old, he had developed into a "dandy little (at 5'6", 121 pounds) shortstop," and as the season passed its midpoint, was hitting .275.[8] However, the league itself was failing and McGraw began to look elsewhere for employment. By chance, a more important opportunity opened up that allowed McGraw to join the highest level of professional baseball faster than even he had expected.

McGraw's reputation had spread as far as Baltimore, and when Cedar Rapids played Rockford later in the season, that opportunity appeared in the form of shortstop Bill Gleason. Gleason had played six seasons at shortstop for the St. Louis Browns of the (major league) American Association. Gleason was friends with Bill Barnie, who was managing the Baltimore Orioles of the American Association. Barnie had heard of McGraw and wanted Gleason's opinion about the scrappy young Canarie. McGraw's own opinion: "I'm just about as good as they come."[9] Gleason was satisfied, and informed Barnie that McGraw would be a quality addition to the Orioles. As a result in August 1891, John McGraw arrived in Baltimore as a major league ballplayer and earned $200 per month, provided he was with the team for the remainder of the season.

McGraw faced several problems, baseball being what it was in the 1890s. First, he was small even by the professional standards of the time, and wearing a hand-me-down uniform several sizes too large did not help his appearance. Even Barnie was surprised how small the ballplayer he had heard about actually was. Second, he had replaced a veteran on the squad; the other players, knowing the same situation could happen to any of them, were never thrilled with the appearance of any rookie. The game itself differed in a number of ways from that which would be observed even later the same decade. The pitcher threw from a box fifty feet away; the current distance of a pitching rubber, placed 60 feet 6 inches from the batter, was established two years later. Home "plate" was a foot wide, not the current 17 inches. Fielding gloves, increasingly common by 1891, barely covered the hands and errors were common. Perhaps one of the biggest impacts on play at the time was the presence of only a single umpire on the field. Since the arbiter could not observe everything at all times, stretching of the rules was common. It was not unknown, for example, for a player to shorten his trip around the diamond by cutting past third base. Arguments were frequent, and an umpire had to be tough, literally, to survive not only player fights, but objects and even fists from irate fans. McGraw was in his element. The Baltimore Orioles of the mid–90s had a well-deserved reputation as one of the "fightingist" in their league. In a newspaper story headlined "Orioles Played Dirty Ball," the writer described, "A riot was almost precipitated by dirty ball-playing on the part of [pitcher Tony] Mullane and shortstop McGraw. The former tried to hit [Cincinnati's Arlie] Latham with a pitched ball, and the latter deliberately jumped on his hand with his spiked shoe, after he had made a head-first slide into second base."[10]

McGraw's first months in the big-time were anything but spectacular. Once again scrappiness was not an immediate solution to his inexperience at that level. His first appearance on the field was August 26, facing the Columbus Solons, then a major league team as well. Starting at shortstop, he made an error that allowed a run, but made up for it with a sixth-inning single and reached second base on an error by the fielder. McGraw scored his first run on a single by Wilbert Robinson. Playing in 33 games the last month or so of the season, McGraw managed to bat .270, with 31 hits in 115 at-bats, including five triples. At shortstop, he produced 17 errors in his 90 chances, a fielding average of .811, poor by any standards. McGraw's fielding at times was so poor, Manager Barnie moved him to right field. Baltimore finished the season in fourth place.

Despite McGraw's problems, Orioles owner Harry von der Horst offered him a contract for the next season. Bill Barnie had quit as manager near the end of the season, replaced by outfielder George van Haltren, who agreed that "Little McGraw" would remain with the team as a substitute.[11]

Two significant changes took place as the 1892 version of the Orioles began the pennant race. The first, with the greater implication for major league baseball, was the merger that took place between the two leagues, the National League and American Association. Teams in both leagues had been losing money, a problem exacerbated by the experiment with the Players League in 1890. The result was that one twelve-team circuit, a "big league," was created, with four teams from the AA dropped. Baltimore became part of what was officially called the National League and American Association, but informally called simply the National League.

The second change occurred one week into the new season, when after the team lost eleven of its first twelve games, van Haltren was replaced by Ned Hanlon as manager. It would take time for Hanlon to overhaul the team, and Baltimore managed a record of 46–101, 8½ games behind the eleventh-place St. Louis Browns. McGraw did manage to show improvement, albeit primarily as a utility player, coach and even ticket taker — his $1,200 yearly salary was for more than simply sitting on the bench. Appearing in 79 games, McGraw averaged .269, approximately the same as the year before. But his fielding significantly improved. McGraw split his time evenly between the infield and outfield, but as a second baseman, his fielding average improved to .925.

Among the changes that took place as the 1893 season of appeared on the horizon was the elimination of the pitcher's box. It was replaced by a rubber slab, placed 60 feet 6 inches from the batter, on which the pitcher had to place his foot while delivering the pitch. Not surprisingly, batting averages increased that season, and averages higher than .400 would not be rare until pitchers adjusted to the new distance. Manager Hanlon also made significant changes to the team by beginning the formation of what would become known as the "legendary" Baltimore Orioles team of the mid–1890s. McGraw had already become friends with Orioles catcher Wilbert Robinson, who was later immortalized as the lovable Uncle Wilber, manager of the Brooklyn Dodgers. From Louisville, Hanlon obtained shortstop Hugh Jennings, the future long-time manager of the Tigers. Other acquisitions and signings that year included another future Hall of Famer, outfielder Joe Kelley, as well as 5'7" second baseman Henry "Heinie" Reitz.

McGraw quickly developed a reputation as a scrappy, quarrelsome player, one who was not averse to stretching or breaking rules in a day when only a single umpire was present. In an exhibition game at Chattanooga, McGraw, playing shortstop, prevented a runner on second base from advancing by holding his belt.[12] Writers had their own nicknames: "Mickey Face," which he seems to have tolerated, and "Muggsy," a name that would result in a fight if used in his presence.

The Orioles were still less than a .500 club, though their record did improve to 60–70, good enough for eighth place in the 12-team circuit. The team's single noteworthy achievement for the season was the no-hitter thrown by Bill Hawke against the Washington Nationals on August 16. Only "Dummy" Hoy and Duke Farrell reached base, both due to walks, as Hawke struck out six in a 5–0 performance in front of a "crowd" of 872. The difficulties faced by the umpire was exemplified by what did, and did not occur, during the course of the game. McGraw was fined $5 by umpire Bob Emslie for arguing a lead-off strikeout. "This little evidence of the supremacy of the umpire had its fruit in no further unnecessary backtalk or kicking. Emslie had rather an easy game to umpire, and but one close decision arose, when Hoy was called out at second. It looked as if McGraw had dropped the ball, but as he appeared with it directly he emerged from the collision the umpire may have been correct in his ruling."[13] Jennings was ill much of the early season, and McGraw became the regular shortstop. His fielding remained suspect, with 67 errors and a fielding average of .894 at the position. However, his batting improved to .321, albeit during a year when averages were often inflated, and he stole 38 bases.

During the preseason, Hanlon continued to put together a team that would exhibit the epitome of "inside baseball." From Brooklyn came first baseman Big Dan Brouthers, at 6'2" the giant on the team, as well as the diminutive 5'4" outfielder Wee Willie Keeler. Jennings was healthy again, allowing McGraw to move to third. The infield now consisted of McGraw, Jennings, Reitz and

Brouthers, with only Brouthers taller than 5'8". Hanlon believed in speed coupled with inside baseball and strong defense, rather than raw power. The outfield consisted of Kelley in left, Keeler in center and "Steve" Brodie, late of St. Louis, in right. Wilbert Robinson took over the regular catching duties, while Sadie McMahon was the primary pitcher.

That winter, Hanlon assembled his team in Macon, Georgia, for spring training, a time used primarily to work on the brand of baseball he emphasized. Using two-a-day drills, the team practiced bunting, hit-and-run plays and hitting fouls (not counted as strikes before 1901 if "unintentional"). On defense they worked on small but critical plays such as how to properly cut off throws, backing up on plays, and covering bases. After weeks of such intensive practice, the team was ready.

The Orioles opened at home, facing Amos Rusie and the New York Giants on April 19, with McMahon as the Oriole pitcher. In front of a crowd of 15,500 (13,800 paid), the revamped Orioles pounded the Giants, 8–3. McGraw scored the first run in the third inning, leading off with a walk and stealing second base when Giants catcher Duke Farrell overthrew the second baseman. Keeler struck out, but when Farrell lost the pitch, McGraw advanced to third. He scored when the next batter, Steve Brodie, grounded out. The following day, Baltimore made it two in a row, as Tony Mullane limited the Giants to six hits in a 12–6 triumph; three errors by each team resulted in most of the scoring. Leading off the first inning, McGraw was hit by a pitch, eventually coming around to score the game's first run. The Orioles made it three in a row with a 4–3 victory behind Bert Inks on April 21. McGraw played a critical role in the victory. In the seventh inning, with the Giants in front 3–1, McGraw singled in the tying runs, then went to third on a hit-and-run single by Keeler. He scored on a sacrifice fly. Manager John Montgomery Ward of the Giants blamed his losses on the better conditioning of the Orioles: "The Baltimores have been playing together for several weeks, and in the matter of conditioning have the advantage of any team in the League."[14]

Baltimore was not the only team to play "dirty" baseball.

In Baltimore, Tuesday, [Boston outfielder Tommy] McCarthy played a new trick. The "trap" ball may be a thing of the past in the infield, but "Tommy" has uses for it in the outfield. In the third inning Robinson was on second and McGraw on first, with only one man out. Keeler, who followed McGraw, hit a fly to McCarthy. To everyone's surprise he dropped it. The two base runners hugged their bases, and, before they knew what was up, McCarthy had thrown the ball to [third baseman Billy] Nash. The latter snapped it to [second baseman Bobby] Lowe who, in a flash, tagged Robinson and forced McGraw. This play was wildly hissed and stigmatized as dirty baseball by the Baltimore spectators.[15]

McGraw became particularly adept at getting on base in the leadoff spot. "Standing upright in the left-hand batter's box, his hands about six inches from the end of the bat, and swinging with a chopping motion, McGraw became expert at fouling off pitch after pitch ... [until] a base on balls.... Once on base, McGraw would flash the hit-and-run sign to Keeler, batting second, and take off with the pitch. More often than not, Wee Willie would be able to punch the ball through the space the second baseman or shortstop running to cover the base had just vacated. McGraw would easily pull into third, and an Oriole rally would be in the offing."[16]

The Giants and Orioles kept the race tight throughout the summer until the final month, when Baltimore won 27 of their final 30 games taking over first place permanently. They clinched the pennant on September 25 with a victory in Cleveland. Hungry for a victory at last, fans went wild. At Ford's Opera House in Baltimore, 3,000 men and boys sang "B B C, B B C, The champion baseball club are we." A silk pennant in orange and black, fifteen feet long and reading "Baltimores, Champions 1894," was brought out to the building's stage.[17] At the railroad station, the chant was more risqué: "B B C, B B C, Baltimore baseball cranks are we. Rah, Rah, Rah, Sis Boom Bam, Baltimore, Baltimore don't give a damn."[18]

Baltimore finished with a record of 89–39, an improvement of 29 victories from the previous year, and three games in front of the Giants. Playing in 124 games, McGraw batted .340, batting in 92 RBIs, and stealing a career-high 78 bases. Fielding was still a problem for him. Playing mostly at third base, McGraw had a fielding average of .892, the result of 46 errors. Keeler hit .371, Jennings .335, Kelley .393 with 111 RBIs, and Brouthers .347 with 128 RBIs. Batting averages for the year must be placed in perspective; with the pitching rubber having been moved, the league average was .310. Hugh Duffy was batting champion with an average of .440.

Sadie McMahon was the staff ace at 25–8. Kid Gleason, acquired from St. Louis during the season, produced a 15–5 record. Duke Esper was 10–2, and Bill Hawke, 16–9. But baseball did not end for the Orioles with the completion of the season. During that summer, coal baron and Pittsburg Pirate owner William Temple offered to donate a silver cup to the winner of a postseason series between the first- and second-place teams. The Temple Cup Series, as it was known, was played from 1894–1897, after which it was discontinued.

The 1894 Series between the Orioles and second-place Giants began October 4 in Baltimore. The series was marked by controversy even before it began. Temple's original idea was to split receipts between the winners and losers at 65 percent–35 percent. The division was unacceptable to the Orioles in general, and McGraw in particular, who refused to play unless the division was changed to 50–50. In the end, the players agreed to divide the pot equally, and McGraw agreed to play.

Thirty-six-game winner Amos Rusie of the Giants faced Duke Esper in the opening game. Sadie McMahon would miss the series with a sore arm. The "official" crowd of 11,720 watched New York slug its way to a 4–1 victory, a score which belied the dominance of the New York team. Three players, van Haltren, Dirty Jack Doyle and George Davis, tripled, and Rusie doubled in his own cause. The Giants held a 4-0 lead as the ninth inning started. The Oreoles' Giants' only run came in their last at-bat, when McGraw singled, went to second on a grounder by Brodie, and scored on a single by Reitz. A crowd at the Opera House, equally divided among partisans, followed the game. "Take him out of de game" was rang out when it was announced that McGraw "was indulging in one of his usual senseless kicks against the umpire."[19]

The second game pitted the Giants' Jouett Meekin, 33–9 for the season, against Kid Gleason. A crowd of nearly 12,000 saw their Orioles twice jump to a lead in the course of the game. But a three-run triple by Giant outfielder Mike Tiernan put the Giants in front in the ninth, as they won, 9–6. McGraw went hitless. The series moved to New York on October 6, with a similar outcome. With a crowd of 20,000 cheering them on, Rusie and the Giants won their third straight of the series, out-pitching George Hemming in the 4–1 final. McGraw had a single hit, and did not figure in the scoring. The Giants finished their sweep two days later as poor weather held the crowd to about 10,000. The game was stopped after eight innings, the Giants behind Meekin defeating Hawke by a 16–3 score. McGraw managed one hit and one run. Financially, the teams earned approximately $21,000 for their efforts, the Giants receiving about $800 apiece, the Orioles $450. Of course, in many instances players made their own private financial arrangements.

Hanlon made a significant change as the 1895 season began. Dan Brouthers was sold to Louisville after the start of the season, replaced by George Carey at first base. McMahon's arm was slow in healing — he would win ten games during the season and in his place Bill Hoffer was added to the staff. Hanlon decided upon Hemming as his ace.[20] Meanwhile, the *Baltimore Herald* named McGraw as the outstanding third baseman in the league, an opinion far from universal.[21] Robinson had another year under his (substantial) belt, while Jennings was expected once again to be healthy. However, a crowd of some 14,000 saw Philadelphia defeat Baltimore, 7–6, in the opener on April 18, with Esper taking the loss. Baltimore evened its record two days later, as a crowd of more than 11,200 watched Gleason and the team pound the Phillies, 23–4. McGraw had three hits and scored four runs.

By the end of June, the Orioles were a respectable 30–19, good for second place behind Boston, which stood at 32–18. The bottom fell out for Boston as the season progressed, playing less than .500 ball the rest of the way. Baltimore became hotter, going 57–24 for the remainder of the season despite briefly falling to fourth in July, as they finished three games in front of Cleveland. Hoffer clinched the second consecutive flag for Baltimore on September 28, a 5–2 victory in New York, for his 31st win. The team, however, had problems. Reitz broke a collar bone and was limited to 71 games. McGraw dealt with ill health — malaria — for much of the season, though he still managed to bat .369 in 96 games and stole 61 bases. His home run against Rusie and the Giants as the season ended provided some icing on the Orioles' cake. In the Temple Cup Series, Baltimore once again went down to defeat, as the Cleveland Spiders won four of five games.

For the 1896 season, Carey was replaced at first with Jack Doyle, obtained from New York in a trade for Gleason. In March, McGraw traveled to Macon, Georgia, for training and preparation for the upcoming season. Rumors suggested that McMahon's arm was dead. "You can't blame a player for resting as much as possible," said Doyle in denying the rumor.[22] While the media considered Baltimore to be in fine shape for the upcoming season, McGraw's health problems continued. Ill for much of March and early April, it was announced on the 15th of the latter month that he would likely miss much of the season. This time he battled typhoid fever, a life-threatening illness in pre-antibiotic days. It was August before he would be able to play once again. Meanwhile, Hanlon turned down Washington's offer of $10,000 for McGraw.

Pitted in a close race with Cincinnati much of the season and with Cleveland the last two months, Baltimore hung on for their third consecutive pennant, this time finishing 9½ games in front. They faced Cleveland again in the Temple Cup Series. McGraw was limited to 23 games at season's end, batting .325. Hoffer won 25 games; rookie Arlie Pond posted 16 victories. Another rookie, Joe Corbett, younger brother of boxing champion Jim Corbett, contributed three victories near the end of the season. Sadie McMahon, his arm gone, managed an 11–9 record. Among regular position players, team captain Hugh Jennings batted .401 and led the league in fielding at shortstop, Kelley hit .364, and Keeler .386. The Orioles extracted revenge on their adversaries from the previous series, sweeping the Spiders behind two victories each by Hoffer and Corbett. In the 6–2 third-game victory behind Corbett, McGraw scored two runs, one following a successful hit-and-run, and singled in another. Without question, the Orioles were now league champions.

The year 1897 began with several high points for McGraw. First, he had fully recovered from the typhoid that laid him low the previous year, and he was ready for the upcoming season. Second, he joined the ranks of matrimony on the evening of February 3 when he married Minnie Doyle, daughter of a widowed clerk for the Appeals Tax Court in a ceremony at St. Vincent's Church. Hugh Jennings served as best man, with Joe Kelley and Willie Keeler as ushers. Among the couple's gifts was a silver service from the Baltimore Baseball Club.[23]

The Orioles reported to spring training in Macon in mid–March with largely the same team that had won the 1896 championship. Steve Brodie, whose hitting had fallen off, was traded to Connie Mack's Pirates, bringing Jake Stenzel to Baltimore. Stenzel had hit .361 the previous year. Meanwhile, the twenty-four-year-old McGraw was developing a reputation as one of the more astute (read: outspoken) players in the game.

A trim dapper little gentleman is Johnnie McGraw, the diplomatic trickster who tends the left corner cushion for the Orioles. Johnnie looks the spoon-in-the-mouth, cake-fed heir of a pampered coupon clipper, rather than a long-headed and nimble-witted operator on the diamond. But when Johnnie opens his face in a baseball argument the apron string delusion immediately proceeds to evaporate.... McGraw has a faculty of saying things every time he talks, and can vent more cold-blooded practical knowledge on the game in five minutes than could be knocked into the ossified top piece of many a ball tosser we wot of by the medium of a surgical operation on the cerebellum.[24]

The season opened at home on a high note, as Baltimore defeated the Boston Beaneaters, 10–5, behind Bill Hoffer. The Orioles produced 13 hits, though none from McGraw, who led off and played third. Willie Keeler contributed two hits in the game, the first of 44 straight in which he would hit safely and set a National League record that still stands. Baltimore swept three consecutive games in the opening series against Boston.

By mid–June, the Orioles had opened a 2½ game lead over Boston on the basis of a 27–9 record. But several factors contributed to Baltimore's inability to maintain that pace. First, members of the team developed the usual collection of sprains and other assorted injuries that limited their effectiveness. Second, the Boston team included stars of their own: Jimmy Collins, "Sliding" Billy Hamilton, Hugh Duffy and Kid Nichols were all future Hall of Famers. A third contributing factor was the dissension that developed among Orioles players. A significant portion of that problem seemed to center on McGraw. Reports included a (naked) wrestling match between McGraw and Willie Keeler, the latter taking exception to being cursed out for failing to prevent a run. Even Hanlon received criticism by his third baseman.[25]

By the end of August the race came down to four teams: Baltimore, Boston, Cincinnati and New York. Boston was in front of Baltimore by three games (69–31 versus 64–32) with 4½ games separating the second-place team from the fourth-place Giants. At least one fan was unhappy with the Orioles' play. St. Louis brewery magnate Adolph Busch, a name that would become more prominent in baseball at a future time, offered $500 to each Chicago [Colts] pitcher who defeated Baltimore, as he does not "want to see rowdy ball triumph."[26] Not to be outdone, other breweries took note of the free advertising. "Money to the sum of $500 has been offered to every Louisville and Chicago pitcher for every game that they win from the Baltimores.... Money is the only factor used to defeat a superior team which cannot be done by honest toil. Superiority in every line leads everything to the front ranks, so it is with [Washington's] Heurich's Beer; it has led and will always lead all others, no matter what obstacles are thrown in its way. Heurich's Beer is the purest and most wholesome beer in the United States."[27]

The season came down to a three-game series between Boston and Baltimore, beginning on September 24. Kid Nichols out-pitched Joe Corbett in the opener, holding Baltimore off, 6–4, despite a two-run rally in the ninth inning by the home team. A crowd of 12,900 was on hand. McGraw singled in a run during the rally, which fell short when Keeler lined into a double play to end the game. The next day, a record crowd of more than 18,000 watched Hoffer out-pitch Fred Klobedanz, a 26-game winner that season, by a 6–3 score. McGraw started a double play in the ninth to help seal the victory. In the rubber match of the series, Boston's Nichols won a slugfest, as Boston pounded Corbett, Jerry Nops (20–6 that season), Hoffer (22–11) and Morris "Doc" Amole for 22 hits and a 19–10 score. Boston left town with a record of 91–38, in front of Baltimore with a record of 88–38. New York and Cincinnati were no longer factors in the race. Boston held on to win the pennant with a record of 93–39, two games in front of Baltimore at 90–40. Boston's Kid Nichols led the league with 31 victories. For the Orioles, McGraw recovered to hit .325. Willie Keeler, after hitting safely in the team's first 44 games, produced a then-record 239 hits and a .424 batting average. Jennings hit .355, Kelley .362.

Baltimore met Boston in the fourth and final Temple Cup Series. The Orioles won four of the five games, the last game a 9–3 victory behind Hoffer in front of a crowd estimated at 750 persons. Both teams appeared listless, and only exhibition games interspaced in the series allowed a profit to be made.[28]

Despite having finished either first or second the previous four seasons, Hanlon continued to try to improve the team. Amole, Reitz and Doyle went to Washington in exchange for infielders Dan McGann and Gene Demontreville, a .341 hitter in 1897. As well, "A pair of compounders of Kentucky prescriptions in Johnnie McGraw and Robbie [Wilbert Robinson] to give the troops a juicy flavor."[29] However, outside events would take their toll. On February 15, the battleship U.S.S. Maine exploded and sank in Havana Harbor with the loss of 260 men. Though the disaster was eventually determined to be a tragic accident, the event still became the impetus to a war with Spain. In Cleveland, a streetcar strike resulted in a boycott of the Spiders' games. The season schedule was increased to 154 games, but most teams still lost money. On the field, the Brush rule, named for the president of the Cincinnati club who introduced the stipulation, stated that "any player who addressed an umpire or a fellow player in a villainously filthy manner would be brought before a three-man board of discipline and, if found guilty, banished for life."[30] Another change involved increasing the number of umpires at the game from one to two.

The season opened for Baltimore on April 16, as the home team Orioles jumped to a 6–0 lead after two innings on the way to an 8–3 triumph behind Doc McJames, the first of his 27 victories that year. McGraw had one hit and scored one run. Only 6,500 persons were on hand, the largest crowd of the season.[31] As April came to an end, the Orioles were playing good ball, having won 6 of 8 games and tying for first place with Cincinnati. May was a different story, with a 9–10 record dropping them to fourth, three behind third-place Boston. Cincinnati continued to maintain its lead with a record of 21–7.

Additional changes took place. Jake Stenzel, despite hitting .353 the previous year, seemed to lose his batting eye and was traded to St. Louis on June 10. Arlie Pond enlisted in the Hospital Corps of the army, and after shutting out Philadelphia on July 6 for his only victory of the season and the last of his brief major league career, left for duty in the war.

As July became August and the summer waned, the Orioles righted themselves sufficiently to climb as high as second place. Twice they won twelve consecutive games, including a streak the third week of September that brought them within striking distance of first-place Boston. The streak was broken by Chicago on September 23, a game in which McGraw "vented his spleen on everybody."[32] The reality was that the Beaneaters, a team that included the same four Hall of Famers as the previous season, along with stars such as Fred Tenney and Bobby Lowe, were simply too strong. Baltimore ended the season with a record of 96–53, their highest victory total in its history to date (albeit in an expanded season). But Boston had a record of 102–47. Oriole players still had nothing of which to be ashamed. McGraw batted .342, leading the league in runs scored with 143. Willie Keeler won his second consecutive batting title, hitting .385. Jennings dropped to .328, his last .300 average in a full season. Kelley hit .321 and Demontreville, .328.

The 1899 season became notable in one particular aspect for what had been a continual problem in professional ball: "syndicated" baseball. Several owners had controlling interests in more than one professional club. The lack of competition for the customer's money meant owners could transfer at will players from one team to another, thereby strengthening one at the expense of the other. Culmination of such practices was seen in 1899, with the best members of the Cleveland Spiders, including Cy Young, being sent to St. Louis by owners Frank and Stanley Robison, and in Baltimore, when Ned Hanlon and Harry von der Horst purchased interest in the Brooklyn team. The Cleveland Spiders became the classic example of futility that season, posting a record of 20–134. Baltimore fared much better. With McGraw and Wilbert Robinson having business interests in the city, they remained as the nucleus of a club that stayed competitive through most of the season.

Hanlon became manager of Brooklyn, and during the first week of March, the twenty-five-year-old McGraw was named manager of the Orioles. Even though stars such as Jennings, Keeler and Kelley went to Brooklyn, McGraw still retained several players of note. In addition to himself and Robinson, the starting catcher, Baltimore reacquired Steve Brodie from Pittsburgh, as well as outfielders Jimmy Sheckard from Brooklyn and James "Ducky" Holmes. McGraw's young pitchers included future Hall of Famer Joe McGinnity, called "McGinnerty" in the media.[33]

Jerry Nops opened the season for Baltimore as they hosted the New York Giants on April 15 before a crowd of some 4,000 patrons. Baltimore won, 5–3, as McGraw contributed a single and run, along with two stolen bases. McGinnity posted the first of his twenty-eight victories for the season in an 8–4 triumph on April 18, as Baltimore swept the opening three-game series from the Giants. The Orioles finished the month with a respectable 6–6 record, good enough for sixth place in the young season.

McGraw demonstrated a natural leadership ability early on, and kept his team hustling and focused. Nops was fined and suspended for drinking.[34] And the team, "The meek and lowly Orioles, composed of two ballplayers [presumably McGraw and Robinson] assisted by seven men of lesser caliber but filled with the same spirit," remained in the race well into the season. The end of July found the team tied with St. Louis in fourth place with a record of 50–35, 8½ games behind first-place Brooklyn. By mid–August, they closed the gap to 5 games behind, with a 58–38 record. A week later, the record improved to 62–40, and at 5½ games, well within striking distance for the pennant. As manager, McGraw showed no indication of mellowing in his aggressiveness towards the authorities on the field. His fighting spirit was at least recognized, even admired to a point, by the league's arbiters.

> "Mr. McGraw of the Baltimore club may be a trifle unkind to my umpires at times, and greet their decisions with conversations that Chesterfield would never indorse. But after all he pays for the privilege, and as a rule he pays promptly," says President [Nick] Young. "Every other day or so — perhaps not quite so often but pretty near it — I receive a five dollar note wrapped up in a business-like letter reading: 'Dear Mr. Young: Inclosed please find $5, which I pay for the privilege of calling Umpire So-and-so a stiff. I think he was a stiff on this particular occasion, but we all have our faults, heaven knows. Please acknowledge receipts and oblige. Sincerely, John J. McGraw. P.S. Kindly offer my regards to Umpire So-and-so, who complled me to separate from the inclosed five-spot.'"[35]

But then tragedy struck. Minnie McGraw had been troubled by abdominal pain through much of the previous months. On August 26, the pain had become so severe that physicians were called to the McGraw home, where they quickly diagnosed appendicitis. Despite emergency surgery, there was little that could be done in those pre-antibiotic days, and on August 31, the twenty-two-year-old died.

McGraw remained absent from the team until September 11, during which time the team barely played .500 ball. While the manager did regain his focus on baseball as the season drew to a close, the talent simply was not there, and McGraw's Orioles finished with a still respectable record of 86–62, remaining in fourth place and 14½ games behind Brooklyn. McGinnity paced the staff with a record of 28–16 while pitching 366 innings in his rookie season. Nops won 17 of 28 decisions. Despite his personal tragedy, McGraw hit a career-high of .391, leading the league with 124 walks and an on-base percentage of an astounding .547. Robinson batted .284. Infielder Bill "Wagon Tongue" Keister, Jennings' replacement, batted a career-high .329.

Attendance for the season in Baltimore barely exceeded 120,000, beating only Cleveland, Louisville and Washington, and resulting in a loss of some

$35,000.[36] During the first week of March 1900 the league voted to drop the four franchises, resulting in a more manageable (and hopefully profitable) eight teams. Most of the men who had been playing for Baltimore were shifted to the Brooklyn franchise.

McGraw's fate as a professional baseball player, and for that matter the fate of Robinson since the players were linked both by friendship and Baltimore business interests, was in question as the league contracted. At least one rumor had the two being sold to Brooklyn for some $15,000, with half going to the principles involved.[37] McGraw announced he would go nowhere unless he received a portion of the purchase price as well as a raise in salary; Robinson included himself in the ultimatum, stating, "We will sink or swim together."[38] In the end, the contracts of McGraw, Robinson and utility man Bill Keister, a .329 hitter for Baltimore in 1899, were sold to St. Louis for $15,000. Following negotiations with owner Frank Robison, the players signed — McGraw for $10,000 and the aging Robinson for $5,000. The contract also was noteworthy for what it did not contain: a reserve clause.[39]

McGraw and Robinson reported late and as the season moved into May, St. Louis could play no better than .500 ball (6–6), good enough for fourth in the eight-club National League. It was May 12 before McGraw and Robinson appeared on the field in St. Louis, ironically to face Joe McGinnity and the rest of Hanlon's Brooklyn team. A crowd of 7,500 watched the Cardinals (among other nicknames) fall, 5–4, as McGraw's ninth-inning error contributed to the visitor's three-run winning rally. St. Louis fell to sixth with a record of 8–9. Despite the addition of McGraw, who batted .344 in 99 games, with an on-base percentage of .505, the team finished fifth with a record of 65–75, nineteen games behind Brooklyn. Robinson, who turned 37 that season, managed only an average of .248 in 60 games.

In the interim between the 1900 and 1901 seasons, American League president Ban Johnson continued his attempts to compete with the older league by placing a franchise once again in Baltimore. McGraw and Robinson became stockholders in the re-established Oriole organization. While relations between the two leagues left much to be desired, that between McGraw and Johnson was remarkably amiable. Among the changes that Johnson attempted to institute in the new league was the elimination of gambling as well as ending the disrespect players and fans exhibited towards the umpires. In time, these restrictions would lead to a break between the two men. But for now each showed respect for the other. Indeed, in February, Johnson and McGraw together helped break ground for a new ballpark in the city.

As player-manager, McGraw spent much of the preseason signing players for the new version of the Orioles. There was still Robinson, of course. Among others he signed were the "Iron Man," Joe McGinnity, outfielder "Turkey" Mike Donlin, a compatriot from St. Louis and a future movie star, and future Hall of Famer Roger Bresnahan.

On April 24, the new league opened with an 8–2 victory by the Chicago White Stockings against Cleveland. Baltimore's debut came two days later, as a crowd of 10,371 watched a malaria-stricken Joe McGinnity pitch a complete-game 10–6 victory against Boston. Ban Johnson threw out the first pitch. McGraw contributed two doubles and scored a run, while Donlin had two triples, scoring twice.

McGraw's "honeymoon" with Ban Johnson lasted only until the first week of May. On May 6 and 7, McGraw so angered umpire Jim Haskell in Philadelphia that the aggressive manager was tossed from the game on the latter date. McGraw's complaints to Johnson had little effect. On May 17, Johnson had had enough of McGraw's outbursts, and suspended the Oriole for five days. "Mr. McGraw will not even watch the games from the bench for five days. I ordered him kept away from the grounds as a penalty for using foul and profane language on the diamond to Umpire [Joe] Cantillon."[40] The suspension accomplished little, since it overlapped a week's worth of rainouts, and McGraw and Baltimore continued their fighting ways with both league officials and President Johnson. One disagreement concerned the contract of former Oriole Hugh Jennings. Jennings had initially agreed in May to sign with Connie Mack and the Athletics. After talking with McGraw, Jennings announced his preference to sign with the Orioles. Johnson announced Jennings' contract belonged to the Athletics, and any game in which he participated with McGraw was threatened with forfeiture.[41] In the end, Jennings signed with Philadelphia. Then on May 31 in Detroit, the Tigers' "Ducky" Holmes hit an inside-the-park home run in the ninth inning, diving under Robinson's tag and tying the score. When Robinson and pitcher Harry Howell argued vociferously, they were thrown out of the game by umpire Jack Sheridan. At that point, the entire team surrounded the arbiter, screaming and threatening. Mike Donlin even threw a bat at Sheridan. Sheridan forfeited the game to Detroit. On June 14, McGinnity was tossed for arguing with the same Sheridan.

Though only twenty-eight, McGraw no longer played a role as a full-time player. Yet he could still catch his opponents flatfooted when necessary. On June 22, for example, in a home game against Detroit, he stole home while the pitcher, holding the ball, could only stand and watch. By mid–July, McGraw's Orioles found themselves in third place with a record of 33–26. At this point, a series of injuries to McGraw further curtailed his playing time. In Philadelphia, the collie owned by Athletics first baseman Harry Davis chased McGraw around the bases. In July, a collision with a Washington player dislocated his knee. His replacement in the field, Jack Dunn, was injured in mid–August, forcing McGraw's return before the leg had healed. The result was a torn cartilage when McGraw turned while returning to a base. On August 20, McGraw announced he was quitting as an active player.

Despite all the problems with injuries and fighting, Baltimore still managed to finish with a record of 68–65, good for fifth place in the fledgling league.

John McGraw (1911) managed 33 years, nearly all in New York, compiling a record of 2763–1948, while winning 10 pennants and three World Series. He was as tough as they came, but if you played to win, he was on your side (Baseball Hall of Fame and Museum, Cooperstown, New York).

McGraw batted .349 in 73 games. Though his playing career was not quite finished, McGraw's time as a regular was over. His personal life, however, was on an upswing. On January 8, 1902, McGraw married twenty-year-old Blanche Sindall in a ceremony at St. Ann's Church in Baltimore.

The McGraws traveled to Hot Springs, Arkansas, in February, where John hoped the heated waters would help his knee recuperate. The treatment appeared to be successful, and McGraw was so pleased with the results that he released his substitute for the previous season, Jack Dunn, who signed with New York. McGraw also took up golf with the media hoping he would use some of his excess "exuberance" on the links rather than on the baseball diamond.[42]

Still, he could not completely escape the problems on the field. Mike Donlin, a .340 hitter the previous season, was arrested for striking a woman — Mamie Fields, an actress appearing in a stage version of *Ben Hur*— in Baltimore. Donlin was expelled from the league, and would play only briefly that season in Cincinnati. Donlin's "interest" in the female entertainment industry later came to fruition with his marriage to Mabel Hite.

Baltimore opened the season in Boston on April 19, losing to Cy Young as 14,000 fans watched their team rally for four runs in the ninth inning for a 7–6 victory. McGraw was ejected by umpire Tom Connally for arguing. On April 23, the Orioles lost their own home opener before a crowd of 12,723, as McGinnity was hit hard in an 8–1 loss to Washington. An injunction served during the game prohibited Philadelphia players Bill Bernhard, Chick Fraser and Nap Lajoie from playing for the Athletics, part of the dispute between the two leagues on the legality of player contacts. (See Chapter 1).[43]

Baltimore had split its first four games of the season when McGraw placed himself back in the lineup on April 28, and quickly demonstrated that taking up golf had not caused him to mellow in the least. In a game at Baltimore on May 1, McGraw claimed he was hit by a pitch thrown by Boston hurler Bill Dineen in the ninth inning. Umpire Jack Sheridan did not agree, and eventually tossed McGraw from the game after an argument. Roger Bresnahan singled as McGraw's batting replacement, but nevertheless the Orioles lost, 6–4. Following the game, only intervention by police officers allowed Sheridan to leave the field intact. One officer was injured by a brick thrown by an irate fan.[44] McGraw received a five-game suspension from Johnson for his actions.

McGraw's attitude towards Ban Johnson, the league's umpires, and the American League in general continued to deteriorate. Over the next few weeks he continued to bate the arbiters, Johnson, and other players. Spiked in the leg by Dick Harley of Detroit during the last week of May, precipitating another brawl, McGraw once again was unable to play as the injured knee became badly infected. In June, he decided to abandon Baltimore and the American League, and despite denials on the part of representatives of the New York Giants, began talks with Giants owner Andrew Freedman. On July 7, it was announced that McGraw was released from his contract with Baltimore, and would sign on as manager of the National League team at a salary of $10,000. Speculation also centered on whether the American League would place a team in New York the following season — most likely the Baltimore franchise, the only one allegedly losing money in 1902.[45] McGraw's actual salary was probably higher, making him the highest-paid manager in league history.[46] For the record, Baltimore finished in the league basement that season, the city's last appearance as a major league franchise for a half-century, with a record of 50–88. McGraw hit .286 for the twenty games in which he appeared. He was now a New York Giant, and his primary legacy would be established in that city during the next three decades.

McGraw quickly began a significant overhaul of his new team, by then only a shadow of the competitive squad from previous years. Pitchers Joe McGinnity and Jack Cronin, as well as Roger Bresnahan and Dan McGann, came along with McGraw from the Orioles. Joe Kelley and Cy Seymour also moved from Baltimore, going to Cincinnati, a team owned in part by John Brush during those days of syndicate baseball. McGraw subsequently signed George Browne from the Phillies and Roscoe Miller from Detroit.[47] The effect was that "Freedman, Brush and McGraw systematically destroyed one franchise (Orioles) and manipulated a second (Cincinnati) to benefit a third (Giants)."[48] By the end of the 1902 season, Brush was forced to sell his interest in Cincinnati to the "yeast magnates"—the Fleischmann brothers, and George Cox, a political hack in the city—in response to threats that a street would be run through the Reds' ballpark, "Palace of the Fans."[49] At the same time, Brush acquired controlling interest in the Giants.

The "new" Giants under McGraw made their first appearance on July 19, facing the Philadelphia Phillies. The team was solidly in last place, with a 28–50 record and 5½ games behind seventh-place Cincinnati. In front of a crowd of 16,000, McGinnity gave up only five hits. But it was not enough as the Giants went down to a 4–3 defeat. McGraw managed one single at the plate. New York won its first game under McGraw on July 23, as Luther "Dummy" Taylor, a deaf mute who produced 116 victories in his career, defeated Brooklyn, 4–1. Brooklyn's only run scored on an error by McGraw at third during a steal by Willie Keeler. McGraw was later thrown out at home while attempting to score.[50]

Even with the addition of a nucleus of what would become a competitive squad, there was little that McGraw could do with the team. The Giants finished last with a record of 48–88.

The most significant event for baseball as the 1903 season appeared on the horizon was the signing of a "peace agreement" between the two leagues—the national Agreement as it was called. The leagues were to be considered equal, with player contracts to be honored, thereby ending the raiding of clubs for players. A three-man National Commission — Harry Pulliam as National League president, Ban Johnson as the American League counterpart, and Reds owner Garry Herrmann — would oversee the leagues.

The agreement meant Christy Mathewson and Frank Bowerman, two players who accepted bonuses to sign with the St. Louis Browns, remained with McGraw. Mathewson's relationship with McGraw would blossom over the years, and the two, along with their respective wives, became the best of friends, traveling and often living together. A graduate of Bucknell College near Harrisburg, Pennsylvania, the tall and handsome Mathewson became a role model for the fans during these years, and would remain so until his death in 1925.

The Giants opened their 1903 season at the Polo Grounds, with Christy Mathewson facing the Brooklyn visitors with a crowd of greater than 20,000.

This was not one of Mathewson's better days, as Brooklyn scored four runs in the first inning on the way to a 9–7 victory. McGraw, his knee once again injured during spring training, did not appear in the lineup. Clearly his playing days were approaching the end. The following day, McGinnity evened the score, defeating Brooklyn, 6–1, in front of 13,000 fans. On April 22, McGinnity again defeated Brooklyn on his way to a league-leading 31 victories and 434 innings pitched; Mathewson would be close behind with 30 victories.

As August began, "Iron Man" Joe McGinnity lived up to his nickname, albeit one based not on his baseball experiences but on an earlier profession, winning both games of a doubleheader against Boston; Boston totaled twelve hits for the day. The two victories moved New York briefly into a tie with Chicago for second place in the National League race. The fight for second place behind the league-leading Pirates jockeyed back and forth between the Colts and Giants for the next few days. Chicago shut out Cincinnati the following day to regain the spot, only to lose it by a percentage point when New York defeated Boston, 4–1. The Giants ended the week with two doubleheader victories, first against Philadelphia and then versus Brooklyn, and by August 9 had pulled a half-game in front of Chicago, only to lose it again. On August 28, New York took over second place, and while the race would remain close until the end of the season, the Giants maintained their position. Pittsburgh clinched the pennant on September 18: New York finished 6½ games behind the league champions, and 1½ in front of Chicago. McGraw had improved the Giants by 36 victories (84–55) in only a single season. McGraw was limited to 12 games as a player, with three hits in eleven at-bats.

The peace agreement between the leagues resulted in the beginning of another tradition, a post-season series between the champions of the two leagues. In September, owner Barney Dreyfuss of National League champion Pittsburgh agreed to meet Henry Killilia's Boston Beaneaters, the American League winner. Boston defeated Pittsburgh, five games to three, in the first modern World's Series.

The Pittsburgh-Boston matchup was not the only potential post-season affair that year. Other teams followed suit with their own intra-city contests, pitting natural rivals such as those in Chicago. The New York Highlanders, off-spring of the defunct Baltimore team that had been wrecked through the machinations of McGraw and others, had finished fourth with a record of 72–62. Manager Clark Griffith proposed to Brush and McGraw a similar contest for the championship of New York. Angered over Ban Johnson having placed competition for the fans' money in the city as well as having lost a dispute concerning the contract of potential star Kid Elberfeld, McGraw and Brush would have none of it. Their decision would have implications a year later.

McGraw was quite happy with the team's turnaround during the 1903 season, but still recognized weaknesses that existed at several positions. From Brooklyn, he obtained shortstop Bill Dahlen. Playing primarily with Chicago and Brooklyn, the thirteen-year veteran had consistently hit in the .290–.300 range in earlier years. Now thirty-three years old, Dahlen's best years were behind him. Still, he could anchor a key infield position for a time. Third base was another problem. McGraw was finished as a player, and appeared only in five games that season. As a replacement, he found Arthur Devlin, a three-sport man at Georgetown University noted mostly for his prowess on the football field. Devlin would anchor third for McGraw from 1904 to 1911. To provide additional arms for a pitching staff consisting primarily of McGinnity, Taylor and Mathewson, McGraw added George "Hooks" Wiltse and Red Ames.

The Giants opened their 1904 season before 17,500 fans in Brooklyn on April 14. The season began auspiciously enough as the automobile in which the team was traveling was struck by a horse-drawn wagon while crossing the Brooklyn Bridge. Players were dumped onto the pavement, but fortunately no one was badly hurt. The players were more successful that afternoon. Christy Mathewson allowed three hits while striking out four, as the Giants defeated their cross-town rivals, 7–1. At least one paper already conceded the pennant.[51]

McGraw limited himself to appearing in five games during the season. As described by Charles Alexander in his biography of McGraw, at least one of these appearances resulted in controversy.[52] On May 7 in a game in St. Louis, the Giants went into the ninth inning on the short end of a 1–0 score. Pitcher Jack Taylor, no slouch given that four times in his career he won more than twenty games in a season, had limited the Giants to seven hits at that point. Catcher Jack Warner singled, and McGraw ran for his slow-footed receiver. Whether McGraw with his bad legs was an improvement could be questioned; given Warner's average for the season of .199, one might think McGraw would have allowed him to enjoy the scenery from a rarely visited vantage point. Roger Bresnahan batted for pitcher Luther Taylor and smacked a solid drive deep into left field. McGraw took off from first as soon as it was clear Bresnahan's hit would fall safely. What is less than certain is why Billy Gilbert, coaching at first for the Giants, took off after McGraw on the basepath. One must remind the reader that players did not have numbers on their backs in those times. And while Gilbert was a mere 5'4" tall, Bresnahan at 5'9" was no Giant himself.

McGraw scored the tying run easily as the other Giant players congregated along the baseline. But Cardinal outfielder Jake Beckley mistook Gilbert rounding third for Bresnahan, and threw the ball home. With catcher Mike Grady up the basepath, Beckley's throw arrived at an unguarded plate, and Bresnahan scored the go-ahead run. McGinnity shut down the Cardinals in their half of the inning and the Giants won, 2–1. Manager Kid Nichols protested the game, arguing that Rule 56, Section 17 prohibited players from leaving the bench. The Giant response was that the players left the bench only after Beckley had made his throw. Whether Gilbert was in violation was unclear since he was already on the field. Regardless, National League president Harry Pulliam turned down the protest and Beckley was tagged with an arguably unfair error.[53]

By the end of May, New York was in first place with a record of 25–11, a mere half-game in front of Chicago and one game in front of third-place Cincinnati. The Giants then prepared for a sixteen-game road trip, finishing up with a series against the Colts. On June 13, Mordecai Brown outpitched Mathewson, and Chicago passed New York in the close race. The lead was lost for only a short time. During the last weeks of June and the first week of July, McGraw's men went on an eighteen-game winning streak, finally stopped on July 5 by Philadelphia in a 6–5 extra-inning loss. McGraw, running for Warner, was thrown out at home in the ninth with what might have been the winning run.

The hard-fighting Giants were a reflection of McGraw, considered by some as the "meanest man in baseball."

> Ask any National Leaguer who is the meanest man now playing baseball, and chances are better than even that if he be not a member of the New York team, he will answer, after a moment's thought: John J. McGraw. The verdict will be unanimous. Ask any member of the Giants who is the greatest leader the game has ever seen, and the answer will be just as ready and just as emphatic: John J. McGraw. Versatile in his play, a baseball general all of the time, a nice fellow off the field, the devil himself on it, never scorning any trick to score a point, out to win baseball games, he cares not how, tutored by Ned Hanlon, and having kept his eyes open since, this doughty little third baseman, captain and manager of the New York Baseball Club is this year achieving his pet ambition which is: To win the National League pennant.... Umpires hate McGraw worse than they hate their job. Part of a manager's duty, according to "Muggsy" [a nickname he despised] is to make umpires earn their salary through the sweat of their brow, and so miserable does he make the life of a judge of play that some find it easier to give the Giants a shade than stand and swallow the caustic comments of Manager McGraw on the side lines.[54]

But even his enemies had to concede that the growing popularity of baseball had much to do with McGraw's leadership and prominence in the game.[55]

The winning streak effectively put an end to the National League race, and by the end of that week the Giants, with a record of 52–18, had opened a 9½ game lead over Chicago. By the beginning of September, the lead was stretched to 15 games. Not all had yet conceded: "The New York Nationals may take a slide to the bad soon — if McGraw discharges all his pitchers and makes his sluggers only hit with one hand free in the batting clinches."[56] More serious was the reported dissension on the New York club. The failure to participate in a post-season series the previous year had hit the players where it hurt, in their pocketbooks. At least two, McGinnity and Bresnahan, had threatened to leave the team. After McGraw and Brush had announced they would continue their boycott of the postseason, this time potentially the new World's Series, the players once again voiced their strong disapproval. "McGraw's players are beginning to grumble loudly over the prospect of losing their share of the receipts of a world's championship series which they had counted on if they won their pennant.... The players cannot see why they should be compelled to help field the ancient grudges of McGraw and Brush, nor why those private grudges against the American League should be allowed to defy the best interests of the players, the game and the public."[57]

On August 6, McGraw reacquired another old problem: Turkey Mike Donlin. Movie-star handsome — a fact reinforced when he joined Hollywood in the years following his retirement from baseball — Donlin had a running problem with the "bottle." When sober, he could hit. Playing with Cincinnati, he barely missed winning the 1903 batting title, hitting .351 to finish closely behind winner Honus Wagner. He was hitting .356 in 1904, when once again he was suspended by Reds manager Joe Kelley, the former Oriole and no stranger to such behaviors. McGraw was willing to provide Donlin with another chance, to the extent of later inserting a "no drinking clause" in his contract.[58] Donlin managed to hit .280 for the Giants over the remainder of the season. In exchange for Donlin, McGraw sent Moose McCormick to the Reds.

The Giants officially clinched the pennant on September 22, defeating Cincinnati, 7–5, for their 100th victory in front of a "crowd" of 4,200. Other than the obvious, the game was noteworthy for another reason. Catching for New York was 54-year-old Orator Jim O'Rourke. The former star and future Hall of Famer caught all nine innings while also producing one hit in four at-bats. The season ended on October 8, as Wiltse shut out Brooklyn, 5–0, New York defeating their cross-town rivals for the 19th time in 22 games that year. The victory, Wiltse's thirteenth in his rookie season, completed a record season of 106–47 the number of games having been increased to 154 for the leagues. The Giants finished 13 games in front of Chicago. McGraw's aces, McGinnity and Mathewson, had won 35 and 33 games, respectively, once again leading the league in that category. McGinnity's 408 innings pitched and 1.61 ERA also led the league. Taylor was fourth in league victories with 21.

Boston edged out the Highlanders for the American League pennant, in part the result of a wild pitch by Highlander pitcher Jack Chesbro. Chesbro won 41 games that season, a modern record. But while facing Boston on the last day of the season, his wild throw in the ninth inning of a tie game allowed Boston to defeat New York and clinch the pennant.

What about the postseason? As early as July, Brush and McGraw, with support from Chicago Colts owner Jim Hart, announced plans for a world tour consisting of ten players from each of their respective clubs; neither team would participate in a post-season series.[59] At the time, it was not clear whether New York or Boston would be the series' American League representative. But to McGraw, it mattered little. His dispute was with Ban Johnson, and the fact he and Brush remained upset about the addition of the Highlanders to the city really mattered little. McGraw produced several excuses: "If we didn't sacrifice our [pennant] race in our own league to the box office we certainly are not going to put in jeopardy the highest honor in baseball simply for the box office inducements."[60] McGraw clearly had in mind the Temple Cup losses for Baltimore some ten years earlier. In other words, the competition was unworthy. Even a petition signed by 10,000 New Yorkers and the displeasure of his own players, who once again lost out on post-season money, would not change the minds of McGraw and Brush. It would be 90 years before another series was cancelled.

The 1905 team was largely the same as that which won McGraw's first pennant the previous year. Even though he would produce dynasties at least twice more during his long tenure at the helm of the Giants, McGraw always believed the 1904–05 squad was his best. Certainly his pitching was dominant, even given the strong pitching throughout the leagues during those years. Mathewson and McGinnity were the best-known hurlers on the team, with Red Ames and Hooks Wiltse providing strong backup. With McGraw finished as a player, Art Devlin now played a solid third base. Mike Donlin, while not the epitome of sobriety, was at least under control. Including himself, McGraw had eight former Orioles with him.

The season opened once again on April 14 on a high note. Following a parade and the hoisting of the 1904 pennant, the Giants and Joe McGinnity easily defeated Boston, 10–1, before a reported crowd of 40,000 fans — a number likely inflated. Donlin contributed three hits, including a double and the season's first home run. The following day, Mathewson and Wiltse combined to shut down Boston, 15–0. Mathewson allowed two hits in his six innings of pitching, and even contributed a home run in his own behalf. First baseman Dan McGann also homered under the center field ropes. By the end of the month, the Giants led second-place Pittsburgh by a half-game, New York having won nine of its first twelve contests. Even so, McGann was already under a ten-game suspension for a fight with Philadelphia catcher Fred Abbott on April 22. During the same fight, Mathewson allegedly bloodied the lip of a boy selling lemonade near the Giants' bench.[61]

Sportswriter Joe Vila of the *Morning Sun* estimated that intimidation of umpires by McGraw and other Giants had resulted in at least twenty-five victories the previous season.[62] McGraw continued with his attempts at intimidation throughout this new season. Among his victims was umpire Bill Klem. Klem would eventually be considered among the greatest of baseball's arbiters, and would be honored with election to the Baseball Hall of Fame. But in 1905 he was still a rookie, and his first run-in with McGraw took place in early May. On May 5, McGraw was tossed from a game by Klem, thus beginning a period of intimidation. Klem quickly realized that if he were to survive, he must learn to stand his ground.

On May 19, McGraw began what became known as the "Hey Barney" affair. The previous day, McGraw had been tossed from the game against Pittsburgh for taunting. When McGraw entered the field the following day as well as the next, he observed Pirates owner Barney Dreyfuss sitting in the grandstand, and proceeded to yell, "Hey Barney," followed by implications that Dreyfuss had welched on gambling debts and that President Pulliam was one of his pawns.

Dreyfuss proceeded to file a formal complaint with the league office. McGraw, unable to keep his mouth shut, compounded the problem by phoning Pulliam and repeating his allegations. Eventually, the league's board of directors exonerated McGraw, while an injunction removed even a fine and suspension levied for the phone call.[63] Ironically, Dreyfuss was reprimanded for indulging in the controversy.[64]

All told, McGraw was tossed from thirteen games that season, including three consecutive games in August.[65] He was requested by Pulliam to stop referring to umpires as thieves.[66] Several times, he nearly brawled with fans, with only the presence of police keeping them separated. But his aggressiveness was having its desired effect. By the beginning of July, New York was again running away with the pennant with a record of 47–19, 6½ games in front of Philadelphia. By early August, a record of 70–30 placed the Giants seven games in front of Pittsburgh. The final standings had New York owning a record of 105–48, nine games ahead of Pittsburgh. This time profit won over principle, and Brush and McGraw agreed to face Connie Mack's Philadelphia Athletics for the first time in a World's Series.

On paper, the pitching for the respective teams appeared about evenly matched. Rube Waddell had won 27 games and was considered among the best in the business. Backing the left-hander up was Eddie Plank, Chief Bender and Andy Coakley. But as related in the first chapter, a freak injury removed Waddell from the series competition. For McGraw there was Mathewson, winner of 31; McGinnity, who "slumped" to a mere 21 victories; Red Ames, winner of 22; and the young Hooks Wiltse, winner of 15 in his second season. The receiving corps was a toss-up: Bresnahan and Bowerman for the Giants and Osee Schrecongost for Mack, backed up by Doc Powers. In the hitting department, the Giants were clearly superior. Bresnahan, McGann and Donlin all topped .300, with Turkey Mike hitting a career high .356 and leading the league in runs scored with 124. The two managers, while hardly the equal in temperament, were still considered two of the top strategists in the business. Each said the proper things as the series got underway, Mack confident "that as he had the best team in the American League, it will prove just as successful in the series for the world's championship." McGraw was equally confident, adding, "We can beat the Philadelphians in batting, and furthermore we can beat them running the bases. The only thing left open for argument, then, is the pitching."[67]

Dressed in new black uniforms with white stockings, the Giants took the field on October 9 before a crowd of nearly18,000 fans at Columbia Park in Philadelphia. Mathewson was McGraw's choice, facing Plank. The Giants' pitcher was superb, holding the Athletics to four hits and three doubles while shutting them down, 3–0. "In the box, Mathewson did everything that was desired. His speed was terrific, his control perfect. He alternated slow and fast ones. He used the wet ball. He curved them in, out, down and over. Philadelphia was at his mercy. Not a single base on balls did he grant."[68] Fielding was nearly perfect, with most outs recorded from ground balls; McGann made 14 putouts at first.

Philadelphia returned the favor the following day at the Polo Grounds before a crowd of nearly 25,000. Bender was Mack's choice to face McGinnity. The Iron Man pitched well enough to win, allowing only six hits, but his defense let him down. Philadelphia's three runs were the result of Giant errors in the third and eighth innings. Bender, meanwhile, allowed only four hits and shut the Giants down. Bresnahan led off the bottom of the first for New York with a double, but George Browne, Mike Donlin and Dan McGann all went down easily, McGann missing three swings and throwing his bat down in disgust. The Giants missed a second chance in the second inning when with one out, Bill Dahlen and Art Devlin walked. Dahlen, however, was thrown out attempting to steal, effectively ending the rally.

Mathewson returned for the third game back in Philadelphia with only two days rest, facing Coakley. Again he shut the Mackmen down with a four-hit shutout, 9–0, fanning nine and walking one. The temperature was cool, holding the crowd to a mere 11,000. Bresnahan led off and took first when hit by Coakley's pitch. After Browne fouled out, Donlin singled Bresnahan to third. McGann singled off the fence in right-center, scoring Bresnahan and sending Donlin to third. Sam Mertes smacked a ball too hard for outfielder Danny Murphy to handle, and the Giants were up by two. The Giants put the game out of reach in the fifth inning with five more runs, and now led the series two games to one.

McGinnity was the choice for the fourth game as the teams seesawed between New York and Philadelphia. He faced Plank, who had lost the opener to Mathewson. Once again Plank pitched well enough to win, holding the Giants to four hits. McGinnity, meanwhile, scattered five hits, and held on for a 1–0 shutout. The Giants' run, unearned, came in the fourth. Sam Mertes hit a ground ball to shortstop Monte Cross, who fumbled the ball. After Dahlen flied out, Devlin sacrificed Mertes to second from where he scored on Billy Gilbert's single.

McGraw sent Mathewson out for the third time as the teams returned to New York. Bender was once again the choice for Mack. This time Matty allowed six hits, but for the third time shut down the Athletics when necessary. The Giants scored their first run in the fifth inning. Both Mertes and Dahlen walked and advanced on Devlin's sacrifice. Gilbert scored Mertes with a sacrifice fly, Dahlen being thrown out advancing to third. While a single run proved to be all that was necessary, the Giants earned an insurance score in the eighth when Mathewson walked, went to third on a double by Bresnahan, and scored on a ground ball by Browne. Mathewson had achieved a feat never duplicated — pitching three shutout victories in a World's Series. Mack and the Athletics were simply outclassed by their National League rivals, lacking the "snap" that had resulted in their league victory.[69] Although the loss of Waddell might account for part of the Athletics' difficulties, the reality is that no team can win if they cannot score runs.

McGraw's on-field success, coupled with the financial windfall for owner Brush, resulted in a new three-year contract for the Giants' manager, reportedly for a salary of $15,000 per year.[70] Changes were also introduced once the Giants met for spring training in Memphis at the beginning of March. After a winter layoff, players traditionally worked out by running or distance walking. Among McGraw's innovations was the introduction of the medicine or push ball as a means of conditioning.[71] Players were assured that any soreness would disappear in 48 hours.

McGraw had other problems more serious than conditioning. Mike Donlin was at it again, spending a night in an Albany jail for drunken conduct, including brandishing a pistol while on a train. Christy Mathewson became ill with what was eventually determined to be diphtheria, causing him to miss the beginning of the season. Bresnahan lost four teeth when hit by a bat swung by Henry Mathewson, Christy's brother. Still, the nucleus of the team was intact, and despite the problems, this was still the same team that had won two consecutive pennants and a World's Series. One transaction in which McGraw was involved made for an interesting historical footnote. On March 20, the contract of outfielder Archibald "Moonlight" Graham, who had appeared in one game the previous season, was sold to Memphis of the Southern League. Graham initially refused to report for the offered salary.[72] He did appear in the lineup for Memphis several days later. Graham would be depicted in the 1989 movie *Field of Dreams* in a part starring Burt Lancaster.

The Giants opened their defense of the pennant on April 12 in Philadelphia. Bresnahan led off the season by being struck by lefty pitcher Johnny Lush's first pitch. He was forced at second on a grounder by Browne, who was caught stealing for the second out. But Mike Donlin singled and scored on a triple by Dan McGann, who also scored when Sam Mertes followed with a double, and the Giants were quickly on top, 2–0. Red Ames, taking up some of the slack for the ill Mathewson, held the Phillies to four hits in a 3–2 victory. Lush would have better days for Philadelphia, winning eighteen games that season. Philadelphia evened the series the next day, defeating the champions 5–4, in ten innings. Ames also was the winning pitcher in the home opener in an 8–2 victory against Brooklyn on April 20. A clearly weak Mathewson threw out the first pitch.

It only required a week before McGraw was again in the news as a result of his temper. On April 26 he was accused by a spectator of punching the man in the eye.[73] On May 1, McGraw, Bresnahan and McGann were tossed from a game for rowdyism. The three were suspended for three games by Pulliam. Even the "fates" seemed to be against McGraw, as the manager was mildly injured on May 7th, when a tire came off the car in which he was riding to an exhibition game in Newburgh, New York, causing the auto to run into a tree.

Then on May 17, McGraw was accused in Pittsburgh of using a whip on a boy for allegedly throwing stones at the team. The boy had no marks on him, and McGraw denied the accusation.[74] At least this case was tossed from court, as the judge determined it was an attempt at a "hold-up" on the part of the boy's father.[75]

Mathewson made his first appearance of the season on May 5 against Boston. Before he tired after seven innings, the Giants' ace allowed seven hits, including two doubles and two triples, and three runs. When he was replaced by Joe McGinnity in the eighth, the Giants still led, 4–3. But in the ninth inning, Donlin dropped a fly ball, allowing Boston to score three times and earn the victory.

Despite the challenges, McGraw still managed to lead the team to a record of 96–56, certainly respectable in most years by any measure of success. However, 1906 was the year the Chicago Cubs, under manager Frank Chance, won 116 games, still the record for a 154-game season, losing only 36. New York finished 20 games behind Chicago. Mathewson recovered sufficiently to win 22 games, second on the team to McGinnity's 27. Even with his fast start, Red Ames only managed a record of 12–10. Luther Taylor went 17–9. Cecil Ferguson, of whom much had been expected, won exactly twice. Mike Donlin was hitting .314 when he broke his ankle in mid–May. Bresnahan slumped to .281. In July, outfielder Cy Seymour rejoined New York when his contract was purchased from Cincinnati. Seymour had been the 1905 batting champion with an average of .377, and managed to hit .320 for McGraw in 72 games. Whether a healthy Mathewson would have made any real difference is questionable. Historically, one more victory on his part would have placed him in front of Grover Cleveland Alexander as the National League leader in career wins; the two are currently tied with a total of 373. Christy's brother, Henry, did have one opportunity to emulate his older brother, as McGraw allowed him to start against Boston on the last day of the season, his second appearance for the year — he had relieved brother Christy on September 28 against St. Louis, allowing no hits or runs. Henry pitched nine innings, walked 14, and lost his only big league decision, 7–1.

Even before the start of the 1907 season, McGraw ran into trouble. Thrown out of an exhibition game against the Athletics in New Orleans, McGraw refused to leave the field, resulting in a first-inning forfeit. Several days later, the Giants skipped out on a game, forcing Brush to pay $1,000 in recompense. And once again Mike Donlin was the source of problems. His entertainer wife, Mabel Hite, had convinced Donlin his future lay in that industry, not baseball. After receiving a bonus paid out of McGraw's pocket, Donlin reported briefly for the 1907 spring training season, even producing a triple against the Athletics in New Orleans on March 27. But he subsequently changed his mind, and did not play in the 1907 season. "Spike" Shannon, obtained from St. Louis the year before, replaced Donlin in the outfield. McGraw also suffered from a recurrence of the sinus problems that would plague him the rest of his life, forcing the manager to miss the beginning of the season.

The season began at home on April 11 with the Giants facing Philadelphia. The Phillies' Frank Corridon out-pitched Joe McGinnity and Red Ames for eight innings and led, 3–0. However, police commissioner Theodore Bingham refused to place his officers on the grounds, and Brush refused to hire any security. The 16,000 fans shivered for most of the two-hour game, and in the eighth many crossed the field to reach the sun. When the fans did not clear the field, umpire Bill Klem ruled the game a forfeit. After several days of rain, the Giants won their first gone on April 15, as Ames and Taylor defeated these same Phillies, 6–5. The victory represented the first of seventeen straight, and by the last week of May, New York and defending league champion Chicago were tied in the race with identical 25–6 records, 6½ games in front of third-place Philadelphia. Whether McGraw was cognizant of the absence of security on the field, or was simply demonstrating that miracles are possible, his "gentlemanly" behavior was noted by the press.[76]

A loss to the Boston Doves on May 24 dropped the Giants to second place. Roger Bresnahan saw the game from the stands, having been suspended by McGraw for "insubordination," and Frank Bowerman, normally "Matty's catcher," replaced him behind the plate. The Cubs, having taken two of three from New York in their recent series, were considered the "class" of the league, "and class tells in all, particularly in baseball."[77] Already the press was predicting that Chicago would make a repeat appearance in the World's Series, even though the season was barely a full month old.

This time the press was correct. By the end of the first week of June, the Giants owned a record of 28–14 and had fallen 5½ games behind Chicago. The Cubs had defeated the Giants in five of the six games in which they met. Even seventh-place Brooklyn, with only 13 victories for the season, had beaten McGraw twice in a row. By mid–July, following a 12–3 pounding at the hands of the Cubs once again in which even pitcher Mordecai Brown contributed a home run, the Giants had fallen 12 games back. A record of 47–30 left them only a half-game in front of third-place Pittsburgh. The Giants ended the month with a double-header loss to Cincinnati, McGraw being slugged by a ground security officer, former pugilist Frank Kramer, with whom he had been arguing, after the game.

The last two months of the season McGraw appeared to merely go through the motions. At one point he announced he would retire at the end of the year. The team had aged faster than anyone expected. McGinnity still pitched over 300 innings, but his record fell to 18–18 in what would be his next to last season. Mathewson still produced 24 victories, but Red Ames fell to 10–12, Taylor to 11–7 and Wiltse to 13–12. Shortstop Bill Dahlen was through. A broken arm limited McGann to 81 games and a batting average of .298; he would be in Boston the following year. The end of the season found New York in fourth place with a record of 82–71 as Chicago won its second consecutive pennant.

The 1908 season would not only provide one of the most exciting pennant races in major league history, it would also produce one of the most famous/ infamous, and controversial, plays in baseball history. A young first baseman, despite a long and respectable career, would be tarred with the undeserved nickname of "Bonehead." But that was months later. McGraw chose as the site of spring training the out-of-the-way small Texas town of Marlin, some one hundred miles from Dallas. The isolation allowed the team to train without the distractions of larger towns or cities, yet still had adequate rail lines for transportation, allowing exhibitions with other teams. McGraw and a young outfielder from St. Vincent's College, Fred Snodgrass, of whom more would be heard later, arrived on February 22 for early practice. During an intra-squad exhibition, McGraw even took the mound, legging out a single when at bat. Mike Donlin reported, sans a few pounds, and even managed to comport himself in the manner desired by McGraw. While Chicago remained the favorite in the pennant race, and Pittsburgh also was expected to contend, McGraw expected an improved squad with youngsters such as Fred Merkle, replacing McGann at first, Al Bridwell obtained from Boston, Buck Herzog and Larry Doyle in the infield, to be competitive. Cy Seymour, though aging, still anchored the outfield. The pitching remained strong. McGinnity was nearly finished, though he still managed 11 victories that season. There was a healthy Mathewson, as well as Ames, Doc Crandall and Wiltse.

The Giants opened their season on April 14 at Philadelphia; Mathewson was McGraw's choice. Matty held the Phillies to four hits while striking out seven, as the Giants won, 3–1. Mathewson knocked in the two winning runs in the sixth.

The home opener on April 22 against Brooklyn pitted Mathewson versus Harry McIntire for the visitors. Mathewson had clearly recovered from his long illness of the previous year, and held the visitors to seven hits, while striking out eleven. But in the bottom of the ninth, Brooklyn still led, 2–1. Leading off, Fred Merkle, pinch-hitting for Mathewson, doubled, and was sacrificed to third by "Spike" Shannon.[78] Merkle was caught off third base on Fred Tenney's grounder, leaving Tenney on first with two out and Donlin at bat. Donlin smacked the pitch over the fence in right field, giving the Giants a come-from-behind 3–2 victory as the chanting crowd of 25,000 went wild, carrying Donlin off the field.

> Donlin, Donlin, he is It;
> Donlin, Donlin, made THE hit;
> Though some others made the run,
> Donlin's was the only one.[79]

The victory kept New York in first place, tied with Chicago with identical 6–1 records. McGraw showed that despite concerns the previous year that he might retire, he had not mellowed. On April 28 in Boston, former Giant Dan

McGann ended a home team rally by hitting into a double play. McGraw referred to McGann with the pejorative phrase "Ice Wagon," a vehicle known for its lack of speed. Both McGraw and McGann were staying at the Copley Square Hotel, and that night the two came to fisticuffs.[80] Neither one was particularly popular among league umpires. Hence: "If some of the National League umpires could decree, they would tie McGann and McGraw together by their coattails, fling 'em over a clothesline, and let 'em fight it out Kilkenny style. The Mc duality isn't popular with the arbiter contingent."[81] One sad note that week occurred when Henry Chadwick, considered by some as the "Father of Baseball," died in Brooklyn.

By the beginning of May, the Giants were barely above .500 (8–7), falling behind both Chicago and Pittsburgh. McGinnity made his first start on May 11 in Pittsburgh, losing a 5–2 decision despite allowing only five hits. He lost again in St. Louis on May 23rd, allowing ten hits and six runs in five innings. Even some sportswriters were discounting New York's chances. When the Cubs pounded Mathewson for seven hits and five runs in two innings on May 25 in an 8–7 loss, the Giants fell below .500 — their record of 15–16 placed them on the top of the second division. But McGraw kept the team fighting. "The spirit of rowdyism with which John J. McGraw has imbued the New York Giants bids fair to live as long as he does, at least as long as do the men he has taught to bulldoze umpires and behave themselves like Bowery roughs both on and off the diamond. In defense of his teachings McGraw points to his two National League pennants, and it is true his team has not shown championship form since it was compelled by President Pulliam to comport itself decently on the ballfield."[82] To his credit, in a May 2 loss to the Phillies, McGraw even kept his temper in a disagreement with umpire Bob Emslie when the arbiter changed his mind on a decision; Donlin, however, was tossed.[83] Calm would not last long. McGraw received a three-game suspension for his behavior in early June.

A 21–10 streak in June brought the surprising Giants back into the race. Victories included two of three against Chicago and doubleheader sweeps of Boston — Wiltse and Mathewson earning victories— and then Brooklyn, Mathewson saving the first for Wiltse and winning 5–2 in the second. Their record of 36–26 left the Giants two games behind both Pittsburgh and Chicago. Donlin was leading the league with an average of .326. A doubleheader sweep of Philadelphia on July 4 included a ten-inning no-hitter by Hooks Wiltse. The gap closed to one game on July 13, as McGinnity and Mathewson pitched the Giants to a doubleheader sweep of Pittsburgh. They briefly passed Chicago into second on the 19th.

On August 24, the Pirates scheduled a makeup game as part of a doubleheader against the Giants. McGraw, arguing that he had not received a 24-hour notice, announced he would not play a second game. Fortunately for the Giants, he changed his mind, as they swept the home club, moving past the Pirates into first place with a record of 67–42. Wiltse held the Pirates to four hits in a 4–1 victory in the first game, while Mathewson allowed only six hits in a 5–1 second-game triumph. As the season moved into September, the Giants went on an eleven-game winning streak to stay in front of both Chicago and Pittsburgh. The scheduling of seven games in five days for the Giants at the beginning of September did not bode well. They came through, however, twice sweeping Boston in doubleheaders, splitting with Philadelphia, and defeating Brooklyn.

September 19 found the Giants with a record of 87–46, 4½ games in front of Chicago and five in front of Pittsburgh, and a pennant race seemingly over. But the Cubs kept winning and New York did not. On September 22, Chicago swept a doubleheader in New York, winning the first game, 4–3, as Orval Overall and Mordecai Brown out-pitched Ames and McGinnity, and the second, 3–1, with Brown again out-pitching Crandall. The Cubs were now one game — six percentage points — behind New York, setting the stage for one of the most famous major league games in history.

The precedent for the controversy in the game on September 23 could be found in an article entitled "Take Nothing for Granted in Baseball," published some two weeks earlier.

Posted in conspicuous places in the office of President Pulliam of the National League are several signs which read "Take Nothing for Granted in Baseball." None but an experienced baseball man like Mr. Pulliam knows how essential it is to remember that injunction at all times. For in baseball there was never yet a certainty that could be taken for granted beyond all possibility of an upset until every possible avenue of escape from that certainty had been closed. If Umpire [Hank] O'Day, dean of Pulliam's staff, had permitted the motto, which he has seen so often in the league's New York headquarters, to become photographed on his memory, he would not have taken for granted certain things in Friday's game of baseball between the Chicago Cubs and Pittsburgh. He would not have taken for granted that Wilson's hit to center field, with the bases full and two out, in the tenth inning would score the only run needed to end the game in Pittsburgh's favor. The chances were 1,000,000 to one that hit would win the game, so O'Day took it for granted that it did win the game, and started off the field with the crowd. In consequence he did not see that the one chance in a million prevented that hit from winning the game by rights. Instead of looking to see if the other base runners besides the one who scored advanced and touched the bases beyond the ones they were occupying he took it for granted they all knew the rules and would do so. Consequently, O'Day did not see first baseman Gill of Pittsburgh leave the field before touching second base on that hit. He did not see Evers of Chicago call for the ball and force out Gill, thereby saving a defeat for the Cubs with the chances 1,000,000 to 1 against them. And because O'Day neglected his duty, Chicago lost even that one millionth chance.... On skill and luck the game belonged to Pittsburgh. But Pittsburgh had on first base a slow thinking player, who did not know enough baseball to realize that if he did not run and touch the base he could be forced out on a base hit at the end of the game. Chicago had a second baseman who knew that, and, because he knew it, succeeded in retiring the Pirate numbskull. In the department of brains, therefore, Chicago clearly was the stronger team. Yet, although the Cubs took advantage of a weak spot in the Pirate makeup, they were not allowed the fruits of their own preponderance of brains, simply because a major league umpire, supposed to know all there is in baseball, forgot his job in a crucial moment and was found wanting. Not only is the double umpire system needed, but there is equally great need of umpires who will remember not to "take anything for granted in baseball."[84]

The basis for the editorial came about in the tenth inning of a scoreless game between Chicago and Pittsburgh on September 4. Manager and left fielder Fred Clarke led off the bottom of the inning for the home club Pirates with a hard grounder that Cub third baseman Harry Steinfeldt could not handle, and Clarke was on with a single. Tommy Leach sacrificed Clarke to second. Honus Wagner bounced a pitch towards right field, but Johnny Evers made a "brilliant stop," saving a run. The Pirates now had men on the corners with rookie first baseman Warren Gill coming to bat. Even though Gill had been in the majors only since the end of August, pitcher Mordecai Brown walked Gill, loading the bases. After Ed Abbaticchio struck out, right fielder Chief Wilson come to bat. Wilson smacked the first pitch past Evers to short center, scoring Clarke.

> Gill, who was on first base when Wilson singled, ran only half way to second base and as soon as he saw the ball hit safely he returned and ran back to the Pirates' bench in a hurry to get his punctured slats manicured as soon as possible, never thinking it was necessary for him to touch second base in order to make the victory complete. He did not go within thirty feet of second at any time. Evers, seeing Gill break for the bench, yelled for [Jimmy] Slagle to throw in the ball. Jimmy did and Evers touched second base with it, then wheeled to claim a forceout on Gill, only to see Umpire O'Day making fast tracks for an exit with his back turned completely to what had been pulled off. Evers ran after O'Day and made his claim for the out, which actually retired the side and consequently wiped out the run which Clarke had scored. But the veteran umpire only remarked: "Clarke was over the plate, so his run counted anyway."[85]

The Cubs appealed the ruling, but since O'Day never actually saw Gill's error, he could not make a ruling.

Several points should be noted both from the editorial as well as in the game summary. First is the most obvious: Players on base must proceed to the next base to eliminate the forceout. The second point, easily overlooked, was the necessity for a second umpire to be present.

And so the stage was set for the battle between the Cubs and Giants in the "rubber" match of the series. Mathewson was McGraw's choice, facing Jack Pfiester. This time, two umpires were present: O'Day and Bob Emslie. A home run by shortstop Joe Tinker in the fifth inning was the Cubs' only run, as Matty held Chicago to five hits while striking out nine. The Giants tied the game in the sixth and the score remained knotted going into the home half of the ninth inning. Cy Seymour led off with a groundout to Evers. Art Devlin singled, but was forced at second on a ground ball by Moose McCormick. Devlin slid hard into Tinker, and the two had some choice words for each other. With two out,

Fred Merkle came to bat. The nineteen-year-old was in his second season with McGraw. Purchased from Tecumseh in the South Michigan League the year before, he had limited major league experience at this point. Merkle was playing in place of the injured Fred Tenney.

Merkle singled to right, sending the slow-footed McCormick to third. Al Bridwell followed with a solid single to center field, and McCormick trotted in with the winning run. But what about Merkle? Apparently forgetting the controversy that erupted in Pittsburgh several weeks earlier, or perhaps being unaware of it, Merkle came within about fifteen feet of second when he turned and ran towards the center field clubhouse. Evers had not forgotten, and called for outfielder Art Hofman to throw him the ball, at the same time yelling to Umpire Emslie to watch the play.

At this point, things became hazy. Joe McGinnity apparently realized the situation, and grabbing the ball while wrestling with Hofman, threw it towards left field. Evers retrieved a ball — whether this was the same ball was never established — and stepped on second base. Merkle also realized the significance of what he had done, and attempted to return to second with several Cubs hanging on him. Meanwhile, the crowd had stormed the field. It was Emslie, the umpire at second base, who by rights had to make the call. But neither he nor O'Day saw what happened. As one student of the game said, "If the protest of Pittsburgh was decided against Chicago on the ground that the umpire did not see the play — and Emslie did not see the play today and Merkle is positive he touched the base — why, it strikes me as a parallel case."[86] Hank O'Day, the official representative on the field, would have to make the decision.

O'Day decided the run did not count and the game was a tie. Pulliam would later uphold O'Day's decision and Merkle would be tagged with the nickname of "Bonehead." To his credit, McGraw never blamed his first baseman, and supported him throughout a long and respectable career. McGraw went so far as to give Merkle a $300 raise for his 1909 contract, no small benefit for a man who had been primarily a substitute throughout the previous two seasons. Even the man arguably considered the greatest umpire of all, and a man who had no love for McGraw, Bill Klem, thought the Giants should have been awarded the game.

The next day, Cubs manager Frank Chance attempted to gain a forfeit for the previous game by putting his players on the field earlier in the afternoon. But no umpires were assigned by the league, and the Cubs' attempt for an easy victory was ignored. The actual game started about 3:30 P.M., and Wiltse, with a save by Mathewson, defeated Chicago, 5–4.

The season ended for Chicago on October 4, as they defeated Pittsburgh behind Mordecai Brown, 5–2, holding first place with a record of 98–55. New York, with a record of 95–55, still had three games left with Boston. On October 5, the Giants defeated Boston, 8–1, behind Ames and McGinnity, and a day later they won, 4–1, behind Wiltse. The Giants tied Chicago in the standings the following day with a 7–2 triumph, again behind Ames.

With the game of September 23 declared a tie, it was ruled that the Giants and Cubs would replay the game on October 8. The decision was discussed among the Giant players, who agreed to the replay. McGraw and Brush never changed their minds that they had already won the pennant fair and square. Mathewson was the obvious choice to face Pfiester. The Giants missed a chance to break the game open in the first inning. Fred Tenney led off the home first and was hit by Pfiester's first pitch. Buck Herzog walked. Bresnahan struck out, and Herzog was caught napping at first — Cubs catcher Johnny Kling picked him off. Donlin doubled to score Tenney. Seymour walked, and Manager Chance brought in Mordecai Brown who struck out Art Devlin to end the inning.

Mathewson, winner of a league leading 37 games that year, did not have it this day. The end came in the third. Tinker led off with a triple, and scored on a single by Kling. After Brown sacrificed and Evers walked, Schulte doubled in Kling. Chance doubled to drive in the Cubs' last two runs for the day. The Giants managed one more, but lost the game and the pennant, 4–2. Mathewson admitted, "The Cubs beat me because I never had less on the ball in my life. What I can't understand to this day is why it took them so long to hit me."[87]

Owner John Brush, hardly one in a category of philanthropist, donated the $10,000 he received for hosting the playoff game to the players. Despite the disappointing finish, the team had performed well both on the field and at the box office. With an attendance record of over 760,000 fans, Brush earned a reported profit of at least $200,000.[88] Mathewson set a personal high of 37 victories, losing 11. He also led the league in strikeouts (259), innings pitched (390), and ERA (1.43), and even tied McGinnity for saves with five. McGinnity finished his career with a record of 11–7. Taking up the pitching slack were Hooks Wiltse (23–14) and Doc Crandall (12–12). A young left-hander also appeared once in a loss; more would be heard from Rube Marquard in the future. Mike Donlin finished with a batting average of .334. Though Donlin led the league in this category for much of the season, Honus Wagner eventually passed him to win the title with a .354 average. Donlin's six home runs tied him for fourth in the category. The youngster Larry Doyle was the other regular to hit over .300, finishing at .308. No, the Giants did not appear in the World's Series, but considering how far they had fallen the previous season, McGraw's team had nothing of which to be ashamed.

McGraw continued to replace veterans with younger players as the 1909 season approached. Joe McGinnity departed. The Iron Man had been with McGraw for most of the decade, and had won 246 big league games. He was released in February, and still managed to pitch in the minors another 14 years. Luther "Dummy" Taylor was only 33, but Marquard appeared ready to take over his spot. Taylor played seven more years in the minors, later returning to Kansas City to work with the deaf. Bresnahan, with a managerial job available in Cincinnati, was traded to the Reds for outfielder Red Murray and twenty-six-year-old pitcher Arthur "Bugs" Raymond. Murray would be a solid out-fielder in years to come, while Raymond, a man with enormous potential, could never overcome the challenges of the "bottle." But the Giants would miss the experienced Bresnahan with only rookie Chief Meyers to replace him, perhaps spelled by Snodgrass and Art Wilson, also a rookie. Donlin was gone, decid-ing a career in vaudeville working with his wife, actress Mabel Hite, would be more to his liking. While he would briefly reappear in the majors some years later and would also attempt a minor league comeback, his baseball career had effectively ended. Hite would die of cancer in 1912, and Donlin would finish his entertainment career in the 1920s and early 1930s as a bit player in the movies.

McGraw was hopeful that the pitching staff could make up for any defi-ciencies at the plate. McGinnity was gone, but Mathewson, Wiltse, Ames and Raymond made for a potent rotation, with Marquard and Jake Weimer, obtained from Cincinnati, in support. New York opened at home against Brook-lyn on April 15 and 30,000 fans saw the Giants shut out, 3–0, by Irvin "Kaiser" Wilhelm. Wilhelm won only three games during the 1909 season, and picked the opener for one of them. George Schlei was McGraw's choice to catch Ames, a decision that did not go over well with the crowd, which chanted, "Give us Meyers! He can hit a ball. Put in the Indian."[89] McGraw was not present. A line drive had split his index finger of his left hand, and the digit had become badly infected. Mathewson likewise had an injured hand, the result of a line drive off the bat of Moose McCormick. One could not fault Ames for the loss. Mathew-son's substitute pitched nine innings of no-hit ball, losing in the 13th having allowed seven hits while striking out ten. Wilhelm did not allow a hit until the eighth inning. The Giants returned the favor the next day, winning 3–0 behind Raymond's four-hitter and a save by Ames. Larry Doyle knocked in two runs in the ninth and scored the third for the win. The team, which in reality had played over its head the previous year and had not been significantly improved for 1909, suffered further difficulties with a series of injuries throughout the first month. Mathewson's hand still bothered the man McGraw had counted on to be his ace. Doyle suffered from tonsillitis, while Bridwell had a sprained ankle. Cy Seymour, already suspended once by McGraw for a fight with coach Arlie Latham, collided with right fielder Red Murray and suffered an injured shoulder. Even with the "$17,500 battery" in place — Marquard and Meyers — the team was not in the pennant race. By the end of April, New York was 4–6, in sixth place, 2½ games behind Chicago.

Mathewson made his first appearance on May 4, giving up nine hits in six innings in a 5–2 loss to Philadelphia. McGraw's hand continued to bother him, and it was May 11 before he could appear on the bench with consistency. While the Giants were respectable, competing for the pennant was simply not realistic. May 15 found them in seventh place with a record of 9–15, 5½ games behind Pittsburgh. A streak of 8–2 brought them to .500 by the end of the month, though it only put them seven games behind Pittsburgh. Mathewson recorded his first shutout on May 17, a 6–0 victory over Cincinnati. His home run in the second game of a holiday doubleheader on May 30 was the key to a 5–4 victory over Philadelphia. With a return by Mathewson as well as Raymond, when sober, being equally effective, the Giants continued to play better than .500 ball, and by the end of June resided in third place with a 33–23 record. But Pittsburgh, on track for 110 wins that year, had increased its lead over New York to ten games and seven over second-place Chicago.

Raymond, however, could not remain sober. After a 2–1 victory against Cincinnati, Raymond and McGraw got into a scrap on the sleeper train the night of June 16, the result of some over-exuberant celebrating on the part of the pitcher. Raymond suffered a split lip in the process. Whether a punch would be more effective than fines was a subject for conjecture.[90] Raymond would continue to be a problem, and when fines proved ineffective, McGraw suspended him near the end of the season.[91]

It seemed that the better the Giants played, the better the Pirates played as well. An 18–12 record for July left New York with a record of 51–35, but now twelve behind Pittsburgh. A doubleheader loss on July 9th, as both Marquard and Raymond failed, followed by an 8–2 pounding of Wiltse a day later, were contributing factors. Mathewson temporarily stopped the losing streak in Pittsburgh on July 12th , holding the Pirates to four hits in a 3–2 victory in the first game of a doubleheader. In the second game, however, Marquard was again hit hard, giving up eleven hits, hitting three batters, and losing, 9–0.

Tragedy intervened as the season moved through July and August, perhaps in the process placing sport in some perspective. National League president Harry Pulliam had suffered nervous exhaustion, what today would probably be diagnosed as clinical depression, for a long time. Repeated conflicts with players and owners certainly contributed to his difficulties, and as a result Pulliam had taken a leave of absence from the pressure. On July 28, while alone in his apartment at the New York Athletic Club, Pulliam shot himself in the temple. He was found alive the next morning, but died several hours later. Pulliam was buried on August 3 in Louisville. League secretary John Heydler was chosen to carry out the duties of president.

New York's record of 69–46 by the end of August only resulted in falling sixteen games behind the Pirates and nine behind Chicago in what was really no longer a pennant race. In the end, New York finished with a 92–61 record, 18½ behind Pittsburgh and 12 behind Chicago. Considering the challenges, McGraw had done well. Mathewson was 25–6, with an ERA of 1.14. Wiltse also passed the twenty-victory mark, going 20–11, with an ERA of 2.00. Raymond, despite a suspension amid bouts with the bottle, went 18–12. Much was expected of Marquard, but the youngster only managed a record of 5–13. Larry Doyle led the team in batting, hitting .302 with six home runs, one behind league-leader Red Murray. Murray hit .263 in this, his first season with McGraw. The only other full-time players to approach .300 were Al Bridwell at .294 and Moose McCormick at .291.

The Giants again traveled to Marlin, Texas, to open their 1910 spring training season, a trip that would continue through 1918. McGraw continued to fine-tune a team that clearly was competitive, but had in the past lacked experience among its younger players. Bugs Raymond arrived sober as training began. Thirty-eight-year-old Fred Tenney was replaced at first by Fred Merkle; Tenney was hampered by growths, probably plantar warts, on his foot, which prevented him from playing, and waivers were asked the beginning of May. Snodgrass was also ready as a full-time outfielder. Veteran Wee Willie Keeler returned for one last season with McGraw. The pitching staff was anchored by Mathewson, of course, with Ames, Wiltse and Raymond also in the rotation. Louis Drucke had been signed by McGraw out of Texas Christian University, one of many college men in the major leagues by this time. He had won two of three decisions the year before, and was ready for a steady role in 1910.

Raymond started out pitching as effectively as McGraw had hoped. On March 20, for example, he held Houston to two hits in five innings. But as the team began to play its way north towards the end of March, Raymond fell off the wagon when he discovered a table full of cocktails during a Dallas banquet.[92] His pitching through the rest of training camp was erratic enough to arouse McGraw's suspicions that Raymond had fallen once again for the bottle.

The season opened for the Giants in Boston on April 14. Red Ames pitched hitless ball for seven innings and held the Doves to four hits in eleven innings, but an error by Devlin allowed the winning run to score, and the Giants lost, 3–2. Raymond and the Giants also lost the following day, 5–4. Mathewson finally put the Giants in the win column on the April 16, striking out nine in a 3–1 triumph; Matty even homered to help his cause. The Giants also won their home opener on April 20, as Wiltse tossed a three-hit shutout against the Doves, 4–0. As April drew to a close, the Giants with a 9–3 record were actually one-half game in front of Pittsburgh, though the Pirates were percentage points in front by having played three fewer games (7–2). The Giants briefly increased their lead to a full game before a four-game sweep by St. Louis in mid–May brought the Giants back to earth. Mathewson once again served as a "stopper," defeating Cincinnati on May 18. The Reds managed eleven hits and six runs, but the Giants scored ten.

Raymond was erratic to say the least. On April 28, for example, he struck out twelve, walked eight, but pitched all thirteen innings in a 5–2 victory over Philadelphia. Next time out, on May 5, he allowed ten hits in three innings against the same Phillies, ultimately losing, 9–3. On May 9, he lost 2–0 to the Cubs. On May 14 it was St. Louis' turn, with Raymond giving up five hits in

Art Devlin (1911) was the regular Giant third baseman from 1904 to 1911. His forte was defense, though he averaged .269 over his career. He hit only 10 career home runs. The first was a grand slam in his first appearance for the Giants (Library of Congress, Bain Collection).

the first inning in a 9–3 loss. On May 31st, Raymond scattered ten Philadelphia hits to win, 4–2. But on June 7, it was a 5–4 loss again against St. Louis The winning pitcher was ironically named Johnny Lush. Two events finally demonstrated McGraw's patience with Raymond was at an end. On June 17, Raymond relieved Drucke in a game with the Pirates. Drucke had held the Pirates to one hit in six innings, and the Giants led 3–2 in the ninth. After Drucke allowed the first two batters to reach base, McGraw brought in Raymond. Raymond proceeded to hit the first batter, filling the bases. The Pirates' Tommy Leach was thrown out on a grounder, allowing the tying run to score. A wild throw to first, two more hits and a hit batsman later, and the Pirates had scored four runs. McGraw discovered Raymond was drunk; the pitcher had exchanged a baseball for drinks at a local saloon while supposedly warming up. After a month-long suspension, McGraw gave Raymond another chance. But on July 22, he was again drunk at a game, and McGraw suspended him for the season. Raymond finished with a 4–11 record, while McGraw continued to become prematurely gray.

The Giants were clearly in the race by the end of June. Their record of

36–22 put them a close 1½ games behind first-place Chicago. Mathewson was 13–2. A 7–3 defeat of Chicago behind Wiltse on the ninth of July, followed by a 10–9 slugfest victory the next day—Raymond pitched seven innings in relief of Drucke and Ames—placed them only one-half game behind the leading Cubs. This was as close as McGraw would come to the pennant that season as five straight losses dropped them back as low as third place. As July moved to a close, their record of 51–36 still left the Giants seven games behind the Cubs. On July 28, McGraw was again chased for arguing a call by umpire Mal Eason.

A 16–12 record for August dropped them to third place, now twelve games behind Chicago. On August 21, long-time outfielder Cy Seymour was waived, ending up with Baltimore in the Eastern League; Fred Snodgrass permanently took over the position. The team went 19–11 through September, moving past Pittsburgh into second place, but still ten games behind Chicago. The Giants finished second, their record of 91–63 placing them thirteen behind Chicago, but 4½ in front of Pittsburg. Mathewson, with a record of 27–9, again led the league in wins, while his ERA of 1.89 was the third lowest. Wiltse was 14–12 and the unsung Doc Crandall went 17–4 with five saves. Drucke and Ames each won 12 games. Fred Snodgrass led the team in batting with a .321 average, good for third in the league. Josh Devore was the only other regular to hit above .300, finishing .304. Willie Keeler appeared in nineteen games, hitting .300 with three hits in ten at-bats in what was his last season. Fred Merkle had played admirably in replacing Tenney, hitting .292 and defensively producing a fielding average of .981. McGraw even agreed to play the Yankees in a post-season series that October after their American League opponents also finished second. The Giants won four of six games, with Mathewson winning three and saving one in relief of Drucke, as crowds totaling 100,000 watched.

"Youth will be served."[93] McGraw's youth movement finally paid off in 1911, as the Giants produced their first extended dynasty. As spring training began, the Giants had virtually the same team that had finished second the previous year. Raymond was back for another try, reportedly having not touched a drink for three months. Instead, his appetite appeared to have returned, for the man who "hoped to be another Mathewson" had added significant weight. Louis Drucke, also once considered a possible Mathewson [the contemporary standard of excellence it would appear], had been injured in a subway accident. Though he would continue for another year with McGraw, his pitching never recovered. Marquard, whom McGraw had purchased from Indianapolis in 1908 for $11,000, won only four games the previous season, but McGraw's confidence in him was about to pay off—literally. Labeled as a "lemon," Marquard would win 24 this season. Art Fletcher batted .224 in 51 games the year before but was now ready to be the full-time shortstop. McGraw conceded the Cubs were probably the pennant favorites, although he argued with good reason the Giants would be right up there.[94] In addition to being a spring training prognosticator, McGraw also had the opportunity to umpire a game. On March 13,

Merkle's arguing during an intrasquad game resulted in umpire Leroy Hansell leaving the field; McGraw finished the game in his place with Mathewson taking over as manager. McGraw apparently also had his own problems with arguments during the game.[95] Perhaps McGraw was learning to mellow — he was tossed from only seven games during the upcoming season.

The Giants opened at home on April 12, facing the Phillies. Earl Moore shut down the Giants, 2–0. The results were the same the following day, as Christy Mathewson lost, 6–1. That would be the last game at the old Polo Grounds as a fire broke out early the following morning, destroying most of the grandstand. The Giants played their home games at the Yankees' Hilltop Park until the Polo Grounds could be rebuilt later that season, with a $500,000 steel and concrete structure replacing the wooden one. On April 15, the Giants, playing at Hilltop Park defeated Brooklyn, 6–3, behind Crandall. Crandall contributed a triple and scored a run for the Giants' first win. The next day Bugs Raymond, relieving Wiltse in the second inning after the starter was injured by a hit, held Brooklyn to a single run as he won his first game in nine months, 8–1. Philadelphia was off to a fast start, winning 11 of 14 by the end of April. New York, 8–5, was tied for second with Pittsburgh and Chicago.

May 13 began with the Giants in second place, with a record of 14–9 behind Philadelphia. That day one could witness additional records being set. The visiting Cardinals were scoreless in their half of the first. The Giants then proceeded to score ten runs before a man was retired. First "Slim" Sallee and then Bob Harmon, a 23-game winner that season, were knocked from the slab. Third baseman Lou Lowdermilk was then brought in. Before the inning was over, the Giants had scored 13 runs. Fred Merkle had six RBIs on a double and inside-the-park home run. He scored the last run as part of a double steal. McGraw decided that with a 13-run lead, there was no reason to have Mathewson risk an injury by continuing to pitch. Rube Marquard was brought in to pitch the rest of the game and responded by striking out 14 to set the National League record for strikeouts by a reliever. A young rookie catcher named Hank Gowdy replaced Merkle at first.

Marquard was an example of how a pitching talent could be brought to fruition under the tutelage of McGraw and his coaches. The lefthander had never won more than five games in a season prior to 1911, and had earned the sobriquet of "lemon." McGraw's friend, fellow Oriole and coach Wilbert Robinson, had worked with Marquard all spring, helping him to develop a variety of pitches. It paid off that season, as Marquard ultimately won 24 games and was on his way to the Baseball Hall of Fame.

On July 21, McGraw made a move to solidify his infield. Al Bridwell and Hank Gowdy were traded to Cincinnati for Buck Herzog. Herzog was a man who had no problem standing up to McGraw. He had already been traded once by the Giants' manager, but he hustled and played strong defense. McGraw placed Herzog at third, replacing Devlin. A young Art Fletcher took over the

Charles "Buck" Herzog (shown here in 1911) and John McGraw had one thing in common: a desire to win. Three times Herzog was traded by McGraw, but he always managed to return. He appeared in four World Series with the Giants, hitting .400 (12-for-30) in 1912 (Library of Congress, Bain Collection).

shortstop position permanently. With Doyle at second and Merkle established at first, McGraw's infield was set.

McGraw's other change was that of Bugs Raymond. Once again he lost his battle with the bottle, and in the last week of June was again suspended and fined. On June 24 he turned up in Winsted, Connecticut, to pitch an exhibition against Torrington. Even here he was removed after seven innings. Raymond went 6–4 in the 17 games in which he appeared in 1911, his last season. In September 1912 Raymond was kicked in the head during a fight in Chicago and subsequently died from the injury. Raymond was one of many "might have beens" in baseball history, a man who ultimately lost a battle to the "bottle." Despite such difficulties, McGraw had the Giants solidly in second place by the end of July with, a record of 56–36 and 1½ games behind Chicago.

Beginning on August 12 while in third place with a 59–41 record, McGraw's Giants won eight of their next nine, passing both Pittsburgh and Chicago to take over first on August 22. Despite briefly falling back for a day, they maintained that position through the end of the season. As Johnny Evers of the Cubs admitted, "The Giants are a second-division team with a first-division manager. Without McGraw they wouldn't be heard of."[96] A twelve-game winning streak through mid–September all but sewed up the pennant. A 6–2 victory over Cincinnati, Mathewson's 25th victory, on September 23 moved the Giants eight games in front of Chicago. September ended with two victories over second-place Chicago, a 3–1 win behind Ames followed by a 5–0 shutout by Marquard. The pennant was officially clinched on October 4 when Mathewson blanked Brooklyn, 2–0. Mathewson's 26th victory was also his fifth shutout of the season.

New York finished with a record of 99–54, 7½ games in front of Chicago. Mathewson won 26 of 39 decisions, second only to rookie Grover Cleveland Alexander, who won 28 for Philadelphia. Marquard won 24, losing seven. Doc Crandall was 15–5 with five saves, Wiltse 12–9 and Ames 11–10. Chief Meyers led the team in batting with an average of .332. Doyle hit .310, including 13 home runs, while Fletcher batted .319. It was on the base paths that the Giants really shined. The team stole a record 347 bases. Eight players stole 19 or more, Josh Devore leading the team with 61, followed by Snodgrass with 51, Merkle with 49 and Murray with 48. McGraw was confident he could handle Mack in the World's Series.

The series was scheduled to open on October 14 in New York. Though the modern World's Series dated to 1903, this year marked the first year for several changes. The results of the match would receive extensive press coverage. Players would write, or have ghostwritten, their views and perspectives on the series. Among the writers was Mathewson, who was hired by both the *New York Herald* and *Washington Post*. Whether Mathewson contributed any significant verbiage is open to question, since John Wheeler of the *Herald* served as his ghostwriter. Mathewson's—or perhaps Wheeler's—comments would shortly create a level of controversy. Mathewson's *Post* articles were to supplement those of Joe Jackson, sporting editor for the paper.[97]

Washington manager Jimmy McAleer probably came closest to predicting the outcome.

> The Athletics are the best team in the American League, and they are the strongest combination that ever represented the American League in the big series. Mack has his three pitchers—Jack Coombs, Chief Bender and Eddie Plank—all working nicely, and I don't think he will have to use another man to win.... Coombs, Bender and Plank will keep the Giants so close to first or second base that they will not be able to steal many bags, and Thomas and Lapp will toss them out unless they get a break on the start of the pitcher. Pitching will win the series and I think that Connie Mack has the best pitching staff on earth.[98]

Others made their own prognostications. Cobb predicted Mack would win on the basis of offense, but McAleer's was right on the mark. For the Giants, the "Three M's" would be the determining factor.

> The three M's of Muggsy McGraw's squad will be the big factors in the world series of 1912 [*sic*]. The combination is winning the National League flag for New York. It

reads like this: Mathewson, Marquard, Meyers. These three on the line dented, then demolished, the pennant hopes of the Cubs and Pirates. They pulled the Giants to the top of the heap in the parent organization. Mathewson, Marquard and Meyers. Two months ago they were calling Marquard an $11,000 lemon; Mathewson, a grand old veteran who is pitching his last year in major league baseball and who has lost all his former ability, and Meyers was not called much of anything outside of "Chief" and "The Indian." And today you hear and read, "Christy, the greatest of them all," Marquard the sensation of baseball and the leading pitcher of either league in 1912 [sic]. Meyers, the "big chief to whom most of the credit is due...." When the Giants and Athletics met in their other world series, the White Elephants were badly smothered by the New Yorkers. It was the peerless Mathewson who sent Mack's men back to their league, beaten. This year it will be Mathewson and Marquard...." Not only is Meyers a good catcher, but he is one of the best hitters in the National League.... The three M's will be the strength of the Giants in the world series of 1911.[99]

The 1911 World's Series represented the second time these two managers faced each other in the postseason. The pitching staffs showed the least turnover — Mathewson, Ames and Wiltse were on both of McGraw's squads, though Wiltse did not appear in the 1905 Series, while both Bender and Plank pitched in 1905 for Mack. Position players in both series included Harry Davis, Bris Lord and Danny Murphy for Mack. McGraw had no doubt who would open: Mathewson. Mack was still, allegedly, undecided for the opener. Speculation centered on Bender. While Coombs was as likely a choice, the belief was that for Bender to have sufficient rest between starts, he would have to pitch the opener.[100]

"The Giants were all togged out in brand new uniforms of black [trimmed in white], and they hung crepe on the Philadelphia round-house door."[101] The game started about 2:15 P.M. in front of a "seated" crowd reported as 38,281. Among changes instituted this year was that fans could not stand on the playing ground itself. The Athletics' Bris Lord, facing Mathewson, took two strikes, fouled off three pitches, and swung and missed for the first out. Two hours and twelve minutes later, Harry Davis grounded out to Art Fletcher and McGraw and Mathewson had won the first game, 2–1. Though the Athletics finally scored on the big right-hander, Mathewson won his fourth straight series game. Marquard "reviewed" Mathewson's performance for the *Times*, mainly reporting the game as it transpired on the field. There was an attempt to explain McGraw's "inside baseball." In the fourth inning, Fred Snodgrass was on second base, the result of being hit by Bender's pitch and a grounder by Murray. McGraw signaled a hit-and-run to Herzog, who grounded to Eddie Collins. Collins fumbled the ball, and Snodgrass, being on the move with the pitch, rounded third and came home with a slide under the "surprised" Ira Thomas.[102] In his ghost-written column, Matty described the victory in part as the result of crossing up an opponent that had been stealing the Giants' signals. "The turning point in the game today came in the third inning, when the Giants crossed the Athletics and threw them in the air. In the second inning they thought they had our signals, and perhaps they had. In the third they attempted to employ their information thus obtained, and they found they had been crossed. It was at this point that they stopped winning, and we began."[103]

The teams traveled to Philadelphia, and two days later — games were not played on Sunday — Marquard had his turn to face the Athletics and Eddie Plank. The score was tied at one apiece when Philadelphia batted in the sixth inning. Bris Lord and Rube Oldring both flied out. Eddie Collins doubled, and Frank Baker appeared at bat. Marquard had already struck Baker out on three curves in the first inning, and retired him on a grounder in the fourth. Marquard described the events of the sixth.

My jump ball was working fairly well, though I did not have the best of control.... Baker is a bad man and I had been warned against him [by McGraw], and I had the right dope, too, but at the last moment I switched, because I thought I was working it too hard.... When he came up in the sixth I fully intended to follow instructions and give him curved balls. But after I had one strike on him and he refused to bite on another outcurve which was a little too wide, I thought to cross him by sending in a fast high straight ball the kind I knew he liked. Meyers had called for a curve, but I could not see it, and signaled a high fast ball. Either he knew the signal from Collins, who was on second, or he outguessed me, for he was waiting for that fast one, and sent it over the fence, scoring Collins ahead of him.[104] Baker's home run was the critical factor in the Athletics' 3–1 victory.

Meyers was convinced the Athletics were stealing signs. In Lawrence Ritter's interviews, Meyers described such events surrounding the series. "They're getting our signs from someplace, I told McGraw. That coach on third base, Harry Davis, is calling our pitches. When he yells 'It's all right, it's a fast ball.' He must be getting them off you, McGraw said. But they weren't getting them from me. I went to Rube and to Matty and said, 'Pitch whatever you want to pitch, I'll catch you without signals.' And still the guy [Davis] was hollering 'It's all right' for the fast ball. He knew something. I never did find out how he did it."[105]

Mathewson, or his ghostwriter, was equally critical. "That ball was right in the heart of the plate, came up the 'groove,' and Baker hit it over the fence for a home run. If the ball had been pitched on the outside, or had been a curve, the result would probably have been different.... Meyers [suspecting the stealing of signals] walked out to the pitching box and said to Marquard, 'Pitch him two curve balls, no matter what I sign for.' [After throwing two curves] Marquard thought he could sneak a fast one over the plate ... but Baker was all set up there waiting for it.... Baker hit that ball over the rightfield fence, and that cost us the game."[106]

The teams returned to New York for the Tuesday game. Mathewson was McGraw's choice, this time facing Coombs. After four victories, Mathewson's, streak was finally broken. He pitched well, and came into the visitor's ninth leading by one run. Again it was Baker who played the foil. "Mathewson Repeats

Marquard's Mistake with Baker and Another Home Run Saves the Athletics"
was the headline for the *Times*.[107] After Collins grounded out, Baker came to
bat.

> Matty had evidently not soliloquized enough about John Franklin Baker, the
> Maryland fence breaker. He knew well that this slugger had spilled the beans on
> Marquard, but was the Big Train afraid of him? Not at all. He fooled him for two
> strikes with curve balls and might have fooled him again with a curve, but Math-
> ewson evidently guessed that Baker expected a curve so he decided to peg him a
> fast straight one, just as Marquard did in Philadelphia on Monday. Baker leaned
> against the ball with the gentleness of a battering ram. The ball went high and dry
> into the right wing of the new Brush stadium and Baker cantered around easily,
> touching each base with his spikes of joy. The score was tied.[108]

Two unearned runs in the 11th gave the Athletics a 3–2 victory, and Baker
would shortly have a new nickname. The Giants' activity on the basepaths also
proved McAleer's predictions to be correct: Athletics catcher Jack Lapp cut
down five runners.

After several days of rain, the series resumed on October 24 in Philadelphia. Bender and Mathewson, the opening day pitchers, again faced each other.
The Giants opened the scoring with two first-inning runs, but Bender held
them scoreless the rest of the way. Meanwhile, the Athletics went ahead in the
fourth with the help of three doubles and won, 4–2, to lead the series three
games to one. Marquard, with help from Ames and Crandall, closed the gap
with an extra-inning 4–3 victory on October 25 in New York. In Game Six, the
Athletics broke open the game against Red Ames, Wiltse and Marquard with
four runs in the fourth and seven in the seventh, and won the series with an
easy 13–2 pounding of the Giants. Mack and McGraw had now each won one
series against the other.

During November, the McGraws and Mathewsons as well as a coterie of
writers and players barnstormed their way from Jacksonville to Key West and
then on to Cuba. Four other teams had visited the island nation during the previous several years, most recently the Phillies. As if to belie the argument that
black or Latin players could not play at the same level as white players, the
Cubans had always fared well in competition with major league players, often
coming close to breaking even in victories and sometimes winning more than
their share. McGraw, for all his bluster and emotion, appeared willing to at
least support the notion that black players might have a place in the majors.
But outside of one attempt to sign such a player, even he would not be willing
to breach the color line. Only a few light-skinned Cuban players were able to
join major league teams during this era.

The Giants began the defense of their National League title with spring
training again down in Marlin at the beginning of March. This time they were
the favorites to repeat. "McGraw has a scrappy bunch of youngsters and a pitcher
like Christy Mathewson, according to Washington manager Clark Griffith."[109]

George Burns (1912) spent 11 seasons patrolling left field at the Polo Grounds, a job he carried out so well that the bleachers there became known as "Burnsville." Leading off for McGraw much of his career, Burns led the league five times in runs scored. In 1913, his first full season, Burns batted .286 (Library of Congress, Bain Collection).

McGraw's primary additions were pitcher Jeff Tesreau, late of Toronto, and a young outfielder named George Burns. Burns had briefly appeared with the club the previous year, and would acquire some needed experience during the upcoming season. His primary role would begin another year in the future.

The Giants opened their season by pounding Brooklyn, 18–3, at Washington Park on April 11. Between 25,000 and 30,000 fans were present, overflowing so that they lined the outfield. Any ball hit into the crowd was a double. Consequently, the Giants hit a record 13 ground-rule doubles among their 22 hits before the game was called on account of darkness in the sixth inning. Rube Marquard was the benefactor of all the hitting; his three hits and two runs scored were all part of the action. Jeff Tesreau made his debut the following day, holding Brooklyn to three hits, but three errors by Tillie Shafer, temporarily at shortstop, were the key factors in Brooklyn's 4–2 win. Brooklyn took the rubber match of the series, 5–2, scoring three fast runs off Ames in the first inning. McGraw made it as far as the fifth inning before receiving the heaveho by umpire Garnet Bush.

Mathewson made his first appearance on April 15th, a cold day in Boston.

But the Giants continued their slow start as Hub Perdue held them scoreless, 3–0. McGraw had other problems as well. Fred Merkle had been playing without a contract thus far, and informed McGraw on April 15 that he would hold out until he received a new contract for higher pay. The newspapers could not resist reminding their readers that Merkle had failed to touch second base in 1908 on a play that cost the Giants the pennant.[110] Readers were more concerned with the fate of the passengers from the ship *Titanic* which had recently sunk.

Once again Marquard came through for McGraw the following day — April 16, beating Boston, 8–2. Merkle also came to undisclosed terms on his contract and played that day. Wiltse followed that with a 4–1 victory, Merkle providing a portion of the offense with his first home run of the season. The Giants were now above the .500 mark for the first time that season. The game marked the beginning of an eight-game winning streak, including Mathewson's first win of the season, a 6–2 victory over Brooklyn, which brought the club into second place as the season moved into the month of May; their 10–3 record placed them one game behind a surprising Cincinnati team. The team only became hotter from there. Through May and June, fueled by a sixteen-game winning streak, the Giants went 44–9 until stopped by Brooklyn in both games of a July 4 doubleheader as both Mathewson, who lasted three innings, and Wiltse were hit hard. The day before, Marquard had won his nineteenth straight game in a 2–1 duel with Brooklyn's Nap Rucker. Even with the doubleheader loss to Brooklyn on the holiday, the Giants were still 14½ games in front of second-place Chicago. Mathewson redeemed himself the day following the doubleheader loss, defeating Brooklyn, 6–1, in a game that also represented his 300th career win.

The Giants' fortunes began to decline as the second week of July began. On July 8, Chicago stopped Marquard's streak, which had reached 21 victories over two seasons, by a 7–2 score. Mathewson evened the series the next day with a 5–2 win against Mordecai Brown to earn his 12th win of the season. But as the season moved through July, the Giants slowly began to lose momentum. Marquard suffered the ignominy of losing both games of a July 14 doubleheader. By the end of July, the 67–24 Giants were still ten games in front of Chicago. Two weeks later they were six games ahead, not so much because the Giants were playing that badly — they split their first twelve games in August — but Chicago had won thirteen of fifteen. While Mathewson and Marquard devolved to the level of baseball mortals in August, the 6'2" rookie spitballer Jeff Tesreau kept New York and McGraw on track. "In big Jeff Tesreau the Giants see great hope, for he has already shown that he will be a valuable asset from now until the season's end. Under the constant coaching of Wilbert Robinson, Tesreau has gradually overcome his lack of control, the only flaw that he has shown in his mound work this season. With big Jeff working along with Marquard and Mathewson, New York has three pitchers who probably have the call on any other pitching staffs in the league."[111] For example, on August 2, he shut down

Cincinnati, 4–0, on five hits. On August 16, it was another five-hitter, this time against New York's main rival, Chicago. But it was September 6 on which Tesreau reached his peak that season. Only two days before, Tesreau had allowed eight hits by Philadelphia in a 5–2 triumph for New York. But in the first game of a doubleheader, one of three in three days for McGraw, Philadelphia was helpless. Dode Paskert, a .315 hitter that season, led off with a short infield pop fly that Merkle almost gloved, only to have the ball pop out at the last second. The play was ruled an error. That was the only event close to a hit that day, as Tesreau completely shut the Phillies down for a no-hitter. Tesreau won 17 games that season, and even though Marquard won 26 and Mathewson 23, it was Tesreau who was a primary factor in New York holding onto the league lead into September. The day after Tesreau's masterpiece, an era for McGraw came to an end. Bugs Raymond was found dead in his room at the Hotel Veley in south Chicago. While heat was the suspect in his death, it was just as likely the result of an injury during a drunken brawl some days before.

The lead fell to 4½ games as the month began. But a run of thirteen victories in eighteen games by the Giants, while Chicago lost nine of fourteen in the first half of the month, all but wrapped up the season for New York. On September 26, a doubleheader sweep of Boston behind Mathewson and rookie Al Demaree made it official. Mathewson would not pitch the rest of the season as McGraw decided to rest his ace for the upcoming series. The Giants finished at 103–48, a safe ten games in front of Chicago.

Boston was McGraw's opponent that year in the World's Series. The American League champion, led by "Smokey" Joe Wood's 34–5 regular-season record, won 105 games, finishing fourteen in front of Washington. Prior to the start of the postseason, in a series of nine articles, New York sportswriter Hugh S. Fullerton compared the two teams "position by position."[112] For example, he "cross-questioned" pitching and hitting opponents of the two teams, answers for which entered into Fullerton's analysis.

> The only chance I can see for New York is that Big Jeff Tesreau develops into the one-man hero of the series.... You may think it odd that I figure Mathewson as having a very small chance to beat the Red Sox. In fact, I am led to think that his style of pitching is just the kind the best hitters on the Boston team like to hit. I think Crandall would be much more likely to stop them than Matty, yet it is the opinion of many that McGraw, pinning his faith to the nerve and brain work of his grand veteran, will start the series with Matty. It will be Wood for Boston in the opening game, almost beyond a doubt. All the Boston experts are picking Wood to beat the Giants. I believe Wood will stop them almost completely.[113]

Fullerton rated Boston as superior in seven of the nine positions, also noting that Chicago and Pittsburgh, the primary competition for New York, had regularly beaten the Giants.[114] Fullerton was not far off in his pitching analysis. Wood did open the series for Boston, though it was Tesreau who was McGraw's choice. Wood would win three games in the series. Fullerton was hardly the only pundit who felt Boston was the better team. Among other writers, and even the gamblers, Boston was the slight choice.[115]

Tesreau was McGraw's choice to open the series. Under the glare of hindsight, McGraw's choice would be subject to criticism, but at the time it made sense.[116] Tesreau had been the most effective member of McGraw's staff the second half of the season. Having developed control under Robinson's tutelage to go with an effective spitball, Tesreau won 17 of 24 decisions. His 1.96 ERA was the best in the league. McGraw considered his young right-hander "the peer of Ed Walsh, the famous spit-ball pitcher of the Chicago Americans."[117]

A crowd of 35,730 attended the October 8 opener in New York, witnessing a game undecided until the final out. The Giants opened the scoring in the third inning. After Tesreau fanned, Josh Devore walked and Larry Doyle, the Giants' leading hitter that year at .330, doubled him to third. After Snodgrass fanned for the second out, Red Murray singled the runners home. Tesreau held the Red Sox hitless through five. Boston's first run came in the sixth inning, as Snodgrass misjudged a fly by Tris Speaker, the ball rolling to the fence for a triple. Speaker scored on a ground ball by Duffy Lewis. The Sox went ahead to stay in the seventh, as Harry Hooper's double sandwiched by three singles scored three runs. Tesreau, or likely his ghostwriter, blamed his overconfidence for the Sox' rally, believing that his opponents would fail to hit pitches higher in the strike zone than had been called for by Meyers.[118] The final score was 4–3, as the Giants came close in the ninth. But Wood's last two strikeouts, his tenth and eleventh of the game, snuffed the rally.

Mathewson was picked by McGraw to start Game Two in an attempt to tie the series as the teams went to Boston; McGraw's ace had last pitched in a game that counted back in the last week of September. He allowed ten hits by Boston, but it was primarily the lack of defensive support that kept the Giants in the hole. Boston jumped to a 3–0 lead in the first, the result of an error by shortstop Art Fletcher. Fletcher would have his problems all day, though he was hardly the only one at fault, as five errors kept the Red Sox in the game. The Giants went ahead in the tenth on Merkle's triple and a sacrifice fly. But again the Sox tied the game when Speaker tripled to center, and helped by a Giant juggling act with the ball, continued to race home. Catcher Art Wilson allowed the throw to get past him, and Speaker slid in with the tying run. Umpire Silk O'Loughlin called the game due to darkness in the eleventh, finishing the 6–6 tie.

Returning to Boston on October 10, McGraw called on Marquard in another attempt to tie the series. Facing him was Boston's 20-game winner Buck O'Brien. This time Rube came through, scattering seven hits in the 2–1 triumph. The Giants only managed six hits in the eight innings he pitched, but the hits came when they counted most. Equally important, this time the defense came through — particularly as the game ended in the ninth. Boston had two runners on base when Sox catcher Hick Cady hit a shot between right and center fields, above the heads of Josh Devore and Fred Snodgrass.

In the deafening roar, Devore had been forgotten. He was running faster than he had ever run in his life towards the fence, with one eye peeking keenly over his left shoulder. No one dreamed he could ever reach that ball. The Boston crowd was already celebrating a second victory and counting the series won. The bands were blaring, the bass drums were rumbling, and the cymbals were crashing. The grandstands and bleachers were afire with waving red flags. Devore continued his wild tearing dash. Little Josh [at 5'6"] knew what that crisis meant.... On and on he kept in the daring, desperate attempt. One last glance over his shoulder, and he saw the ball about to whiz over his head, seemingly out of his reach. But in the instant he gathered all the power of his frame and leaped forward with both hands stretched up.... That sphere was firmly clutched in Josh's hands.... That was the last out of the ninth inning and the end of the most nerve-racking rally in a series which had already seethed with feverish excitement.[119]

McGraw was confident the Giants were on the right track. They had lost (blown?) the first two games of the series primarily due to their sloppy defense. He felt vindicated in his prediction that inexperience would undo his opponents. "Both the base runners and their coaches were far too excited to use cool judgment in taking advantage of their one great opportunity."[120] Further vindication was found in the excellent defensive game played by Art Fletcher, another man who had come under fire earlier. McGraw refused to remove him, and was proven correct in his judgment. As seen years earlier in his treatment of Merkle, and would be seen again with Snodgrass, McGraw was a man who could forgive anything but lack of hustle.

With the series now tied, McGraw came back with Tesreau, the adversary from the opening game. Boston was leading 2–0 in the seventh when McGraw made an error that may have been the difference in the game, and perhaps even change the momentum of the series. With the already gray skies darkening more — even the umpire requested a new white ball to replace the discolored one in play — Buck Herzog singled, and after Meyers flied out, Fletcher doubled over first to score Herzog. Moose McCormick, batting for Tesreau, singled past shortstop Steve Yerkes. McGraw, coaching at third, waved Fletcher on. Yerkes recovered the ball, threw a strike to Cady, and Fletcher ran the catcher over. Cady held the ball and Fletcher was out. Instead of the potential tying run on third, the Giants were now retired and still one run down. The Sox scored once more in the ninth to produce the final score of 3–1.

For Game Five in Boston, McGraw came back with his "stopper" Mathewson, with twenty-game winner Hugh Bedient his opponent on the mound. Mathewson allowed five hits, and supported most of the game by excellent defense, again pitched well enough to win. But Bedient held the Giants to three hits. The Sox scored all they needed in the third inning when Hooper and Yerkes tripled in succession, followed by an error on Speaker's grounder that rolled under Larry Doyle's glove. The 2–1 loss put the Giants behind three games to one.

With the Giants now only a single game from elimination, McGraw came back with Marquard. As he had in Game Three, Rube again produced. The

Giants scored five times in the first inning, and took a relatively easy 5–2 victory. The next day it was Tesreau's turn, again facing Joe Wood, the man who had already bested him twice. This time the Sox' ace lost it, and the Giants' six first-inning runs allowed Tesreau to coast to an easy 11–4 triumph. With the series now tied at three games apiece, it all came down to the final in Boston on October 16.

Despite the excitement and significance of the eighth game — including the 6–6 tie in Game Two— the attendance was just a hair above the 17,000 mark. A mixup in ticket allotment resulted in the Royal Rooters booster club boycotting the game. They missed one of the most exciting contests in series history. With no tomorrow, McGraw picked Mathewson to again win the big one. Bedient was the surprise choice by Boston manager Jake Stahl. Excellent fielding kept the game scoreless for two innings. The Giants broke through in their half of the third when Devore walked and later scored on Murray's double. The Sox tied the game in the seventh on a double by Olaf Henriksen, scoring Stahl.

The score remained tied into the tenth. Wood had relieved Bedient in the eighth inning, and had held the Giants scoreless for two innings. However, a double by Murray and a single by Merkle put the Giants into the lead going

Fred Snodgrass (1910) was most famous for a catch he didn't make in the 1912 World Series against Boston. But he was a solid outfielder in a nine-year career. He hit a respectable .291 in the 1913 season (Library of Congress, Bain Collection).

into the bottom of the inning. Mathewson remained in the game despite having been hit hard. Clyde Engle led off for the Sox and hit a lazy fly ball to center. Outfielder Fred Snodgrass settled under the ball, and dropped it. No excuses—not the weather nor the sun nor interference from a teammate. He simply dropped it, and Engle was now on second base. Harry Hooper followed with a smash to center that Snodgrass ran down and grabbed, partially redeeming himself. A tiring Matty walked Yerkes, bringing Tris Speaker to bat. Speaker had hit .383 during the regular season, and had already produced eight hits, including two triples, in this series. With the possible exceptions of Ty Cobb and Shoeless Joe Jackson, Speaker was arguably the best player in the American League.

Matty threw a slow inside curve to the future Hall of Famer, who swung and lofted an easy foul towards first. "Anyone could have caught it. I [Fullerton] could have jumped out of the press box and caught it behind my back—but Merkle quit. Yes, Merkle quit cold. He didn't start for the ball. He seemed to be suffering from financial paralysis. Perhaps he was calculating the difference between the winner's and loser's end [$1500]. He didn't start. Mathewson saw the ball going down. Meyers saw that it would fall safe, and they raced toward it, too late, and the ball dented the turf a few feet from first."[121] At this point, a visibly angry Mathewson simply ran out of luck. Speaker hit the next pitch on a solid line to right, scoring Engle with the tying run and sending Yerkes to third. Lewis walked to load the bases, and Larry Gardner came to bat. Gardner hit a hard drive over Devore's head. The right fielder again made a long run to haul it in, but he was simply too deep. A desperate heave fell short as Yerkes scored the winning run. "Snodgrass Drops Easy Ball, Costing Teammates $29,514" read the headline in the *Times*.[122]

The "Snodgrass Muff" joined the ignominious plays of baseball history. Snodgrass himself recognized the significance: "Snodgrass came to the bench after the game, and picked up his blazer. He did not speak to anyone. He acted as if he thought that he was a criminal, and then he walked off the field alone. I [Tesreau] rode back to the hotel in the same taxicab with him, and there were tears in his eyes. He did not speak to Josh Devore, who was in the cab, or me, until we almost got back to the hotel. Then he said, 'Boys, I lost the championship for you.'"[123] The truth, of course, was that is exactly what happened. But no teammates ever held it against him, nor did McGraw. Snodgrass was a hustler, and that is what counted—not an error which could happen to anyone. Indeed, when McGraw later discussed the defeat, ironically it was Merkle on whom he placed the loss, the failure to catch Speaker's pop fly being the deciding factor.

CHAPTER THREE

The American League Race

Boston was the 1912 world champion, and so the obvious question was whether they could repeat. "Smokey" Joe Wood, winner of 34 games, was back, as was the supporting staff of Ray Collins and 20-game winner Hugh Bedient and the most notable position players, Boston outfielders and future Hall of Famers Harry Hooper and Tris Speaker, as well as Duffy Lewis. William Phelon, in his analysis of the 1913 season, felt that Boston really had not stood out from the pack, and that it was hustle as well as some particularly exemplary seasons on the part of Wood and others that resulted in the pennant.[1] Philadelphia was expected to provide the strongest opposition, with Washington in the mix as well. The Athletic pitching staff of Plank, Bender and Coombs was certainly the match of anything other teams could throw against them. Both offensively and defensively, "the $100,000 infield" of future Hall of Famers Frank Baker and Eddie Collins, along with Jack Barry and Stuffy McInnis, was the best in the league. Washington had Walter Johnson on the cusp of greatness, supported by 24-game winner Bob Groom and such position players as speedy outfielder Clyde Milan and his 88 stolen bases in 1912 and infielder Chick Gandil, whose "date with infamy" would be years in the future. The Cleveland Naps likewise could not be ignored. Phelon's hardly inspired choice was that Philadelphia would dethrone Boston.

After training in San Antonio, the Mackmen came north in the beginning of April and faced the National League Phillies in what was becoming an annual city series. While the Phillies were a darkhorse contender at best in the upcoming season, they nevertheless represented legitimate competition. The pitching staff anchored by Grover Cleveland Alexander and Tom Seaton would keep them in contention, and a lineup that included slugger Gavy Cravath, Dode Paskert and Sherry Magee could be formidable. Nevertheless, the Athletics provided a preview of what their American League opposition would face by winning five of the six games versus the Phillies, the other ending in an eighteen-inning 2–2 tie.

The Athletics' season opened in Boston on April 10, the opposition being the 1912 world champions. "Smoky" Joe Wood started for the Sox, while Jack Coombs was the choice for Mack. It was no pitchers' duel as the teams combined for 22 hits, five by the Athletics' Eddie Collins, and nineteen runs. In the end,

Philadelphia won by a score of 10–9. Wood allowed nine hits and seven runs in his five innings of pitching, while Coombs allowed a "mere" eight hits and five runs in the same span. In the sixth inning, Coombs became involved in a play more typical of early spring training. Catcher Jack Lapp singled before stopping at third on a double by Coombs. Eddie Murphy grounded to shortstop Heinie Wagner, who threw home to catch Lapp. Lapp, however, returned to third, only to find Coombs standing on the bag with Murphy now at second base. The Red Sox catcher tagged Lapp, but since it was he who was actually entitled to the bag, Lapp was safe. Meanwhile, Coombs had returned to second and Murphy ran to first. A throw to first baseman Hal Janvrin went wild, and in the end Lapp scored and both Coombs and Murphy moved up.[2]

Two days later, Coombs tried, but again provided another performance that left much to be desired. The Red Sox scored four times in the first inning off Coombs and reliever Herb Pennock. Coombs faced only five batters before leaving, four of whom reached base. The Athletics had scored four times in the top of the inning, so the Sox merely tied the game. Eddie Plank took over in the second for Pennock, pitching eight shutout innings in what became a 5–4 Athletics victory. Eddie Collins contributed two hits in four appearances at the plate and scored the eventual winning run in the third on a single, steal of second and two ground outs.

Connie Mack had more to concern himself about Coombs than just two poor outings. The man was clearly ill with what was at first thought to be the "grippe," a catchall term encompassing anything resembling "flu-like" symptoms. John Wesley Coombs had been born November 18, 1882, in a small farming area in Iowa. The Coombs family moved to Maine when Jack was a child, and he grew up on a farm near Kennebunk. Enrolling in Colby College in 1902 and majoring in chemistry, Coombs earned both a nickname and a reputation as an outstanding athlete in numerous sports, including baseball, football, basketball and track. He once reportedly ran a 100-yard dash in 10.2 seconds. During the summers, he played semi-professional baseball throughout New England. During his senior year, by now a solid six-feet tall, 185-pound athlete, Coombs pitched Colby to the college baseball championship of Maine.

In December 1905 Coombs was signed by Tom Mack, Connie's brother, to a contract with the Athletics, agreeing to join the team following his graduation the following June.[3] Coombs made his debut on July 5, 1906, pitching a seven-hit shutout against Washington.

Coombs' condition merely worsened, and in mid–April as the 1913 season was just underway, he was sent back to Philadelphia for treatment. It was initially believed he would be out at most for a week, and for a brief period appeared to be recovering. However, the fever quickly worsened and on April 19, Coombs was admitted to Northwestern General Hospital in Philadelphia, ironically occupying the same bed that former Athletics catcher Mike Powers

Bush McInnis Barry Collins Baker Mgr. Mack Oldring Thomas

Middle Row: Daley, Schang, Lapp, Brown, Bender, Wyckoff, Davis, Orr. *Bottom Row:* Houck, E. Murphy, Plank, Strunk, Bailey, D. Murphy, Walsh, Taff

PHILADELPHIA AMERICANS

had used several years earlier. The eventual diagnosis was significantly more serious: spinal typhoid, which in those pre-antibiotic days could easily be a death sentence. Coombs did recover, but only after months of hospitalization and a loss of nearly 60 pounds from his playing weight of 180. For Coombs, the 1913 season was over.

Play resumed for the Athletics on April 17, this time facing the Red Sox in a series at home. Chief Bender faced Ray Collins, and the Athletics won their third in a row, 6–5. Bender was knocked out in the third inning while Boston scored all five of their runs. Reliever Joe Bush held Boston scoreless the rest of the way, and Philadelphia eventually tied the game with three runs in the eighth inning. In the home half of the ninth, a bases-loaded walk to Rube Oldring by Sox reliever Buck O'Brien, a 20-game winner in 1912, forced in the winning run. The following day, Carroll "Boardwalk" Brown took the mound for Mack, facing Rube Foster. Brown had entered professional baseball several years before with an independent team in Atlantic City, New Jersey, acquiring both experience and a nickname. After pitching for Bridgeport in 1910 and 1911, he was signed by Mack and won 13 games in 1912. He joined the rotation as a replacement for Coombs. Brown held Boston hitless for four innings before the Red Sox broke through with two runs. Byron Houck replaced Brown in the seventh, with Bender coming in for the ninth inning. Boston pounded Bender with three doubles and two singles, producing four runs and an 8–5 victory, Boston's second of the year and Philadelphia's first loss.

Eddie Plank made his first start of the season for Mack on Saturday, lasting only three innings as Boston scored four runs on eight hits and three walks off Plank and Weldon Wyckoff. Pennock entered the game in relief in the fifth, holding Boston scoreless for the remainder of the game. Meanwhile, the Athletics limited Red Sox starter Buck O'Brien to two-thirds of an inning, scoring seven times in four innings against O'Brien and Charley Hall, and winning their fourth game with a 7–5 score. The series with the Sox ended Monday. Boston led 3–2 into the seventh, when a single by Murphy and two Boston errors allowed the Athletics to load the bases. Frank Baker drove in two runs with a single, and Tom Daley, replacing an injured Amos Strunk, drove in two more with another base hit. Athletics starter Byron Houck walked nine batters and hit one, but nevertheless scattered most of Boston's seven hits until relieved by Eddie Plank with two outs in the ninth. Joe Wood lasted only into the third for Boston when he was replaced by Bedient. The victory improved Philadelphia's record to 5–1, with only undefeated Washington at 5–0 ahead of the Athletics in the race.

Boardwalk Brown took the mound for the Athletics on April 22, as the Yankees came to Philadelphia for a four-game series. Even under manager Frank

Opposite: The 1913 Philadelphia Athletics. The team won four pennants during the five years between 1910 and 1914 (Baseball Hall of Fame, Cooperstown, New York).

Carroll "Boardwalk" Brown (1912) earned his nickname while pitching with an independent Atlantic City team. Brown's 17 victories in 1913 were critical to the Athletics' pennant hopes due to the loss of Coombs for the season (Library of Congress, Bain Collection).

Chance, for eight years manager of the Chicago Cubs and as tough as they came, the New Yorkers were mired in the American League cellar in the young season. Manager Chance chose George "Slats" McConnell to oppose Brown, and through three innings held a 3–2 lead. But in the fourth a Stuffy McInnis home run started a four-run rally, and the Yankees never caught up. Frank Baker's eighth-inning homer on a ball that bounced into the left field bleachers completed the scoring. Brown pitched a complete game, the first of the season for Philadelphia.

"Bullet" Joe Bush took on Ray Keating the following night, and the Yankee spitballer held the Athletics to three hits and the first shutout of the year for the Mackmen. New York scored in the second inning on a walk to Birdie Cree, who reached second on a groundout and scored on a single by Bill McKechnie. The visitors scored twice more in the sixth, while Yankee first baseman Hal Chase singled in the fourth and final run in the ninth. Chief Bender exacted revenge in the third game, limiting New York to five hits in a 4–1 triumph, marking Bender's first victory of the season. Eddie Plank made it three out of four for Philadelphia with another 4–0 shutout in the Friday finish of the first meeting of the clubs this season. The right-hander held the Yankees to a mere three hits while striking out ten. The game was scoreless until the sixth when Philadelphia broke through for three runs. Eddie Collins opened the Athletics' half with a double, one of three the second baseman hit that day, in addition to a single. Baker walked, but McInnis flied to Cree for the first out. Tom Daley singled to center for two runs. Jack Barry grounded out to pitcher Russ Ford for the second out. Catcher Jack Lapp was intentionally walked, bringing Plank to bat. But Plank crossed Ford up, singling in Daley with the third run of the inning. The final score was a 4–0 shutout, Plank's first of the year and his first complete game.

Washington was next in town for a battle to see who would at least temporarily lead in the pennant race. The Saturday game at Shibe Park featured Boardwalk Brown facing Tom Hughes in front of a crowd exceeding 20,000 persons. Nationals ace Walter Johnson had been scheduled to start, only to be laid low by a case of food poisoning. Hughes certainly did his part, and the score was tied 1–1 through seven innings, after which Byron Houck took over for Brown, who had been removed for a pinch-hitter. Washington broke the tie in the eighth, scoring once on a single by infielder Ray Morgan, a wild pitch by Houck, and a dropped fly by Eddie Murphy. However, Philadelphia came back to score twice. Murphy was hit by a pitch. Rube Oldring forced Murphy at second, but then scored on a triple by Collins. McInnis followed with a double to score Collins with the third and eventual winning run.

Byron Houck, twenty-one-year-old, six-foot right-hander from Prosper, Minnesota, might have been among the greatest had he any idea where the pitch was actually headed. Connie Mack signed him out of an independent league, and Houck managed to split sixteen decisions in 1912. With Coombs out, Mack was counting on Brown and Houck to take up much of the slack in the rotation. The 1913 season would prove to be Houck's finest in a short big league career that produced a record of 26–24. Only after he developed a spitball in the minor leagues years later with Vernon in the Pacific Coast League would Houck live up to this potential.

During this visit to Philadelphia, the Nationals made a discovery that allegedly accounted for the recent success of the Athletics' pitchers: the height of the mound. "The pitcher's box at the grounds here is raised several inches above the rest of the diamond, giving the twirlers a distinct advantage over the batters. The centers of all diamonds are sufficiently elevated to afford proper drainage, but at Shibe Park the mound is several inches higher than in other cities.... Mr. Griffith [Nationals manager] is so thoroughly opposed to alibis that he will make no official report on the contour of the field."[4] Contours aside, the game was postponed due to rain.

Johnson finally had his chance to pitch on April 30, and with veteran Eddie

Plank as Mack's choice, the game featured two of baseball's greatest hurlers. The crowd was treated to a true pitcher's duel, as the game remained scoreless into the ninth before Washington broke the scoreless tie. Clyde Milan singled to lead off. Following a fly out, Chick Gandil singled Milan to second. Morgan fanned for Plank's twelfth strikeout of the day. When Milan and Gandil attempted a double steal, second base was uncovered, and Lapp's throw went into center field. Milan scored on the error and Gandil went to third. Catcher Eddie Ainsmith singled in Gandil with only the fifth Washington hit for a second run. The final score was 2–0. Johnson fanned ten while allowing four hits. Philadelphia, with a record of 9–3, closed out the month ½ game in front of Washington and Cleveland.

The merry month of May began with a visit to New York, as the Yankees hosted the visitors for a four-game series. Brown opened for Mack, with Keating pitching for New York. The Yankees led after five, 2–0. But in the sixth inning, the Athletics finally got to Keating. With one out, Brown singled and Murphy sacrificed him to second. Oldring beat out a grounder in the infield, with Brown moving to third. Oldring then promptly stole second base. Collins singled both runners in to tie the score. Baker grounded back to Keating, but when the pitcher threw poorly to Chase at first base, and Collins went to third and made a break for home. Chase threw wildly to the plate and Collins scored the go-ahead run. Baker saved the game in the seventh, not with his bat, but in the field. With a man on second and two out, Ed Sweeney hit a "rope" towards left field. "The ball was high over Baker's head — don't know how high, but high enough to be out of reach without a ladder. The first thing that about 3000 pairs of eyes knew, Baker could be seen, his gloved hand shooting cloudward like a weathervane. But where was the ball? The populace was still wondering when Baker decided to drop down from the dizzy heights. Sure enough, there in his hand was the ball. There ought to be a law against that sort of thing."[5]

Byron Houck took the mound for the second game of the series. Mack probably wore a groove through the turf with his parade of pitchers. "At the head of the procession was Byron Houck. He rode on a float called 'trying to hand the game to the Yankees.' Next came Joe Bush in an allegorical picture entitled 'I haven't got a thing today.' Closely following came Lefty Pennock, whose banner was entitled, 'I may not be a pitcher, but I'm sticking in the league.' And last of all came the old Chippewa medicine man, Chief Bender, chanting his favorite war hymn, 'I know I'm getting old, but just see who I'm pitching against.'"[6]

The Athletic hurlers actually limited the Yanks to a mere three hits. But Houck played wild man, and walked six of the twelve batters he faced before being replaced, first by Bush, then Pennock and finally Bender. In the end, the Athletics scored four times in the fourth, and then plated the sixth and winning run in the eighth inning when Baker singled, stole second and scored on a single by Daley. The final score was 6–5.

Byron Houck (1913). When he was on his game, he could be unhittable. But too often the catcher had no more idea of where the ball was going than did the batter. Still, his 14 victories in 1913 were a major factor in the Athletics' title. Eight of the victories came in relief (Library of Congress, Bain Collection).

Houck came back to try again the next day, Saturday, and fared about as well. The Yankees scored three times in the first four innings, by which time Joe Bush was back on the mound.

The daily explosion of the Yankees occurred in the fifth inning. "The Peerless Trailers, led by the Peerless Leader [manager Frank Chance] up to that time were in front by a score of three to nothing and the big crowd of some 15,000 were rejoicing to think that at last the luckless crew had shaken off the mantle of depression and were going to shock the baseball world with a victory. Now comes a word of sadness. The Yanks say "They ain't no such animal as victory...." They have been battered down so often that the fickle baseball fan has commenced to jeer." [What! New Yorkers jeer? Say it ain't so!] Yes, the fans jeered the Yankees in the midst of their misfortune.[7]

It came apart in the fifth. With Lefty Schulz on the mound, second baseman Jack Barry beat out an infield hit. Schulz seemed to have everything under control when Ira Thomas flied to center and Bush struck out. Jimmy Walsh walked, and with two strikes on him, Oldring doubled in both men. Collins was hit by a pitch, and Baker was safe when Bill McKechnie fumbled his grounder, Oldring scoring. Collins and Baker then attempted a double steal, and when catcher Sweeney threw the ball past third base, Collins scored. An error on Stuffy McInnis' ground ball allowed Baker to score the fifth run of the inning. Danny Murphy singled, and that was all for Schulz. The Yankee pitcher did leave to a cheering crowd. Ray Keating came in and ended the scoring when Barry grounded out. The Athletics scored a sixth time in the seventh on a triple by Collins, who scored when Sweeney dropped the ball on a play at the plate. The Athletics scored twice more in the eighth to lead 8–4, putting the game out of reach even with two Yankee scores in the ninth inning.

Following the Sunday off-day, the Athletics completed the sweep behind Eddie Plank as Ray Fisher was the victim of Monday's battering. For seven innings, the young Fisher held the Athletics to five hits, their only run coming in the fourth after Baker singled, stole second, and continued on to third when Sweeney's throw went wild. McInnis was hit by a pitch, and when Baker and Stuffy attempted a double steal, first baseman Hal Chase took Sweeney's throw and chased McInnis towards second base. Baker scored and McInnis was likewise safe. Chase was the target of derision by the crowd. Sweeney redeemed himself in part with a home run in the next inning, one of the two hits New York managed against Plank. But once again the Athletics placed the game out of reach with a late rally. Scoring four in the eighth inning and three more in the ninth, Philadelphia won its fourth straight by a score of 8–1.

Playing much of his career with mediocre Yankee teams, Ray Fisher still managed to win 100 big league games. Born in the mountains of Vermont in 1887, Fisher developed into a solid athlete at just under six feet in height and 180 pounds. At Middlebury College, Fisher participated in track and field, establishing a school record in the shot-put, football and basketball, in addition to becoming a star pitcher. In 1908, he joined Hartford in the Connecticut League, producing pitching records of 12–1 and 24–5 in 1908 and 1909, respectively with 243 strikeouts. In 1909, the Yankees purchased his contract. As did the Robert Redford character in *The Natural*, Fisher even brought a homemade bat with him to New York.

Fisher's pitching repertoire included both a curveball and a spitball, which according to his catcher Ed Sweeney, "is just as dangerous as the one [Jack] Chesbro exhibited."[8] Fisher's best seasons with New York took place between 1913 and 1916, a period in which he went 51–47 for a team that finished seventh twice and as high as fourth place only once. Illness reduced his effectiveness, and a year off in the army seemingly made him expendable. In 1919, Fisher was waived to Cincinnati. Fisher still managed a record of 14–5 for the pennant-winning Reds that year. The 1919 World Series was famous, though infamous is probably the better designation, as the one in which eight players on the Chicago White Sox were involved in throwing the series to the Reds. Chicago did manage to win three of the eight games in that series, one being a shutout thrown by Dickie Kerr in which Fisher was the losing pitcher. In

1921, Fisher retired, moving to Ann Arbor, Michigan, to coach the University of Michigan baseball team. Fisher had already signed a contract with Cincinnati, and in the dispute that followed was declared ineligible by the new commissioner of baseball, Judge Landis. The ruling stood until 1980, when Bowie Kuhn reversed the ruling. Fisher coached at Michigan for 38 years, producing a record of 636-295-8.[8]

Philadelphia next traveled to St. Louis to face the Browns in a four-game series. Boardwalk Brown opened for Philadelphia on May 7. Philadelphia quickly scored on Roy Mitchell when Murphy walked to start the game, advanced to third on a wild pitch, and scored when Oldring singled. Collins followed with a walk, and Oldring scored on McInnis' single. The lead went to three runs in the fourth when Baker homered. Brown started slowly, walking the first three batters to face him in the first, but Lapp threw two runners out attempting to steal. St. Louis scored twice in the fourth to cut Philadelphia's lead to 3–2. Brown pitched shutout ball the rest of the way. The Athletics' streak became six consecutive victories as Chief Bender scattered eight Brownie hits, while five St. Louis errors, including two by catcher Sam Agnew, a new recruit from the Pacific Coast league, contributed to six Philadelphia runs. The Athletics jumped off to a fast two-run lead when Oldring and Collins singled in the first inning, followed by a Baker double that scored both runners. Bender struck out nine in the 6–3 victory. After the game, Connie Mack was the subject of a rare treat, as members of the Century Boat Club, a prominent St. Louis business organization, invited him to a luncheon. Mack was the first baseball manager to be honored as a guest by the organization.[9]

The Athletics' winning streak ended at six the following day, as neither Houck nor Wyckoff in relief could stop the Browns. St. Louis led 5–0 after the first inning, and that for all intents and purposes decided the game. Two singles and two walks ended Houck's day, and Wyckoff was greeted by a triple off the bat of "Bunny" Brief. Brief scored the fifth run on a sacrifice fly. The seventh inning was witness to an unusual call, one in which an umpire reversed his own ruling. Wyckoff was on third for the Athletics with two out. Oldring hit a low line drive that shortstop Bobby Wallace dropped. Wallace grabbed the ball and threw a low toss to Brief at first base. Brief was on his stomach as he grabbed the throw, and having tagged the bag, tossed the ball to the pitcher's box. However, umpire Charley Ferguson called Oldring safe, believing Brief's foot was not on the bag. The Browns surrounded Ferguson as they protested his call. At this point umpire Silk O'Loughlin overruled Ferguson and called Oldring out. Now it was the Athletics who surrounded O'Loughlin. Eddie Collins threw his "cap in the air, sent his bat after the sky-piece and acted like a wild man. Ira Thomas rolled his mask across the diamond.... Then O'Loughlin ruled his overruling was wrong and reversed himself."[10] After ten minutes, the Browns took the field once again, Collins went out on a weak grounder, and the game proceeded from there. The final score was 7–3.

Eddie Collins managed "only" one hit in four at-bats this day, hardly typical of his play thus far in the young season. Coming into the game, he was hitting a league-leading .463, with 31 hits in 67 at-bats. Boston's Olaf Henriksen was second in hitting, 51 points behind, though only having batted 17 times. Joe Jackson of Cleveland was a more realistic rival, as indeed were the Indians in the pennant race, with an average by Shoeless Joe thus far of an even .400. Collins was also leading the league in runs scored with 22.

The 5'9", 175-pound Collins was in the midst of the peak years of a Hall of Fame career by 1913, coming off averages of .365 and .348 the previous two seasons. Collins was born May 2, 1887, in Millerton, New York, growing up in Tarrytown, a small town north of New York City. Despite weighing only 135 pounds when he enrolled at Columbia University, Collins started at shortstop for the baseball team and quarterbacked the football team. Despite his alleged amateur status, Collins played semi-professional baseball while at Columbia until he was discovered by Philadelphia Athletics pitcher Andy Coakley. Coakley passed the information on to Connie Mack, who signed Collins to a contract. Under the alias of Eddie Sullivan, Collins made his debut with the Athletics on September 17, 1906. Facing the White Sox's Big Ed Walsh, Collins/Sullivan struck out twice, but managed a bunt single and stole the first of an eventual major league total of 741 bases.[11] In the field, he handled six chances. His professional status was shortly uncovered by the Columbia authorities, and he was declared ineligible for his senior year. By 1908, Collins had become Mack's regular shortstop.[12]

Saturday, Eddie Plank took the mound, facing the Browns' Dwight Stone. St. Louis again jumped to a first-inning lead when outfielder Burt Shotton singled, advanced on a sacrifice, and after Gus Williams walked, went to third on the front end of a double steal. Lapp's throw went past Baker at third, and Shotton scored. Williams scored when Del Pratt singled. The Browns picked up a third run in the fourth, but Philadelphia tied the game with three in the fifth inning. McInnis and Walsh singled and Barry walked to fill the bases. Lapp walked, forcing in one run, and after Plank hit into a double play, a single by Eddie Murphy knocked in two runs to tie the game. The Athletics scored three more times and were leading 6–3 going into the home half of the ninth. But the Browns tied the game, and with the bases loaded, Del Pratt smacked a line drive over second. Jimmy Walsh, playing a shallow center, came running in to snag the potential game-winning hit. The Athletics scored twice in the tenth, once on a single by McInnis to score Collins, and again when Baker scored on a squeeze play. The Browns went out easily, and the Athletics had another victory in the books. Once again, the umpires had a difficult time. Jimmy Austin took issue in the tenth with a call by Silk O'Loughlin, and after implying a lack of eyesight on the part of the umpire, left the game without completing his batting appearance.[13]

Now it was on to Chicago, where in a Sunday match Ed Walsh held

Philadelphia to seven hits, including three by Murphy, while striking out six. Despite a McInnis home run, the Sox scored four times off Brown to win, 4–3. Bender came back the next day, holding Chicago to six hits in a 3–0 shutout. Only one run was earned, as the Athletics managed a mere three hits against "Reb" Russell. Heavy rain washed out the rest of the series.

Working its way through the league, Philadelphia's next stop was Cleveland, where the Athletics faced the second-place Indians, now two games behind Philadelphia with a record of 17–9. Plank was Mack's choice. Instead, Cy Falkenberg won his seventh straight, shutting down the Mackmen on three hits in the 2–0 shutout. Cleveland's two runs came in the first two innings; Wyckoff and Bush held them scoreless the rest of the way, but Philadelphia's bats were helpless.

Boardwalk Brown returned to the mound the next day. Cleveland quickly scored three times in the first, and Brown was replaced by Houck. But Cleveland's Vean Gregg was hit equally hard, allowing thirteen hits in 6⅓ innings, and helped by a triple play (Barry to Thomas to Baker to Houck to Barry to Collins to Baker to Oldring), Philadelphia won an 8–5 slugfest.[14] On Saturday May 17, youngster Herb Pennock took his turn against the Indians, and once again Cleveland quickly led after one inning, 3–1. Scoring four more times against three relievers, the Indians took an easy 7–3 victory. Sunday, the Athletics earned a split of the four-game series. Wyckoff lasted only two innings as Cleveland scored twice. Bender came in and shut down Cleveland the rest of the way while striking out five. Jack Barry drove in three runs, and Philadelphia won, 4–2. Each team had now won 19 games, but Cleveland had 11 losses, four more than Philadelphia.

Wyckoff returned to the mound in Detroit the next day as he faced the 10–21 Tigers. This time he lasted into the third inning. Meanwhile, led by Ty Cobb's three hits and a home run by Ossie Vitt, Detroit scored five times in three innings on the way to an easy 9–3 victory. Ed Willett limited Philadelphia to six hits. Willett's performance this day required only one hour, 48 minutes to complete. But games often ran longer. Willette had his own solution to a problem that is encountered even today: the length of a ball game. "Edgar caught his idea while watching Sam Crawford amble around the bases recently after smashing the ball into the bleachers for a home run. 'Why not permit Crawford to run to first and then return to the bench, instead of consuming a minute or so walking around the sacks?' says Edgar. 'There are, we'll say, fifty home runs hit in the American League each season. That means an hour wasted. Everyone knows the hit is a home run when it drops into the bleachers or goes over the fence, so what's the use of wasting time and effort?"[15]

The Tigers followed up their opening-game victory with a second one the following day. Houck started, facing Al Klawitter. Cobb once again was the Athletics' nemesis with three hits and a third-inning steal of home. The Athletics led 6–3 going into the home half of the eighth, only to see the Tigers score

Ty Cobb (ca. 1910), perhaps the greatest player of all time, is certainly one of the most controversial. His .366 career average and 4,189 base hits were only two of the many hitting records he held after 24 seasons in the major leagues, nearly all with Detroit. He batted .390 in 1913, failing to reach the .400 mark for the first time in three seasons (Library of Congress, Bain Collection).

four times to retake the lead. Philadelphia tied the game with a ninth-inning home run by Oldring. In the home half of the tenth, Cobb lined a pitch to center for a hit, but when Walsh was slow in fielding the ball, continued on to second. Three consecutive walks by Brown in relief allowed Cobb to score the winning run. The series loss was only the first for the Athletics thus far in the season. Eddie Plank finally ended the short losing streak, as he blanked Detroit on three hits. Philadelphia scored seven times.

After a travel day, Philadelphia returned home for a long series to face Washington, now in third place with a record of 18–12. "By two inches, two errors and two runs, the crippled, maimed and battered Nationals lost the opening battle with the Athletics, 4–2."[16] Wabash George Mullin was on the mound for Washington, while Boardwalk Brown had what was now a regular turn in the rotation — if nothing else, this was certainly an era for nicknames — and Mullin, recently acquired from Detroit, certainly requited himself well. The Athletics had a mere seven hits, two after Washington errors provided extra chances for the home team, while Brown allowed ten. The Athletics scored all they needed in the sixth on a single by Barry to drive in Baker, and a grounder by Jack Lapp that went through second baseman Joe Gedeon's legs drove in two more. Brown singled in Barry with the fourth run of the inning. Washington came within inches in the ninth when with the bases loaded and Bender pitching in relief, Germany Schaefer hit a shot just foul past third, then another back of shortstop. Jack Barry barely reached the potential hit, but barely was good enough and the Athletics had a 4–2 victory.

Jack Lapp was the latest in a line of catchers that the former tall receiver, Connie Mack, had recruited for the Athletics. There was Doc Powers, of course, but his tragic death allowed one to overlook any deficiencies in the hitting

Jack Lapp (1912) was one of several catchers on Mack's four pennant-winning teams from 1910 to 1914. The 5'8" backstop played eight years in Philadelphia, batting a high of .353 in 1911 (Baseball Hall of Fame, Cooperstown, New York).

department. Ira Thomas, "Paddy" Livingston and Lapp had taken turns behind the plate in recent years, but Thomas had aged and Livingston went to Cleveland. Lapp more or less took over the position by default. Only 5'8", 160 pounds, on first glance Lapp hardly looked the part. But looks were deceiving, and he did provide hitting potential, batting .353 in 1911, albeit in 167 at-bats, and .292 the year before. But he distinguished himself in the 1911 World Series, and, "On fly balls, he is without a superior in the American league."[17] Lapp was born in Frazer, Pennsylvania, in 1885, and after playing amateur ball for Berwyn in the Maine Line League (1905–1906), and bouncing around with Hazleton (Pennsylvania), Portsmouth (Virginia), Allentown and Chester (Pennsylvania), he settled with Syracuse of the New York State League by 1908. Surviving a bout with typhoid fever, he was signed by Mack, and appeared in 13 games during the 1908 season. By 1913, Lapp had become the regular catcher.

After a Sunday day of rest, the two teams matched up for a doubleheader, Houck versus Bob Groom in the opener, and John Taff facing Walter Johnson in the second. Houck limited the Nationals to three hits, dwarfed by eight bases on balls, but he came through when needed. With two runs in both the fifth and seventh, Philadelphia took the opener, 4–0. In the second game, Walter Johnson's pitching and Washington's slugging — both Chick Gandil and Johnson homered — produced an easy 9–2 victory for "The Big Train." The teams followed up the doubleheader split with another pair the following day. This time it was Joe Engel and Tom Hughes for the Nationals; each was a quality pitcher but neither was a Johnson. For Philadelphia, it was Eddie Plank and Chief Bender. Engel lasted three innings, allowing only one hit, but three errors and a balk put Philadelphia ahead by three. Plank only allowed two hits in what became an easy 8–0 triumph. Bender had it almost as easy later in the afternoon, allowing five hits in a 7–1 victory. By winning four of the five games, Philadelphia moved 5½ games in front of Washington, which fell to fourth place. But Cleveland had won three of its last four and was only a game behind in second place.

Philadelphia now earned a "breather" in the form of the 9–24 Yankees coming to town for a four-game series. On May 29, Boardwalk Brown faced Ray Keating in a rematch of May 1. Although Brown did not repeat his shutout performance from earlier in the month, the result was identical. The Yankees led 5–2 into the sixth inning, but Philadelphia scored two in the sixth, and a home run by Home Run Baker tied it in the seventh. Baker's hitting won it in the ninth, as the Athletics' third sacker doubled with two out, and scored the winning run on a single by McInnis. Brown lasted only four innings, but Joe Bush pitched shutout ball the rest of the way for the 6–5 victory.

It was a holiday doubleheader on May 30, as Wyckoff and Houck took on Russ Ford and Ray Fisher. In the morning game, a two-run double in the first inning by Cree provided the visitors with a 2–0 lead. Russ Ford pitched one-hit ball for eight innings, and it appeared that the game would end thusly, particularly after Daley fanned for the first out in the home half of the ninth. But Eddie Murphy singled past second and after Oldring flied for the second out, Collins hit an easy grounder to Hartzell at second that should have ended the game. But Hartzell fumbled the ball, and both men were safe. Frank Baker singled, scoring Murphy with the tying run and sending Collins to third. McInnis hit an easy grounder to Roger Peckinpaugh at third, but once again what should have been an out was fumbled, and Collins scored the third and winning run. Wyckoff pitched equally well, and despite the early runs held the Yankees to three hits. The second game was anticlimatic. Houck held New York to seven hits and four runs, along with nine walks, while Philadelphia, behind a home run once again by Baker, scored seven times. A total of 39,000 fans saw the two games.

Philadelphia completed the sweep as the month of May ended. Chief Bender and seventeen Athletic hits, including home runs by McInnis and Baker — the slugger's third of the series — finished the series with an easy 12–2 win. But even with the Mackmen owning a record of 28–10, the Indians, now having won eight straight, were even closer at a half-game behind.

Monday saw a brief trip south on the part of Mack and his men to take on the Washington Nationals in a doubleheader. Boardwalk Brown and Byron Houck were scheduled to face George Mullin and Walter Johnson. In the opener, the Athletics pounded out 15 hits and nine runs. Mullin was gone by the second inning as Philadelphia quickly jumped out to a 5–1 lead. The final score was 9–4, with both Amos Strunk and Rube Oldring leading the attack with three hits apiece. Even Chief Bender, coming on in relief of Brown and Joe Bush, contributed two hits and a run scored. In the latter game, Baker smacked a fourth-inning homer off Johnson as the visitors swept the doubleheader, winning 4–3. Brown relieved Houck in the sixth when Washington scored three times to take a 3–2 lead, and received credit for the win when Philadelphia scored twice in the eighth inning. The Athletics' winning streak stood now at eight.

Back in their home grounds, Mack and the Athletics prepared to take on the visiting Tigers for four games, hosting Detroit's first visit of the season. Eddie Plank and Hooks Dauss represented their respective teams in the first matchup. It was not pretty. "In honor of the first visit the Detroit Tiger has paid to our fair city during the present season, old Mr. Plank and young Mr. Dauss started in to have a regular pitcher's battle yesterday, but the thing was all gummed up by the supporting casts before it got very far along. Just how gummed up by the supporting casts can be deduced when we chronicle the fact that with anything like able aiding and abetting of the pitchers by their associates the Tigers would have copped by a 1–0 count, whereas the Athletics actually won out by a score of 7–3. Considerable difference is putting it conservatively."[18]

Cobb began the scoring with a second-inning triple, and after Bobby Veach fanned, scored on a long double by Del Gainer. The Tigers made it 2–0 in the fourth when Strunk and Murphy played "Alphonse and Gaston" on a fly by "Wahoo" Sam Crawford, which landed on the turf simultaneously with Crawford landing on third base.[19] Crawford scored on a sacrifice fly by Veach. Meanwhile, a mere first-inning single by Eddie Murphy was the extent of Philadelphia's base runners through five innings. But in the sixth, Lapp and Plank walked, and advanced on a sacrifice by Murphy. Oldring followed with a grounder to third baseman George Moriarity, who threw to the plate in an attempt to cut down Lapp. But Lapp scored when the catcher muffed the throw, and Plank and Oldring ended up at third and second, respectively. Oldring was picked off second for the second out, but then Eddie Collins followed with a rare home run — a ball that bounced into the bleachers — and the Athletics led 3–2. Philadelphia scored three more times in the eighth. Oldring singled and stole second before advancing to third on a wild throw by Detroit catcher Oscar Stanage. Collins hit a fly ball, and this time Cobb and Veach did the "Alphonse and Gaston" act, with Collins making it to third base. Baker grounded to Vitt, but Collins beat the throw home for a second run. Vitt's throw home was wild, and Baker went to third, scoring shortly thereafter on a single by Strunk. The final was 7–3, and the streak was now nine wins in a row.

Wednesday featured Wyckoff against Jean Dubuc. Sixteen Athletic hits, including three doubles and three triples, produced an easy 14–6 victory. Murphy started the attack in the home first with a single, scoring on a triple by Oldring. Collins singled in the second run. Baker was walked, with both runners advancing on McInnis' sacrifice. Strunk doubled, followed by a single by Barry, and that was all for Dubuc. Fred House was brought in, and after retiring Lapp, was greeted with a Wyckoff single and a triple by Murphy, his second hit of the inning. The Athletics scored five more runs in the third, and the game was a laugher the rest of the way.

Philadelphia continued its offensive onslaught the next day against Ed Willett. For the Mackmen, it was Ensign Cottrell, the 5'9" lefty from Hoosick Falls, New York, and most recently from Scranton of the New York State League. To date, Cottrell had averaged one appearance a year in the majors: 1911 with Pittsburgh, and 1912 with Chicago. This represented his first major league start (and one of only two in his career). Though battered by the Tiger bats for thirteen hits and six runs, he nevertheless made the most of it. Pitching his only complete game for his only major league victory, Cottrell struck out two batters, and contributed to his victory with a sixth-inning bases loaded double to drive in three runs. The final score was 10–6.

The Athletics completed their four-game sweep of Detroit on Friday, though this time it took ten innings to do so. Eddie Plank started, and in his six innings of pitching, Detroit amassed twelve hits, including five doubles and a triple, but led only 7–5 at that point since Philadelphia scored five times in the fourth and fifth innings against Joe Lake. Brown replaced Plank and held his opponents scoreless into the ninth. Further effective relief on the parts of Wyckoff and then Bender completed the job. The Athletics tied the game in the ninth. Danny Murphy, pinch-hitting for Brown, singled, with Wally Schang sent in to run. But Eddie Murphy hit a shot to center that Cobb grabbed before throwing to first to double off Schang. With two out, Oldring walked and scored on a double by the reliable Eddie Collins. Baker was walked. but the strategy backfired when Stuffy McInnis lined a single, his fourth hit of the afternoon, to score Collins. The Athletics won in the tenth. Bender, who was brought in to finish the top of the inning when Wyckoff was in trouble, singled, Murphy walked, and Oldring knocked Bender in with the winning run with a single. The win was the twelfth in a row for the Athletics.

St. Louis now came to town, with "Bullet" Joe Bush matched against George Baumgardner. By scoring three runs in the opening inning and five more in the fifth, the "McGillicuddy whalers" had an easy time of it. Each team had nine hits, but for the Mackmen, three of them included a single, triple and a first-inning, two-run home run on the part of Oldring, who accounted for five of the Athletics' ten runs. The game was never as close as even the 10–5 final score implied. On Monday June 9, it was Bender's turn to have fun at the expense of the opposition. Only thirty Brownies faced Bender this day, two reaching base on hits, one on a walk. The Athletics produced eleven hits, one being a fourth-inning home run by Baker once again to start the scoring. Bender struck out five, and the winning streak reached fourteen.

Brown took the mound the next day, and for five innings permitted only two base runners, one on a hit, the other a walk, and a single run. In the sixth, three hits and a hit batter set the stage for three runs by St. Louis, and Eddie Plank entered to prevent any possible disaster. Plank did his job, the Athletics scored ten runs, and the streak was now at fifteen. The record for the season now stood at 37–10, with the lead over the second-place Cleveland "Naps" being four games.

All good things come to an end — even some day in the future Casey Stengel's Yankees would occasionally lose — and for Philadelphia that loss came on June 11 against the Browns. Byron Houck had nothing for which to be ashamed. For seven innings the Brownies managed only two hits. The Athletics scored once in the third against lefty Walt Leverenz. Catcher Wally Schang walked and was sacrificed to second. Jimmy Walsh smacked a hard grounder to Browns third baseman Jimmy Austin, who attempted to tag Schang but missed. In an ensuing argument, Austin was tossed from the scene. Oldring proceeded to single Schang home. The Browns went ahead in the eighth on a walk to Mike Balenti and an attempted sacrifice by Bobby Wallace, which he beat out for a hit. Both runners advanced on a double steal, and Balenti scored the tying run when Schang's return throw to Houck went wild. Houck was unnerved at this point, and was relieved by Bender. Burt Shotton greeted Bender with a single to score the second run. Three more in the ninth produced the final score of 5–2, ending the win streak at 15 games.

Cleveland, now three games behind, came to Shibe Park for a four-game series that could determine the league leader during this portion of the season. Eddie Plank would take the mound first, with Cy Falkenberg on the hill for Cleveland. The home club drew first blood in the third inning when Lapp reached second on an infield error and came home on a single by Eddie Murphy. In the sixth inning, Murphy scored the second run with a single, advanced to third on Falkenberg's wild pitch, and scored on a second wild pitch. The Athletics put the game away with four in the eighth on singles by Oldring and Collins, both advancing on an error by Shoeless Joe Jackson on Collins' hit to right field. Baker was walked to load the bases, but McInnis singled Oldring home. Jack Barry cleared the bases with a double, and only a ninth-inning homer by Joe Jackson prevented another Plank shutout.

The following day pitted Bender against Bill Mitchell. Philadelphia quickly scored in the first when Jimmy Walsh, replacing Eddie Murphy with lefty Mitchell on the mound, scored from third base on a wild throw by Cleveland catcher Grover Land on a "botched" squeeze play. That was the extent of the

Shoeless Joe Jackson (1911). One of baseball's greatest "natural hitters," Jackson was banned for his role in the 1919 Black Sox scandal. His .356 career batting average is topped only by that of Ty Cobb and Rogers Hornsby. In 1913, he hit .373 with Cleveland, his lowest batting average in four seasons (Library of Congress, Bain Collection).

scoring until the ninth, when Cleveland tied the game on two hits and a throwing error by Baker. In the bottom of the thirteenth, however, Barry led off with a double. Schang bunted along the first base line, beating out the hit. But Barry continued past third, and diving into the plate, beat George Kahler's wild throw to score the winning run.

That Wally Schang was behind the plate this day was no surprise. With Lapp injured several days earlier the young receiver had become Bender's *de facto* regular catcher. Born in the small farming community of Wales Centre, New York, some 35 miles from Buffalo, Wally was one of four brothers and five sisters working 170 acres of farmland; brother Robert had a brief major league career as well. His passion for baseball developed early. "From the moment I crawled out of bed my thoughts had to do with baseball, with the result that I raced the poor nag to the creamery every morning. I wanted to get my job over as early as possible so I could drive back home, walk the two miles to the school and get in forty-five minutes to an hour of baseball before the bell called us to our studies."[20] Riding a horse to the games, Schang earned his first "professional money" as a catcher for the Roycroft club in East Aurora, receiving 50 cents

Wally Schang (1914) played 19 seasons in the majors, batting .266 in his rookie season of 1913. For four seasons, he was Mack's regular catcher before being sold to Boston. In his time, he was considered among the top defensive catchers, and provided a strong bat on offense (Library of Congress, Bain Collection).

per game. Jack Tarnish was the team's regular pitcher, and Willie Shumaker his catcher, with the pair being paid $2 per game. The battery was offered $3 per game by an opposing team, and went on "strike" unless the Aurora team would match the offer. However, Mayor Clarence Lamb had seen the Schang brothers play, and offered the two positions with the team as replacements. They accepted. Wally produced four hits the first day, including the "longest hit ever made at Hamlin Park grounds."[21]

The ballfield was not the only site at which the Schang brothers had an impact. As a member of the East Aurora bowling team with brother Bob, Wally "caused a panic ... by dreaming that he was playing baseball. He tagged Ty Cobb in his sleep, awakened everybody in the hotel, and nearly strangled his brother in an argument with the umpire. 'He's out! He's out! I touched him when he was two feet off the bag.' It was all in the dream, but when the other members of the bowling team broke into the room.... Wally had a stranglehold on brother Bob and very nearly choked him black in the face."[22]

After putting in playing time at third base for Buffalo in the semi-professional Pullman Buffalo City League — his brother was the catcher for the team until he split a finger — Schang was signed by the Buffalo team of the International League. Not only did he produce 41 assists while playing with a broken finger, Schang also managed to hit .334 in 48 games in 1912. Though he was fast on his feet, Schang was passed up by Yankee manager Frank Chance in the draft when a scout reported he had a weak arm; the Yankees instead drafted the "famous" Paddy Green. Mack did not make the same mistake. Schang made his first appearance when he pinch-hit on May 9, 1913, and by late June was sharing the catching duties with Jack Lapp. While the Athletics had catchers who could play defense, Schang contributed to the offense as well, and by the end of the season had become the regular receiver.

Joe Bush attempted to make it three straight against Cleveland on Saturday, but the inability to produce hits when needed, and the ability to produce errors when not needed, resulted in a 3–0 shutout by Cleveland southpaw Vean Gregg. Each team produced only four hits. Cleveland scored the only run necessary in the fifth when Buddy Ryan singled, stole second and scored on a single by left fielder (and future Indians broadcaster) Jack Graney. Two more runs in the eighth and ninth proved unnecessary. After taking Sunday off, the Monday game proved a replay of the opening game in the series with Falkenberg facing Plank. With a backdrop of 38 gamblers arrested in the grandstand and bleachers on Monday, the Athletics made it three out of four with another victory, this time 3–2.

With Old Man Ed Plank southpawing with his customary éclat, Recruit "Wally" Schang shooting down the foe along the runways when danger threatened and the balance of the cast interpolating base hits, not with any degree of frequency, but at psychological periods where they would benefit the cause the most, the Mackian crew closed up shop with the Cleveland Naps yesterday by grabbing the last fuss of the series in a 3–2 finish. This makes it three out of four on the series which was doped to plaster the handwriting on the wall, and it looks like nothing but the big yawn and monotonous wait for the ides of October now.... It may be entirely irrelevant, but we'd just like to edge in here with the statement that while Athletic pitching may be somewhat unkempt, as has been stated, in the series just closed it has been good enough to set down Joe Jackson with a batting average of .133 for the series, "Shoeless Joe" being up fifteen times and securing exactly two safe blows. And Joe came here with a batting average of .431, whaled out of the other pitchers of our league. Demon Ty Cobb also hit our peaceful village with a batting average of .470 that he had accumulated while dallying with the pitchers around the circuit, and in a four-game series against Athletic pitching Ty mauled the missile for the terrific figures of .187, striking three safe blows in 16 chances. Must have been the scoreboard again.[23]

Plank held Cleveland to six hits, three by Nap Lajoie. Jackson's sole hit that day did count, as he doubled in the second inning and came home on a single by Lajoie. The brief lead lasted until the fifth, when the Athletics tied the score on a triple by Strunk and a single by Baker. Baker knocked in the winning run in the eighth, his single scoring Eddie Murphy, who reached second base with a double.

The Chicago White Sox came to town Tuesday, and Byron Houck went to the mound to face off with Jim Scott. Home Run Baker homered in the second, one of his three hits and two runs for the day, while he and his teammates produced thirteen hits and seven runs. Houck limited Chicago to three hits, with the Sox's only score a fifth-inning home run by Ping Bodie spoiling a shutout. Two of the aces faced off the following day, with Big Ed Walsh going for the Sox and Bender for Mack. A pitching duel was expected, but the reality was anything but. Chicago produced 12 hits, Philadelphia 10, and Chicago led 4–0 after three innings, at which point Bender was replaced by Wyckoff. Neither J. Weldon nor John Taff after him proved any better, as the final score of 9–5 indicated. On Thursday, Boardwalk Brown took the mound with the goal of winning the rubber match of the three-game series. Philadelphia scored in the second inning when Baker's shot stuck in the scoreboard, and umpire Silk O'Loughlin ruled it a triple, before Baker scored on McInnis' sacrifice fly. Brown just missed a home run when center fielder Wally Mattick grabbed his long fly. The Athletics scored again in the sixth, while Brown held Chicago to four scattered hits in a 2–0 shutout.

The reigning champion Boston Red Sox came to town for three games, the last in the long eighteen-game homestand at Shibe Park. In the June 20 opener on Friday, the Red Sox bunched two runs in the sixth on a triple by Duffy Lewis with Harry Hooper and Tris Speaker on base and four more in the seventh inning against Bush, driving him from the mound, and enjoyed a 6–1 victory. Joe Wood limited Philadelphia to four hits while striking out nine. On Saturday, Byron Houck took his turn, short though it was. The Red Sox immediately began mischief as Hooper led off with a walk, followed by singles from Steve Yerkes and

SPEAKER– BOSTON

Tris Speaker (1911), one of the greatest outfielders in baseball history, was Cobb's primary rival for hitting honors during this period. A key player for the Red Sox, both on offense and defense, Speaker hit .363 in 1913 (Library of Congress, Bain Collection).

Tris Speaker to score Hooper. Lewis walked, and Houck was gone, Eddie Plank coming in for relief. A pop foul and double play ended the Sox threat. The Athletics gained the lead when Danny Murphy, starting the first time this season after recovering from a knee injury, was safe on an error. Collins was safe on another error. Baker singled, but Murphy was caught on a throw to catcher Red Carrigan. McInnis singled, and Oldring followed with a double to score both Collins and Baker. The Athletics still led 4–2 into the eighth inning, at which point an error by Baker on Speaker's grounder followed by four consecutive hits tied the game. In the ninth, with Bender now on the mound, Hooper singled, Yerkes' fly ball was dropped by Oldring, and Speaker singled to score Hooper. The Athletics failed to score in their half, and went down to a 5–4 defeat.

On Monday, June 23, the Athletics salvaged one game out of the three with a 13–4 pounding of starter Ray Collins and two relievers. Jack Barry produced two home runs in the game, and Baker included a triple in the fifteen hit attack. Houck, starting again after his short stint two days earlier, and Brown who relieved him in the second inning, scattered seven Boston hits, with their final two runs coming in the ninth when the game was out of reach.

Having lost the series to the Red Sox, Philadelphia left on a road trip, first heading down to third-place Washington for six games against the Nationals, a visit that included two days of doubleheaders. On Wednesday, Joe Bush opened, with Walter Johnson as his worthy opponent. Initially, a doubleheader was scheduled, but the poor condition of the field limited play to a single game. Trouble started in the third inning for the "Big Train" when, after fanning Jack Lapp, Bush doubled and scored on a single by Eddie Murphy. Walsh grounded out, but Collins singled to score Murphy, who had advanced. Next to bat was Home Run Baker. Baker smacked the pitch over the right field wall, "one of the most vicious clouts ever seen at the Georgia Avenue field."[24] Washington scored once in the fourth and again in the sixth, when Clyde Milan homered. After Gandil followed with a single, Bush was removed in favor of Bender. Philadelphia pounded out ten more runs in the final three innings, winning an easy 14–2 opener. Johnson would win a career-high 36 games this season, but this day marked one of his seven losses for the year.

On Thursday, Philadelphia continued to pound Washington pitching, as they took both games of the doubleheader. The Athletics won the first, 11–2, as Plank limited the home squad to five hits while striking out five. Washington starter George Mullin was chased in the seventh as Philadelphia scored six times and took a commanding lead in the game. In the latter game, Boardwalk Brown lasted into the third inning, at which point he was relieved by Bender when Washington scored twice. Philadelphia led 3–2, but scored seven more runs in the fifth, sixth and seventh, winning 10–3. Lapp's home run was one of eleven Philadelphia hits. Washington's third run came in the ninth inning when catcher Eddie Ainsmith singled before stealing second, third and home on what today might be called "indifference."

Another doubleheader followed on Friday. Johnson again took the mound for Washington, opposed by the Athletics' Boardwalk Brown. Brown had pitched briefly the day before, and given the stress on Mack's pitching staff, seemed a reasonable choice to take the mound again. To his credit, Brown pitched well enough to win, and had anyone but Johnson been his opponent, he might have done so. Washington was limited to three hits and a mere two runs. But Johnson likewise held Philadelphia to three hits while pitching a shutout. Washington right fielder Danny Moeller led off the first inning with a single, stole second, advanced to third on a groundout, and scored on Clyde Milan's sacrifice fly. Washington scored once more, but a single run was all they needed. A great running catch by Moeller in the eighth inning on a ball hit by Amos Strunk helped preserve the shutout. In the second game, Byron Houck lasted only an inning as Washington scored four times. Joe Bush came in, holding Washington to a single run the rest of the way. Philadelphia scored twice in the first on a double by Eddie Murphy, a walk to Collins, a sacrifice fly by Baker and a McInnis double. The Athletics went ahead to stay in the second. Schang led off with a home run, and before the inning was over, two more runs had come across. The game's final score was 11–5.

Clyde Milan (1912), one of the greatest outfielders of the Washington franchise, was among the fastest players of his time. He hit .301 in 1913, while his 75 stolen bases led the league (Library of Congress, Bain Collection).

Having taken four out of five from Washington, Mack sent Byron Houck to the mound to try again after his one-inning stint the day before. Houck continued where he had left off the previous day, walking four and allowing two hits in the four innings in which he appeared. At that point Washington led 2–1. The Nationals scored four more times against John Taff, who had replaced Houck, on the way to an 8–3 victory. Joe Boehling won his fourth in a row for Washington, limiting Philadelphia to eight scattered hits.

Leaving Washington, the Athletics returned north to New York where they would face the last-place Yankees in a four-game series. Eddie Plank was the choice for the Monday opener. In front of a small turnout of 5,000 fans, each team held its opponent scoreless through five innings. The Athletics scored in the sixth when Yankee pitcher Al "Heinie" Schulz walked Plank, who went to second on a sacrifice. Murphy singled, with Plank holding at third. Collins followed with a hard grounder, and Plank came in with the first run of the game, Murphy advancing to third. Baker singled, and the Athletics led, 2–0.

Philadelphia scored four more runs in the final three innings, producing a 6–0 final as Plank limited New York to three hits and struck out seven. "Bullet" Joe Bush and Byron Houck made it two in a row in New York on Tuesday, July 1, out-pitching Ray Fisher and George McConnell to win by a score of 2–1. The game easily could have gone the opposite way, except for a fourth-inning play that ultimately limited New York to a single run.

Umpire Bill Dineen got his head in the way of a throw by Jack Barry at the Polo Grounds yesterday, and then ruled that a base hit is not always a base hit. Two months ago Bill Klem showed New York fans that a hit cannot be made unless a player is properly introduced [see Chapter Four], but Dineen showed something that had never before been suspected, that a player, already in the game for four innings, can take his regular turn at bat and hit a legally pitched ball for a single, only to be ordered back to the plate to try again.... The peculiar ruling was made on a play that came up in the fourth inning, and later developments led to the belief that it cost the Yankees a run, just enough to force the Athletics into extra innings [had it been allowed]. Hartzell had reached first base by beating out an infield hit to Barry, and he moved along to second while Eddie Collins was tossing Peckinpaugh out at first. ["Babe"] Borton hit a sharp grounder down toward second base and Collins made a fancy stop behind the base. He was in no position to make a throw to first base, so he snapped the ball to Barry at second base to make the throw for Borton. Such a play is a baseball rarity, but this skillful pair of Athletics have made it before. Barry wheeled and let the ball go towards McInnis at first base. Dineen was but a few feet from Barry and on a line with first base. The ball hit the big umpire on top of the head and bounded high in the air. It landed behind the first base line and then rolled to the stand, Hartzell racing home from third base and Borton going down to second before the ball was recovered.

Then came a long argument. Connie Mack decided it was too warm to get excited, but the Philadelphia case was well argued by Connie's assistants, Danny Murphy and Harry Davis, with all the privates joining in. Chance led the argument for the Yanks, but two triumphed over one, and the Murphy-Davis side got the verdict. Dineen finally decided that Borton must bat again, and Hartzell return to second base. Big Bill [Dineen] had been standing in the hot sun for four innings, and Jack Barry's carom off the umpire's head had plenty of speed, so perhaps Bill's head was badly muddled.

With the scene shifted back to its original form, Borton grounded to Baker and was safe on the latter's bad throw to first, Hartzell moving up to third on the error. [Ezra] Midkiff followed with a clean single to left, scoring Hartzell and putting Borton on second. The same hit, under the conditions which Dineen had reversed, would have chased Borton home from second with the second Yankee run."[25]

As it was, the Athletics scored twice in the sixth inning. Baker tripled and scored on a single by McInnis, advancing to second on a late throw by Cree, who was hoping to catch Baker at home. Strunk singled, and McInnis came home on a wild throw by Borton. Despite four walks, Houck, who had relieved Bush in the fourth, held the Yankees scoreless the rest of the way.

The Yankees had now fallen to 19–47. This time it was "old reliable" Chief Bender who took the hill, with Russ Ford as the opposing pitcher. Despite the

Yankees' poor performance, Ford had managed to put together a winning streak of five games. New York even provided a lead for Ford, scoring twice in the opening inning with the help of an Oldring error. But it was not to be. The Athletics produced at least one hit in every inning. Eddie Collins scored twice and drove home two others with a triple and two singles. Frank Baker had three singles, scoring twice and driving in a run. But the most potent hitter in the Mack attack was catcher Wally Schang, who contributed a double as well as a sixth-inning home run. Amos Strunk tripled in the final two runs in the ninth, as Philadelphia took an 8–5 victory.

Thursday, July 3, featured the Yankees Ray Keating and Philadelphia's Boardwalk Brown facing each other. Philadelphia jumped out to the lead in the first inning when Eddie Murphy singled, stole second and scored on a short infield pop by Oldring that was just over Keating's head. The Athletics scored again in the second when Lapp tripled and Brown singled him home. Oldring led off the third inning with a home run, and by the time the inning was over, Philadelphia had a 5–0 lead. With Brown scattering six Yankee hits, the final score was 8–4. The four-game sweep had improved the team's record to 51–17, the lead over second-place Cleveland now at 9½ games, a lead that was quickly becoming insurmountable.

The Athletics traveled on to Fenway in Boston, with a holiday doubleheader on tap. The opener pitted Sox ace Smoky Joe Wood against Byron Houck. Boston jumped out to a fast 1–0 lead, increasing that to 4–0 in the third, helped to a significant degree by four consecutive walks on the part of Houck. At that point Wyckoff replaced Houck, only to watch Tris Speaker, the Sox runner on third, steal home. The Athletics tied the game with four runs of their own in the fourth. Strunk and Barry walked and moved up when Lapp was safe on an error. Wyckoff struck out, but the pitch eluded catcher Nick Cady and two runs scored. Eddie Murphy was safe on another error as Lapp scored, and Murphy came in when Oldring doubled. But then the bottom dropped out for Philadelphia as Boston scored seven times in its half of the inning. With the score reaching 13–6, and the heat becoming excessive, the two teams agreed to halt the game after seven innings. In the second game, with Eddie Plank on the mound, Boston again started off to a first-inning lead. Hooper hit the first pitch over right fielder Eddie Murphy's head and circled the bases for a home run. Yerkes smashed a pitch in back of third, on which Baker made a beautiful play for the out. But a Speaker double and a Lewis single scored a second run. Each team scored once in the third, and the score remained 3–1 into the eighth inning. Oldring led off the inning with a walk. After Collins flied deep to center, Baker singled Oldring to third. McInnis followed with another single to score Oldring. Strunk hit a line drive to Hooper, normally as reliable a fielder as one could find, but not this time. Hooper dropped the ball, and both Baker and McInnis scored, giving Philadelphia the lead. The Athletics scored another in the ninth for good measure, to make the final score 5–3. Boston put together eleven hits, but could not manage to do so when it counted.

Smoky Joe Wood (1912), pitching hero for the Boston Red Sox, won 34 of 39 decisions in the regular season, then three of four in the World Series against the Giants. In his prime, Wood had a fastball which rivaled that of Walter Johnson. In 1913, an injury to his thumb in spring training limited him to 11 victories, a key factor in Boston being unable to repeat as champion. Wood was never the same after recovering, but later made a comeback as an outfielder (Library of Congress, Bain Collection).

Saturday pitted Bush against Dutch Leonard. The outcome clearly showed the managerial ability of Connie Mack, as he outmaneuvered his Red Sox counterpart Jake Stahl to forestall a Sox rally.[26] It was Boston that scored first, as Hooper led off the first inning by smacking a Bush changeup into deep right field for a triple. Hooper scored on Yerkes' grounder to Collins. Philadelphia went ahead in the third. Walsh singled, Collins walked, and Baker doubled, scoring Walsh; Collins scored when Hooper's throw home bounced past Carrigan. Boston scored in the fifth to tie the game, and then again in the sixth to take a 3–2 lead. But in the seventh inning, the Athletic offense again shifted into high gear. Barry singled, Schang walked, and Bush attempted to sacrifice, but everyone was safe when Leonard's throw to third was late. The Red Sox brought their infield in with Stahl hoping for a play at the plate. But Oldring punched the ball into right, scoring Barry and Schang, with Oldring ending up at second base. After Walsh grounded out, Collins flied to Speaker in center, but Tris muffed the ball, allowing Collins to reach second and Bush to score. Baker knocked in both runners with a single to right. Five runs were in, and Leonard was gone. The Sox attempted to rally in their half of the inning. Larry Gardner led off with a triple. Clyde Engle doubled to score Gardner, and Heinie Wagner singled. Mack had seen enough, and quickly brought Bender in to stem the tide. Carrigan grounded to Collins, but the normally sure-fingered infielder fumbled the ball, allowing Engle to score. Wagner was thrown out at third on an attempted sacrifice, but Carrigan scored when Hooper followed with a single. With Hooper on first with the tying run, Yerkes grounded to Barry, who quickly turned a double play to end the threat. Bender held the Sox scoreless over the last two innings for a save and an Athletic 7–6 victory.

July 6, a Sunday, was an off-day, and the two teams returned to Fenway Park for a Monday doubleheader. Boardwalk Brown held the Sox off for eight innings in the opener, limiting his opponents to two hits, both in the first two innings. In the ninth with Philadelphia ahead 7–1, three walks, a double and single added two runs to Boston's score. Bender was brought in, and once again the veteran shut Boston down. Ray Collins started for Boston, but the Mackmen made short work of the hurler. Oldring led off the game with a single, then promptly stole second. He advanced to third on a grounder by Walsh and scored on Collins' single. Collins stole second and Baker walked. Collins scored when McInnis doubled, and both Baker and McInnis came in when Strunk also doubled. Two more runs in the third made the score 6–1, a lead Boston never overcame. In the second game, Joe Wood scattered nine Athletic hits as Boston scored seven times in the first three innings off Plank and Houck, winning 8–3 and earning a split of the doubleheader.

Philadelphia now took the train to Cleveland for a three-game set with the second place Naps. With Cleveland eight games behind, the series was critical for determining whether the Athletics would run off with the pennant. Joe Bush was on the mound, and though Cleveland threatened throughout the game, producing twelve hits, they only managed to score three times. Three hits and two runs came in the ninth, sufficient to only make the outcome close. Philadelphia jumped off to a fast lead in the first when Walsh and Collins walked, Baker singled to load the bases, and McInnis hit a long sacrifice fly to Graney. Three runs in the sixth solidified the win for Philadelphia. Baker walked, and after McInnis and Strunk flied out, stole second. Three runs scored when Schang followed with a home run to center field. The final score was 5–3.

Cleveland evened the series the next day as Cy Falkenberg outpitched Eddie Plank, 4–1. Only a ninth-inning run, the result of a single by McInnis and double by Lapp, prevented the shutout. On Friday, Chief Bender and George Kahler faced off in the rubber match. It quickly ceased to be a match. The Athletics scored once in the first inning, and if not for a baserunning snafu, could have produced more. Eddie Murphy was hit by Kahler's pitch, and Oldring sacrificed him to second. After Collins walked, Baker smacked a pitch off the right-field screen, but Murphy, fearing the ball would be caught by Joe Jackson, advanced only to third. Collins had no such fear, and did not stop at second. Jackson threw home to Steve O'Neill, who threw to Ray Chapman to cut down Collins. Murphy, realizing the plate was uncovered as O'Neill came up the line, dashed for home. Lajoie managed to reach the plate in time to cover, but Chapman's throw was low, and Murphy scored. In the second, the Athletics scored three times when Strunk beat out an infield hit and Barry doubled, with both players scoring on a triple by Schang. Bender then hit a sacrifice fly to Graney, and Schang scored. It was 11–1 by the eighth when Cleveland scored four more times to produce the 11–5 final. The Athletics' lead over Cleveland was now nine games.

The next stop for the Athletics was Detroit for a five-game marathon. Saturday pitted Boardwalk Brown against Jean Dubuc. Brown frequently exhibited control problems, but the 6184 fans who sat through a three-hour game that day watched Brown exceed even himself in that area. Five times through eight innings the Tigers loaded the bases, in no small part the result of fifteen walks. Even so, the Athletics held a 10–1 lead going into the home inning. In that half of the eighth, the Tigers produced five hits and five runs, and Plank was finally brought in to end any further hemorrhaging. Philadelphia came back with six more runs in its half of the ninth. With a lead of 16–6, Plank let up on the Detroit batters, who managed another three runs before the game ended, 16–9. Baker led Philadelphia with four hits, with three others contributing two apiece. Sam Crawford led the Detroit attack with three hits, including a triple.

The teams met for a Sunday doubleheader on July 13, and by the end of the day, the Athletics would probably have preferred the time off. Hooks Dauss limited Detroit to five hits in the opener, while Detroit produced ten hits with five walks against Houck. Detroit's only run came in the eighth, bringing the score to 3–1 at that point. Collins walked and came around to score following singles by Baker and McInnis. Detroit put together four more runs in the bottom of the inning, and won, 7–1. In the second game, Joe Bush had a 4–1 lead against Willett as late as the beginning of the sixth inning. But Crawford opened the frame with a single, and Cobb tripled him home. Bobby Veach singled to score Cobb. Veach was forced on a grounder by Del Gainer, and Oscar Stanage fanned. After Moriarity walked, Hugh High, batting for Willett, singled in the tying run. At this point, Bender came in and fanned Donie Bush. Detroit scored its fifth and winning run in the eighth when Vitt tripled, and scored on a sacrifice fly by Crawford. Final score: 5–4.

At this point the doubleheader loss had little effect on the pennant race.

But the pennant was far from a sure thing with more than half the season yet to be played, and a prolonged losing streak had the potential of allowing a surprisingly strong Cleveland team, if not the defending champion Red Sox or even Washington, a chance to close the gap. Bender could be hot or cold, though he had generally come through when needed in relief, and it would be his turn to attempt a reversal of the Philadelphia skid. But Bender proved no more capable of doing so than had either Houck or Bush the day before. Philadelphia scored first against Marc Hall when Murphy and Daley started the game with hits and were sacrificed along by Collins. Baker followed with a fly to score Murphy. The Tigers countered with three runs: Donie Bush singled, Vitt walked and Crawford singled Bush home. Errors by Daley and McInnis on the play allowed Vitt to score and Crawford to take third. Crawford then scored the third run on a sacrifice fly by Cobb. The score was 7–4 in Detroit's favor by the eighth inning when Joe Bush relieved Bender. Detroit picked up a single run in the eighth, and led 8–4 as the last inning began. Daley led off for Philadelphia with a walk and advanced to second on Collins' groundout. Baker then hit a short fly to center that Cobb seemed to grab at his shoe top, but umpire George Hildebrand ruled the ball a trap, and sent Baker to first base. Cobb argued so vehemently that he was tossed from the game, yet the decision stood. McInnis fouled out. Had Baker's fly been ruled an out, the inning would have been over. Instead, Danny Murphy batted for Strunk and grounded to Donie Bush, who fumbled the ball, and Murphy was safe. Walsh ran for Murphy, whose leg was still a problem. Barry followed with a double, Lapp contributed a single, and the score was tied. But in the bottom of the inning, a Vitt single and Crawford triple brought in the ninth, and winning, run. Detroit had now won three of the four games in the series. Cobb, who seemingly had been stopped by Philadelphia pitching earlier, had hit safely seven times in fourteen official at-bats in the series.

Plank then took the mound on Tuesday. Hall was Detroit manager Hughie Jennings' pick to try again. This time he would be without the services of Ty Cobb, who was under suspension for his tirade the day before. Plank allowed nine hits, but none when it really counted. Hall allowed ten in his six innings of pitching, but they accounted for six runs. Oldring and Murphy each scored two runs, and Oldring contributed three hits in a 7–0 shutout. Philadelphia had salvaged two of the five games, and now traveled on to Chicago.

Philadelphia and Chicago opened their six-game matchup with a Wednesday doubleheader. Boardwalk Brown and Eddie Cicotte were the opposing pitchers in the opener, a game that proved to be a true pitchers duel. Through nine innings the game was scoreless, with Brown limiting the Sox to only three hits—two by Morris Rath and one by Cicotte—while the Athletics produced a mere five hits. In the tenth inning, singles by Barry and Lapp, and after a groundout by pinch-hitter Amos Strunk, another by Eddie Murphy scored the game's only run. In the second game, Bob Shawkey was Mack's choice to face

Buck O'Brien. The Athletics quickly jumped into the lead with a lead-off double by Murphy, a sacrifice by Daley and a Collins single. Collins came around to score a second run by stealing second base and coming in on McInnis' single. Collins scored the Athletics' third run in the third when he singled, stole second, and again crossed the plate on a single by McInnis. Philadelphia continued to lead by a 3–2 score into the eighth, when Bender relieved the youthful Shawkey. But Chicago broke loose for three runs to take the latter game, 5–3.

Joe Bush followed up the next day, with Jim Scott serving as the Sox pitcher. For six innings, the game was another pitchers duel, Bush allowing four hits until that point and Scott a mere two, both in the fourth inning. The Sox scored once in the fourth inning on a Hal Chase single, a sacrifice, and a single by Ray Schalk. Most of the scoring came in the seventh. In the visitor half, Baker led off with a single and was forced on a grounder by McInnis. Oldring followed with a single, sending McInnis to third, but Rube was thrown out trying to stretch the hit into a double. Jack Barry then beat out a hit, scoring McInnis and tying the score. But in the bottom half of the inning, Chicago scored all it needed. Schalk singled and went to second on a Ping Bodie sacrifice. Jack Fournier hit a grounder to Eddie Collins, but the second baseman fumbled the ball, and Schalk scored to put Chicago ahead again. After Buck Weaver made the second out, Scott singled to score Fournier. Rath walked and Lord tripled, scoring two more and increasing the Sox lead to 5–1. A McInnis ninth-inning home run for Philadelphia ended the scoring for the day.

Chief Bender faced "Reb" Russell as the crowd of 8,000 anticipated not only another fine game, but the debut of Larry Chappell, the highly touted rookie who cost Chicago some $18,000. Chappell struck out twice in his four appearances, and twice lined to the outfield. The rest of his teammates performed about as well. Bender limited Chicago to five hits, and only second-inning singles by Chase and Fournier, sandwiching Schalk's sacrifice, resulted in a White Sox run. The Athletics scored three times in the fourth inning. Eddie Collins walked, Baker doubled and McInnis' single scored both runners. After Danny Murphy flied out, Barry walked and scored when Schang doubled. Philadelphia scored once more in the eighth to make the final score 4–1. Oldring also managed a hit despite recovering from a "touch of ptomaine."

With each team having won twice, Philadelphia and Chicago faced off in the second doubleheader in four days in front of a crowd that exceeded 30,000. The opener pitted Brown and Cicotte in a rematch of the earlier shutout by the Philadelphia pitcher. The "$18,000 beauty,"[27] rookie outfielder Larry Chappell, made his second appearance in a Sox uniform one to remember, starting off the home half of the first with a triple. Rath followed with a double to score Chappell. Rath scored when Harry Lord bunted and Brown overthrew the ball to first. Houck took over in relief of Brown the following inning. Philadelphia scored in the fourth when Oldring reached second on an error, went to third on a Collins groundout, and came home following Buck Weaver's wild throw of Baker's grounder to third. The Athletics picked up two more in the sixth inning to lead 3–2. Eddie Collins and Frank Baker both doubled, with Collins scoring. Baker came in when Strunk singled. The White Sox tied the game in their half of the inning when Harry Lord singled, stole second, and came around on a single by Ray Schalk. Chicago scored the winning run in the seventh. Cicotte led off with a walk and Chappell singled. Rath walked to load the bases, and Lord's sacrifice fly scored Cicotte.

Boardwalk Brown returned to the mound in the second game, Mack deciding he had not been overworked earlier in the day. Facing him was Ed Walsh. Brown repeated his quality pitching of several days before, limiting the White Sox to five hits and one run in twelve innings. The score was tied at 1–1 in the visitor half of the twelfth. Collins singled and Baker doubled off the wall, with Collins holding up at third. McInnis then followed with a hit that just eluded Chappell, scoring both runners. The final score was 3–1, and the teams had produced an even split of the series.

From Chicago, the Athletics traveled on to St. Louis to face the 37–56 Browns, who were tied for sixth place, in a Sunday game. Eddie Plank started the series on a winning note for Philadelphia, limiting St. Louis to six hits while striking out nine in an 8–0 shutout. Six Athletic hitters had two hits apiece in the fifteen-hit onslaught. The next day, Bob Shawkey was on the mound to try again. But after St. Louis had scored twice in the first three innings, and with runners on base in the third, Shawkey was removed in favor of Joe Bush. St. Louis led 2–0 into the fourth inning when Philadelphia scored three times to take the lead. Walsh walked and Collins singled him to third. Baker hit a long fly to score the first Athletic run, and singles by McInnis and Danny Murphy scored a second. Barry then carried out a perfect squeeze play for the third run. The Athletics broke the game open in the sixth. Eight hits produced seven runs, the key hits being a two-run double by Barry and a bases-loaded single by Baker, which scored three. Despite a four-run rally by the Browns in the ninth, Philadelphia recorded an easy 11–8 victory.

With a record of 63–26, Philadelphia was now 10½ games in front of Cleveland and 12 ahead of third-place Washington. At least one opponent was ready to concede: the manager of the last-place New York team. "The Athletics are the class of the American League," said Frank Chance, manager of the New York Highlanders, when asked for his opinion of the prospects of the Mackmen. "They have the pennant as good as won," the former "Peerless Leader" of the Chicago Nationals continued. "Who is there to stop them? I consider the team playing for Connie Mack this season far better as a machine than the one which wrested the world's championship from the Chicago Cubs in 1910."[28]

Even the best major league teams lose one-third of the time. On Tuesday, Boardwalk Brown faced Roy Mitchell, and the Browns' hurler pitched and fielded his way to a 4–0 shutout victory. Brown did not pitch badly, allowing nine hits in six innings, but in the process, the Browns scored four times. Critical to the Athletics' pennant pursuit was an injury to Wally Schang, who suffered a dislocated finger from a foul ball, forcing him to be sidelined for the near future. The Athletics produced seven hits; surprisingly, two were off the bat of Brown, doubling his total for the year.

When in doubt, the Athletics called on Bender, and that is exactly what Mack did for the final game of the series. The Athletics broke through with three third-inning runs. Bender and Oldring singled, though Bender was picked off second base for the first out. Walsh singled, and both Oldring and Walsh scored when Collins doubled. Baker followed with a fly to right fielder August Williams, but when "Gloomy Gus" dropped the ball, Collins scored the third run of the inning. In the seventh, Baker contributed a home run, and the Athletics left St. Louis for Philadelphia with an 8–1 victory.

After the travel day, Philadelphia opened a three-game set with the visiting Tigers. Bob Shawkey was Mack's choice, the youngster needing the experience. "What we'd like to know is, what in thunder's the use of these other guys offering any resistance? They might slip over a ball game once in a while when they're lucky, but insofar as exerting any influence over the ultimate entries for the World's Series stakes is concerned they're merely running for Sweeney."[29] The Tigers' Jean Dubuc limited Philadelphia to three hits, but they came when it counted and resulted in four runs. Shawkey in turn allowed but five hits, none of which resulted in a score. All of Philadelphia's runs and hits came in the seventh inning. McInnis led off with the first hit for Philadelphia. Oldring followed with another, off the glove of Dubuc. Barry sacrificed the runners into scoring position, and a walk to Lapp loaded the bases. Shawkey hit a shot that bounced off Dubuc, scoring a run and leaving the bases full as Shawkey beat out the hit. Eddie Murphy walked, forcing in Oldring with the second run. Walsh grounded to Donie Bush, who threw to Paddy Baumann for the force at second. But Baumann's throw to first was wild, scoring two more runs. Shawkey fanned seven in pitching the 4–0 shutout.

On Saturday, "Old Master" Plank took his turn. "The tottering old man showed flashes of returning vigor interspersed throughout the fuss, but two vulnerable spots in the conflict proved enough to beat him. Opposed to the 'Old Master' was Edgar Willett, a pitcher of parts who seems to take an uncanny delight in starting a slow ball up from his ankles that moves with such deliberation that the batter gets liver-grown or dies of old age while waiting for it to get close enough to hit at."[30] The Tigers scored three times in the top half of the third inning to take the lead. Willett walked and Donie Bush followed with a single. Bauman scored Willett with a double, putting men on second and third. Bush scored on a Crawford groundout, and when Cobb singled, Bauman scored. Philadelphia countered with two runs in the bottom of the inning. Lapp singled and was forced at second by Plank. Eddie Murphy and Jimmy Walsh singled to load the bases. Collins knocked in Plank by beating out a slow roller, and Murphy scored on a bouncer by Frank Baker that cleared the infield. Walsh was thrown out at the plate while attempting to follow Murphy, and McInnis grounded out to end the inning. The score remained 3–2 until the eighth inning, when Detroit scored three more to win 6–2.

There was no game Sunday, and a Monday rain provided another day off for the players. A doubleheader was scheduled for Tuesday, which included the makeup. The first game, begun under a sweltering sun, pitted Boardwalk Brown against Hooks Dauss. "Cal Brown pitched as though he was out for the express purpose of refuting the allegation that Connie Mack had no pitching force aside from Plank and Bender, and before he got through, the preponderance of evidence went to show that said allegation had been refuted several large sized refutes."[31] The Athletics scored in the second. McInnis doubled and Strunk was safe when Dauss threw his bunt to third in a failed attempt to head off McInnis. Barry grounded to third, and when McInnis remained at the bag, Strunk was run down by Tiger third baseman George Moriarity. Barry advanced to second on the play. Lapp was walked to load the bases. Brown struck out, but Eddie Murphy drove in two runs with a single. Philadelphia scored again in the third when Collins doubled, advanced to third as Cobb fumbled the ball, and scored on a sacrifice fly by Baker. Three runs were more than was needed, as Brown shut down Detroit on six hits. Philadelphia picked up five more through the course of the game to make the final score 8–0. In the second game, Detroit led 2–0 in the third, at which point the rains returned, and umpire Billy Evans called the game. Nobody seemed to mind. "Any guy who pines for more baseball on a day when the rubber in his suspenders is melting ought to be sentenced to circle the bases through eternity in the Bowl of Gehenna."[32]

St. Louis followed Detroit into Philadelphia for four games. With a record of 39–62, the Browns did not appear to provide a significant roadblock for the pennant-chasing Athletics, and indeed Plank seemed to confirm that assessment. In the opener, he limited the Browns to five hits and a single run. Left-hander Carl Weilman was on the mound for St. Louis, and Mack, playing percentages, inserted the right-handed hitting Jimmy Walsh in center, placed Oldring in left and sent Danny Murphy to right field. The platooning paid off. Philadelphia scored in the third on a double by Schang and single by Oldring, and again in the fifth on a double by Danny Murphy, a sacrifice bunt by Barry and a sacrifice fly by Schang. Murphy scored what would be the second, and winning, run with a great slide around Browns catcher Walt Alexander for the 2–1 victory.

Bullet Joe's performance yesterday completes a total of twenty-seven innings pitched by the so-called second string men since the team's return to the home heath, comprising three of the four games played in which the enemy has succeeded in compiling but one run in all three games. Shawkey opened the home stay with a shutout against the Tigers, Brown repeated with another shutout of the Tigers on Tuesday, while yesterday the best St. Louis could do across nine innings of play was to grab the credit of accumulating the only tally that could be scored against "Mack's weak pitchers" in three full games.... If Mr. McGillicuddy didn't have Plank and Bender I suppose some of these other ball clubs would catch his poor little ball club out on the lot sometime and thump them for as many as two whole runs in the short space of one week.[33]

"First-stringer" Eddie Plank followed Bush in the rotation, and were it not for Eddie Murphy and Frank Baker being caught flat-footed on the base paths, Plank might have confirmed writer Jim Nasium's faith in Mack's pitching rotation. "Edward Gettysburg Plank southpawed in opposition to George Baumgardner on the firing line, and the two collaborated in a nip and tuck duel with just about as much nip as tuck."[34] The Browns opened the scoring in the first when Shotton beat out a grounder to Plank, went to second on a groundout, and scored on a single by Pratt. Philadelphia replied with two in its half of the inning. Eddie Murphy walked and Amos Strunk bunted safely as catcher Alexander threw late to second base. Murphy, however, was picked off second, with the Athletics losing a run when Collins followed with a long single. Baker followed with a hit to score Strunk, with Collins stopping at third and Baker going to second on the throw. Collins scored on McInnis' long fly ball. Walsh walked, but Baker ended the inning when he too was caught off base on a pick-off. The Athletics picked up a third run in the third inning when Murphy walked and advanced to third on two sacrifices. Baker's ground ball then scored Murphy when Baumgardner failed to touch first on the infield play. Plank seemed to have the game under control until the sixth inning. Baumgardner started the rally with a double. Shotton fanned, but George Stovall lined a hit to McInnis that was too hot to handle, and Baumgardner scored. Stovall scored the tying run when Pratt doubled, and Pratt scored when Mike Balenti singled. That ended the scoring for the day, as the Browns took the second game of the series.

Bob Shawkey was Connie Mack's choice as the season moved into August, but the youngster only had the opportunity to face one batter. Burt Shotton hit Shawkey's first pitch off the pitcher's glove for a single, and Bender was sent in to relieve. Bender pitched five strong innings, allowing only two base runners, one on a hit, the other a walk. Meanwhile, Philadelphia scored three times in the fourth inning. Walsh singled, and after Collins flied out, Baker singled Walsh to third. Walsh was thrown out at the plate on a grounder by McInnis to third baseman Jimmy Austin, but Baker scored as Oldring followed with a hit. McInnis scored when shortstop Doc Lavan scooped up a grounder by Jack Barry and threw wildly to Bunny Brief at first. Brief juggled the ball long enough for Oldring to score. St. Louis came back with four runs in the sixth inning to take the lead, and scored another in the seventh. By then clouds had descended, and it grew too dark to play, at which point the umpires called the game with the Browns victorious, 5–3.

The fourth and final game of the series with the Browns pitted Boardwalk Brown against Earl "Lefty" Hamilton. St. Louis immediately jumped into the lead in the opening round when Burt Shotton hit Brown's first pitch into left for a single and advanced on the next pitch to Balenti that went wild. Balenti then attempted to sacrifice, but Brown heaved the ball over McInnis' head, enabling Shotton to come in to score. After that, Brown settled down, limiting St. Louis to only three hits the remainder of the way. Philadelphia tied the game in the bottom half of the inning as Eddie Murphy led off with a double. Walsh and Collins both flied out, but then Hamilton walked three consecutive batters, forcing in the run. In the fourth inning, Brown gave his team the lead with a line drive into the left-field bleachers. Two more runs scored in the fifth inning as both Collins from third and McInnis on second came in on a squeeze bunt by Jack Barry.

Sunday was an off-day as Cleveland came to Philadelphia for what could be considered a "crucial series." Cleveland was riding a seven-game winning streak, which reduced Philadelphia's lead to 6½ games. Bob Shawkey took the mound for Mack, with Cy Falkenberg on the hill for the Naps. Falkenberg lasted three innings, giving up two walks and six hits, which resulted in four runs. In the opening inning, Eddie Murphy walked, moved to second when Amos Strunk flied to Jack Graney, and the left fielder threw wild to first while attempting to double off Murphy. Eddie Collins walked. Home Run Baker smacked a bad hop single past Nap Lajoie at second base to score Murphy, sending Collins to third. Collins then scored on a grounder by McInnis. The Athletics picked up two more in the third when with two out: Baker and McInnis singled and Oldring doubled them in. Dutch Kahler relieved Falkenberg for the fourth inning, holding Philadelphia scoreless until the eighth, when they produced three more runs. Cleveland was limited to two singles, scoring its only run in the second inning when Jackson was safe on an error, Lajoie singled, and Amos Strunk made a great catch of a long fly by Terry Turner.

Former University of Michigan pitcher Fred Blanding turned the tables on Philadelphia and Eddie Plank the next day, throwing a 5–0 shutout. Philadelphia amassed eight hits, but none occurred when needed, as indicated by twelve men left on base. Cleveland had seven hits, but they included a run-scoring double and a two-run homer by Nap Lajoie. Final score: Cleveland 8, Philadelphia 0.

The pendulum swung back again for Philadelphia on Wednesday, as "Bullet" Joe Bush outpitched Vean Gregg, winning by a score of 7–1. The game was scoreless until the third, at which time Schang reached first when hit by a Gregg pitch, stole second, advanced to third on a grounder by Eddie Murphy, and scored when Oldring grounded to Turner at third, Schang beating the throw home. Cleveland tied the game in the fifth when Lajoie walked and advanced to home on hits by Graney and Steve O'Neill. Philadelphia put the game away in the fifth. Eddie Murphy was safe on an error, advanced to second when Oldring grounded to third base and Nap Lajoie dropped Turner's throw while attempting the force. Collins was safe on a bunt single, scoring Murphy. Home

Run Baker then did it again, poling a pitch over the right-field wall for a three-run homer. The Athletics picked up single runs in the seventh and eighth for the 7–1 triumph.

The following day, Bender made it three of four against Philadelphia's closest competitors with a 7–3 victory. After a shaky first inning in which Cleveland scored twice with three of their nine hits for the day, Bender limited his opponents to a single eighth-inning run. Frank Baker once again had an outstanding day, knocking out a single and two doubles, one of which just missed heading over the right-field wall, scoring three times, and driving in three others.

Chicago then arrived at Shibe Park for four meetings, the last games in the 2½ week long homestand. Boardwalk Brown opened against Jim Scott. Philadelphia seemed poised to continue its attacks on any and all opponents, for about two innings. The Athletics opened the scoring in the second with a McInnis single and Strunk double, but that was the extent of their scoring for the day. In the fourth, a two-run homer by Ping Bodie put Chicago on top, 2–1, where the Sox remained the remainder of the game. Chicago scored twice more, winning 4–1. The Athletics managed only five hits, but sixteen fly balls ended whatever scoring chances they might have had. On August 9, Bob Shawkey faced off with "Reb" Russell. Shawkey once again was superb, limiting Chicago to seven hits and a single run. Unfortunately for Mack, Russell was just a little better. Philadelphia knocked out eight hits, including doubles by Baker and Schang, but was unable to score. Singles by Buck Weaver, Russell and Larry Chappell in the sixth inning scored the only run of the game.

On Monday, Joe Bush and Eddie Cicotte were on the hill for their respective teams, Bush hoping to end Philadelphia's short losing streak. For a time, it appeared Chicago would continue to lengthen that streak. The Sox scored five times in three innings, producing seven hits, including another home run by Bodie, and three walks. "Bullet Joe "was replaced by Byron Houck after being removed for a pinch-hitter in the home half of the third. Houck came through, holding Chicago scoreless the rest of the game. Philadelphia made the scoreboard in both the fifth and sixth, scoring one run in each inning. In the home half of the seventh with the score 5–2, Schang opened with a double and Houck walked. Cicotte had a two-ball count on Eddie Murphy when he was relieved by Russell. "Reb" completed the walk to Murphy, but then proceeded to walk Oldring and Collins, forcing in two runs and leaving the bases loaded. Jim Scott relieved Russell, only to have Baker triple to score three more runs. Baker scored when McInnis grounded out. The Philadelphia rally produced an 8–5 victory. Scott returned on Tuesday to face Brown in the fourth game of the series. Brown lasted three innings before being removed for a pinch-hitter, with Bender pitching the last six innings. Chicago led 1–0 at that point, thanks to another Bodie home run, his third in the four-game series. Bodie began a seventh-inning rally against Bender with a single — Scott's single with the bases

Frank "Ping" Bodie (1912). Bodie was an average outfielder, primarily with the White
Sox and Yankees in nine seasons. He hit .264 with the White Sox in 1913, with a career-
high eight home runs. Four of them came in mid–August and early September against
Athletics pitching (Library of Congress, Bain Collection).

loaded produced two runs in that inning — and Bodie's sacrifice fly in the eighth
produced another run. Philadelphia scored once in both the seventh and eighth
innings, losing 4–2.

    With a Wednesday travel day, the Athletics rode the rails into Cleveland
to face the second-place Naps, still seven games behind. For the second time
in ten days, Eddie Plank and curveballer Fred Blanding were the opposing pitchers, and for the second time in ten days, the result was the same: a Cleveland
victory. For the fourth time this season, Plank failed to stop his Cleveland opponents. Blanding held Philadelphia scoreless for six innings while his teammates
produced five runs against Plank and another off Houck. Lajoie, Ray Chapman
and Turner all fielded flawlessly to block any potential rallies. At one point
Collins, after being thrown out on another sterling play by Chapman, threw
his bat in the air and yelled, "We might as well pack our bats; we can't beat
such playing."[35] Three runs in the fifth sealed the verdict. Plank hit Turner
with a pitch, but Turner was thrown out at second on an attempted sacrifice
by Graney. O'Neill followed with a double to score Graney, and a double by
Joe Birmingham scored O'Neill. Birmingham later scored on a single by Chapman. Philadelphia produced its only runs in the seventh on a double by Schang
followed by a Houck single, and in the eighth when Baker homered. Philadelphia

Eddie Cicotte (1919), one of the early knuckleballers in the game, had a record of 18–12 in 1913 in the breakout season of what could have been a Hall of Fame career. He went on to win more than 20 games in a season with Chicago three times, including 28 in 1917, and a career high of 29 in 1919. Following the 1920 season, Cicotte was one of eight White Sox players banned for their roles in the 1919 scandal (Library of Congress, Bain Collection).

evened the series the next day with an easy 12–5 victory behind Plank and Shawkey. Mack's strategy was to start Plank, hoping Cleveland would play fewer left-handed hitters. After retiring lead-off hitter Nemo Leibold, Mack brought in Shawkey, who continued for the remainder of the day. Cleveland scored twice that first inning to take the lead, but three Athletic runs in the third inning and five more in the fifth started what would be a twelve-run outburst. Eddie Murphy had four hits and Collins three to lead the seventeen-hit attack.

On Saturday, Cleveland reversed the attack, knocking out ten runs and eleven hits, mostly off the hurling of Joe Bush. Ray Chapman contributed a seventh-inning, three-run homer and Joe Jackson a solo sixth-inning four-bagger to lead the attack. Philadelphia's single run off Willie Mitchell came in the fourth inning when Collins' liner was misjudged by Joe Jackson, resulting in a double, and McInnis doubled him home. Cleveland made it two victories in a row, and three out of four in the series, with a 6–2 win on Sunday. Facing Chief Bender, the Naps produced eleven hits in the first seven innings, scoring six runs and forcing Mack to replace Bender with Wyckoff in the eighth. Philadelphia scored its only two runs in the ninth inning. Collins led off with a double, and after Baker and McInnis flied out, scored on a single by Walsh. Schang and utility shortstop Billy Orr followed with singles to score the second and final Athletic run. With the lead now 5½ games, the Athletics continued west as they moved on to Detroit.

Eddie Plank faced Jean Dubuc as Philadelphia hoped to return to a winning track. For 4½ innings, all was going well for the Mackmen. Philadelphia scored in the opening inning when Eddie Murphy started the game with a single and stole second. Collins walked, and Baker followed with a single to score Murphy. Detroit tied the game in its half of the inning when William "Baldy" Louden singled, stole second and scored on a Cobb single. Philadelphia regained the lead with a fourth-inning run when Baker singled, went to third on a single by McInnis and a walk to Strunk, and scored on a grounder by Lapp. The score went to 4–1 in the top of the fifth. Murphy ended up at second on a throwing error by Louden. Oldring walked and Collins beat out a bunt to score Murphy. Baker grounded to first for the first out of the inning, with Oldring advancing to third. McInnis hit a foul fly that left-fielder Bobby Veach gathered in. But Veach mistook the catch for the third out and headed to the bench while Oldring raced home for the Athletics' fourth run. But in the bottom of the inning, Detroit scored three times on three hits, the first hit resulting when Plank slipped while attempting to grab Del Gainer's bunt. The game was tied at four in the bottom of the ninth. Gainer led off with a bunt that Plank again was unable to field. Stanage walked, and Moriarity ended the game with a line drive past McInnis to score Gainer.

With the Philadelphia losing streak now at three, Bob Shawkey took his turn, with Marc Hall the opposing pitcher. Mack made an additional change by sending Oldring to shortstop, replacing Barry, and Walsh to Oldring's position in the outfield. Another change was unintended. Catcher Jack Lapp injured his finger on a pitch in the fourth inning, and Wally Schang was sent in as his able replacement. Shawkey lasted a mere three innings as Detroit scored three times. It was Philadelphia that opened the scoring in the second inning. Baker doubled and continued to third when Veach threw wildly on the return. Baker scored on a sacrifice fly by McInnis. But Detroit scored three times in the third. After the Tigers loaded the bases with nobody out, a Crawford sacrifice fly scored one run, and after Cobb walked to again load the bases, Veach followed with a single to score two more. Philadelphia regained the lead in the sixth inning. With one out, Oldring singled and stole second. Louden fumbled a grounder by Collins and Baker walked to load the bases. McInnis scored Oldring with a sacrifice fly to Veach. Veach's throw home went past catcher Stanage and Collins scored, with Baker moving to third. Strunk singled and Baker scored the fourth, and ultimately winning, run.

With each team having won once, Philadelphia and Detroit faced off on Wednesday, August 20. Boardwalk Brown allowed ten hits in his eight innings of pitching, and Detroit produced two runs. Philadelphia scored once in the fifth as Walsh singled and stole second. Pitcher Hooks Dauss attempted a pick-off play, but since neither the shortstop nor second baseman was aware of his decision, the throw went into centerfield; Cobb held Walsh at third base. Walsh later scored when Eddie Murphy doubled. Detroit tied the game with a run in the sixth, but in the following inning Philadelphia blew the game open. Strunk started the rally with a single, and came all the way around to score when Dauss picked up Walsh's sacrifice bunt and threw the ball into right-field. Walsh went to third on the error. Schang doubled to score Walsh before ploting another run when Brown followed with a single. Murphy forced Brown, but came around to score when Oldring singled and Rube Bauman threw Collins' grounder into the Philadelphia dugout. Final score: 5–2.

The Athletics then traveled to Chicago to face the White Sox for a three-game series. In the opener, Chicago managed only five hits off Shawkey, scoring only in the second when Mack's bane, Ping Bodie, singled and came around on hits by Buck Weaver and Sox pitcher Joe Benz. Collins had four hits for Philadelphia, scoring two runs. The key hit was a bases clearing triple in the sixth inning by Wally Schang as Shawkey earned an easy 7–1 victory.

Trying to extend the winning streak to four, Byron Houck took the mound to face "Reb" Russell. For seven innings, Russell was the better man in a pitchers duel, with a lead of 1–0. But a Buck Weaver mistake opened the door to Philadelphia scoring. With two out, Oldring was on third, Collins on first, and McInnis was at bat. With two strikes on McInnis, Mack signaled for a double steal. Collins raced to second base, where Weaver took the throw. Both he and Collins dove for the bag, with Weaver tagging the runner just after Collins' leg hit the bag, and Umpire Connolly signaled safe. For unknown reasons, Oldring remained at third. Weaver, however, thought he had tagged Collins for the third out, and rolled the ball slowly towards the mound. At that point, Oldring scored. According to Chicago writer I.E. Sanborn, it was "the worst bonehead play I ever saw."[36] McInnis then singled and Collins scored the second and eventual winning run. Chicago had seven hits against Houck and Plank, who pitched the final 1⅔ innings for a save.

On Saturday, Cicotte and Brown faced off in the final game at Comiskey Park between the two teams this season. Chicago jumped out to a 2–0 lead Brown with a single by Weaver, a walk to Joe Berger, a single by Chase and Bodie's infield out. A two-run triple by Bodie in the third knocked in another two runs, and Bodie scored a third on a single by John Collins, increasing the Sox lead to 5–0. The Athletics scored twice in the fifth. Joe Bush, now pitching in relief, doubled with two out. Eddie Murphy bunted safely, and when Lord's throw hit the grandstand, Bush scored and Murphy went to third. Oldring singled him in with the second run. In the fifth inning, Mack sent Harry Davis in to catch and the newly acquired infielder from St. Louis, Doc Lavan, to short. By the ninth inning, the Sox held a 7–2 lead. Philadelphia briefly rallied when Bush tripled with one out and scored on Murphy's fourth single of the day. Murphy scored the final run when Lavan tripled, his only three-bagger for the season, with the RBI likewise being Lavan's only one for the season.

On Sunday, Philadelphia opened a three-game series in St. Louis. Not only was Chief Bender at the top of his form, shortstop Jack Barry returned after missing two weeks with an injury. The Athletics quickly put the game out of reach. Eddie Murphy led off with a bunt, reaching first base safely as second baseman Del Pratt fumbled the ball. Oldring followed with a second bunt, which Carl Weilman booted, allowing Murphy to advance to third on the play. Noting a pattern, Collins followed with his own bunt and reached first safely as Murphy scored. Baker flied out, but McInnis smacked Weilman's pitch into deep left field for a double. Oldring and Collins scored the second and third runs of the afternoon. Jimmy Walsh flied to Shotton in center, but Burt lost the ball in the sun, and Walsh ended up on second base, with McInnis holding up at third with McInnis scored on a squeeze play by Barry. Schang doubled, and Walsh scored the inning's fifth run. By the fourth inning, the Athletics' lead had reached 7–0, and only a Collins error on a double-play ball in the home fourth prevented a shutout. The Athletics had fifteen hits in the 9–1 triumph.

On Monday, Eddie Plank took the mound to face Walt Leverenz. Plank threw a total of 149 pitches, none of resulted in a Brownie run, but did produce eleven strikeouts. Each team had five hits, but only in the first did St. Louis produce a serious threat. Shotton and Austin led off with singles, but each of the next three hitters grounded out. The Athletics scored all three of their runs, the result of all five of their hits, in the fourth inning. Baker singled and reached second when McInnis sacrificed. Walsh singled to score Baker, and when the ball rolled past Jimmy Johnston in center, Walsh raced to third. Barry's sacrifice fly scored Walsh. Schang doubled on a flyball over second base, scoring when Plank followed with a single. The 3–0 lead remained unchanged the rest of the way.

Boardwalk Brown continued the Athletic mastery of the Browns the following day, as he too shut down Brownie bats in an 8–0 whitewash in St. Louis. The Athletics scored in the first inning. With one out, Oldring hit a short fly ball to center that Shotton lost in the sun — a seemingly common occurrence for the Brownie outfielder — with Oldring reaching second on the play. Collins lined to Shotton for the second out, but Philadelphia scored when Baker's ground ball went between Pratt's legs and Oldring came around. The Athletics effectively put the game away in the third inning. Eddie Murphy led off with a single, and went to third on Oldring's double. Collins flied to Balenti at short, who let the ball drop — the infield fly rule not being in effect, and loading the bases. Frank Baker hit a slow roller to Balenti that the Athletic third baseman beat out, scoring Murphy. McInnis singled in two more runs. Walsh sacrificed to advance the runners, and Baker scored the fourth run of the inning on a double squeeze. The final score was 8–0, as Brown limited St. Louis to seven hits while walking only one.

With the three-game sweep, the Athletic lead over second-place Cleveland was again nine games, and with the Giants in front of Philadelphia by twelve games, it became more likely that the matchup in the 1913 World's Series would once again find McGraw and his Giants facing Mack and his Athletics. The Athletics returned east on Wednesday, traveling to the Polo Grounds to face the last-place Yankees in a three-game series before heading home in September. Bender had the opening game honors, and even the 9–3 score belied the ease with which the victory was accomplished. Philadelphia pounded fourteen hits off starter Al Schulz and reliever Jack Warhop and stole bases with seeming ease, victimizing catcher Ed Sweeney seven times. New York scored three times in the eighth to avoid a shutout.[37]

Rain washed out the game August 29, forcing the teams to meet in a doubleheader on Saturday. It has been said of baseball that on a given day even the most pathetic of professional teams can rise to the occasion. This seemed to be one of those days. In the opening game, Bob Shawkey faced Ray "Slim" Caldwell. The Yankees put together eight base hits to score five runs. But even if Shawkey had been more effective, the outcome might have been the same as Caldwell held the Athletics to two hits— singles by Barry and Murphy — while striking out six. New York scored twice in the third inning, and then put the game away with three more in the eighth inning. New right fielder Frank Gilhooley singled in two of those runs in the eighth and played a fine defensive game in his debut. In the second game, the Yankees scored twice in each of the opening two innings off Boardwalk Brown, and two more in the fourth off reliever Joe Bush to provide starter Ray Fisher with a 6–1 lead. The Athletics produced their first score of the afternoon in the top of that inning when Baker doubled and McInnis followed with a single. Philadelphia made it closer with three runs in the eighth, but went down 6–4 in the end. The Athletics might have been able to continue their rally in the eighth, but umpire Charles Ferguson called Stuffy McInnis out on a play in which the Athletic may have beaten a throw by more than a step. It was a call with which 20,000 seated umpires agreed.[38] The two losses represented the only time the Yankees had defeated the visiting Athletics in their home park this season.

The Athletics returned to Philadelphia for a three-week homestand, the longest of the season. Their first opponents were the third-place Washington Nationals, whom they would face in a Monday doubleheader. Washington's aces were on the mound: Joe Boehling, who had started the season with eleven consecutive victories, and "The Big Train," Walter Johnson, on his way to a 36-victory season. Facing Boehling in the early match was Chief Bender. Washington started things off in a manner that suggested Philadelphia might go down to its third consecutive defeat. First batter Danny Moeller flew out to Walsh but Eddie Foster beat out a grounder to Baker and Clyde Milan did likewise on a ball hit Jack Barry. The two attempted a double steal, but Wally Schang threw Foster out at third, with Milan going to second. Chick Gandil scored Milan with a hit, and Ray Morgan followed with the team's fourth consecutive hit. Bender settled down at this point, getting Howie Shanks on a fly to Murphy. As things turned out, this was the extent of Washington's scoring for the morning, as Bender would limit the Nationals to a single hit the rest of the way. The Athletics responded with three runs in their half of the inning. Eddie Murphy and Rube Oldring drew walks. Eddie Collins sacrificed the runners along, and Murphy scored when Baker grounded out. McInnis lined a pitch over Clyde Milan's head in center to score Oldring on the triple. McInnis scored when shortstop George McBride threw the relay over the third baseman's head. Another run by Philadelphia in the fifth completed the scoring, as Bender pitched a complete game in the five-hit 4–1 victory.

In the afternoon game, Boardwalk Brown started against Johnson. Philadelphia led after two innings by a 2–0 score. Baker doubled and went to third on a sacrifice by McInnis. Jimmy Walsh grounded to Ray Morgan at second, with Morgan pegging the ball to home in hopes of catching Baker. But Frank turned and slid safely back to third while Walsh went to second. Jack Barry then pulled a double squeeze, bunting Johnson's pitch and scoring both runners. Washington tied the game in the third, the result of one of the hardest hit balls seen in Shibe Park. "One monumental whack by Walter Johnson, a blow that will live longer than most blows, inasmuch as it was the longest whack ever poled at Shibe Park and probably the longest that will be poled for a long time to come, grabbed those two runs right back again for the enemy in their half of the third. After McBride had fanned, [Eddie] Ainsmith slapped a base knock to left and walked home when Johnson followed with a clout that would have gone clean over the wall back of the left field bleachers had not a spectator reached up and knocked the ball down."[39] The Athletics came right back in their half of the third with two more runs. Murphy was hit by Johnson's pitch. On a hit-and-run play, Murphy took off for second while Oldring smacked the pitch past the second baseman's position and into right, Murphy continuing to third. Murphy scored on a Collins grounder. Oldring scored on another hit-and-run as he came around on Baker's single. Washington tied the game again with single runs in the sixth and ninth, sending the game into extra innings. Johnson was still on the mound, with first Houck and then Bush in relief for Philadelphia. In the visitor half of the tenth, Washington scored on a Milan double and a single by Morgan. In the home half, Schang grounded out and pinch-hitter Tom Daley struck out. Eddie Murphy kept the fans' hope alive with a single. Rube Oldring followed with a smash into center that bounced past Milan, rolling to the wall. Murphy scored the tying run, and Oldring stopped at second. Eddie Collins slapped a pitch into right and Oldring rounded third base and continued home, just beating the throw with a head-first slide for the sixth and winning run.

The Athletics hoped to make it three straight against Washington, as Bob Shawkey faced off against Joe Engel. Once again Philadelphia scored first. In the third inning, Schang led off with a walk. Shawkey struck out, but Eddie Murphy's easy fly ball to center was dropped by Clyde Milan, putting two runners on base. Schang moved to third on a ground ball by Oldring, which forced Murphy at second. On the next pitch, Oldring raced towards second, and when McBride ran to cover, Eddie Collins punched a hit past where the shortstop had been playing to score Schang. Baker followed with a solid shot up the line past first base, but Chick Gandil made a diving grab for the ball, holding on for the third out of the inning. Shawkey limited Washington to two hits until the seventh. In the home half of that inning, Eddie Foster led off with a walk, advanced on a grounder by Gandil, and scored the tying run when Morgan singled. The return throw by Walsh went past Schang to the grandstand, and Morgan advanced to third. Washington catcher John Henry's single scored Morgan with the second and eventual winning run in what at least one writer considered to be a dreadful game.

> One of the slowest, dreariest exhibitions we have had the misfortune to lamp this season.... "Slow Joe" Doyle was a marvel of activity compared with this guy Engel, who worked in yesterday's somnolent affair. Engel would have a little "dead march" all to himself after each pitched ball, then he would stand several feet back of the hurling slab and fix his dreamy gaze in a faraway look on some spot in the grandstand for an eternity or two until the audience went to sleep, then he would slip up and strike a pose like Apollo Belvidere on the pitching slab for another week or two, after which he would consent to let go of the ball providing the weather conditions were just right.... We have a suspicion that he took an unfair advantage of the batter by waiting till he went to sleep before pitching the ball.[40]

For the record, the game took two hours, five minutes to complete.

Wednesday, September 3rd, was originally a scheduled off-day; instead, a make-up game was played. Boardwalk Brown took the hill to face Bob Groom. Washington quickly opened the scoring with two runs in the first. Moeller singled and stole second. After Milan grounded out, Foster singled to score Moeller, with Foster coming in to score when Gandil followed with a double. Philadelphia gained the lead in the second. Walsh opened with a walk and advanced to third on Barry's single. Foster mishandled the return throw to third, allowing Walsh to score and Barry to advance to second. Schang flew out and Brown struck out. But Eddie Murphy came through with a single, and when Henry allowed the throw from the outfield to roll past him, Barry scored and Murphy ended up at third. Oldring then singled to score Murphy. Brown left for a pinch-hitter in the sixth, to be replaced by Bender. Washington promptly tied the score in the seventh when Morgan singled, advanced on a grounder, and scored on McBride's single. But Philadelphia quickly regained the lead in its half of the seventh. Murphy singled, later advancing to second on Collins' ground ball to Gandil. Frank Baker then singled to score Murphy with the fourth Athletic run. Bender held Washington scoreless for the 4–3 victory.

The reigning champion Boston Red Sox came to Shibe Park for their last series of the season, starting with a holiday doubleheader. Eddie Plank started the morning game, and by the third inning had allowed six hits and four runs. Plank was removed for a pinch-hitter in the home half of the third, with Herb Pennock coming in for relief. Pennock gave up another run in the sixth, the visitors now leading 5–0. In the sixth, the Athletic bats finally came to life. Oldring singled and Collins sacrificed him to second. Baker doubled to score Oldring with Philadelphia's first run, and McInnis then doubled to score Baker. Walsh singled and continued to second on the return throw. Barry completed the inning's scoring with a double squeeze, his bunt along the first base line allowing both runners to come in. Philadelphia scored twice in the seventh to take the lead. Brown singled, and after Murphy fanned, a walk to Oldring and Baker's single loaded the bases. McInnis singled to score both Brown and Oldring, and Philadelphia led 6–5. But Boston came right back in the eighth. Yerkes walked and Wagner was hit by a pitch. Carrigan bunted, but Baker dropped the throw from McInnis to load the bases. Charley Hall fanned, but Harry Hooper singled to score both Yerkes and Wagner as Boston regained the lead. Tris Speaker's single scored Carrigan with Boston's eighth run, making the final score 8–6. The afternoon game pitted Byron Houck against Earl Moseley. Philadelphia scored in the first as Eddie Murphy led off with a triple and scored on Collins' single. Boston tied the game in the second when Houck walked his opponent Moseley with the bases loaded. Philadelphia quickly regained the lead. Walsh walked, went to second on Barry's grounder, stole third and scored when shortstop Heinie Wagner threw wildly to the plate on Lapp's ground ball. The lead was not to last. Boston scored single runs in the third and fourth and two more in the ninth, winning 5–2 for a sweep of the doubleheader.

On Friday, Eddie Plank came out to try his luck again, with Ray Collins on the mound for Boston. Boston led 1–0 after two innings. In the second inning, Duffy Lewis singled and advanced on a Plank balk. Plank then struck out Gardner and Yerkes. But when Lewis attempted a steal of third, Schang's throw went past Baker, and Lewis scored. Philadelphia tied the game in the third. Murphy walked then advanced to second on Oldring's sacrifice and to third on Collins' grounder. Baker followed with a single off Clyde Engle's shin and the game was tied. Philadelphia took the lead in the fifth. Murphy and Oldring singled. Collins bunted and beat the throw to load the bases. Baker hit a long sacrifice fly ball to Speaker to score one run, and McInnis bounced a hit off Larry Gardner's arm to score another. But the lead did not last. Boston put a run on the board in the sixth and three more in the seventh to lead 5–3. A Boston insurance run in the ninth merely finished the scoring at 6–3, the third loss in a row for Mack, stalling his drive for the pennant.

Philadelphia finally managed to salvage one game of the series on September 6 behind Bob Shawkey. Boston produced ten hits, but scored only twice. Philadelphia in turn scored twice in the second, fourth and fifth innings, and three more in the seventh to gain an easy 9–2 victory. Frank Baker led the hitting with two hits and two walks, stole three bases, and scored three runs while knocking in two more. The Athletics began their scoring in the second inning as Baker walked and advanced to third on McInnis' double. A single by Barry and force by Schang scored the two runners. The Mackmen scored two more in the fourth with another double squeeze. Collins opened the inning with a double and Baker walked. McInnis sacrificed them along, with both men scoring when Barry bunted down the first-base line. Boston managed single runs in the fourth and eighth innings, but by then the game was effectively out of reach. The victory was important for on other reason: The lead over second-place Cleveland was now a "mere" 6½ games.

Chicago arrived next in town as the pennant race came down to its final weeks. "Reb" Russell faced off against Chief Bender. Bender certainly pitched well enough to win, allowing eight hits and striking out six. Unfortunately, the Athletic bats were again silent, while the Athletic nemesis, Chicago center fielder Ping Bodie was not. Bodie had swatted three home runs during his previous visit, and continued where he left off. In the second inning, Bodie smacked a Bender pitch into the bleachers, giving the White Sox the lead. The Sox produced an insurance run in the fourth inning when Jack Collins scored on a single by Bodie. The best the Athletics could do was six singles in a 2–0 loss. On Washington defeated Cleveland in a doubleheader, however, so the Athletics actually gained a half-game on their closest rival. Wednesday, Eddie Cicotte made it two losses in a row for the Mackmen by outpitching Boardwalk Brown for a 5–3 White Sox victory. The Athletics did produce nine hits against Cicotte, including a fifth-inning home run by Oldring that briefly gave Philadelphia the lead, 3–2. Chicago tied the game in the sixth inning, and with the score tied at three after nine innings, the game went into extra innings. In the visitor tenth, Joe Berger led off with a single, advancing to second on a sacrifice by Cicotte. After Weaver grounded out, Harry Lord and Jack Collins walked to load the bases. The two deciding runs scored when a hard grounder by Hal Chase went through Brown's legs into center.

Philadelphia finally returned to the victory column on Thursday, as Bob Shawkey limited Chicago to six hits — none by Brodie this day — and a single run. Philadelphia scored in the fifth, as Shawkey "decided" if you want it done right, do it yourself. Barry opened the home half with a walk, advanced to second on a grounder by Schang, and scored when Shawkey knocked a Jim Scott pitch off Buck Weaver's leg into right field. Philadelphia produced two more in the seventh after Chicago had tied the game in its half of the inning. Shawkey beat out a hit for a single. Walsh ran for Shawkey and was sacrificed to second by Eddie Murphy. After Oldring grounded out, Walsh scored on a single by Collins. Collins came around to score when Baker singled, and the return throw from the outfield by Jack Collins went past third to the grandstand. Bender shut down Chicago the last two innings for a save.

Eddie Plank took the mound on the 12th, hoping to earn Philadelphia a split for the four game series. Chicago quickly jumped on the Athletics' southpaw with two first inning runs. Weaver walloped Plank's second pitch for a double and scored when Harry Lord followed with a single past Barry. After Jack Collins sacrificed, Lord scored on a single by Chase. At this point, Herb Pennock replaced Plank. Pennock shut down Chicago until the third, when Weaver homered into the left-field bleachers. Philadelphia scored in the second inning on a Baker single, the Athletic third baseman advancing to third on a grounder by Daley and an error by Lord on a Barry grounder and scoring on an Ira Thomas single. By the home half of the seventh, Chicago led 5–1. In the seventh, the Athletic bats again came alive. Jack Barry opened the home half with a walk, and veteran catcher Ira Thomas singled off the mitt of pitcher Joe Benz. Bill Orr ran for Thomas, and both runners advanced on a wild pitch by Benz. Wally Schang, batting for relief pitcher Byron Houck, walked to load the bases. "Reb" Russell replaced Benz, but ended up walking Murphy to force in Barry with the Athletics' second run. Rube Oldring then picked on a Russell pitch, driving it over Ping Bodie's head in center, the ball rolling to the scoreboard as three runs scored to tie the game; Oldring ended up on third base with a triple. Oldring scored the lead run when Eddie Collins hit a sacrifice fly to Bodie. Frank Baker then unloaded another home run, giving the Athletics a 7–5 lead. Joe Bush pitched two scoreless innings, and with Washington defeating Cleveland, 6–1, behind Walter Johnson that day, Philadelphia increased its league lead to 8½ games.

On Saturday, Cleveland came to town for a three-game series, one in which the Athletics could finally finish off any lingering hopes their closest rival might have at catching Philadelphia in the race. Bender was Mack's first choice, with

Cy Falkenberg on the mound for Cleveland. Philadelphia opened the scoring in the first inning. Eddie Murphy singled, only to be forced at second on a grounder by Oldring. Ray Chapman's throw to first while attempting to complete a double play went wild, and Oldring advanced to second. Eddie Collins grounded to Lajoie, with Oldring moving to third from where he scored on a single by Baker. Three runs in the fourth by Cleveland proved to be the difference. Chapman singled and advanced to second on a sacrifice by Joe Jackson. Lajoie scored Chapman with a single, after which he stole second. Doc Johnston knocked a Bender pitch down the right-field line for a triple, scoring Lajoie. Johnston scored the third and final run when Terry Turner singled. Falkenberg limited the Athletics to eight singles.

Despite the loss, the Philadelphia lead over Cleveland was still 7½ games. Almost certainly the World's Series' rivals would be Philadelphia and the New York Giants. The Giants this season would steal 296 bases, in no small part contributing to their success in the pennant race. Eight players stole more than twenty bases apiece. If the Athletics were to defeat New York, Philadelphia pitchers of course would have to limit the number of Giant base runners, while Philadelphia catchers would have to limit the ability of any runners to run wild on those base paths. Wally Schang, the *de facto* first-string catcher, certainly appeared up for the job. By mid–September, he had thrown out 57 runners in 114 attempted thefts, a success rate of 50 percent. Jack Lapp, the other likely series catcher, had been successful in throwing out 58 men out of 139 attempted thefts, a success rate of about 42 percent.[41] It would appear the catching staff was ready for McGraw and his Giants.

Philadelphia gained a measure of revenge the following Monday. Joe Bush started, with Vean Gregg the opposing pitcher. The Athletics appeared to break the game open in the third inning. Murphy opened with a walk, one of seven permitted by Gregg this day. Murphy advanced to second on a grounder by Oldring that bounced off Gregg's glove, the ball rolling to Chapman, who threw Oldring out. Eddie Collins beat out an infield grounder to put runners at the corners. Baker singled through the box to score Murphy, sending Collins to third. McInnis grounded out to score Collins, and a single by Walsh scored Baker. Barry's double then scored Walsh with the fourth run. Bush limited Cleveland to a single hit until the fourth inning while striking out five. But in the fourth, Bush fell apart, and with two runs already in and the bases loaded, Eddie Plank was brought in to stem the tide, only to have Jack Graney double in three more runs. Graney scored on a single by Gregg, and Cleveland now led by a 6–4 score. But Philadelphia would not be stopped. In the fifth, the Athletics scored twice to tie the game. Baker was hit by a pitch, proceeded to steal second, took third on a Walsh single and scored when Walsh stole second and catcher Steve O'Neill's throw went wild. A passed ball by O'Neill allowed Walsh to score the tying run. Philadelphia went ahead to stay in the seventh. Collins tripled and scored on another passed ball by O'Neill. McInnis was safe on an error by Ray Chapman, scoring when Walsh tripled. Chief Bender worked the final 2⅔ innings, fanning five of the eight men he faced and allowing no base runners in the 8–6 victory, a game that ran over 2½ hours.

Another pitchers duel ensued the following day with much the same result. The afternoon began with Bob Shawkey facing Bill Steen. After two hours and fifty-five minutes, ten innings of play, seventeen walks, and numerous three-ball counts issued by seven pitchers, Philadelphia had an 8–7 victory. There actually was not much hitting: Cleveland had six hits, including a fifth-inning home run by Joe Jackson, while Philadelphia produced ten. The score was tied at seven after nine innings, though if not for a disputed call Philadelphia might have won in regulation. In the eighth inning, Barry walked, went to second on a groundout by Schang, and appeared to have scored on a wild pitch. Catcher Steve O'Neill pegged the throw to pitcher Nick Cullop covering the plate, and Cullop applied a tag after Barry had slid safely. Barry, however, was called out. In the tenth inning, McInnis led off with a double, his fourth hit of the contest. With the infield drawn in, Jimmy Walsh lined a shot past first base, and McInnis came in with the eighth and winning run. Among the participants in the contest was Harry Davis, former Athletic captain and long-time slugger for Connie Mack teams who is best remembered as a hero of the 1911 World's Series. Davis had most recently managed the Cleveland Indians before being replaced by Joe Birmingham and returning to the Athletics. His token appearance this day as a pinch-hitter in the sixth inning for Byron Houck resulted in an RBI double, tying the game at 7–7, and eventually leading to the tenth-inning heroics during which Philadelphia effectively eliminated Cleveland from the race.

St. Louis appeared in Philadelphia for the last time in the season, with September 17 representing the debut of Branch Rickey as Brownie manager. The Browns started out looking like the future baseball magnate's managerial debut would be a complete success by jumping to a four-run lead. In the opening round, Burt Shotten started things off with a bloop double as three Athletic players converged on the hit but could not quite reach the ball. Boardwalk Brown then hit Austin with a pitch. Del Pratt followed with a slow grounder that Brown grabbed but threw wide to McInnis. Pratt and McInnis collided, wrenching the elbow of the Athletic first baseman, and allowing Shotten to score. On the same play, Brown injured his knee. McInnis was able to remain in the game for another two innings, but Brown was finished for the day, and was relieved by Herb Pennock. Pennock gave up a single and sacrifice fly as St. Louis scored three times in the inning. Another run in the fifth gave them a four-run margin. By then Byron Houck was on the mound for Philadelphia.

The Athletics came back to tie the game in the sixth. Collins opened the home half with a bunt single and advanced to second when the throw went wild. Baker's grounder to pitcher Roy Mitchell was fumbled to give Philadelphia runners at the corners. Harry Davis, replacing the injured McInnis at first, came through again, singling to right to score Collins. A double by Walsh scored

Herb Pennock (1913) broke in with Philadelphia in 1912, winning a total of three games in two seasons as a spot starter and reliever. After he moved first to Boston and then to the Yankees, his Hall of Fame career became established. He eventually totaled 240 victories (Library of Congress, Bain Collection).

Baker, followed by a single off the bat of Jack Barry to score both Davis and Walsh. In the eighth inning, the Athletics broke the game open. Davis again provided a key hit, starting things off with a single and advancing to second on a passed ball. Walsh flied out, but Barry singled, Davis stopping at third. Orr ran for Davis and scored when Lapp singled. Daley, pinch-hitting for Houck, tripled in both runners, and scored the final run of the inning when Eddie Murphy singled. In the ninth, Lapp replaced Davis at first base, Bush replaced Houck, and three Brownie batters later the Athletics had won, 8–4.

It was at first feared that the injuries to Boardwalk Brown and Stuffy McInnis were serious enough that both players would be out for some weeks. McInnis, would mend quickly and return in several days. Brown took a little longer to recuperate, but would be available when the World's Series started in three weeks. The report that came in on Jack Coombs was not as optimistic.

While the pitcher's life was no longer threatened by the typhoid which had settled in his spine, his back still was not healed and he remained in a plaster cast. Coombs would attend the series, but only as an observer.

Meanwhile, there was still a pennant to clinch for things to be official. Bob Shawkey took his turn for Philadelphia, with Walt Leverenz serving as the Brownie pitcher. Shawkey limited his opponents to two runs and two hits through eight innings, striking out five. But again the Athletic offense was minimal, producing a mere four hits over that span and no runs. Three more runs in the ninth by St. Louis completed the 5–0 shutout.

Friday's game was rained out, so the final series with Detroit began on Saturday, with Byron Houck being asked to tame the Tigers. Tiger pitcher Ed Willett's wildness started his problems in the first. Eddie Murphy walked on four pitches and promptly stole second. Daley flied to Crawford before Willette walked Eddie Collins. Home Run Baker singled to score Murphy and send Collins to third. Stuffy McInnis, returning from his injury in the previous series with St. Louis, hit a fly to Bobby Veach to score Collins. Both pitchers then settled in for eight innings of dueling. In the eighth inning, Donie Bush walked to start the Detroit half of the fame. Bush stole second base and was on the bag when Detroiter "Paddy" Bauman smacked his fourth hit of the afternoon, a single to center. Tom Daley gathered in the ball and tossed it to Jack Barry covering second, while Bush advanced to third on the play. "Barry didn't turn around to see what was going on. He just held to the ball with his back to the diamond and stopped to hold elegant converse with Eddie Collins, while Bush paused, and then seeing Jack wasn't alive to the occasion, made a fresh dash to the plate and scored when Jack's belated heave arrived too late."[42] Shortly thereafter, Bauman scored the tying run. Barry made up for being "asleep" in the home half of the inning. With two out, Baker and McInnis singled, and Walsh walked to load the bases. Barry then slammed a line drive past third for a double, scoring both Baker and McInnis. Pennock and Bender shut down Detroit in the ninth, and Philadelphia had a 4–2 victory.

Sunday was an off-day, and a Monday doubleheader was scheduled for both the regular contest and a makeup game. Joe Bush was scheduled for the opener, facing Hooks Dauss, with Herb Pennock in the afternoon game and Jean Dubuc as his opponent. Several things were noteworthy this day. First, both Philadelphia pitchers threw shutout ball, though Pennock's performance lasted a total of two innings. The youngster was removed for a pinch-hitter, and Plank took over for the remaining seven innings. More importantly, the double victory officially made Philadelphia the American League champions, the third time in four years. In the opener, Bush scattered eight Detroit hits. Philadelphia scored twice in the second inning, providing all of the runs Bullet Joe would need. Baker singled, McInnis was hit with a pitch and Amos Strunk sacrificed the runners to second and third. Once again, a "double squeeze" proved successful. Jack Barry bunted to score Baker, and as Dauss tossed the ball to first to retire Barry, McInnis never stopped at third and continued in to score a second run on the play. Philadelphia scored twice more in the game, winning 4–0. In the second game, Philadelphia scored the lone run in the second. McInnis walked and was forced at second by Walsh. Walsh stole second base, and scored on a single by Jack Lapp.

The Tuesday finale with Detroit was as close to a laugher as any game during the season. Herb Pennock returned to the mound. Whether or not Philadelphia won the game was moot though young Herb once again appeared destined to have a short afternoon. Detroit scored twice in the first when Bauman walked and Crawford homered over the right-field wall. The Tigers increased their lead with four more in their half of the second. But then the Athletic offense went to work in the home half of the second. Ten hits and a hit batsman later, Philadelphia had scored ten runs, the big hit being a bases-loaded triple by Eddie Murphy. The Athletics continued to score in every inning after that, producing a final score of 21–8. The 25-hit attack was led by McInnis and Walsh with four hits apiece, while Murphy, Baker and Barry had three each. The long homestand now completed with the pennant in hand, Philadelphia was off for Boston as the season was winding down.

With the pressure off, Mack started Weldon Wyckoff, with Dutch Leonard the pitcher choice for Boston manager Bill Carrigan, whose team was fighting for a berth in the first division. Philadelphia required only a few minutes to establish a lead. Leonard struck Eddie Murphy out to start the game. But Oldring followed with a single, and when reserve center fielder Wally Rehg fumbled the hit, Oldring advanced to second. A passed ball and single by Collins scored the first run. Collins stole second and Baker walked. Collins made a dash for third, and when the throw was fumbled, Baker also advanced. McInnis singled both men home for two more runs. The fourth and fifth runs in the inning followed, as Walsh doubled and Barry singled. Boston picked up its first two runs in the fourth inning on two walks and an error, and the teams continued to exchange scores through the eighth inning, at which point Philadelphia led 10–5, the tenth run coming in the top of the eighth on an Oldring single, a steal of second, and a single by Collins. Boston closed the gap to a single run in the home half of the inning on an error, walk and four consecutive hits. At that point, Wyckoff settled down, holding Boston scoreless the remainder of the way. Despite nine hits, twelve walks and a hit batsman, Boston fell one run short.

The following day, Bob Shawkey faced off against Earl Moseley. Philadelphia once again led after their turn at bat. Murphy singled, stole second and third, and scored on a fly by Collins. After Boston tied the game in their turn at bat, Philadelphia again led by one in the third inning when Murphy was safe on an error and Oldring followed with a triple over Hooper's head. Oldring ended the inning when he was caught attempting to steal home. Boston scored twice in both the fourth and sixth innings on the way to a close 5–4 victory.

With the pennant won, Connie Mack decided to rest his regulars and allow substitutes and prospects to get some work, while at the same time having the opportunity to watch them in game situations. On Friday, September 26, Charlie Boardman, a young left-hander from Waterbury, Connecticut, had his chance to start against Boston's Dutch Leonard. It was auspicious. Boardman barely lasted one inning, as three hits resulted in a 2–0 lead. Byron Houck and Herb Pennock were little better, and Boston led 9–0 after four innings on its way to a 10–4 victory. On Saturday, Byron Houck took on Ray Collins, the results being much the same as Philadelphia lost their its in a row. The victory meant little more than bragging rights, as Boston had the "satisfaction" of at least splitting the season series with the new American League champions, each team having won eleven games. Philadelphia made it close in the ninth by loading the bases with two outs. But pinch-hitter Amos Strunk could only manage a short tap in front of the plate that catcher Wally Snell, a recruit from Brown University, grabbed, and diving to the plate, made the final putout of the game.

From Boston, the Athletics traveled south to Washington for the final away series of the regular season. Facing them was Walter Johnson, already the winner of thirty-five victories this season. Johnson was at his best, though the team he faced was a champion in name only given the status of the players that day. One might recognize the names of such starters as Tom Daley or Jimmy Walsh. But others included Harry Fritz at third, hitless this day of his debut in four at-bats; Press Cruthers, starting for the first time at second base; George Brickley in right field; and Wickey McAvoy at catcher. Weldon Wyckoff certainly had nothing to be ashamed about, limiting the second-place Nationals to three hits and a single run. Washington scored the game's only run in the seventh when Gandil singled, stole second, went to third on an infield hit and scored on a ground ball by catcher Rip Williams.

Philadelphia made it five losses in a row on Tuesday, as Charlie Boardman made his second start of the week. Joe Giebel, a draftee from Savannah in the South Atlantic League, made his debut as Boardman's batterymate. To their credit, Giebel produced one of the four Athletic hits while Boardman held Washington to seven hits. Once again Philadelphia was shut out, but two of Washington's three runs were the result of errors on the part of Athletic first baseman Billy Orr. Shortstop Monte Peffer, who had started the day before, was injured when hit in the eye during fielding practice before the game, and he was replaced by former University of Michigan player Johnny Lavan. Lavan was hitless in four at-bats.

As the season entered October, Mack picked the right-hander from Missoula of the Union Association, Pat Bohen, to make his debut. Had Philadelphia actually scored, Bohen might have at least entered the record books with a victory — he did limit an equally inept Washington team to three hits. The only run of the game scored in the eighth inning. Eddie Ainsmith singled and Howie Shanks doubled to put runners on second and third. Bohen struck out the next two men, but with the 17-year-old Cuban Merito Acosta at bat Bohen threw a wild pitch, allowing Ainsmith to score.

Philadelphia returned home to finish the season, with New York the opponent. Mack had to balance the need to keep his players sharp for the upcoming series matchup with John McGraw's Giants with the danger of an injury to one of his starters. With a rainout on October 2, a doubleheader was scheduled for the following day, one which started out cold and windy. Eddie Plank started the opener against the Yankees' Ray Caldwell. With their regulars back in the lineup, the Athletics produced fifteen hits, two being home runs by Eddie Murphy and Eddie Collins. The game was a slugfest, tied at 10 runs each into the home half of the sixth inning, Philadelphia scored twice in its half and once more in the seventh inning to take a 13–10 victory, and end its six-game losing streak. The Yankees took the rain-shortened second game, as Ray Fisher outpitched Weldon Wyckoff and his team of irregulars, 2–1, in six innings.

The long season ended October 4, as three Athletic pitchers—Brown, Shawkey and Houck—allowed eight New York hits and thirteen walks, including eight by Houck, resulting in ten runs. Philadelphia produced eight, falling short by a score of 10–8.

Home Run Baker proved to be the hitting star for Philadelphia during the season, swatting a league-leading twelve home runs while also pacing the circuit in RBIs and 117 and batting at .337. Eddie Collins led the team with an average of .345 and 55 stolen bases. Jack Barry batted .275, but finished fifth in the league with 85 RBIs. He was also the only member of the team to have a two-homer afternoon. Despite the absence of Jack Coombs, the Athletic pitching staff proved more than adequate. Chief Bender led the team in victories with a record of 21–10, leading the league as well in saves with 13, though this was not an official statistic for the times. Bender also yielded only a single home run, that to Ping Bodie of the White Sox. Eddie Plank was second in victories on the team with a record of 18–10, with Boardwalk Brown close behind at 17–11. The balanced staff also featured Byron Houck at 14–6, and Joe Bush with a 15–6 record. And so with the regular season over, it was time to prepare for the World's Series.

Give My Regards to Broadway

While strolling along 'mid the city's vast throng,
I saw a few friends just ahead.
They were bidding goodbye to some other guy,
And these were the words that he said:
Well, boys, I'm off for the Big Town,
It's me for the Great White Way.
Have you a message to send to a New York friend?
And then I heard Frank Baker say:
CHORUS
"Give my regards to Broadway,
Remember me to Coogan's Flat.
Tell Matty and Rube, or any other boob,

That I'm swinging the same old bat.
Tell Demaree and Jeff that I'll meet them
Out there in the thick of the fray.
Tell McGraw and his bunch that I still lug the punch
And give my regards to Broadway."
Then I stepped over near, where a fellow might hear
That was there being spoken.
As the guy asked again: "Haven't you other men
Some message to send as a token?"
Then just for a minute nobody got in it;
Twas as silent as among the dead.
Till out from the rank stepped one Eddie Plank,
And these were the words that he said:
CHORUS
"Give my regards to Broadway,
Remember me to Johnny McGraw.
Tell those guys who've been told that I'm getting too old,
I'm still able to swing my left paw.
Just say I'll be there on the firing line,
And though my dome may be sprinkled with gray,
I'm still able to totter and baffle the swatter,
And give my regards to Broadway."[43]

Final Standings

	W	L	Percentage	Games Behind
Philadelphia	96	57	.627	—
Washington	90	64	.584	6½
Cleveland	86	66	.566	9½
Boston	79	71	.527	15½
Chicago	78	74	.513	17½
Detroit	66	87	.431	30
New York	57	94	.377	38
St. Louis	57	96	.373	39

CHAPTER FOUR

The National League Race

Could McGraw repeat in 1913? Writers were skeptical. Among the thorough analyses was that of William Phelon.[1] Phelon's primary questions about the Giants' chances concerned defense and pitching. In the new day of "lively ball," the Giants given their rather porous defense, had to score their runs in bunches instead of simply playing for a single run as in previous years. Certainly they could run and hit. Phelon predicted a second-place finish for McGraw, behind Pittsburgh.

Pitching was a legitimate question. Mathewson was still the ace, but was no youngster. Nor was Ames. Tesreau was coming off a fine rookie year. Would he continue to be as dominating as he had been the last half of the 1912 season? McGraw had purchased the contract of Al Demaree from Mobile of the Southern League the previous August. A curveballer, Demaree had been purchased for a reported $8,000 after a season in which he went 25–10, including 11 shutouts.[2]

Demaree made his impressive major league debut on September 26, in the second game of a doubleheader against Boston. Mathewson had already pitched the pennant clincher earlier that day in an 8–3 triumph. Demaree tossed a 4–0 shutout, allowing only seven hits and striking out nine.[4] Much was expected of Demaree.

In an attempt to further improve the team — or at least attendance — McGraw signed 1912 Olympic pentathlon and decathlon champion Jim Thorpe in the beginning of February. Thorpe had been designated "the greatest athlete in the world" by King Gustav of Sweden following his triumphs. It was soon revealed, however, that Thorpe had been paid for playing minor league baseball. Naïve behavior on the part of Thorpe or not, the Amateur Athletic Union declared Thorpe a professional and therefore ineligible for Olympic competition. As a result, Thorpe was stripped of his medals.

McGraw admitted he had never actually seen Thorpe play baseball, and was not even sure whether he was left- or right-handed; he based his decision to sign Thorpe upon the recommendations of others. Thorpe's minor league career, for which he had been paid $60 per month, not much but sufficient to dub him a professional, had certainly been less than extraordinary. During the

Al Demaree (1913) won 13 games in 1913, his first full season. Of his 80 career victories, 15 were shutouts (Library of Congress, Bain Collection).

1909 season, he had played with Rocky Mount of the Eastern Carolina League, producing a 9–10 record as a pitcher, while batting .253 in 44 games as a part-time outfielder and first baseman. The following season with Rocky Mount and Fayetteville, Thorpe went 16–10 with a batting average of .250. "Manager McGraw pays little attention to averages. It is known that at times Thorpe played brilliant baseball in the South. The Indian is not what is known as a scientific batter. He swings at the ball freely and isn't satisfied unless he hits it out of the lot."[5] He was considered an adequate fielder, and as a hitter was a "free swinger" who had trouble with breaking pitches. McGraw outbid five other teams, and reportedly signed Thorpe for the sum of $6,000.[6]

Outfielder Claude Cooper, who batted .267 with Fort Worth of the Texas League, was also signed for possible use as a utility player. Fred Merkle, unlike the previous year when he had threatened to hold out, signed his contract early. Fred Snodgrass was also signed, and at an increase in salary, an act that ran counter to those who blamed him for the loss of the 1912 Series, and in one case, the loss of a home.

> Here is a man in a Pittsburgh police court who blames the Giant center fielder for the destruction of his home and for his own downfall. This one made a bet on the Giants, and is now trying to hold Snodgrass responsible for his loss: "Until I began

betting on the last world's series I had a happy home and was getting along very well in life. I had never bet on ball games to any extent previous to that time, and when a friend persuaded me to wager a goodly sum on the Giants to win the championship I began my downward course. After I had lost several hundred dollars on the different games I resolved, if possible, to get even, and I wagered every dollar I could beg, borrow or steal on the final contest. I thought I had won it until the report came in over the ticker that Snodgrass had dropped the fly. After that I went from bad to worse, and my wife finally left me. It hurts to think I must go to jail because Snodgrass muffed that fly."[7]

The Giants traveled south to Marlin in mid–February in order to have an early jump for spring training. McGraw had a new contract, a five-year deal for $30,000 per annum. Two players not joining the team for the trip south were Rube Marquard and Tilly Shafer. Shafer was undecided on his baseball career, while Marquard, in the midst of a three-year contract, had "theater obligations" which might keep him from the team until May. Shafer decided to forego a career as an automobile salesman for a time, and agreed late in February to a three-year contract. For a time, the shortstop position would be based upon a competition between Shafer and Art Fletcher. Fred Snodgrass was also unavoidably delayed while in the midst of a legal dispute and would not arrive until mid–March.

Among the youngsters McGraw was watching was utilityman Henry "Heinie" Groh. The contract for the diminutive (5'7", 160-pound) Groh had been purchased from Oshkosh of the Wisconsin-Illinois League some years before, and after Groh hit .333 for Buffalo in 1911, McGraw promoted him to the Giants for 1912. Groh made his major league debut in April of that season. One story, perhaps apocryphal, was that his debut came as a pinch-hitter against the Cubs on April 12. When Groh appeared at the plate, a voice from the Cub dugout asked if McGraw was sending up the batboy to hit. Even umpire Bill Klem allegedly asked if Groh was under contract.[8] Groh appeared in 27 games that year, hitting .271. But an infield of Merkle, Doyle, Fletcher and Herzog was a difficult one for a rookie of unproven talent to displace, and though there was later criticism when Groh was traded prior to becoming a Hall of Fame infielder, the level of his talent was not immediately apparent. Groh was noted for his use of what was called a "bottle bat," one with a thick barrel and thin handle, specially made for Groh's small hands.

McGraw also announced, to the possible consternation of purists, that the Giant uniforms would be cream colored with a violet monogram, and a violet band on the stockings. McGraw felt the team should honor the source of the colors, New York University. He was not the first to so honor a college; the official colors of the Pittsburgh Pirates were red and blue, the colors of the University of Pennsylvania, even though Penn was a college that was on the other side of the state.[9]

As spring training proceeded, McGraw became increasingly hopeful for the upcoming season. Cooper and Thorpe were both proving impressive. In an intra-squad game, Thorpe homered off Mathewson, hitting what McGraw called, with some exaggeration, "the longest hit in the world."[10] Demaree was at times dominating on the mound. Marquard finally reported to the team in Houston during the latter part of March, further shoring up the staff. And while the opposition was not that which they would face in a month, the team still won an impressive eighteen straight games.

The Giants' 1913 season opened at home against Boston. The big spitballer, Jeff Tesreau, was McGraw's choice, facing the Braves' Hub Perdue. Perdue was at his best while Tesreau would have better days. The Braves scored twice in both the fourth and fifth innings, the latter two on a home run by catcher Bill Rariden, on their way to an 8–0 shutout. The Giants only managed two hits— one each by George Burns, a sharp grounder past third base in the bottom of the fourth for the team's first hit of the season, and Red Murray.

Burns had been a catcher and outfielder with the minor league Utica club when, in 1911, former Oriole Sadie McMahon recommended him to McGraw. Burns' contract was purchased, and the young outfielder appeared in several games at the end of the 1911 season. During most of 1912, Burns spent his time sitting with McGraw and learning the game, not unlike the experience undergone years later by Mel Ott. By 1913, he was considered ready, and with Josh Devore being benched for perceived indifference, Burns became the regular left fielder.

Among the crowd of some 22,000 were the "rah rah" boys of NYU, cheering their colors and chewing peanuts, and Blossom Seely, Mrs. Rube Marquard. "The cold damp weather endured by the players was typical of that covering much of the country; three games were postponed elsewhere that day. The day ended with the Braves in first place, allowing for at least one prediction. According to Boston manager George Stallings, when asked about the Braves' pennant chances, "We expect to finish among the first eight teams."[12]

The rains that had washed out the games in the Midwest moved through the East Coast the next day, causing the same havoc. It was not until April 14 that the Giants had a chance to redeem their opening day loss. Red Ames faced Brooklyn and pitched a shutout into the eighth inning while striking out ten. The Dodgers scored their first run in the top half of the eighth inning on an error by Merkle, but the Giants went ahead in the bottom of the inning, 2–1. Doc Crandall singled as a pinch-hitter for Ames during the rally, and Jeff Tesreau came in to pitch the ninth in search of what would one day be called a "save." After striking out the first two batters, Tesreau gave up a single to Jake Daubert, who went to second when Cooper fumbled the hit. James Carlisle "Red" Smith, the red-headed third baseman for Brooklyn, came to bat.

> Some time ago ... Smith promised his wife that he would never play baseball again and right here, let it be known, that if Mr. Smith had kept his word with Mrs. Smith, as a good husband should, this same "Red" Smith would not have slammed

one of Jeff Tesreau's curves into the grandstand at the Polo Grounds for the home run which fractured the game and beat the Giants by a score of 3–2. When Mrs. Smith said, "Oh promise me that you will never play baseball," the well-known husband said he wouldn't, and then changed his mind. And now he's glad and Mrs. Smith is glad too, and Mr. Ebbets and everybody concerned is also glad he didn't live up to the 'Oh promise me' talk.... Now comes "Oh promise me" Smith. Smith waived his bat once, and then again, and missed both times. Then Jeff smiled to himself and said to himself "Oh this is too easy." So he let up a bit and thought he would allow Smith to at least get a glimpse of the ball as it whizzed by.... He reached out his bat and dented the ball where it was healthiest. When the ball recovered from the tickle, it was in the right field grandstand, and Smith was running around the bases as if he was trying to catch the last car. [13] The game was noteworthy for another reason as it marked the major league debut of Jim Thorpe. Typical of the times, Thorpe's description clearly smacked of a racist attitude: "As a last straw with two down in the ninth, McGraw sent Jim Thorpe in to bat. The Indian went the way of his white brothers and was tossed out at first base after hopping a grounder to [George] Cutshaw."[14] The season was two games old for the Giants, and the team had only two losses for Tesreau to show for it.

The Giants finally entered the win column on April 17. It was opening day at South End Grounds in Boston, and before a small crowd of 7,500 or so, Christy Mathewson took on Hub Perdue, the spitballer who had shut the Giants down a week before. For eight innings, Mathewson shut Boston down, allowing nine hits and baserunners in six of those innings. Each time, however, he worked out of it. Meanwhile, New York had scored twice on Perdue, once in the fourth on Herzog's sacrifice fly, and in the eighth on a home run by Larry Doyle. But in the ninth, Boston broke through to tie, with former Giant Cy Seymour's double driving in both runs. In the tenth, Fletcher walked, was sacrificed to second by Burns, and scored when Doyle singled in what became the winning run with his fourth hit of the game.

The victory marked the first of what developed into a seven-game winning streak. Al Demaree started the next day, the Giants had ten runs by the end of the second inning, and the rookie cruised to an easy 13–4 victory. Doyle already had two hits before being tossed in a dispute with umpire Bill Byron.

Doyle, the team captain as well, drew a three-game suspension for his tirade. His absence had no discernible effect on team play as the Giants proceeded to sweep a Saturday double header from the Braves. With Tilly Shafer replacing Doyle at second, Red Ames had an easy time of it the first game, 7–2, and Tesreau finally recorded his first victory in the second, 10–3. Merkle's bases-loaded triple put the game out of reach in the fifth. Two days later, since there was no Sunday baseball, Marquard completed the sweep with his first victory of the season, 4–3. A leaping catch by shortstop Art Fletcher in the fifth saved at least one run, and probably provided the margin of victory.

The Giants returned home on April 22 to begin a four-game series with the Phillies. Tesreau took the mound and lasted as long as the second inning, when Fred Luderus, "with a pair of shoulders like Zbyszco, whaled the ball into the right field stand for a home run."[15] Hooks Wiltse came in to relieve and remained on the mound the next eleven innings, allowing only a single run in the third. The Giants tied the game in the sixth on consecutive singles by Snodgrass, Shafer and Burns, the second run scoring when catcher Otto Knabe threw wildly to third while trying to catch Shafer. The Giants had an opportunity to win in the eleventh when with Burns at first, Merkle rocketed a solid double to the left field fence. But Burns held up thinking the ball would be caught, and only made it as far as third. Meyers walked to load the bases before pinch-hitter Moose McCormick fanned to end the threat. The game was finally called because of darkness in the thirteenth, leaving the game a 2–2 tie.

The Giants attempted to return to their winning ways in the second game of the homestand against the Phillies, as Christy Mathewson faced Ad Brennan. Brennan had no love for either McGraw or the Giants, and as would become apparent later in the season, was not averse to engaging in a brawl with the Giants' manager. Animosity between McGraw and Brennan, or between McGraw and anybody for that matter, was no surprise. What was a surprise was the strong play of the Phillies during this first week of the season. With a 4–1 record, the Phillies were in first place, percentage points ahead of Chicago and New York. The relative positions of the teams was just another irritant for McGraw. Mathewson came through again, his five-hit, 3–1 victory moving the Giants past both Philadelphia and Chicago into first.

Red Ames stretched the Giants' streak to seven games the next day, out-pitching Earl Moore and the Phillies by a 7–1 score. Moore lasted a mere two innings, allowing five hits and all seven runs, three on a second-inning home run by shortstop Tilly Shafer. The Giant defense, thought to be one of McGraw's weaker areas at the beginning of the season, came through again. In the second inning, with Sherwood Magee on first, "Cozy" Dolan lined a solid shot towards right field. Second baseman Larry Doyle "wished himself over toward the south about ten feet, climbed into the air, and clutched the ball, doubling up Magee before he could get back to first base. It looked like a case of grand larceny."[16] The Phillies certainly did not help themselves, either. In the sixth, Philadelphia outfielder Doc Miller pulled the "bonehead offering of the afternoon" by neglecting to touch second base while running out a triple.[17]

The teams completed their four-game series on Friday, when Al Demaree faced Grover Cleveland Alexander. The Phillies' tall, thin right-hander had won 28 games as a rookie two years earlier, and was on his way to becoming a leader in career National League wins. The war and the epilepsy that either resulted from his service, or was triggered by it, were years in the future. The man who became known as "Old Pete" had arguably replaced Mathewson and Mordecai Brown as the dominant pitcher in the league. He was at the top of his form this day, holding the Giants scoreless through eleven innings. His opponent on the mound, Al Demaree, was even sharper, limiting the Phillies to three hits through ten innings. In the end, the game was a scoreless tie. And while McGraw and umpire Bill Klem had no shortage of confrontations, this game represented one time in which the Giants' manager did indeed have a legitimate grievance and could argue correctly that he was robbed of a victory.

The dispute came in the tenth inning. With the game scoreless and nobody out, the Giants loaded the bases with Merkle, Herzog and Wilson. Moose McCormick was sent up as a pinch-hitter for Demaree. The *Times* writer described it best.

> This never happened in baseball before. In the tenth inning against the Phillies at the Polo Grounds yesterday, the Giants won the game, and then they got no better than an even break.... Alexander the Great, who was spinning the twists for the Phillies, looked at Harold [McCormick] and you could tell right off the reel that he hated him. While Umpire Bill Klem turned his back to the game to announce that McCormick was batting for Al Demaree, the Mobile reaper, Alexander was impatient and turned the bulb over, and McCormick slashed it to left field for a single, scoring Merkle. Up jumps Mr. Klem and says: "No! Positively No!" Here's the idea. Alexander and McCormick should have waited until Mr. Klem had told the 10,000 or maybe more inhabitants of the stadium that "Mac" was going to pinch hit. The ump was right, according to the rules. So, now, don't get peevish because the Giants didn't win. The best they did was to tie the Phillies in an eleven-inning tilt by the unproductive count of 0–0. Any mathematician knows that a 0–0 score gets you nothing. Can you beat it? No neighbor, not without cheating. So back comes Harold McCormick to the bat. He had raced to the clubhouse and was ready for the shower bath when an A.D.T. messenger boy, paid for by "Ump" Klem, said, "Harold, you must bat all over again." Say, they wouldn't believe it, and neither would you. If the bitter truth be told, McCormick batted over again, according to the dictates of Mr. Klem. He holds the same position in baseball that the Czar of Russia holds in his balliwick. The fact is, you can't beat him.[18]

And so in his second chance at the plate, McCormick grounded to Luderus, whose throw to home started a double play. Snodgrass followed with a ground-out. The Giants were retired without scoring, and the game remained a tie when it was called due to darkness after eleven innings. The fans in the end took it calmly, though for a time the field resembled "a strike of the mill hands at Lawrence, Mass."[19]

The series with Philadelphia, though it produced two victories and no defeats, was far from satisfactory for the mental health of "Mac." As had been shown repeatedly through his (now) long career, the only thing McGraw hated more than losing was being "cheated" of a victory he thought he won. He felt no better when the Giants crossed the river to face the 5–5 Dodgers on Saturday, only to lose by a 5–3 score in the new home for Brooklyn, Ebbets Field. The victory, Brooklyn's first in the new park, was sealed in the seventh by a winning blow off the bat of "Jake Stengel, the limber-legged Teuton who clutches prospective base hits in centre field for Bill Dahlen's Superbas."[20]

Casey's blow off reliever Doc Crandall went over the head of Fred Snodgrass, landing at the flagpole in deep center and breaking a 3–3 tie.

The Giants had an opportunity for revenge the following Tuesday, as Mathewson was once again the "stopper," facing Brooklyn ace Nap Rucker. Rucker held the Giants hitless through seven and scoreless through twelve. Mathewson had his difficulties as Brooklyn repeatedly put men on base, but each time the right-hander shut them down. The Giants finally broke through against Rucker in the thirteenth. Larry Doyle led off with a double, and Murray followed by beating out a bunt. Merkle was safe on a fumbled grounder by second baseman George Cutshaw, and Doyle scored the first of six runs in the inning. Mathewson shut them down in the bottom of the inning for the victory. The thirteen innings of shutout ball also extended Mathewson's streak to 22 innings in which he had not walked a batter.[21]

Red Ames faced Pat Ragan in the "rubber match" of the three-game series. For the majority of years Ragan spent in the majors — eleven — he was rarely more than a journeyman pitcher. His lifetime total was a mediocre 77–104, but this season would represent one of his best, finishing with fifteen victories for a sixth-place Brooklyn team. One of his victories came this day: a decision of 5–3. Ames did not pitch badly, and went into the seventh with a 3–1 lead. But four hits, including one by Stengel, resulted in four runs, and there went both Ames and the game. Ames did labor under a handicap that day. "Once Leon Ames used to wear a green necktie. He did this because some wise soul told him that the emerald hue would croak any jinx which might pursue him. Ames, when he left fashionable upper Eighth Avenue yesterday couldn't find the green cravat in his dresser, so he wore one of deep purple. No wonder he lost the game."[22] For the record, McGraw was not around at the finish either, having been tossed in the ninth by umpire Charley Rigler.

Ames had been with McGraw since 1903. A steady if not spectacular pitcher, he had won 106 games for the Giants, including twenty-two in the championship season of 1905. A curveballer who sometimes had trouble finding the plate, Ames also produced thirty wild pitches that year. Born in Warren, Ohio, in 1882, Ames had been playing with the Ilion Typewriters of the New York State League, leading that league in strikeouts for the 1903 season, when he was signed by McGraw. His debut that September 14 against St. Louis was auspicious, as he threw five hitless innings in a 5–0 rain-shortened game. His next start on September 24 resulted in a five hit, 7–2 victory over the Pirates. During the 1908 season, the year of the "Merkle boner," Ames won seven of his eight decisions in the final weeks of the season despite having missed much of the year with a kidney ailment. "It is safe to say that McGraw and his Giants would have been in a sorry case in the last 10 days of the desperate fighting had it not been for the splendid work of Leon Ames."[23]

The green necktie was the result of a plea in the *Times* some two years earlier following a series of challenging losses. "Won't someone please send Mr.

Ames the left hind foot of a churchyard rabbit, a few swastika pins and some old rusty horseshoes."[24] Ames did receive the green necktie, which he wore under his uniform during games, along with a four-leaf clover, from a "prominent actress."[25]

The beginning of May found Chicago in first with a record of 12–4, two games in front of New York. Managed by "the Crab," Johnny Evers, the Cubs were McGraw's primary competition during these years, winning pennants from 1906–1908, and again in 1910, while finishing second in 1909 and 1911. Not even the Giants could match that record. By 1913, Chicago was a team that was wearing down. Former Giant Al Bridwell was acquired to replace Joe Tinker, he of Evers to Chance fame; Chance too was gone. Mordecai Brown was gone, and Orval Overall, one of baseball's greatest names if not exactly a "name pitcher," was at the end of his career. Larry Cheney was now the ace, having recorded a 26-victory season in 1912, aided by the youngster Jimmy Lavender, a 16-game winner the previous year. Roger Bresnahan, another former Giant, was acquired to spell Jimmy Archer. Bresnahan was 34, not much older than Archer, who was no "spring chicken" at 30. The Cubs could be tough, but the likelihood they would be in the race to the finish was questionable.

The Giants traveled to Philadelphia and the "bandbox" known as Baker Bowl as the merry month of May began. With the Phillies right behind New York, McGraw started Tesreau, who had the unenviable task of facing Pete Alexander. Tesreau was certainly up for the task, allowing only four hits in seven innings. The Giants managed six. But again the Giants' defense let down, as Philadelphia scored the only run of the game in the sixth when Alexander reached base on an error by Shafer, later scoring on a double by Knabe. Chicago also lost, so while the Giants remained two behind the leading Cubs, they were now only a half-game in front of the Phillies.

Tilly (or Tillie, as it was sometimes spelled) was one of many idiosyncratic players with whom McGraw dealt over the years. A college man, he had attended Stanford and Notre Dame, and was a standout at St. Mary's College in California when he was signed by McGraw on the recommendation of Fred Snodgrass. He was a man of considerable talent, but one who never had an interest in baseball as a career. McGraw once said that "if Shafer had to play ball as a livelihood and not as a recreation, he would develop into one of the best players in the game."[26] Repeatedly "retiring" to join his father in business back in California, and no fan of the long seasons, Shafer was enticed to "unretire" this season with a three-year contract.

It was Al Demaree's turn the next day — Friday, May 2 — with Tom Seaton as his opposing pitcher. Once again, a fine pitching performance by the starter went for naught. Demaree allowed six hits and one run in his six innings, leaving with the score tied. But in the seventh, a three-run, inside-the-park home run by Gavvy Cravath meant the difference, as the Giants lost their third in a row, 4–3.

Now it was Matty's turn, the "stopper" before the term had its current meaning. For seven innings he did just that, leading 2–0. But in the eighth, a pinch-hit two-run homer by Cravath — another of the nineteen home runs he would hit that season — tied the score, and Luderus' run-scoring double in the ninth ended it. On Monday, it was Marquard who would attempt to end what was now a four-game losing streak. Alexander was again the opposing pitcher. Pete was not quite as effective as he had been several days earlier, but he did not have to be. Outfielder Sherry Magee hit two of his season's eleven home runs that day, and Giant nemesis Cravath hit another, his third in the series, and the Giants went down, 6–3. Only a sturdy Giant defense, which robbed the Phillies several times of hits, kept the game as close as it was. The Giants had come to Philadelphia with a record of 8–4, good enough for second place. They left with a record of 8–8, finding themselves in sixth place and 1½ games behind Brooklyn, while the Phillies were now in first.

On May 6, the Giants returned home to face the 4–15 Reds in a four-game series. Having lost five in a row, McGraw gave the assignment to Jeff Tesreau to end the skid. The big right-hander could not find the plate this day and walked six while allowing ten hits in six innings of work. However, the Giants' offense came through with three triples and a four-run fourth, and led 6–3 in the visitor half of the seventh. Two walks and a single loaded the bases for Cincinnati, and Demaree came in for relief. A sacrifice fly scored one run. But another fly ball and a strikeout ended the threat. Shafer was the star of the game with four hits, scoring two runs and knocking in another.

The next day marked Ames' turn on the mound for New York, and he lasted only into the second inning. After Ames loaded the bases and allowed one run to score, McGraw had seen enough and brought in Mathewson to shut down the Reds. A ground out was all it took, and with the Giants scoring six runs, Mathewson had his fourth win of the young season. Even though Tesreau had pitched six innings two days before, McGraw brought him back for the third game of the series. The Reds' Johnny Bates hit the first pitch of the game into left, where George Burns could not hold on to it, with Bates ending up with a triple. Manager Joe Tinker singled him home, and that was all the Reds needed as George "Chief" Johnson shut the Giants out on six hits. Four Giant double plays killed any chances of a rally, as they went down, 4–0.

Rube Marquard took the mound for the final game of the four-game series. Marquard went eight innings, in seven of which the Reds failed to score. But one inning, the sixth, did Rube in. Buck Herzog started the Giant scoring with a second-inning home run off an Art Fromme curveball. For five innings the lead held. But in the Cincinnati sixth, Bates once again tripled, and following a foul out by Beals Becker that Meyers handled, Manager Tinker doubled in the first run. An error by Shafer put runners on the corners and a wild pitch scored Tinker from third with the leading, and ultimately winning, run. The final score was 3–1. The Reds had won two in a row, but with a record of 6–16, they remained in the league cellar.

Cincinnati had finished fourth the year before and was considered a dark horse in the 1913 race. Joe Tinker had taken over as manager, and the team was felt to be improved from the previous year. Outfielder Mike Mitchell, a .280 hitter, had twice led the league in triples the previous three years, not including the 22 he hit in 1912. The Cuban, Armando Marsans, light-skinned enough to pass for white in those segregated times, was a .300+ hitting outfielder as well. Dick Hoblitzell held down first base. and Eddie Grant played third for Cincinnati, each a solid hitter. Pitching was questionable. Art Fromme's victory was his first of the season, but he was coming off 16 triumphs the previous year, and had won as many as 19 in 1909.

On Saturday, May 10, Chicago came to town for a four-game series. With a 14–10 record, the Cubs were one-half game behind the leaders; Al Demaree faced Larry Cheney in the opener. A delegation from Troy, New York, was on hand to cheer and honor its hometown boy, Chicago manager and second baseman Johnny Evers. Evers had hit a career-high of .341 in 1912, and despite turning 32, was still one of the best defenders in his position. Evers had two of Chicago's four hits this day, scoring the first run of the game in the sixth, and driving in the second and winning run in the eighth. Demaree again pitched well enough to win, allowing four hits, but his teammates could only manage a single run against Cheney. Rubbing salt on the wounds of defeat, a largely Cuban team defeated a Giant squad the following day, a Sunday, in an exhibition in Long Branch, New Jersey.

On Monday, Matty faced Lew Richie, winner of 31 games the previous two seasons for Chicago. Matty extended his streak of innings without a walk to 47 as he held Chicago to three hits for his fifth victory. The Giant bats finally were unlimbered, knocking out ten hits against Cheney in five innings, led by a fifth-inning inside-the-park home run by Herzog. Only an error by Shafer allowed Chicago to score, the game ending with the Giants in front, 5–1. Now it was Tesreau's turn, and with two triples by Merkle in support, he came through with an 8–2 triumph. Chicago managed six hits, but the right-hander struck out seven, and other than struggles in the first innings, had no significant difficulties throughout.

With the Giants returning to winning ways, Marquard took his turn, with Cheney again his opponent. This time it was a slugfest. Nearly nine thousand fans sat for 2½ hours and watched the visitors score eight runs in the opening two innings. Cheney did not last through the second as the Giants came back with seven runs in those same two innings. The game may have been longer than usual, but several members of both teams were not around at the end. McGraw was gone in the third after an argument as to whether Art Wilson had been out on a play at third. For the Cubs, Evers was already serving a suspension, and Al Bridwell was tossed in the first. Klem spent considerable time warning the Cub bench, and finally levied a fine on reserve outfielder Otis Clymer. Moose McCormick, batting for Marquard in the sixth with two men on base, drove in the tying run with a single; Shafer followed with a single to drive in the go-ahead run. The final score was 14–11, not pretty, but still representing a notch in the win column. The Giants moved into third place with their 13–11 record as they prepared to host Pittsburgh.

McCormick was best known as the man who scored the winning run that did not count — the run negated by the "Merkle boner —" against these same Cubs in 1908. Not the most graceful of runners, though he still managed to steal 19 bases in his rookie season of 1904, McCormick was a man who could be counted on in a pinch, literally. Lifetime, he was 28-for-93 (.301) in pinch-hitting roles. The previous season, he was 11-for-30 off the bench for McGraw. McCormick had been a teammate of Mathewson while an undergraduate at Bucknell, baseball being one of McCormick's four sports there, but left in 1903 to turn professional with Jersey City. He was signed by McGraw the following year, but after 59 games was traded to Pittsburgh by way of Cincinnati, the Giants obtaining Mike Donlin in the deal. After four years as a steel worker, "Moose," the nickname originating from the length of his stride, returned with the Phillies. The following year he came back to New York, where he played as a full-time outfielder for the only time in his career. Trained as an engineer, McCormick periodically worked in the steel industry, retiring from major league baseball after the 1913 season.

McGraw's pitching rotation by now was largely Demaree, Mathewson, Tesreau and Marquard, and would remain so for most of the season. On occasion, Crandall or Ames, while with the Giants, would be thrown into the mix. With seventh-place Pittsburgh in town, Demaree took the mound. Whereas previously it was light hitting that let the youngster down, this time Demaree failed off the rubber. Hall of Fame shortstop Honus Wagner singled in one run in the first and scored another as the Pirates jumped to a 5–2 lead after two innings. In all, Wagner had three hits, including a home run, in the 7–2 Pittsburgh victory. It was also announced that McGraw would be subjected to a three-game suspension for his run-in with Bill Klem several days earlier.

The next day, Friday, Mathewson took his usual turn on the mound. For the Pirates, it was the "$29,000 battery: $22,500 for Marty O'Toole, winner of 12 games the year before, and catcher Bill Kelly, a .318 hitter the year before and a relative bargain at $6,500."[27] For seven innings Matty showed his usual stuff, leading 7–1. But Ham Hyatt, pinch-hitting for reliever Wilbur Cooper, homered for the second run. Five consecutive singles scored two runs and left the bases loaded for the dangerous Owen Wilson. In 1912, Wilson set a still-standing record of 36 triples, and had hit .300 each of the previous two years. With Tesreau warming up, Wilson popped out to Fletcher, and Bobby Byrne struck out to end the threat. Though Matty walked one to end his streak, he still held on for his sixth victory, 7–4. Tesreau and Babe Adams along with few relievers went twelve innings on Saturday, earning only a 1–1 tie in a game called due to darkness. After a Sunday rest, the teams resumed the series, with Marquard facing Howie Camnitz. Only 5'9", Camnitz had been a consistent winner for Pittsburgh, three times winning more than 20 games, including 25 in the pennant-winning year of 1909, and threw a no-hitter against New York in 1907. Twice coming back from a run down, New York finally won in the 14th inning on Burns' double, with Tesreau winning in relief. The Giants' victory was their 15th against 12 losses, moving the team into third place.

St. Louis came to town, with Matty and Tesreau the choices for the short two-game series. Neither pitcher had his best stuff. Matty was battered for eleven hits, while Bob Harmon shut the Giants out with only two hits, 8–0. Tesreau was marginally better the next day. He allowed only four hits by the Cardinals, but his six walks made the difference as New York went down for a second time, 4–3. The Cardinals started the scoring in the first inning, as player-manager Miller Huggins led off with a walk, followed by bases on balls to two of the next three hitters. Huggins scored on a groundout by third baseman Mike Mowrey. The Giants still managed to hold a 3–2 lead into the eighth inning before the Cardinals picked up two. Slim Sallee scattered nine hits, and the Giants went down to the second loss of their brief series with St. Louis.

McGraw had been dissatisfied with the consistency of his pitching to date, which triggered what was later considered a controversial trade. On May 22, Red Ames, Henry Groh and Josh Devore were sent to Cincinnati in exchange for pitcher Art Fromme. Heinie Groh went on to an outstanding career with the Reds. At the time, McGraw had more than sufficient men for the infield, and the reality was that it would have been difficult for Groh to break into the lineup. Ames was probably adequate, and would continue to have several quality years of pitching left in his arm, but McGraw felt he could do better with Fromme. While on paper the pitching staff looked exceptional, Marquard and Tesreau had thus far been inconsistent in the campaign, and Demaree was bothered by a bad back. Devore was on the "outs," and would not be missed.

Fromme's lone victory for the year had come two weeks earlier against the Giants. He had been pitching with Quincy in the Three-I League (Illinois, Iowa and Indiana) in 1907 when he joined the Cardinals. After back-to-back 5–13 seasons, he was traded to Cincinnati in a three-way deal that sent Roger Bresnahan to St. Louis and Bugs Raymond and Red Murray to New York. He won 19 in 1909 and 16 in 1912, but was frequently bothered by "rheumatism," which contributed to his inconsistency. He seemed particularly effective against the Giants, which perhaps entered into McGraw's reasoning. Fromme had a mixture of speed and a wicked changeup, a pitch that writer Damon Runyan called the "Fromme dipsey-do."[28]

A court case involving McGraw was decided that same day, one which had far-reaching consequences. McGraw had sued the Pathé Frères Motion Picture Company, the Universal Film Manufacturing Company and the Commercial Motion Picture Company for unauthorized filming, basing his argument on Section 50 of the Civil Rights Act that prevented using pictures for advertising

John McGraw (left), Miller Huggins and umpire Bill Brennan in 1913. Best known for his years as manager of the Yankees, Huggins started out in 1904 with Cincinnati. In 1913, he became player-manager with St. Louis, a terrible team that finished in the cellar. Huggins, a diminutive 5'6", 140 pounds, still led the league that year in on-base percentage (OBP) at .432. Brennan was in the league from 1909–1913, and again in 1921. He continued in the profession until his death at age 47, after collapsing on the field at Knoxville during a game in 1933 (Baseball Hall of Fame, Cooperstown, New York).

or trade purposes. The court threw the case out, stating that moving picture firms were "at liberty to take pictures of baseball players without their consent."[29] The law would eventually be re-written, hence the phrase "without the express, written consent of major league baseball."

Rain disrupted play for several days, and the Giants finally went back on the road, heading to Boston for a four-game series with George Stallings' Braves. On Monday, May 26, Marquard out-pitched Bill James as the Giants put together seven hits in the fourth to score seven runs, their total in a 7–2 triumph. Eleven men went to the plate, with Larry Doyle contributing a triple to start and later a single. Buck Herzog homered as well.

A double-header was scheduled the next day, with Mathewson and Tesreau facing the side-armer Lefty Tyler and Hub Perdue. Tyler held the Giants scoreless, limiting the visitors to four hits and striking out four. Even so, the Giants lost on a fluke run by Boston in the bottom of the ninth. With left fielder Joe Connolly on second and two out, Bill Sweeney singled. Right fielder George Burns made a perfect throw home as Connolly rounded third, but Burns' throw hit the bat that Sweeney had dropped; the ball bounded away, and Connolly scored. In the second game, three sixth-inning runs on two hits and a Fletcher error resulted in a 5–2 Boston victory. The double loss dropped New York into a fourth-place tie with St. Louis with a record of 16–16.

It was now back to New York where a four-game series with the first-place Phillies awaited. Philadelphia was off to a 22–7 start, having won eight consecutive games, and were leading the second-place Dodgers by five games. It was Al Demaree's turn, with the daunting task of having Pete Alexander as the Phillies' pitcher. The Giants drew first blood as Burns led off with a single in the home half of the first, stole second and later scored on an infield out. A Meyer home run in the seventh provided another run. But Philadelphia put together two runs in each of the second, fourth and sixth innings, and the score was tied 6–6 after nine. The Giants had tied the score in the eighth on a pinch-hit double by Moose McCormick. Remembering the events that took place the previous time he had pinch-hit against Philadelphia, McCormick "would not even approach the plate until he had been properly introduced by Umpire [Hank] O'Day, as his last pinch hit against the Phillies never reached the league records."[30] Crandall, Marquard and Tesreau held the Phillies scoreless through the fourteenth inning, when the Giants broke through against reliever Tom Seaton on Fletcher's double, scoring Shafer with the winning run.

An estimated 56,000 fans came out for the morning-afternoon holiday doubleheader the following day. Art Fromme took the mound for his first appearance in a Giant uniform, and no doubt left McGraw wondering whether he should have simply kept Ames. Fromme gave up thirteen hits in the 7⅓ innings in which he appeared. Another home run by Cravath, two more hits, and Marquard was brought in. A single tied the score for Philadelphia. The Giants regained the lead on Merkle's two-run double in their half of the inning. Marquard held Philadelphia scoreless in the ninth for the 8–6 victory. Tesreau pitched the afternoon game before the capacity crowd, scattering eight hits and hitting a two-run double in the fifth for a 5–1 win. Mathewson completed the sweep of the Phillies as the month came to a close, winning 3–2 in front of another large crowd of over 35,000. Merkle's sixth-inning triple scored Shafer with the Giants' third run, and going into the ninth it looked like this was all Matty would need. A fine leaping catch by Fletcher of a ball off Hans Lobert's bat was the first out of the inning, but a single by Magee and triple by Luderus after Cravath popped out scored one run, and Luderus scored following an error by Fletcher. Matty, however, ended the game with a strikeout of 5'9"

Jimmy "Runt" Walsh. The four-game sweep of the first-place Phillies improved the Giants' record to 20–16, and moved them back into third place, now 3½ games behind in the league standings.

The Giants started their three-week western trek with a Sunday stopover in Cincinnati, Sunday ball being legal there. Marquard scattered nine hits, while the Giants scored all they needed in the opening inning on a walk and two hits sandwiched around a throwing error by Heinie Groh, now a Red. Then it was on to St. Louis, with Tesreau facing Slim Sallee. A 5–3 defeat of the Cardinals was the Giants' sixth consecutive victory, moving them into second place behind Philadelphia. Tesreau and Doc Crandall limited the Cardinals to seven hits, while the Giants pounded out eleven, three by Fletcher. For what it was worth, former Giant Red Ames shut down Brooklyn, 1–0, that day, allowing only three hits.

Matty took the mound on the fourth with hopes of extending the win streak, with newcomer Dan Griner the Cardinals' choice. The burly right-hander had won three games in a short stay the year before. He would do no better than 10–22 for the 1913 season, but on this particular day he had the better

Doc Crandall (left) and Grover Hartley in 1912. Hartley played with five different teams in a 14 season career. Primarily a part-time catcher, Hartley was adept at handling young pitchers (Library of Congress, Bain Collection).

of the Giants. Matty allowed eleven hits and six runs in his six innings of pitching, and the Giants went down, 6–4, to end the winning streak. The final game of the series on Saturday pitted Marquard against Bob Harmon. Harmon had shut the Giants and Christy Mathewson out in an easy 8–0 victory the last time he faced the team. This time it was a slugfest. The Giants came back from an 8–2 deficit with seven runs in the seventh and eighth innings, and pulled out a 9–8 victory. Mathewson, the last of five Giant hurlers, pitched the final two innings in relief to collect his eighth victory of the season. A double by Fletcher in the seventh drove in two runs, and his triple in the eighth brought in the eventual winning tally. From St. Louis, the team moved on to Chicago for a four-game series.

Jeff Tesreau opened the series on June 9 with a well-pitched game. Unfortunately, as had been happening with frequency, his teammates provided minimal offensive support. For nine innings he held the Cubs to four hits and a single third-inning run. The Giants had jumped to a one-run lead the previous inning on a double by Red Murray followed by a triple by Meyers. The score remained tied into the tenth. But a double by Archer, Ward Miller running for the catcher, and singles by pitcher Charley Smith and Evers scored the winning run in the Giants' 2–1 loss. Matty came back the next day, winning an easy 11–3 pounding of four Cub pitchers. Shafer led the 13-hit attack with three of his own, including a double and triple. Mathewson even had a single and stole a base. A six-run third put the game out of reach. McGraw sent Jim Thorpe in to pinch-hit for Matty in the eighth with the score now 11–1. The Olympic champ singled, then replaced Snodgrass in center, catching one fly for a putout. Hooks Wiltse came in to replace Matty, and while simply "lobbing" the ball, allowed the Cubs two runs in the ninth. With the game effectively out of reach, McGraw sent Grover Hartley in to catch the last few innings. He made no attempt to catch attempted base stealers, what today would be called defensive indifference, and the Cubs stole five bases.

Chicago recovered to win the third game of the series in ten innings against Marquard, the winning run scoring when Jimmy Archer singled, advanced to second on a throwing error by Meyers on an attempted sacrifice, and following a double play, raced home on a single by second baseman Art Phelan. Marquard had allowed twelve hits during the regulation nine innings, but Chicago had only managed to score twice. The Giant attack was led by Fred Snodgrass with three hits, including a double.

With the Giants having lost two out of three thus far in the Cub series, McGraw sent Art Fromme out once again in an attempt to put the Giants back on a winning track. Charley Smith, who had out-pitched Tesreau several days earlier, allowed ten Giant hits in nine innings, but managed to scatter most of them harmlessly. The Giants had men on base during eight of those innings, but could score only in the third when Fletcher stroked a two-run single. The Cubs tied the game against Fromme with single runs in the second and seventh.

In the tenth, the Giants scored when Burns led off with a double and moved to third on a bunt single by Shafer. Burns scored on Fletcher's single, his third RBI of the game. Merkle later doubled in the final two runs in the 5–2 victory, Fromme's first as a Giant.

"That's my kind of player."[31] McGraw's assessment of a young Art Fletcher accurately summed up the style of play exhibited by the Giant shortstop for much of his career. Fletcher was born in 1885 in a small town across the Mississippi from St. Louis. Baseball was just a sideline as Fletcher earned a college degree in business. While playing semi-professional baseball, he received an offer from Dallas in the Texas League. Under pressure from his father, Fletcher remained near his hometown until a firmer offer arrived from Dallas.

Fletcher came to McGraw's attention when the Giants played a series of exhibition games with the Dallas club. Fletcher's play — sliding into Giant players with spikes high, and crowding the plate fearlessly — resulted in the purchase of Fletcher's contract from Dallas for $1,500.[32] Fletcher joined the Giants in a utility role for 1909, his first start hardly memorable since he went hitless in five at-bats. Fletcher batted slightly above .220 his first two seasons but McGraw liked his aggressive nature and defensive ability, and in 1911, McGraw replaced his long-time regular third baseman, Art Devlin, with Fletcher. Later moved to shortstop, Fletcher was a solid anchor on defense for a decade while consistently hitting in the .280–.300 range.

Still five games behind first-place Philadelphia, the Giants began a return east with a three-game stop at Pittsburgh. The hard-luck Tesreau faced Camnitz in the opener, and the Giant bats produced thirteen hits in his support. But Tesreau's defense also produced five errors, some of which led to scores, and Pittsburgh led 5–3 after seven innings. Nevertheless, it was the defense that ultimately came through for the Giants. In the eighth inning, with Wilson on third and two outs, Pirate manager Fred Clarke in a pinch-hitting role poked a short Texas League fly into short left-center. Second baseman Larry Doyle sprinted out and grabbed the ball just before it landed on the turf, saving a run and as it turned out, the game. In the Giants' half of the eighth, Shafer doubled with two out, went to third on a smash by Fletcher that was too hot for Honus Wagner to handle, and scored on a single by Doyle. After Doyle stole second, Fred Merkle doubled in the winning runs. Doc Crandall pitched two scoreless innings for the save, and the Giants had won their second straight.

On June 11, Merkle doubled in the final two runs; on June 12, Merkle doubled in the winning runs. The refrain ran through game after game, season after season. Yet the Giant first baseman is remembered primarily among the dwindling number of baseball fans who know the history of the game as the source of the "Merkle boner." Yes, it was he who arguably cost the Giants the 1908 pennant. The events of that day have been covered *ad nauseum* in any baseball history of the period. But who exactly was he?

Carl Frederick Rudolf Merkle was born in Watertown, Wisconsin, on

December 20, 1888, meaning he was not yet 20 years old at the time of the "boner." He grew up in Toledo, Ohio, where he is still remembered, starring in both football and baseball in high school. His entrance into full-time professional baseball began in 1907 with Tecumseh of the Southern Michigan League; Merkle led the league with six home runs that season, batting .271. His contract was purchased by McGraw, and in a brief appearance with the Giants he batted .255 in 15 games. He continued in a reserve role the following season, batting .268 in 38 games, the most notable of which was the day of the "boner." Nevertheless, McGraw raised Merkle's salary, an act hardly based upon the quality of his hitting that year. The event clearly bothered the young first baseman the following year, as he managed only a .191 average in 79 games.

In 1910, McGraw's faith in the tall (6'1", 190 pounds) powerful slugger came to fruition. In a full-time role, Merkle batted .292, the beginning of a Giant career that would continue to 1916. In 1912, Merkle hit a career-high 12 home runs, batting .309. His 1913 season was simply a continuation of the role he had now taken on with the confidence he had developed.

The next game was Al Demaree's turn, with Babe Adams as the Pirate choice. Red Murray stole a home run off the bat of Wilson, Doyle and Shafer "robbed" other potential hitters, and fourteen Giant hits produced a 3–2 victory for Demaree. The winning run scored in the ninth when Meyers doubled, and pinch-runner Buck Herzog scored on Snodgrass' double. Pirate catcher Bob Coleman, in his first major league game, accepted thirteen chances in the game played June 13, 1913. The significance is unclear, for Coleman batted .180 that season. Still it was noteworthy enough to make the newspapers.[33]

Mathewson went for the sweep on Saturday, Marty O'Toole the choice of the Pirates. Matty had better days, allowing five runs, the result of two triples, a home run by Jim Viox, one of his two that season, and another home run in the ninth by Owen Wilson. The Giants, meanwhile, came back with two runs in the second, fifth and seventh innings to hold on for a 6–5 victory. It was the tenth victory for Mathewson — not a pretty one, but it counted. More importantly, the Giants had won their fourth straight.

It was now down to Cincinnati for a four-game series. The Reds were already deep in the cellar, a 19–34 record putting them 16½ behind the leaders, four back of seventh-place St. Louis. Rube Marquard was the Monday choice. The Giants scored twice in the second when Merkle singled, Murray doubled and Snodgrass singled. Marquard held the Reds to nine hits and two runs, and New York had its fifth in a row. The string continued on Tuesday. Tesreau issued six walks into the fourth, and was replaced by Fromme. By that time the Giants had scored six times, the Reds were held to two, and the streak reached six. Demaree faced Chief Johnson on June 18. The Giants opened the game with George Burns bunting the first-pitch, reaching first on an error. Shafer beat out his first pitch bunt, and when Groh mishandled a throw on Fletcher's first-pitch bunt, the Giants had loaded the bases three pitches into the game.

Larry Doyle was now up, and it was again the first pitch which proved beneficial to the Giants. But instead of a bunt, Doyle smacked the pitch into center, scoring Burns and Shafer. Merkle came to bat, and after watching a couple pitches go by, tripled in two more runs. Three Finger Brown replaced Johnson, and retired the Giants without further damage.The fun started again in the second when Burns tripled and Shafer doubled. The final score was 7–2, the streak now seven. Matty faced the Reds for the fourth game of the series, Rube Benton on the mound for the Reds. Mathewson was once again pitching as a mere mortal, giving up twelve hits and six runs. But the Giants scored four times in the second, three on a bases-loaded triple by Snodgrass, and four times again in the eighth, holding on for an eighth straight victory, 8–7 Matty was now 11–4 for the season.

Matty a mere mortal? Perhaps. He did not win every contest in which he pitched — it only seemed that way for a time. But at a time when ballplayers had reputations, not always undeserved, of being uncouth ruffians, and often had difficulty in staying at the best hotels in many cities, at nearly 6'2" Matty literally stood head and shoulders above the crowd. College educated, movie-star handsome and a moral standard for youth, Mathewson was not only the idol of his times, he was arguably the best pitcher in the first decade of the new century. His records speak for themselves: 373 victories, tied for highest in National League history, and 37 wins in 1908, a modern league record and one of four years in which he won more than 30 games. Five times he led the league with the lowest ERA, with a lifetime average of 2.13.

Mathewson was born in northeast Pennsylvania on August 12, 1880. His baseball career began at age 14 with the local Factoryville team, graduating to semi-pro teams from the area. It was during this period he developed his most famous pitch, the fadeaway, now more popularly known as a screwball. In 1898, he enrolled at Bucknell University near Harrisburg where he played both football, and baseball — Eddie Plank of Gettysburg College was among his opponents — was elected class president, and joined a fraternity (Phi Gamma Delta) and the glee club. For good measure, he also played checkers and chess.[34] In the summer of 1899, he signed with Taunton in the New England League, a common practice among college players in those less-stringent days. The following year he signed with Norfolk in the Virginia League where his record of 20–2 brought him to the attention of John McGraw.

Matty had his choice of signing with several teams, but chose the Giants because he felt, correctly, they were in greater need of pitching. McGraw purchased his contract from Norfolk for a sum between $1,500 and $2,000, and Matty joined McGraw in July, 1900, the beginning of what someday would become "a beautiful friendship." His first year gave no indication of his future with the Giants as he lost his only three decisions. He returned to Norfolk, was drafted by Cincinnati, and ended up returning to New York in a trade that brought a washed-up pitcher named Amos Rusie to the Reds. In his first full season with New York, Mathewson won 20 games for a seventh-place ballclub and tossed a no-hitter in July. In 1903, Matty produced his first 30-victory season, his 267 strikeouts being a league record that lasted almost 60 years. He went on to top 30 victories in each of the next two seasons, becoming both McGraw's ace and life-long friend. When McGraw retired after three decades as Giants manager, Matty's picture was one of two that were on his office wall.

Return now to the 1913 season, replace the name Merkle with Snodgrass "three runs on a bases loaded triple by..., etc., etc." add a "muff" to the mix, and you have another quality player unfairly tarnished for a single miscue. Frederick Carlisle Snodgrass was born in Ventura, California, in 1887. Snodgrass was a catcher for St. Vincent's College in 1907, when he was observed by McGraw, in California for spring training.[35] The following year he was offered a contract by McGraw calling for $150 per month, and joined the team as a catcher in June of the 1908 season. A broken thumb, the result of a foul tip in practice, ended his brief season in August. The following year, 1909, Snodgrass was moved to the outfield to take advantage of his speed, and soon became the regular center fielder. His 1910 batting average was .321, good enough for fourth highest in the league. Snodgrass established himself as a solid hitter, strong on defense — ironic considering the reaction to his World Series miscue — and fast enough to steal 51 bases in 1911 and 43 in 1912.

Stopping in Pittsburgh on the way back to New York, the Giants saw their eight-game winning streak end, as Marty O'Toole out-pitched Tesreau in the intense heat of the afternoon. Tesreau allowed four runs and seven hits in his four innings. Fromme and Crandall finished up, as the Giants lost, 7–3. The Giants were now 32–20, two games behind Philadelphia in the race.

The Giants finally returned home after three weeks on the road. Brooklyn was the next opponent as the team across the river came in for a four-game series. Nap Rucker, one of the more underrated pitchers in league history, would face Marquard in the opener. A Georgia boy and son of a Confederate soldier, Rucker entered into professional baseball the tough way, as Ty Cobb's roommate down in Augusta. One story, perhaps apocryphal since there were no witnesses other than the principals, had Rucker getting knocked out of the box early. He returned home to bathe before Cobb arrived. Cobb, angry that he could not be first in everything, attempted to choke Rucker in a fit of rage. In the words of sportscaster Bill Stern, "Perhaps true, perhaps not, but always a good story." Whether true or not, and given the paucity of in-room bathtubs for the time, no one knows. Rucker was eventually purchased by the Brooklyn Superbas, and turned in a 15–13 record his rookie year of 1907. Rucker was always the outstanding pitcher for what were generally mediocre Brooklyn teams.

Rucker pitched 38 career shutouts, the June 21, 1913, game against the Giants being one of them. New York managed four hits, two by Merkle, as the Superbas pushed across a run in the fourth on singles by Casey Stengel, Zack

Wheat and Jake Daubert, and an unneeded insurance run in the ninth. More than 33,000 watched the Saturday afternoon game. Monday, June 23, was a doubleheader, with Art Fromme pitching the opener, and Mathewson the latter game in front of another large crowd reported at 23,000. Fromme and Crandall held the Brooklyns to eight hits in the opener over ten innings. Unfortunately, the last hit was a home run by Zack Wheat with Stengel on base, sending the Giants down to a 4–2 defeat, the fifth of the season against Brooklyn and the third time a home run had decided the match. Larry Doyle had sent the game into extra innings with a ninth-inning game-tying home run of his own. In the second game, Matty limited Brooklyn to seven hits and no walks, reportedly throwing only 11 called balls out of 70 pitched.[36] Only six pitches were needed to retire Brooklyn in the ninth inning. Had Matty not thrown 14 pitches in the eighth, he might have broken the obscure record held by Ben Sanders some 20 years earlier of having only needed 68 pitches in a nine-inning game.

With Brooklyn having won two of the three thus far in the series, Tesreau took the mound. The spitballer tossed a seven-hit, 4–0 shutout in front of a "small" crowd of 10,000. Fred Snodgrass led the attack with three hits, and figured in three of the four Giant runs. However, by splitting the four-game series, the Giants actually fell four back of the league-leading Phillies, who won four straight in that span and now had a 37–17 record. The good news was that sixth-place Boston was now coming to town for a six-game series. The bad news was that there were two doubleheaders scheduled for the next two days.

So good or bad, the games on June 25 matched Al Demaree and Rube Marquard against Dick Rudolph and Hub Perdue. In the opener, the Giants started the scoring in the fourth when Shafer beat out a bunt, went to second on Fletcher's groundout, and scored on a double by Murray. Shafer opened the sixth with a home run, and before the inning was over, the Giants had scored three times. The final score was 5–1, the Braves managing only five hits against Demaree. In the second game, home runs by Bris Lord and Drummond Brown — Brown's sole four-bagger of the year — and a six-hitter by Perdue resulted in a split of the doubleheader, 4–3.

Another day, another doubleheader, with Art Fromme and Christy Mathewson facing Lefty Tyler and Otto Hess. In the opener, the Braves jumped all over Fromme and Crandall, who relieved in the fifth, and led 4–0 going into the sixth, the Giants without a hit against Tyler. But the Giants scored once in that inning on a hit batter and scratch singles, and four more in the seventh, the lead run scoring on Burns' double. Matty came in to pitch the final two innings, earning what would later be called a save. The two innings merely served to loosen Matty's arm as he continued on in the second game. A fifth-inning grand slam by Doyle produced a 9–0 lead, and Matty was removed in the sixth when Jim Thorpe was sent in as a pinch-hitter. Thorpe fanned, but it really did not matter, as the Giants coasted to an easy 11–3 win.

Doyle was again the hero on June 27, as Tesreau, fresh off his recent shutout, took on Bill James. The Giants had a 3–1 lead going into the eighth, as Doyle already had scored one run on Boston's fourth-inning throwing error. The Braves loaded the bases with one out when Connolly smashed a hard grounder between first and second. Doyle grabbed the ball, tagged Boston's Hap Myers running by, and tossed to first for the double play. Al Demaree, the winning pitcher three days earlier to open the series, pitched the Saturday game. The results were the same, even if not as pretty. Boston led 4–1 going into the seventh, having knocked Demaree out of the game by the fourth inning, with Crandall coming in to relieve. But the Giants broke loose with seven hits, including a triple by Merkle, and eight runs in their half of the seventh. Boston managed to make it close with five runs in the last two innings, but the final score of 10–9 was in the Giants' favor. Meanwhile, as the Giants were winning five of six from the Braves, first-place Philadelphia lost four of five, leaving the Giants a mere half-game from the lead. And guess who was leaving town for the start of a four-game series Monday in Philadelphia.

No love was ever lost between McGraw and the Phillies, or for that matter McGraw and anyone facing him on the baseball field (or off it, either). But the Giants' manager had already stirred things up with Philadelphia. The teams had played twelve games out of the twenty-two so far, the Giants winning the six decisions in New York, with two ties—one being the disputed game over McCormick's "non-hit"—and the Phillies had won four in Philadelphia. The Giants certainly had the pitching, with Mathewson, Marquard and Tesreau backed up by Demaree in the rotation and Crandall in relief. The Phillies had Alexander and Tom Seaton and little else. Of the 62 games that Philadelphia had played thus far, including several ties, Alexander and Seaton had appeared in forty-three. Alexander had eleven wins, Seaton twelve. While Alexander had already established a reputation as one of the outstanding pitchers in the league and would later tie Mathewson for most career victories in the National League, Seaton was almost an overnight sensation. In 1910, he won 28 games for the Portland Beavers, but only in 1913 did he become an established major league star. Ad Brennan was the third pitcher for the rotation, joining Eppa Rixey. Stirring the pot even more was a comment allegedly made by McGraw: "If a team like the Phillies can win a pennant in the National League, then the league is a joke. My team is hitting now and we have more good pitchers than Philadelphia can muster."[37] The Phillies had led the league for much of the season, but the Giants had made up seven games in the last month. The winner of this series would be leading the league.

An unnamed writer for the *Sporting News* had his own take on the matter. [Manager] Charley Dooin should get a copy of the *New York Globe* containing manager McGraw's latest expert testimony on the National League race. Then the Phillies leader should take his men into a private room where they could spill language and read the statement of the Giants' boss. Dooin might say, like the general of old: "If ye be men go out there and smit these Giants and every other foe that crosses your horizon." But that should not be necessary. A child with the proper fighting spirit should be able to humble those Giants after reading that roast.... Are Alexander, Seaton, Mayer, Brennan, Rixey, Chalmers and Moore going to permit themselves to be belittled like that...? Now we'll see whether the Quakers have the Spartan courage required to stay in the race to the finish. There is just one thing they should keep everlasting in their minds — the statement of McGraw: "If *** the Phillies can win a pennant *** the league is a joke." Fight, men! Fight, not for personal glory and gain, but for Philadelphia! [38]

Tesreau was McGraw's choice, Seaton the choice of Phillies' manager Red Dooin. The year before, Tesreau had a haircut, then went out and tossed a no-hitter against Philadelphia. Just in case there was something to be said for the practice, the large (235-pound) hurler had a breakfast of steak, pancakes, bacon and eggs, and then went for a haircut. The barber apparently contributing to hunger pangs, Tesreau had a hardy lunch and headed to the park. A haircut did not help Samson once, and did not seem to do much for Tesreau this day either. The tall right-hander lasted into the fourth as Philadelphia scored four runs on six hits before McGraw replaced him with Wiltse. The Giants came back with three in the fourth and three more in the fifth, two scoring on a double by Meyers, and the Giants had a 6–5 lead; Philadelphia tied it at 6–6 the bottom of the fifth on a steal of home by Hans Lobart. The Giants pulled ahead, 10–6, with four in their half of the seventh, only to have Philadelphia come back with three. Lobart was safe on Doyle's error, Magee singled, and both scored on a long double by Cravath, who rapidly developed into a pain in McGraw's side. At this point McGraw pulled Wiltse, sending in Mathewson to hold that line [score]. Luderus flied to Snodgrass for the first out. Mickey Doolin, a .218 hitter, grounded to Merkle, who made an unassisted putout. For some reason Meyers wandered up the line, and Cravath seeing home plate was sitting by its lonesome, ran home with the third Philadelphia run of the inning, making it a 10–9 game. The Phillies tied the game at 10 in the eighth as once again New York lost its concentration. Pinch-runner Cozy Dolan was at first when Dode Paskart lined to Doyle, who while attempting to double Dolan off first, instead hit him in the head with the throw, causing the ball to bound away. Dolan then ran to second, or more correctly ran into Merkle while running to second. Merkle and Dolan started wrestling behind the back of the umpires. Meanwhile, other Philadelphia players got involved, the ball was on the ground, nobody called time out, and Dolan ended up on third. He scored on a groundout, and the game was tied. The Giants finally won the slugfest in the tenth when Snodgrass beat out a slow roller, his fourth hit of the day, went to second on a groundout, and scored on a single by Herzog. Mathewson shut the Phillies down in their half of the inning, winning his 14th of the season and putting the Giants in first by a half-game.

The game was followed by one of those nasty episodes common to the times. As the game ended, some of the 15,000 fans poured onto the field, many expressing their strong dislike for the Giants' manager. McGraw and Philadelphia captain Mike Doolan were walking across the field together when McGraw was attacked from behind. It was not immediately clear who actually began the attack, but McGraw was knocked to the ground and repeatedly kicked. As a mob estimated at 2,000 surrounded the melee, things became ugly very quickly. Doolan did what he could to protect McGraw, but the Giants' manager still came out of the fight with deep cuts to his chin and cheek.

Two of McGraw's players, catchers Art Wilson and Grover Hartley, had been walking about twenty feet behind McGraw. Wilson was not watching closely, and did not see the beginning of the attack. Hartley, however, said later that night that it appeared Philadelphia pitcher Ad Brennan had been walking closely behind McGraw, and may have instigated the attack.[39] Brennan later admitted his role, was fined $100 and served a suspension.

Rube Marquard and the Giants had their revenge for the attack the next day. Marquard held the Phillies to four hits, while his teammates pounded first Alexander, then Rixey, followed by Erskine Mayer and Cy Marshall with seventeen hits, three each by Herzog and Murray, and won an easy 10–0 shutout.

Ad Brennan (1912) was a marginal pitcher — 37 career wins, primarily with the Phillies — best known for his fight with manager John McGraw (Library of Congress, Bain Collection).

McGraw was escorted by several police and there were no further incidents. The third game of the series pitted Matty against George Chalmers. Among the attendees was National League President Tom Lynch, in town to investigate the attack on McGraw. The Phillies managed thirteen hits and four runs against Mathewson. But a three-run homer by Doyle in the fourth put the game out of reach, and the Giants, with seventeen hits, took an 8–4 victory into the clubhouse. Matty allowed no bases on balls, his streak now reaching 34 consecutive innings.

The final game of the series had Al Demaree facing Pete Alexander. McGraw was in the stands serving a five-day suspension for his role, whatever it might have been, in the Brennan fight. For six innings, Demaree held the Phillies to five hits and two fourth-inning runs. Alex was better, and in the seventh the Phillies led, 2–1. In the top of the inning with two out and Murray on third, McCormick pinch-hit for Demaree. Moose hit a grounder to deep short and just managed to beat out Doolan's throw, allowing Murray to score the second run for the Giants. Art Fromme came in for relief, and the Giants scored twice in their half of the eleventh. After Fletcher struck out, Alex's third of the night, Herzog doubled off the wall in right. Merkle followed with a smash through Doolan's legs, scoring Herzog with the lead run. After a walk to Murray and a fly by Meyers for the second out, Snodgrass grounded to Dolan at first. But Alexander, probably tired after the day's exertions, was too late covering the bag. Snodgrass was safe and Merkle scored the second run of the inning. Fromme struck out to end the inning, then proceeded to close down the Philadelphia bats in the home half, and the Giants had swept the four-game series. The win was their eighth in a row, and with a record of 43–23, they were now 3½ games in front of Philadelphia as they moved on to Brooklyn for the Fourth of July holiday doubleheader.

A doubleheader sweep extended their victory string to ten. Jeff Tesreau was the first-game starter, facing Earl Yingling. Some 18,000 fans sat through the heat of the morning sun, estimated as a tongue-in-cheek 99 degrees in the shade, though probably not far off, as Tesreau sweated his way to a four-hit triumph, 5–2. With two out in the ninth, Tesreau succumbed to the heat, and was replaced by Crandall, who struck out Carlisle Smith. John Hummel then sent a shot to deep center field. Snodgrass ran as far as he could, stretched, and caught the ball on the end of his fingers. In the afternoon contest, the Giants backed Marquard with fourteen hits and nine runs against Rucker, as New York won a relatively easy 9–5 game. The 28 hits for the day raised their total to 82 in the last six games, a period in which the Giants scored a total of 47 runs.

Matty took the mound on July 5, and after six innings held a 3–0 lead. The Giant runs were all scored in the home half of that inning as Matty led off with a single and went to second on Shafer's hit. Herzog's double, which stuck in the mud, scored both runners, while Buck came in when Doyle singled.

Brooklyn rallied in the seventh when four singles scored two runs. That completed the scoring as Matty won his sixteenth and extended his string of innings without a walk to forty-three. Snodgrass was not around at the end. In the third, the outfielder waived his arms on a called strike by umpire Cy Rigler. Rigler asked him what that was about, to which the reply was, "You ought to know. Your blue eyes are alright, are they not?"[40] Snodgrass got the heave-ho from "old blue eyes."

After a day off on Sunday, Demaree had the call, facing Cliff Curtis. Brooklyn managed twelve hits off Demaree, but could only score a single run. Meanwhile, the Giants put together ten of their own. They broke the game open in the sixth when with one out, Merkle walked and stole second and third. Murray then walked and stole second. The throw went wild, Merkle scored and Murray was now on third. Murray scored on a single by Meyers, who later scored when John Hummel dropped a fly ball by Burns. The final score was 6–1, the Giants' streak now reaching twelve. With a record of 47–23, they were 4½ games in front of Philadelphia.

On July 8 the Giants returned home to the Polo Grounds to start a four-game series with the Cubs, the team McGraw originally expected would provide most of the year's competition. The Cubs had not been playing badly, but their 40–34 record still left them in third place, nine behind the Giants. Tesreau was on the mound first for New York, with Jimmy Lavender for Chicago. The Cubs drew first blood when in the first inning, a walk to Tommy Leach, an infield hit by Evers, followed by a bunt sacrifice and sacrifice fly scored a run. The Giants tied it in the second when Snodgrass singled in Murray. Chicago scored four in the sixth to move into a 5–1 lead, but in the bottom of the inning, the Giants got one back with another score by Murray on a single by Snodgrass. Four more by the Giants in the seventh produced a 6–5 lead for the home club. Tesreau was replaced by Marquard, who pitched the last two innings for a save. The win was salvaged in the ninth when a long fly by Evers to right was grabbed by Murray for the final out. In a move more commonly observed in recent history, Murray then tossed the ball into the stands for the crowd to fight over. The win was the thirteenth in a row, and gave the Giants thirty-two victories in their last thirty-nine games.

Fresh off his two innings the day before, Marquard went to the rubber with hopes of extending the streak. Facing him was Cheney. Cubs catcher Jimmy Archer had been injured the day before, and former Giant Roger Bresnahan was catching. Bresnahan had apparently been eating well in the years since he left McGraw. "Roger has grown quite large. It is inadvisable to sit behind him when he is catching if you expect to see what is going on in the diamond. Roger is getting so slow that he starts in the morning to catch an afternoon train."[41]

The Cubs managed a mere five hits, two by Cheney, no walks, and only two baserunners managed to get as far as second base. Only once did the Cubs manage to threaten a further advance. "In the fifth inning Roger Bresnahan threatened to reach third. Yes, and if Roger had been carrying fifty pounds less weight he could have done it, too. The late Duke of St. Louis got on in the fifth on an infield hit. Cheney sent a long hit to left, and Roger tried to get up speed. He was puffing hard rounding second base, and about the time a sprinter would be going over the plate Roger was being tagged out at third by Shafer."[42] The Giants scored all they needed in the fourth. Fletcher and Doyle led off with singles, Fletcher stopping at second. Merkle forced Doyle, and the Giants now had runners on the corners. To the surprise of Cheney and Bresnahan, Fletcher and Merkle pulled off a double steal. Fletcher scored, and when Bresnahan missed the next pitch, Merkle advanced to third. Murray walked, and when Cheney uncorked a wild pitch, ended up on third as Merkle scored a second run. Murray was thrown out at the plate on a ground ball. "Bresnahan was so big there was no room for even a ray of light to get through."[43] Final score, 3–0, for win number fourteen in a row.

Now it was Matty's turn again, and who better than he to extend the streak. Matty had now won nine straight. It was close, but it was just not to be. The Giants did produce ten hits, and were leading by a 2–1 score going into the sixth. But with two out and Evers and Vic Saier on base, utility outfielder "Windy" Ward Miller smacked a two-strike pitch between Snodgrass and Murray and ended up on third with a two-run triple. The Cubs' Charley Smith was supported by four double plays, and the 3–2 loss ended the streak at fourteen. The Giants began anew the next day as Tesreau again faced Lavender. Among the crowd of 12,000 was a collection of Russian teachers observing its first American baseball game along with Russian athlete Leon Vagatarian, the man defeated by Thorpe in the previous year's Olympic games ["Hello, Indian. How's every little thing?" "Fine. Remember me to the Czar of Russia and King of Sweden."], and the brass band from the Hebrew Orphan Asylum.[44] The Giants pounded Lavender and two relievers with 22 hits, four each by Fletcher and Murray and three by Doyle, on the way to a 14–4 victory. "Those weak batters who only got two hits don't even get a mention."[45]

Three out of four against Chicago ain't shabby, and now the 31–48, last-place Reds were in town for a four-game matchup. The Giant rotation of Demaree, Marquard, Mathewson and Tesreau was rested and ready for the next five days, with no Sunday ball. On Saturday, Demaree faced former Giant Red Ames. Ames, owner of the roundhouse curve and green neckties, pitched well enough to win, allowing six hits and two runs, but Demaree was even better. The Reds managed only a single score, going down, 3–1. Marquard now up. With two runs in both the second and fourth and another in the fifth, the Giants went into the final inning leading 5–1. But then Bescher and Marsans singled, the Cuban's third hit of the afternoon. John Dodge singled in Bescher, and Marsans scored when Dodge was forced by Hoblitzel. Marquard then got Heinie Groh to pop out, ending the game.

Tuesday, July 15, pitted two of the game's greatest against each other once more. Mordecai "Three Finger" Brown won a lifetime total of 239 games despite, or perhaps due to, having lost part of his hand in a childhood accident. The result was an unusual pitching style that produced an unusual breaking pitch, one difficult for a batter to hit. His glory years had been with Chicago, with whom he produced six consecutive 20+ win seasons. At 37, Brown was more of a spot starter, but one who could still be effective at times. Matty, of course, was Brown's only equal as a contemporary over the previous decade. Brown's catcher this day was another of the Cubbie greats, Johnny Kling. Wisdom may come with age, and if so both Brown and Kling were among the smartest on the field that day. At the same time it wrecks havoc with arms and legs, and the best days for each were behind them. Still, it was a treat for the true baseball fan to have the opportunity to watch some of the greatest in that day's match.

The afternoon began with 300 Boy Scouts accompanied by the 7th Regiment Band parading to the flagpole in the center-field bleachers, where the Giant players hoisted the 1912 pennant up the pole. National League President Thomas Lynch made a speech, wishing the Giants had won the series against the Red Sox. No doubt McGraw was in agreement for once with the man.

The Giants scored in the third inning on a single by Burns, and one out later, a double by Fletcher. Cincinnati took the lead in the sixth when former Giant Josh Devore clouted a long home run to tie the game, followed by a Bescher double and a single by Dodge. The Giants regained the lead for good in their half of the inning. Merkle reached second on an error by Devore, went to third on a sacrifice and scored on Meyer's fly. Snodgrass was safe on an error by Joe Tinker, went to third on a hit by Mathewson, and scored on a Burns single. Snodgrass produced an eighth-inning insurance run on an inside-the-park home run to deep center. Matty now had 17 wins and a streak of 61 innings without issuing a base on balls. Tesreau completed the sweep on Wednesday with a 5–3 victory, limiting the Reds to seven hits. "Jeff Tesreau's slippery elm pitching was on its best behavior. The Bear Hunter is said to have pitched 99 balls during the game, which is a record for pitchers weighing over 230 pounds."[46] The newest winning streak for the Giants had now reached five. Nineteen victories in twenty games propelled the Giants to a 54–24 record, and a 7½ game lead over Philadelphia.

Now it was the Cardinals' turn to face the Giants, a six-game series beginning with back-to-back doubleheaders. Art Fromme and Al Demaree were the choices for the Thursday match, with Bob Harmon and Slim Sallee the Cardinal hurlers. In the opener, New York started the scoring in the second inning when Doyle doubled and scored after fly balls by Merkle and Murray. The Cardinals tied the game in the fifth, and if not for some poor base running might have won it right there. Steve Evans doubled and went to third on a single by rookie catcher Ivey Wingo. Wingo took second on the throw to third. Wingo attempted to steal on the next pitch, but with Evans standing at third, Wingo

Jeff Tesreau (1912) was a Giant in more ways than one. At 6'2" and more than 200 pounds, with a wicked spitball, Tesreau followed his 22 victory season of 1913 with 26 the following season. He retired after seven seasons with 115 wins (Library of Congress, Bain Collection).

had nowhere to go, and was tagged out. With Evans [still] standing at third, Charley O'Leary singled him in. The Cardinals scored three more in the sixth, the Giants managed one in the seventh, and there the scoring ended as the Cardinals won, 4–2. The Giants exacted their revenge in the second game. Demaree held St. Louis to five hits. With the score tied 2–2 in the bottom of the ninth, Merkle singled and stole second before scoring the winning run on a single by Meyers.

Tesreau returned to the mound on Friday with two days rest. He allowed the Cardinals only four hits in eight innings of pitching, but five Giant errors allowed four runs to score, and the Giants went down to a 4–3 defeat. Matty's turn came in the second game, and "Big Six" came through again. He limited the Cardinals to five hits, but his streak of walkless innings came to an end in the eighth with a free pass to Ed Konetchy. His teammates managed ten hits, including home runs by Meyers and Snodgrass, as Matty won his eighteenth, 5–0. The Giant lead increased to eight games over Philadelphia.

Marquard faced Dan Griner in the Saturday game. For five innings only a single Cardinal reached base, a walk to "Possum" Whitted. The Giants broke the scoreless tie in their half the fifth. Consecutive singles by Meyers, Snodgrass and Marquard loaded the bases. George Burns forced Marquard as Meyers scored, and Snodgrass scored on a sacrifice fly by Shafer. The Giants scored two more in the sixth when Burns singled in Murray and Snodgrass. The Cardinals ultimately scored three runs, enough to go down to a 6–3 defeat. It was Marquard's seventh win in a row and twelfth for the season. After a Sunday off, Hooks Wiltse took the mound on Monday for only his second start of the season, facing Harmon. He barely lasted four innings. The Giants jumped to a 4–1 lead, but three Cardinal runs in the fourth tied it, and Crandall replaced Wiltse, who left men on second and third with two out. Crandall retired Ted Cather to end the Cardinal scoring for the day. The Giants regained the lead in their half the inning on a Burns double, a steal and a sacrifice fly by Fletcher. Crandall provided his own insurance run in the sixth with a leadoff triple, then scored on a double by Burns. The final score was 8–4.

With another Giant win streak underway, it was Pittsburgh's turn again to face McGraw's men. The three-game series opened with a Tuesday doubleheader, Demaree and Mathewson facing Camnitz and Adams. A crowd of 35,000 was on hand to watch another visiting team go down to defeat. In the opener, Demaree shut down the Pirates on two hits through seven innings, while the Giants put together two four-run innings, two runs coming on Shafer's fifth-inning home run. The Pirates managed three runs on five hits the last two innings, but it was too little, too late. The second game pitted two of the games' best hurlers— Matty's prowess spoke for itself, while Babe Adams would go on to win 21 games this season and 194 in his career. After nine innings, the teams were tied at one run apiece. Matty was removed for a pinch-hitter in the eighth, with Art Fromme doing the honors through the remainder of the eleven-inning game. In the home half of the eleventh, a Burns single, a walk to Shafer and another single by Doyle loaded the bases. Merkle hit a deep fly to Max Carey and Burns came home with the winning run. Five victories now in a row. Marquard made it six the next day, shutting down the Pirates on two hits, 2–0, extending his own win streak to eight. The Giants had now won 45 of their last 55 games, extending their lead to 9½ over Philadelphia.

With the Thursday game cancelled due to rain, the Giants had an extra day to travel west to St. Louis, opening their road trip with a five-game series there. Doc Crandall was McGraw's choice in hopes of giving the weary arms of the regular starters a rest while facing one of the weaker teams. But Sallee and the Cardinals fooled them. The Giants only managed three hits, while fourteen Cardinal hits along with three Giant errors resulted in a 7–0 loss. Marquard returned on Sunday, scattered nine hits and held on for a 2–1 victory, his streak now at nine. On Monday it was Matty's turn again. St. Louis had four scattered hits, while seventh-inning triples by Snodgrass and Burns, the latter scoring on a single by Shafer, put the game out of reach. A Tuesday doubleheader completed the visit to St. Louis. Al Demaree and Art Fromme made it four victories in five games for the visitors. In the opener, Demaree's sacrifice fly was the only score in a 1–0 shutout. In the second game, Fromme limited

FROMME (CINN.N.)

Art Fromme (1911) won 11 games for McGraw in 1913, but more was expected of a man who won 19 games with Cincinnati in 1909, and 16 in 1912 (Library of Congress, Bain Collection).

the Cardinals to one seventh-inning run and five hits, while Burns' inside-the-park home run was one of seven Giant hits in the 3–1 triumph. The losses dropped St. Louis into the league basement.

The Giants closed out the month by moving on to Chicago and the West Side Grounds. Tesreau opened the series against Cheney. Jeff had one of those days as the Cubs produced seven hits and five runs in seven innings. With Murray run ragged while hauling down several other solid hits, the 5–0 score was not even as close as it seemed. Marquard faced Lavender on Thursday, July 31, hoping to extend his win streak and start the Giants anew. Lavender stopped the Giants cold for five innings, holding them hitless. The Cubs scored right off the bat, literally, when Schulte singled and Heinie Zimmerman tripled him home. In the sixth inning, however, the Giants broke through with four. George Burns was retired to open the inning, though he probably was a bit wobbly after being knocked unconscious two innings before while breaking up a double play. Shafer then produced the Giants' first hit, a single. Fletcher lined to Tommy Leach for the second out, but then Shafer stole second and scored on a single by Herzog, Buck taking second on the throw to the plate. Merkle singled in

Herzog, and when Murray tripled and Meyers doubled, the Giants had a 4–1 lead. The Cubs got one back in their half the inning, then tied the game with two in the eighth. Fromme was sent in to replace Marquard with the score tied. In the bottom of the ninth with Evers on second, Fromme intentionally walked Zimmerman. But Vic Saier crossed up the Giants with a double, ending the game with a 5–4 victory. Fromme, who had relieved Marquard, took the loss.

August began with Matty again playing the "stopper." The tall right-hander came through again, earning his twentieth victory with a 5–2 triumph. The twenty wins represented the eleventh consecutive season Matty had reached that magic number. Tesreau was the choice to finish the series. The Cubs were capable of producing only four hits, one of which was a second-inning lead-off home run by Vic Saier. The Giants tied the game in the third when, with two out, Burns walked, stole second and scored on a single by Shafer. New York went ahead in the eighth when Shafer singled, stole second, and came around to score on a wild throw by Bresnahan. Final score: 2–1.

After Sunday off, the Giants traveled to Pittsburgh. Demaree opened the three-game series. The Pirates managed a mere three hits of Demaree, with nobody reaching base between the third and eighth innings. Meanwhile, the Giants scored once in both the sixth and seventh innings. In the eighth, Demaree weakened. With one out, Chief Wilson tripled and scored on a groundout. Pinch-hitter Art Butler walked. Ham Hyatt was announced as a pinch-hitter for Camnitz, but when McGraw brought in Marquard to relieve Demaree, Hyatt was replaced by Claude Hendrix. Manager Fred Clarke's maneuver failed when Marquard struck him out to end the rally. The Pirates failed to score in the ninth and the game ended at 2–1.

On Tuesday, Marquard reappeared on the mound. A crowd of 10,000 watched as Marquard's streak came to an end. Pittsburgh scored once in the first, but it was in the third inning when the Pirates drove Marquard from the rubber, scoring four runs until Fromme came in to relieve. The Giants managed one in the ninth when Shafer tripled and scored on a Fletcher groundout to Honus Wagner. Yet the score remained 5–1.

On Wednesday, Matty took his turn, and pitched no better than Marquard had the day before. The twenty-game winner allowed two runs in the third, but it was in the fifth inning when the Pirate bats grew even hotter. Five hits, two errors and a walk thrown into the mix resulted in seven runs. The final score was 9–1. The Pirate victory marked the first series in three years Pittsburgh won from New York. The Giants' lead over Philadelphia dropped to six games.

The only consolation was that the Giants moved to Cincinnati to face the seventh-place Reds. Marquard took the mound first. Both he and Reds' pitcher Chief Johnson "pitched remarkable ball," the Giants producing six hits through eight innings against Johnson, and the Reds managing four hits in seven-innings, after which Marquard left for a pinch-hitter. But a triple by Bescher in the first inning followed by a Devore sacrifice fly produced one run, and a seventh inning single by Groh, who eventually scored on a single by Jimmy Scheckard, resulted in a 2–0 lead. The Giants got one back in the eighth when Eddie Grant, running for Art Wilson, scored on a Shafer single. But in the ninth, the Giants pushed four runs across to win, 5–2.

Tesreau went against George Suggs on Friday. The Giants led 6–1 after five innings. Tesreau lasted as long as the sixth, when Cincinnati scored four runs to pull within one. Demaree relieved big Jeff, holding the Reds until the ninth. But with Marsans on base, Dick Hoblitzel poled a "walk-off" home run to right field, and the Reds won 7–6.[47] Former Giant Red Ames held the Giants scoreless in his three innings of pitching for the win.

On Saturday, Mathewson again took the mound looking for his 21st victory and an attempt to redeem his shellacking of several days earlier. This time it was easy. Matty left after seven innings with a 9–1 lead. Hooks Wiltse finished up the 11–2 victory. The Reds managed eight hits, three by Groh. Marquard started the series and on Sunday he was back to finish it. The Giants pounded Johnson for thirteen hits and five runs. Marquard was the only member of the lineup who did not manage a hit. The Reds closed within one with two runs in the eighth, but Marquard held on for the 5–4 victory. Bescher was the hitting star for the Reds with four hits, including a double and home run. Marquard's catcher this day was "Long Larry" McLean, recently acquired from the Cardinals in a strange trade for Doc Crandall. The 6'5", nearly 230-pound McLean was with his fifth major league team in the previous dozen years. The travels did not include stops at minor league cities. The problem was not his defense or his hitting, but rather his hitting the bottle. Both said and unsaid in his career, McLean had a problem remaining sober. When in this condition, he produced averages such as .355 with Portland in 1906, helping lead that team to a Pacific Coast title, and .289 and .298 in two full seasons in Cincinnati. McLean's 1913 season began late, the result of a broken arm acquired in a poolroom fight. In August, McGraw decided he would take a chance. In truth, McLean performed well, hitting .320 during the last two months of the season, and later replaced Meyers when the latter was injured in the series. (See chapters describing the series.)

The trade for Crandall was "strange" for more reasons than just McLean. Several days later, the Giants purchased Crandall's contract back from the Cardinals without the hurler ever actually appearing for St. Louis.

The Giants stopped in Brooklyn on Tuesday on their way back to their home grounds. Brooklyn scored four times on five hits off Al Demaree through the fifth inning when he was relieved by Fromme. The Giants scored once in the first, then tied it in the sixth with a home run by Fletcher. The game entered extra innings still tied at four. In the eleventh, the Giants scored twice. Fromme was safe on an error, with Grant sent in to run. Burns singled and Shafer walked to load the bases. Both Grant and Burns scored on two sacrifice flies, making three for the Giants that day. Matty took over in the bottom of the inning. He was greeted by a triple off the bat of Wheat, who scored on a sacrifice fly, the third of the day for Brooklyn as well. But Matty settled down, Brooklyn did not score again, and the Giants won, 6–5. The day also marked Matty's 33rd birthday as well as one of his two saves that season.

Larry McLean (1913). When sober, he was among the top offensive catchers in the league. But too often, McLean was a mean drunk (Baseball Hall of Fame, Cooperstown, New York).

The Giants returned home to face the last-place Cardinals in a three-game series, beginning with a Thursday doubleheader. Marquard pitched the opener. Doyle began the scoring with a first-inning, two-run homer. Ed Konetchy briefly put St. Louis in the lead, 3–2, with a third-inning double, which probably bounded back on the field after hitting a seat in the stands. Umpire Ernie Quigley called it a double, and so it became. Konetchy tried again in the eighth, and this time there was no doubt about the distance. But three Giants runs in the third and six more in the eighth put the game out of reach. Herzog also homered, another one of the ten Giant hits and Fromme pitched the ninth. In the second game, Konetchy homered again, this time off Tesreau, but Jeff limited St. Louis to six hits, and the Giants won another easy game, 7–3. On Friday, the Giants completed the sweep of the series as Art Fromme limited the Cardinals to four hits, Shafer homered, and the Giants won, 6–1. The six-game winning streak improved the Giants' record to 75–32.

On Saturday the Pirates came to the Polo Grounds for a five-game set, including a Monday doubleheader. Matty opened against Babe Adams, who had outpitched Marquard two weeks earlier. The results were similar this day. The Pirates raked Matty with ten hits and eight runs in three innings of work. The fun started right off when Carey singled and went to third on a wild throw by McLean. Viox singled him home, after which Wagner poled a long home run into the right field stands, increasing the lead to 3–0. Five more scored in the third, and Matty was replaced by Wiltse, who held the Pirates from there. The Giants rallied to score four times in their half of the third, with pinch-runner Jim Thorpe breaking the shutout. A pinch-single by McCormick, who was hitting for Matty, a walk, and a home run by Shafer scored three more. The Giants chipped away at the lead with two more runs, but an 8–6 loss was still a loss. Honus Wagner, who had been discussing retirement, certainly showed no signs of slowing down this day with three singles in addition to the homer. After resting on Sunday, Demaree and Tesreau faced Camnitz and Hank Robinson for the pair of Monday games. Showing the loss by Mathewson was only a temporary roadblock, the Giants took both. In the opener, a sweltering crowd of 25,000 watched both teams knock out ten hits. But other than a two-run homer in the ninth by Mike Mitchell, Pittsburgh's were scattered, and the Giants won, 5–3. In the second game, Tesreau sweated out, literally, with the loss of twelve pounds for the afternoon, an identical ten-hit game. But this time only a single Pirate could score, and the Giants won 5–1. Wagner had four hits for the day, two in each game. Art Fromme took a turn on Tuesday, in part to give the other pitchers in the rotation some time to rest. The strategy did not work. Fromme allowed seven hits and six runs in 1⅓ innings. Max Carey led the assault with two home runs before Doc Crandall came in for relief. Crandall had only recently returned after his trade to St. Louis, and was given a round of applause by the 8,000 fans in the stands. Pittsburgh managed two scores off Crandall, but the tallies did not really matter as the Giants went down to an

8–3 defeat. The rubber match of the five-game series pitted Marquard against George McQuillan. Different pitcher, same result, a 4–1 loss, as the Pirates took their second straight series from McGraw's men. Wagner collected three more hits, bringing his total to twelve for the five games in New York.

Chicago followed Pittsburgh into town. The Giants had no relief here as the always scrappy Cubs were in third place at 62–52. Mathewson took the mound with Eddie Stack as his opponent. A Johnny Evers fifth-inning home run was pretty much the extent of Chicago's offense this day. Meanwhile, the Giants scored four in the third inning and two more in the fourth. Snodgrass started it off with a walk and a steal of second before moving to third on Larry McLean's single. Burns singled, one of three hits for the afternoon by the Giant outfielder, and Snodgrass scored, with McLean holding at second. A single by Shafer sent McLean "puffing like a porpoise" into third. Claude Cooper ran for him. A force by Fletcher scored Cooper, and a double by Doyle scored two more. The final score was 8–2.

On Friday it was Tesreau against Cheney. Zimmerman was the hitting "goat." Twice he was at-bat with the bases loaded, once striking out and once popping out. Perhaps Tesreau felt a modicum of revenge for Zimmerman's comment that "he [Tesreau] was pretty lucky to stay in the league."[48] Meanwhile, the Giants managed eight runs on seven hits along with six stolen bases off catcher Jimmy Archer to win, 8–1. Marquard went out to the rubber on Saturday, the goal being to complete the streak. He was successful. The Giants pushed across runs in both the first and second innings, jumping off to a 2–0 lead. In the fifth with one out, Shafer bounced a slow roller to pitcher Charley Smith. Smith's throw went past first and Shafer ended up on second. Shafer then proceeded to steal third. The play was close, and third baseman Heinie Zimmerman, with help from Evers, put up an enormous fuss, referring to the eyesight of umpire Bill "Lord" Byron.[49] The upshot was, to nobody's surprise, Byron would not change his mind. The call proved significant, as Shafer scored the third Giant run on Fletcher's ground ball to Smith. Two innings later, Zim and Evers were out again, this time screaming at Umpire Rigler about the fifth-inning call. Rigler had enough, and both Zim and Evers were gone. Shafer's run proved significant when the Cubs picked up two in the eighth. That ended the scoring for the day, with the Giants having swept the three games.

Seventh-place Cincinnati followed the Cubs into town for the Reds' last visit to the Polo Grounds this year. Al Demaree opened the series against former Giant Red Ames. Ames certainly pitched well enough to win. In the third, he led off with a single, eventually scoring the only run of the game through 8½ innings. The bottom of the ninth began with a single off Ames' shoe by Herzog. Merkle was up, but McGraw sent a limping Larry Doyle in to bat. Doyle came through with a single, sending Herzog to third. Murray hit a high fly to center, scoring Herzog with the tying run while Doyle took second on the throw.

With Snodgrass at the bat, Ames started to wind up, and Doyle stole third. Cincinnati was dumbfounded. Anyone must admit Larry had an awful nerve. J. Tinker whispered to Ames, and Snodgrass got a pass. McGraw whispered something to [first-base coach] Matty, and Matty whispered something to Snodgrass, and Snodgrass stole second. There's some quiet inside ball for students of the game. All done in whispers, without any signals, either.... "Chief" Meyers, with his smashed thumb all dressed up as if it was a holiday, went in to bat for Olaf Wilson.... J. Tinker also became strategic, and when Meyers was about to wave his bat alarmingly, Josephus whispered to Ames to let Meyers saunter. Meyers accepted the nomination, and the bases resembled an uptown Subway train at rush hours. Old Doc Crandall [who had relieved Demaree in the seventh] poked his head out of the Giants' rathskeller, and McGraw gave him the high sign, so Otey got his bat. McGraw then spoke to Old Doc in a fatherly way. He said, with feeling: "Doc, I did you a good turn once when I saved you from spending your declining years in St. Louis. Now one good turn deserves another." There were almost tears in Crandall's eyes after this little talk, but it was because he was laughing. "I know I'm getting old and gray Mac, but if there's a hit left in me it'll win this ball game...." Old Doc mauled the ball unkindly and pumped a single over the alfalfa back of second, and Doyle scooted in with the winning run.[50]

Matty's turn came the next day, and once again "Big Six" came through with an outstanding game. The Reds managed eight scattered hits; the Giants only had three against Chief Johnson. But one was a seventh-inning Merkle triple, followed by a Murray sacrifice fly. Matty's win was his twenty-third of the year. Art Fromme was McGraw's choice on Wednesday, with Mordecai Brown the Reds' starter. Brown held the Giants to one run and seven hits, three by Merkle. Cincinnati fared better, scoring five times in Fromme's seven innings. Rookie Ferdie Schupp pitched the eighth, one of five appearances he would make in 1913. Schupp would later win 21 for McGraw, but not this year. In the ninth, Dimitri Ivanovitch Dimitrihoff, or as he was known in New York, Rube Schauer, one of only five native Russians to play major league baseball, made his first appearance. Schauer had been pitching for a Garrison, North Dakota, team when discovered by McGraw. On the "what do we care for expense plan,"[51] McGraw paid somewhere between $1.98 and $15,000 for his contract.[52] He won 28 games for Superior in the Northern League, and arrived in New York with McGraw hoping he would provide some needed quality pitching.

Schauer, pronounced "shower," retired the three batters he faced. "When Schauer began to pitch in the ninth inning rain began to fall, so somebody said it never Schauers but it pours."[53] The performance proved atypical for Rube. His only decision this year was a loss, and his major league record was a very unremarkable 10–29.

On August 28 the Giants traveled to Philadelphia for a short visit. Philadelphia had been a surprise this year, and though the Giants were a comfortable 12 games in front, the Phillies brought a record of 67–45 to bear. It would only get better this week. On Thursday, Tom Seaton, who would have a career year in 1913 with a 27–12 record to lead the league in wins, faced Marquard. Twice

Luderus smacked what looked like home runs, only to hear the hits called foul. The Phillies nevertheless pounded Marquard and Crandall for seven runs, producing an easy 7–2 victory. Former twenty-game winner Howie Camnitz, recently acquired from Pittsburgh, faced Tesreau on Friday. The Phillies managed two runs on three hits in their half the first, but that was the extent of their hitting until the final inning. The Giants, meanwhile, tied the game at 2–2, forcing the game into extra innings. In the home half, Bobby Byrne singled with one out, and reached third when Tesreau walked the next two batters. Sherwood Magee, who had homered the day before, smacked a long foul fly to left field. George Burns, forgetting there was a man on third with one out, made a running catch of the ball. Byrne easily trotted home, and the Giants lost, 3–2. Matty faced Alexander for the third game, one that was no classic despite the fact the two men who hold the league record for career wins were opposing each other, although one could make a case for bizarre. The Phillies led 8–6 into the ninth inning. With one out, McGraw complained to umpire Bill Brennan that the spectators in the center-field bleachers were distracting the players and should be removed. Brennan asked Manager Dooin of the Phillies to do so. When the fans refused, Brennan forfeited the game to the Giants, and all Hades broke loose. The fans threw cushions and anything else portable onto the field, and when Brennan and McGraw were attacked while heading to the railroad station for the trip back to New York, a police officer was forced to draw his revolver to maintain order as well as the health of the participants. One man was arrested.

Several days later, league President Lynch reversed Brennan's ruling, and the game was awarded to the Phillies, the score being 8–6. But in mid–September, the league board of directors negated Lynch's reversal, ordering the game to be completed at the end of the season.

The Giants in the interim returned to the Polo Grounds to face the Boston Braves. The series opened with a Labor Day doubleheader, Demaree and Marquard versus Hess and Rudolph. In the morning 10,000 fans watched a pitcher's duel enter the tenth tied 2–2, the Giant score complements of a second-inning homer by Meyers. In the home half, Meyers doubled, and was replaced by Shafer. Snodgrass sacrificed Shafer to third for the first out. Crandall, pinch-hitting for Demaree, bounced a grounder to Rabbit Maranville, whose throw to the plate cut down Shafer. Grant ran for Crandall. Burns' hard single sent Grant to third, and when Hess threw wildly on a relay, Grant scored the winning run. In the afternoon game before 25,000, Marquard and Rudolph went into the fourteenth inning tied at one apiece. In the home half, Fred Merkle popped a Texas League fly behind first base to easily reach second, and when the throw went behind the runner, proceeded into third base safely. Murray singled, and the Giants had swept the day. Merkle was a little worse for wear. In the top half of the inning while chasing a pop foul, he dove headlong into the band that was present, tangling one foot in the base horn, the other in a trombone.

Tesreau took the slab Tuesday, and after three walks and a bases-loaded double, he was replaced by Fromme. After two innings, the Braves led 5–0, the game ending at 5–2. Matty's turn came on Wednesday, and only a fifth-inning double by Connolly produced the Braves' two runs. But Tyler pitched one beauty of a game, the Giants managing only a single hit. In the eighth, pinch-hitter Larry McLean doubled in Murray with two outs for the only Giant hit and run. Murray was on base thanks to an error. Otherwise, the game might have been a no-hitter for Tyler.

On September 4 the Dodgers were back in Manhattan, beginning a five-game series with a Thursday afternoon doubleheader. Marquard took the mound first, facing Frederick Mitchell "Mysterious" Walker. "Mysterious" lasted only into the third inning, as Fletcher and Murray each singled in a run. But the Giants' 2–0 lead lasted only into the sixth, as five hits sandwiched around an error and walk produced six Brooklyn runs. In the second game, the Giants scored twice in the third inning when Meyers doubled and came home on Snod-grass' single. Snodgrass reached third on a poor throw to the plate, scoring when newlywed Larry Doyle singled. A Red Smith home run was the limit of Brooklyn's scoring as Tesreau scattered eight hits. On Friday, Demaree took on Rucker. The game was played on a gloomy, rainy afternoon, which made it difficult to follow Demaree's tosses throughout, particularly from the midpoint on.

> It is getting quite dark now, neighbor, and it's difficult to see just what is going on in this fifth inning. From the darkness it surely looks as if there is a lot happening. There seem to be several players wearing New York uniforms hurrying around the bases and it wouldn't be surprising if they were scoring runs. Yes, that's just what they are doing. Bill Brennan, the umpire who occasionally is wrong, although he won't admit it, says that what happened in that dark inning was something about as follows: Mr. Brennan, mind you, ought to know, because he was right up there watching what was going on. Bill got by yesterday without a kick, because it was so dark that the players couldn't tell whether the ball was coming over the plate or not."[54]

What was happening there in the fifth was Snodgrass had doubled and went to third on Doyle's single. Herzog doubled, and "two ghostly figures" came in to score. The Giants now led 5–0, and shortly thereafter Brennan did call the game due to darkness.

Matty faced Reulbach on Saturday. Two second-inning hits by Burns and Murray were the extent of the Giants' hitting. Meanwhile, Brooklyn smacked eleven hits off Mathewson, though managing to score only twice. McGraw was clearly upset with the Giants' lack of offense, attempting to take out his frustrations on umpire Mal Eason on a dispute about whether Snodgrass was hit by a pitch in the ninth inning.[55] Manager Bill Dahlen had already hit the showers, the result of suggesting that Mr. Eason obtain some green glasses and a tin cup along with a corner to sell pencils. Brooklyn shortstop Bobby Fisher had also been tossed, making three for the day.

More serious was McGraw's concern about the Giant offense. They had now lost eight of their last twelve, though still had an eight-game lead on Philadelphia, down from twelve at the end of August. Was it overconfidence? The Giants were about to head out on their last road trip of the season, not returning until September 25. The season would end with a five-game stint against the Phillies, and there was genuine concern about whether the team could hold up. Mathewson, Marquard and Demaree had been performing up to expectations, with the lack of offensive support frequently being the team's downfall. Tesreau had been disappointing at times. Fromme and Wiltse had been marginal at best.

The Dodger series ended Monday with Marquard against Ragan, and the Giant bats finally unlimbered. At least half the Giants' fourteen hits were straight down the middle of the field. "If a tennis net had been stretched across second base the Giants would have been greatly embarrassed."[56] Fletcher started the scoring with a third-inning home run, but it was in the seventh that everything broke loose. Snodgrass singled, Doyle walked and Fletcher had an infield hit. When pitcher Pat Ragan threw the ball past first base off the grandstand, Snodgrass scored. Doyle was retired at the plate on a grounder by Burns for one out, and likewise Fletcher on Shafer's grounder. With Burns now on third and Shafer on first, Shafer stole second. A single by Murray scored Burns and Shafer stopped at third. Murray stole second, and when Meyers singled, both Shafer and Murray scored. Grover Hartley ran for Meyers, and he scored the fifth run of the inning on a single by Merkle. The Dodgers were hitless until the ninth when they put together four hits and one run, making the final score 8–1. Dahlen once again was not around at the end. When Jake Daubert was picked off first base in the second inning, the skipper could take no more.

> Dahlen sent up a scream that might lead you to think that the mortgage on his old farm had been foreclosed and his family jewels stolen. Umpire Eason then indulged in his daily pastime of benching Dahlen just as "Red" Smith was called out on strikes. After "Red" remarked that the decision was nothing less than grand larceny, Eason told him to take the first train back to Brooklyn. Then Manager Dahlen had his little joke and went out and took Smith's place at third base. The umpire announced that Dahlen was playing in place of Smith. That didn't seem quite true to the crowd but they applauded Dahlen's nerve. They wondered what would happen when bad Bill had to throw the ball to first base. The only way he could get it over would be to charter a taxicab.[57]

The Giants departed on their road trip, with Pittsburgh being the first destination for four games. Tesreau kept the Giants on the victory path with a 5–2 triumph. The Giants led 5–0 into the eighth when Pittsburgh bunched three of their total of six hits, managing to score two runs. Then it was Demaree's turn in the rotation, the result being a 4–1 victory. Pittsburgh managed only six hits, and even the run was a gift. In the first inning, Carey singled and stole second base, one of the 61 with which he led the league that year. Demaree seemed unaware that Carey was on second base, tossing the ball to a surprised Merkle near the first base bag. The throw went wild and Carey scored.

On Friday, the weather was just too gloomy and dark for a game, so Saturday brought another of those doubleheaders that can wear out a pitching staff. McGraw was especially unhappy since there was a long train trip to Chicago to follow the Pirate series. Mathewson pitched the opener, attempting to end a three-game losing streak. He did so, upping his record to 24–9 in a relatively easy 4–2 win. The Giants produced eleven hits off "Wild Bill" Luhrsen and Marty O'Toole, while the Pirates were held to seven hits. In the second game, Claude Hendrix held the Giants to four hits, two by Doyle, while his teammates put together thirteen hits and eight runs. Art Fromme never made it through the first, as Carey led off with a triple, scoring on Dolan's single. Dolan stole second and scored on a double by Wagner. By the time the inning was over, Pittsburgh led, 4–0. Chief Wilson was the hitting star of the game with a triple and home run for Pittsburgh. For the Giants, it was on to Chicago for the Sunday game.

Perhaps feeling the effects of the overnight trip, Marquard allowed three runs and five hits in six innings, while Fromme in relief gave up four more runs. As the crowd of 25,000 settled in for the game, Cubs manager Johnny Evers never made it to the first pitch. As Larry Cheney was warming up, the pitcher rubbed the ball on the grass. Umpire Cy Rigler tossed the ball out, and when Evers argued the decision, he too followed the ball. Snodgrass opened the game with a single, but when he was called out on an attempted steal, he also was tossed for excessive zeal. The Giants produced fourteen hits but could not manage to push a run across. Tesreau evened the score the next day in an exciting thirteen-inning contest. The Giants led 2–0 into the bottom of the ninth, when the Cubs' Vic Saier tied the game with a home run. In the twelfth inning, the Giants pushed through with a run for a 3–2 lead. But in the Cubs half, it was again Saier who proved to be a nemesis for Tesreau. He doubled, scoring the tying run on Archer's single. But in the thirteenth inning, singles by Fletcher and Burns, a wild throw by Archer, and a sacrifice fly by Shafer produced the fourth and winning run for New York.

"Slide to First Base" read the headline. "Arbiters claim it is done to make the play look close in hopes of gaining decision — runner loses time in sliding." Often in amateur baseball and occasionally in the professional ranks, we still observe runners sliding into first, often headlong, with the idea they will more quickly reach the bag. Except on a possible tag play, the idea is a mistake, as a fraction of a second is lost when the player breaks stride for the dive. But the idea is nothing new, as the 1913 headline indicates. Umpires so disliked the attempt, they would sometimes call the runner out simply because of the act. "More sliding to first base probably would be seen in the National League if it were not for the fact that the umpires invariably call out the man who hits the dirt. They do not think it is necessary for a base runner to slide into first base, because he loses time in so doing.... Not long ago an umpire in the American Association called out a runner for sliding into first base when he apparently was safe by five feet.... Most indicator handlers look at the play in the same light and say they will wave out a runner nine times out of ten when he jumps into first base." A high quality slide, when appropriately carried out, was an act worthy of admiration in the view of the writer. "Knowing how to slide into a base makes up a championship ball team. Take all the championship teams of modern years and you will find they had smart base runners and sliders. What makes the Giants so strong? Their ability to run bases and slide. That is one of the first things that McGraw teaches his players, and, if you ever have noticed, each one is well versed in hook sliding."[58]

The Giants moved on to last-place St. Louis for a Thursday doubleheader. Mathewson allowed ten hits, but the Giants were unable to score in ten innings against Slim Sallee. The Cardinals pushed through the winning run on a triple by Ivey Wingo and Finners Quinlan. Wingo had been knocked unconscious on his hit when the throw by Fletcher struck him in the head. Cardinal manager Miller Huggins ran for Wingo, shortly afterwards scoring the winning run. The Giants could only muster four hits. They did not do much better in the second game, producing five hits. They did score twice, on a seventh-inning bases-loaded single by Merkle, and Marquard held the Cardinals scoreless, allowing only three hits.

With a lead of nine games over the Phillies, the Giants had all but officially clinched the National League pennant. The sports writers were already playing the mathematical game of "if the Giants do this, then.." "Of these fourteen [games yet to play] the Giants have only to get an even break to preclude any likelihood of Philadelphia winning the pennant. This would give McGraw's men a season's record of ninety-nine victories and fifty-three defeats. To beat out the Giants in the event of an even break, the Phillies would be compelled to win twenty of their remaining twenty-one games."[59]

The Giants began their move towards the finish line with a double-header split at Crosley Field in Cincinnati. In the first game, Chief Johnson shut the Giants down on six hits. The Reds scored both their runs off Tesreau in the first inning when Bescher led off with a single, taking second on a wild throw by Tesreau. Heinie Groh bounced a pitch back to Tesreau, whose throw to third caught Bescher off the bag. But Bescher slid back safely, Groh was safe at second, and the Reds had men on second and third. A Fletcher error allowed Bescher to score, and Groh scored on a single by Hoblitzel. The Giants broke even in the second game behind Demaree and Marquard. The Giants snapped a 2–2 tie in the ninth with two runs, winning 7–5. The Phillies lost twice that day, and the Giant lead was now ten games.

McGraw and his men returned to New York for a "home and home" series with Brooklyn. In the interim, the Philadelphia Athletics clinched the American League pennant. At the Polo Grounds on Wednesday, September 24,

Mathewson and Reulbach faced off, with Matty the 2–1 winner. Brooklyn produced eleven scattered hits, and had a brief 1–0 lead following consecutive singles by Wheat, Daubert and Smith in the fourth inning. But Meyers led off the home half of the inning with a triple, scoring on a wild throw by Bob Fisher. Singles by Merkle and Snodgrass and a sacrifice fly by Doyle scored the second and winning run. The lead was now 10½ over the Phillies. New York crossed the river to Ebbets Field, extending the win streak to four with an easy 8–2 triumph behind Marquard on Thursday, and a 4–2 victory behind Tesreau the following day. Brooklyn won the final game of the series with a 4–0 shutout by Nap Rucker. Philadelphia, meanwhile, lost that day to Boston, and New York backed into the pennant, the fifth for McGraw. The remainder of the season consisted of playing out the "string," allowing for some tune-ups by the pitchers. September ended with the loss of two of three games in Boston with Giant pitchers Rube Schauer and Bunny Hearn splitting a doubleheader on September 29, and Art Fromme and his "band of unknowns" being shut out, 8–0, the next day. The starting lineup for New York included Art Wilson at first, Eddie Grant at second and Milt Stock at shortstop. The season ended with the Giants

Stuffy McInnis (left), Eddie Murphy, Frank Baker, Jack Barry and Eddie Collins. McInnis, Baker, Barry and Collins represented one of the most famous infields in baseball history. Photograph dated 1914 (Library of Congress, Bain Collection).

hosting Philadelphia for five games. It became six as an October 2nd double-header was preceded by the conclusion of the controversial August 30th game in which Philadelphia had been leading 8–6. For the record, the score remained unchanged, and Matty received his eleventh loss of the season. Otherwise, the Giants won four of the five decisions.

With a season record of 25–11 (2.06 ERA), Matty was one of three Giant pitchers with a twenty-victory season. Marquard finished at 23–10 (2.50 ERA) and Tesreau 22–13 (2.17 ERA). Demaree won 13 against four losses (2.21 ERA). Art Fromme was 11–6 for the portion of the season in New York, his ERA of 4.01 indicating a level of inconsistency. Doc Crandall was 2–4 in what was primarily a relief role that produced a team-leading five saves. Among position players, catcher Chief Meyers led the team in hitting with a .312 average. Larry Doyle led the team with five home runs and 73 RBIs while hitting .280. Merkle slumped to .261 with two home runs, his lowest total since taking over the first base position.

Final Standings

	W	L	Percentage	Games Behind
New York	101	51	.664	—
Philadelphia	88	63	.583	12½
Chicago	88	65	.575	13½
Pittsburgh	78	71	.523	21½
Boston	69	82	.457	31½
Brooklyn	65	84	.436	34½
Cincinnati	64	89	.418	37½
St. Louis	51	99	.340	49

CHAPTER FIVE

Athletics vs. Giants:
Analysis of the Opponents

"The World Series"

Stand forth ye husky hitters,
Ye catcher, pitcher-all
The skillful combination
That goes to make baseball;
Stand forth and let the people
Look on you as you stand
And feed you hot-air pudding
As favorites of this land!
Ten million bleachers love you
And in their own intense,
Enthusiastic manner
Express their sentiments,
While grandstands, full of staggers,
Break loose with all their might
And strain their respiration
In yelling their delight.

Thus does the nation honor
You in a general way,
But that is cold-air flushing
Compared with next week's play,
When two big nines are battling
Day after day to break
The other season's record
And hold the final stake.
Will Philadelphia win it?
Or will the banner fly
Above the Giant players
Of little old N.Y.?
Who'll win the great World Series?
Ten million fans would quit
Their work next week to witness
The fight that settles it.[1]

Both on paper as well as on the field, Mack and his Athletics contained a potent lineup, and if judging both by the baseball writers as well as gamblers, one superior to that fielded by their National League opponent. Both American League statistician Irwin M. Howe and *New York Times* writer Hugh Fullerton provided extensive comparisons of the two lineups in the days leading up to the series. Typical of the era, two factors played critical roles in calculating which was the better team: pitching and defense. Of course, to quote that old cliché,' calculations aside, that's why they play the games. If the game was played on paper, using one example, the 1906 World's Series winner would have been the National League Cubs, not the Sox, and the Giants would have been the reigning champions, while defeating the Red Sox "on paper" the previous year.

The position of catcher is the most critical of the defensive lineup. Plank, Bender, Mathewson, and similar pitchers could throw all the "dipsy-doodle" pitches in their respective repertoires, but without someone behind the plate capable of catching them, all their efforts would go for naught.[2] And in those days of "inside baseball," the steal played a critical role in a team's offensive attack. Among the job descriptions listed under catcher, therefore, was the

John "Chief" Meyers (1912) was one of several Native American players in his time. Meyers caught over 100 games for six consecutive seasons between 1910 and 1915. He hit .312 in 1913, the third consecutive season in which he broke the .300 mark (Library of Congress, Bain Collection).

ability to stifle this portion of the opponent's offensive strategy. Offensively, the Giants' Chief Meyers out-hit any of the competition. The durable Meyers was arguably the best at his job that season, hitting .312, while catching 116 games. "For an opposing player to take chances on injuring this Indian is practically the same as trying to knock the Brooklyn bridge."[3] Substituting for Meyers when necessary, the Giants had the literal and figurative Giant (6'5", 228 pounds) Larry McLean, who caught in 28 games after joining the team midway through the season, batting .320, as well as Art Wilson (.190 in 79 at-bats), and "Slick" Hartley (.316 in 19 at-bats).

Philadelphia could counter with Ira Thomas, no slouch as a backstop but still in the declining years of his career. Thomas was the catcher of choice when Bender or Plank was on the mound, illustrating among other things that Casey Stengel some three and one-half decades later did not invent player platooning. Thomas batted .283 while appearing in only 22 games. Rookie Wally Schang batted .266 while catching 72 of the 79 games in which he appeared in the first season of a long and successful career. Jack Lapp was the third of Mack's backstops, batting .227 in the 82 games in which he appeared. Lapp was generally behind the plate with "Colby Jack" Coombs pitching but the typhoid fever that sidelined Coombs all season made this choice irrelevant. Defensively, Meyers, Schang and Lapp were about equal in ability. Though both teams emphasized stolen bases as part of their offensive strategies, the pitching staffs for each team, as well as their respective catchers, showed remarkable abilities to limit this weapon. Offensively, Meyers and McLean were each clearly superior to Mack's backstops. Give the nod at catcher to McGraw.

First base for the Athletics and Giants was covered by Stuffy McInnis, at 5'9" the shortest starter in the league at that position, and at 23 years of age, also the youngest starter, and Fred Merkle, respectively. A discussion of this position illustrates the difficulty of "paper" comparisons. The tall (6'1") Merkle played in every game that season for the Giants, batting .261, a drop from the .309 (with 11 home runs) the year before. As Howe pointed out, "more ink has been spilled over Fred Merkle [as a result of the 1908 base running error] than all the other first basemen in the league."[4] Still, Merkle had developed into one of the league's better players at that position. A quality fielder, Merkle showed a clear superiority over McInnis only in the area of speed.[5] McInnis batted .324 that season. Though perhaps not as fast as Merkle, McInnis "was on the bases much more often than Merkle that season, with an on-base percentage of .382 vs. Merkle's .315.[6] Both Fullerton and Howe addressed the difference by comparing the two managers' systems. McGraw's emphasized stealing and "run all the time," while Mack's had greater emphasis on hitting (at least as defined by that era's baseball strategy) and on taking fewer chances on the base paths.[7,8] The ability of both first basemen to sprint from home to first was similar, though McInnis was considered to be the better at breaking from the plate. On base, Merkle seemed to have the advantage of breaking from first, as well as his ability to "take the bags" on the base paths. McInnis stole 16 bases that season, while Merkle stole 35. However, Fullerton felt if their respective teams and their systems were reversed, the disparity in stolen bases would be too.[9]

Even when granting the fact that Merkle had an off-season at bat — his career batting average was .273 — McInnis had the clear advantage at the plate. Fullerton also broke down the batting percentages of the two, calculating the relative averages of McInnis against Mathewson/Marquard/Demaree style pitchers, compared to Merkle hitting against those of the Bender/Plank style.[10] Even here, McInnis came out ahead, .274 to Merkle's .177.

A more significant difference, argued by Fullerton, was in the area of intangibles. Though he played on an aggressive team, Merkle was not what Fullerton considered to be an aggressive player.[11] To his credit, Fullerton did not consider the Merkle "boner" in that non-aggressive category, since in Merkle's defense, it was one made by many others. Instead, Fullerton replayed the mental error exhibited by Merkle the previous year in the series: the failure to catch a foul ball hit by Tris Speaker in the last inning of the deciding game. McInnis, in Fullerton's opinion, would have caught that ball, even risking a collision in the process. To further illustrate this difference, Fullerton pointed out that despite breaking his arm just prior to the 1911 World's Series, McInnis insisted on having the chance to play briefly in the final game. Give first base to the Athletics.

Second base was covered by two of the best in baseball: Eddie Collins for the Athletics and team captain Larry Doyle for the Giants. Doyle batted .280, an offseason for the man who would have a lifetime average 10 points higher, and who was considered by some to have only Johnny Evers as an equal in his league.[12] Doyle was also the winner of the Chalmer's Trophy the year before, a reward in part for his aggressive play reminiscent of McGraw and the 1890s Baltimore Orioles. Some considered Doyle as the most dangerous hitter in the Giants' lineup.[13] But Collins was something special. Batting .345 in the eighth season of what would be a Hall of Fame career, Collins even then was considered the best at his position. Defensively, Collins was deemed faster on his feet than Doyle, and covered more ground. Doyle was considered better at handling throws and blocking base runners.[14] In reality, perceptions of any defensive differences were subjective, and merely reflected the superiority on defense of the two fielders when comparing them with the rest of the second basemen in each league.

On the base paths, while Doyle, the best in the league, had no reason to feel slighted, Collins was considered a "speed marvel."[15] While Doyle might be considered the faster starter, Collins covered the base paths faster.[16] Doyle was considered more aggressive in the art of base stealing, arguably to the point of carelessness. To support his position, Fullerton made a comparison of base stealing attempts by the two men over the course of two seasons.[17] He made a point of observing Doyle in thirty-four attempts at either stealing a base, or in advancing an extra base, comparing this with (albeit only) nine attempts by Collins. "In five he had the advantage of the ball; in three others he was stealing unopposed because the catcher did not throw on account of a runner being on third base. In four others the catcher let the ball drop and had no chance to throw him out. In eighteen instances he attempted the steal at the wrong time...; of these eighteen he stole seven bases. In just eight cases he stole when he logically should have tried to steal, and he was thrown out six times." [18] Fullerton's conclusion was that Doyle's successes were due primarily to getting a jump on the pitcher or catcher when his attempts were "unexpected."

Collins, by comparison, was observed attempting to steal nine times, eight of which were at a time when stealing was warranted. He was successful on five of the eight occasions. Fullerton's conclusion was that when an attempt to steal is expected, and presumably the runner is being watched, that Collins was superior. [19]

Both Doyle and Collins, on their best days, could hit any type of pitching. Collins, however, was clearly the better of the two. Fullerton also prepared a comparison of how the two batters fared against the better pitchers in each league. [20] Collins here demonstrated his superior hitting ability. Against the best in their respective leagues, Collins hit in the .270 range, Doyle about .260. Considering who these pitchers on opposing squads had been, not hitting more consistently against the likes of Grover Alexander (22 wins, 2.79 ERA) and Babe Adams (21 wins, 2.15 ERA) in the National League and Walter Johnson (36 wins, 1.14 ERA) or Eddie Cicotte (18 wins, 1.58 ERA) in the American League is no surprise. It was against the second tier of pitchers that Collins showed a clear advantage, hitting .380 as compared to Doyle's .288. Doyle also had a reputation of hitting breaking pitches poorly, while Collins had few if any weaknesses. So in comparing the relative merits of the two starters at second, Collins and Doyle were equal in the field, while Collins was better on the base paths and significantly a greater risk at bat. Nod to Collins.

The shortstop position pitted the Giants' Art Fletcher against Jack Barry of the Athletics. Fletcher already had a reputation as an "erratic" ballplayer, one prone to panic, and had even been referred to as "yellow" by his peers in the National League. [21] As described by statistician Howe, "Fletcher will pull hair-raising plays with such speed and accuracy that he sets the fans wild and the next day and sometimes the next minute he will muss up a chance that will either lose the game or put it so far out of reach that no one but he can pull it back." [22] Fletcher's performance in the previous year's series had not helped his situation. During the second game between the Giants and Boston, Fletcher had one of those days any ballplayer would dread. In the first inning, Boston scored three unearned runs off Giants ace Christy Mathewson, in large part due to an error by Fletcher. In the fourth inning, Fletcher committed a second error on a stolen base attempt by Boston's Harry Hooper, which resulted in another run scored. To complete his date with "infamy," another error by Fletcher on a hit by Larry Gardner allowed Duffy Lewis to score the tying run in the eighth inning. Ultimately, the game ended in a 6–6 tie after being called at the end of the 10th inning.

To save the clearly rattled 27-year-old further humiliation, and probably for his own piece of mind, manager John McGraw removed Fletcher from the game that day. McGraw's response was similar to what he demonstrated with Merkle years previously. Though with a (deserved) reputation as a gruff, no-nonsense manager who expected mental alertness at all times, McGraw returned Fletcher to the lineup the next day. Fletcher may have panicked under the pressure, but he was certainly not "yellow."

When describing Jack Barry, one might justifiably paraphrase a (likely apocryphal) statement made by President Abraham Lincoln when asked early in the war about General Ulysses Grant: "I can't spare him. He fights." In Barry's case, Mack couldn't spare him, he won. Mechanically, Barry may not have been the best in the league. As a hitter, his lifetime average was about .243. He was never seriously considered for the Hall of Fame. But he was considered a "money player, a game, fighting, brainy fellow, willing to do the bulk of the work."[23] Not only did he complement second baseman Eddie Collins well, but his range overlapped that of third baseman Frank Baker, who was considered rather "awkward" in the field. Fletcher was the better hitter, batting .297 for the season (with only 35 strikeouts in 538 at-bats), compared with Barry's career-high .275. Further, Barry had a reputation as one who came through in a "pinch," more so than Fletcher. Whether this was true or merely a reflection of Fletcher's tendency to panic in stressful situations, one can only surmise.

On the base paths, Fletcher was faster and a hard runner, stealing 32 bases that season in the McGraw style of play. Barry, by contrast, stole 15. So on paper, Fletcher compared well with Barry. On the field, however, both by reputation and indeed in the game itself, Barry was ahead. He was considered by many as one of the outstanding "lieutenants" in Mack's lineup. In stressful situations, he was known for "keeping his cool," to borrow a future phrase. When asked whether he would trade Barry for Fletcher had he been born a Mack, a veteran league (albeit unnamed) official replied that such a trade would be akin to trading [Ty] Cobb for George Browne.[24]

At third base, the competition was among three persons: future Hall of Famer Frank "Home Run" Baker of the Athletics, and Buck Herzog and Tillie Shafer on the Giants. Baker had been "virtually unknown until his home runs [two years before] made him a national figure," an illustration of the fame that an unexpected success (or even an unexpected mistake) may bring a player.[25] Largely on the basis of his outstanding hitting during the 1911 Series against Mathewson, Marquard and their fellow Giants, and the source of his nom de plum, Baker had a reputation as a slugger. Certainly his season totals would support his reputation. His career-high total of 12 home runs led the league for the third consecutive season. He was a consistent .300 hitter, with the .337

average (and .413 on-base percentage) during the 1913 season being the second highest in his career. While perhaps limited in range, Baker nevertheless was a more than adequate fielder, capable of firing throws with speed and accuracy. He had a reputation of being "gun shy" when dealing with the spikes of opposing runners; perhaps one should exclude Ty Cobb in this category, given the difficulty most fielders had with this particular individual. The reputation was unfair. In previous series, the Cubs and Giants had tried to run him off the bag, failing in all attempts. In 1911, the Giants' Fred Snodgrass twice cut Baker in plays at third, and each time Baker refused to alter his position while blocking the bag.

The Giants countered with two more than adequate counterparts at the hot corner with Shafer and Herzog. McGraw had platooned the two at third for a time during the year, with each playing approximately half the season in that position until Herzog was permanently replaced by Shafer. Shafer was the more versatile of the two, having played all infield positions except first base during the season. He had a reputation of being somewhat "aloof," even offended by the coarse habits of his fellow ballplayers. Despite hitting .287 in this his fourth season with the Giants, the twenty-four-year-old retired after the series. Despite significant financial offers on the part of the Giants, the "moneyed" Shafer stuck to his decision.[26]

But that would be a month hence. Shafer was a speedy base runner who apparently could run 100 yards in some 10 seconds.[27] He stole 32 bases during the season. In the batter's box, he lacked Baker's power, but still managed five home runs and 12 triples. In the field, Shafer was an aggressive infielder, certainly the equal of Baker. Shafer was arguably the choice of starter for most writers.[28, 29]

Herzog had a reputation as the Series began based upon his performance against the Red Sox the year before. In that series, Herzog led the Giants with a .400 average and a team-leading five RBIs. Herzog had an adequate 1913 season, hitting .286, but rumors of dissent with Manager McGraw followed him.[30] Feelers from the new Federal League had provided distractions, as well as Herzog's disagreement with McGraw over whether he or Shafer should have been the regular third baseman. To say the aggressive Herzog was unhappy with sitting on the bench is to put it mildly. In conclusion, Baker would be the choice as the best at his position.

In summarizing the comparative strengths among the catchers and infielders on the two teams only Chief Meyers would seem to be superior for the Giants at his position. Mack's "$100,000 infield" had earned its pseudonym, with McInnis, Collins, Barry and Baker receiving collective nods over Merkle, Doyle, Fletcher and Shafer/Herzog.

The outfield trio for the Athletics of Rube Oldring, Eddie Murphy and Amos Strunk matched up well with the Giants' outfield of George Burns, Fred Snodgrass, and Red Murray. Of course in a short series, one player can

Rube Oldring (1913) was a regular outfielder for Mack for 10 of his 13 big league seasons. In the 1913 season, he batted .283 (Library of Congress, Bain Collection).

suddenly hit a hot streak — witness Buck Herzog for the Giants in the 1912 Series, or suddenly suffer a defensive lapse, as demonstrated by Fred Snodgrass in that same 1912 Series.

Left field would pit Oldring against Burns. Oldring was an established veteran player at the peak of his thirteen-year career. According to Fullerton, "Oldring's strong point is in driving runners home. [He was] more effective with men on bases than at any other time, ..and more than half of his long hits [27 doubles, 9 triples, 5 home runs] have been made with runners on bases.... He is one of the most dangerous men in the country in a pinch."[31] Oldring also had the advantage of experience, this being his ninth season in the "majors," as well as his second appearance in the postseason. Two years earlier, he started the Series with two doubles against the Giants' Christy Mathewson. (Of course, one might cynically point out that these two hits constituted half of his total for the six games.) Burns, in contrast, would have a distinguished fifteen-year career by the time he retired, but he had only just completed his first full season in the league. Likewise, this was his first appearance in the postseason series. His .286 batting average for the season matched reasonably well with Oldring's .283; the differential between RBI totals was more significant: Burns' 54 RBIs compared with 71 RBIs from Oldring.

Burns was considered a "good mechanical player with few faults."[32] His primary advantage was speed, both on the base paths (40 stolen bases) and in the field, where he was able to effectively cover his own position and capable of lending center fielder Fred Snodgrass a hand (or perhaps a glove) when necessary. This is not to say that Oldring, though less graceful than Burns, was incapable of running. He could "stride with terrific force that is likely to swoop a baseman off his feet."[33] His career-high total of 40 stolen bases that season, out of a career total of 197, could attest to his running abilities, particularly given the Mack style of baseball. The general consensus among Burns' peers, however, was that "Burns is a dangerous man on the bases.... He runs with better judgment and takes legitimate chances."[34] The left field position had not been a strong point on McGraw's teams in the past, and Burns certainly addressed this weakness. His best years, however, would be in the future. In 1913, he was still a young, inexperienced player thrown into a high-pressure situation. If one rated the two left fielders on the basis of defensive ability, Burns would probably be given the advantage. Offensively, Oldring was significantly superior, and in a short series, that could be significant.

Center field for the Athletics was manned primarily by Amos Strunk (81 games in the field), a .305 hitter for the season with limited power, Jimmy Walsh (90 games in the outfield) and Tom Daley, a weak hitter midway through a four year career. Strunk was a left-handed hitter, Walsh right-handed, a difference that might determine which of the two Manager Mack decided to start.[35] "Strunk is a marvelous man covering ground through the outfield and has the advantage in fielding through this fact."[36] Though Strunk lost ground when turning bases, he could more than make up for this with his speed; Strunk had 14 stolen bases for the season.[37] His speed also allowed Strunk to cover the outfield effectively.

Fred Snodgrass was one of the more ironic figures from the earlier years of series competition. A steady if not spectacular player, he is remembered primarily for dropping a fly ball during the 1912 World's Series the previous year, an error that became known as the "Snodgrass muff," or the "$30,000 muff," the difference between the winning and losing team shares. The play is familiar to any historian of baseball. During the 10th inning of the series finale, with the Giants holding a 2–1 lead, the Red Sox's Clyde Engel hit an easy fly ball to center field. Snodgrass simply dropped the ball. Eventually the Sox rallied, winning the game and the series. Criticism of Snodgrass had been unfair. Often forgotten is that on the next play, Snodgrass made a running catch on a far more difficult fly hit by Harry Hooper. For that matter, Red Sox outfielder Duffy Lewis dropped a similar fly ball the week before, allowing the Giants to rally and tie the game. Ironically, the ball had been hit by Snodgrass. Nevertheless, Snodgrass would be immortalized for a momentary lapse.

Again to McGraw's credit, he always defended Snodgrass. As was true with Merkle years before, McGraw would not tolerate sloppy play or lack of hustle, but could be forgiving of human error. And as he had done for Merkle earlier, McGraw raised Snodgrass' salary for the following season.[38] As a defensive outfielder, Snodgrass was considered adequate.[39] He had speed, and could cover a lot of ground in the expansive centerfield area of the park that was the Polo Grounds. "Snodgrass often had difficulty with judging fly balls, usually using his speed to make up for mistakes. He played ball just as McGraw wanted it played."[40] Yet despite having the tools, Snodgrass had a habit of attempting to cut off hard-hit balls to left- or right-center, running towards them at a short angle.[41] If he caught up with the ball, all was fine. However, any ball that was past him had a long way to roll. While the dimensions of the Polo Grounds varied considerably during much of its history, Snodgrass' territory during this period stretched more than 450 feet in left-center, not as far as its peak of 505 feet two decades later, but still a run.[42] A "charley horse" acquired while running out a hit against Brooklyn two weeks earlier threatened to restrict him further during the upcoming series.[43]

Snodgrass hit .291 for the season, though he had considerable problems against pitchers with speed. According to calculations by Fullerton, Snodgrass hit only .157 against such hurlers.[44] While Eddie Plank was not considered a speedball pitcher for Mack, Chief Bender might present a greater problem for Snodgrass. In contrast, Snodgrass performed well when facing curveball or otherwise breaking pitch hurlers such as Babe Adams.[45] One might, as a result, rate Snodgrass and Strunk about equally at bat. Defensively, Strunk should be given the nod.

The third outfield position pitted the Athletics' Ed Murphy, a .295 hitter in his first full season, against Giant right fielder Red Murray, a .267 hitter in the last full season of an eleven-year career. Murray's experience in the postseason had been decidedly mixed. In the 1911 Series against many of these same Athletics, Murray had "gone for the collar," with only two walks in 23 at-bats to represent his chances on the bases; he struck out five times. In contrast, during the previous year's series against Boston, Murray hit .323, with ten hits in thirty-one at-bats, and a slugging average of .516. One might logically wonder which Murray would appear in 1913. During the season, Murray had particular difficulties with left-handers, and given his previous history in facing Eddie Plank, this did not bode well.[46] He also had some difficulty with the fastball, making it equally uncertain as to how he would deal with Bender.

Where Murray did stand out was in the field: "Murray is the most sensational of all the right fielders in his catches, and the way he plays balls against the right field wall at Brush Stadium [i.e., Polo Grounds] is remarkable.... He can go right against the stands, either face forward or with back to the wall, leap and drag them down, and he seems absolutely fearless in breaking against the barriers."[47] The "barrier" those days was only about 255 feet from the batter.[48]

Eddie Murphy, who joined Danny Murphy as the two outfielders on the Athletics with that surname, was a solid batsman, capable of "crippling someone."[49] Murphy did not have Murray's power; Murray had three seasons in which he hit seven home runs while Murphy would have more than a single homer in a season only once. But Murphy could hit any kind of pitching, and was as capable at bunting for a hit as he was at chopping a ball over the infield or lining a drive over the heads of those infielders.

On the base paths, Murray was the faster, as attested by six times having stolen 35 or more bases in a season. Murphy ran the bases well, but was not one to take chances; he did manage to steal 21 bases during the season.

In an informal poll among managers and scouts, Fullerton found 11 of 14 would prefer Murphy over the Giants' Murray.[50] (The other three had not seen both men in action.) Consequently, most analysts would choose the Athletics' Murphy as the better player for the right field position.

The 1913 matchup between Mack and McGraw featured some of the greatest pitchers who ever toed the slab.[51] Previous matchups had likewise featured outstanding hurlers, and certainly one could argue that the 1911 Series between these two clubs was decided precisely on that basis. This time around the Giants featured Mathewson and Marquard, future Hall of Famers, as well as Tesreau, Demaree, Fromme and Crandall.[52] With Coombs still out, the Athletic staff consisted of Plank and Bender, along with Shawkey, Bush, Brown and Houck as backups. The absence of Coombs could prove crucial, leaving Mack with only two hurlers he could count on consistently. He was already the winning pitcher in four World's Series games, three in 1910 against the Cubs and once in 1911 when facing these same Giants. He had also hit .385 in the 1910 matchup. Mathewson, Plank and Bender were "throwbacks," the only remaining veterans of the two teams that had first battled back in 1905.[53] That first matchup, entered into reluctantly by McGraw, had resulted in five shutouts, four for the Giants and three being pitched by Mathewson. In 1911, the teams met again, with that time the Athletics being victorious. Most of the players in the third matchup had participated in that postseason classic of two years earlier.

Writers generally gave the nod to McGraw when analyzing the pitching staffs.[54] The long-time ace of the staff was Christy Mathewson; nothing more needed to be said. For the twelfth time in his career, Matty had won more than 20 games that season, finishing with a record of 25–11. For the tenth time, he had pitched more than 300 innings. In Howe's words, "As a versatile pitcher Mathewson has no equal in the game. Thirteen years ago he brought to the Polo Grounds a magnificent physique, remarkable powers of endurance and intelligence of a high order. With these he perfected the 'fadeaway,' conserved his strength ... and for twelve years he has been McGraw's ace."[55] While there was little indication of whether the strain on his arm would be a problem, the reality was that Matty was 35 years old, not a youngster by the standards of professional sports. Though by league standards he had a good year, he was no longer as dominant as he had been in the past, being hit hard as the season progressed.[56] Nevertheless, Matty came through when necessary and still managed to win close games. Still, he had been less than successful in the 1911 Series when he was two years younger, and writers expected the Athletics would get to him early and hard.[57]

Rube Marquard had completed the year with his third consecutive 20+ victory season. But like Mathewson, he was being hit harder and more frequently than in the past, and was likely showing the results of developing arm damage that would eventually limit his effectiveness. And like Mathewson, his performance during the previous two World's Series had been mixed. He was winless in 1911 as Marquard was "beaten up" by the Athletics in general, and by Home Run Baker in particular, and won twice during the 1912 Series against Boston. Even in the two victories against Boston, some considered Marquard to have been the fortunate recipient of game-saving catches by his defense.[58] Marquard had started the season slowly, but became more effective as the campaign progressed, particularly after mid–June.

The third pitcher on McGraw's staff was the tall right-hander, Jeff Tesreau. Like both Mathewson and Marquard, Tesreau had won twenty games that season, the first of two consecutive such seasons in a relatively short but successful career. A spitball pitcher and owner as well of an effective fastball, Tesreau could be difficult to hit on a good day. In the previous year's series, Tesreau's performance had been mixed, with 15 strikeouts in 23 innings and one victory in three decisions. But Tesreau was a rookie then, and with an additional year's experience under his belt, he could be expected to deal with any pressure in a more timely manner. Nevertheless, there was concern among sportswriters as to which Tesreau would appear.[59]

The final two pitchers in McGraw's collection who might be expected to appear in the series were Al Demaree and Art Fromme. In his first full season in 1913, Demaree had won 13 games, with a respectable 2.21 ERA. Known as a pitcher who rarely lost his "cool," he represented an unknown factor against a team that had never faced him. Fromme was considered an odd pitcher.[60] Acquired from Cincinnati earlier in the season, he went on to win 11 games in 17 decisions for McGraw. When Fromme was on his game, he could be as difficult to hit as any pitcher in the league. But "unfortunately for him and the Giants, he is just right only at rare intervals."[61] His inconsistency meant McGraw would be hesitant to use him against the Athletics.

Even with the absence of Coombs, the Athletics' pitching staff was likewise anchored by two of the game's greatest: Eddie Plank and Chief Bender. Like Mathewson, Plank was a collegian, Mathewson having attended the east-central Pennsylvania college of Bucknell, while Plank had attended Gettysburg College, site of the Civil War battle waged exactly 50 years earlier. Also like Mathewson, Plank had been in the major leagues since 1901. Plank was a hard throwing left-hander with a "cross-fire" style of pitching which made it difficult for the batter to focus on the ball. Along with his speed, Plank also had a sharp breaking curve. This combination of pitches could spell trouble for the

Giants, for "in spite of the fact that the Giants have improved in their batting against left-handers, a good left-hander ought not to be troubled by them."[62] But also like Mathewson, Plank's age could be of concern to Mack, as it was to some sportswriters. "It has been stated with increasing emphasis that Old Man Plank was all in, that he has reached that stage of decrepitude where he totters around feebly and as soon as the games with New York are over he will be laid away to sleep peacefully at Gettysburg with the rest of the old soldiers."[63] Despite his "advanced" age of 38 years, Plank had been the winner in 18 of 28 decisions during the season. Of the 30 games in which he was the starting pitcher, Plank completed 18, a smaller proportion of complete games than in previous years. As the season progressed, he had to be relieved more frequently. But Mack had a strong second tier of pitching for relief if Plank were to tire.

Mack's other ace was Bender, a veteran of 11 major league seasons. Bender had been victorious in 21 of 31 decisions during the year, in addition to a league-leading 13 saves (a statistic not calculated at the time). The right-handed Bender had a good fastball to accompany a sharp curve and the ability to place the ball wherever he desired. Bender was considered by some as "the best one game pitcher in the world."[64] Bender had pitched a complete game shutout back in the 1905 Series against these Giants, the only victorious Athletics pitcher in that series. He had also been the winner of one game in the 1910 Series against the Cubs, and was the winning pitcher in two of three decisions in the 1911 Series. His ERA during that 1911 Series against this Giants team had been 1.04, about as low as anyone could expect against a team as powerful as the one he had faced.

Backing up the two mainstays on the staff were youngsters Joe Bush, Bob Shawkey and Byron Houck. Bush was not yet 21 years old, but had won 15 of 21 decisions during the season, pitching primarily in relief roles. Houck, a 22-year-old in the last full season of a short career in the majors, had won 14 of 20 decisions for Mack, while Shawkey, the oldest of the trio at 23, had just completed his rookie season with six wins in 11 decisions. Shawkey at times had been "brilliant," and was considered as the relief pitcher of choice by the writers.[65] Houck, on the other hand, had a strong repertoire of pitches but was plagued by control problems, as indicated by his 122 walks in the 176 innings in which he pitched. As was the case in general for the entire Athletics' staff, the trio seemed to tire in the late stages of the season.

"It is reasonable to suppose that neither Bender, Plank nor Mathewson will be as effective against the batsmen as they were two years ago. Marquard, as a result of his additional experience and knowledge, should be, on paper at least, better than in 1911. But the fact remains, that the lanky left-hander is not pitching the brand of ball he did in 1912 [when he won 26 games]."[66] In the case of the first three, advancing age could play a significant role in whether they could continue being effective in a World's Series following the long season. Still, in the words of writer Harry Williams, "Although all the others [referring to the cast of the 1905 adversaries] have surrendered their places to players of a younger generation, it is on the work of these three veterans [Bender, Plank and Mathewson] who bore the brunt of the battle eight years ago, on which the result of the coming series is generally conceded to hinge."[67]

CHAPTER SIX

Game One

Even before the series began, a controversy erupted regarding whether the ballplayers should be allowed to write newspaper articles describing events taking place on the field. Ballplayers had written, or at least "ghost written," such articles in the past with few complaints. Johnny Evers, for example, though a member of the 1910 National League champion Cubs, had contributed to news media, as had former White Sox player and manager Fielder Jones."[2] Evers, though a member of the Cubs, had broken his leg near the end of the season, and was unable to play; Jones likewise was not a participant in the series. Even the previous year, several Giants had contributed articles to newspapers, including pitcher Jeff Tesreau and Manager McGraw.[3, 4] So what was the problem?

Apparently the members of the Baseball Writers Association had complained to the National Baseball Commission.[5] It really amounted to a "turf" battle in which the writers perceived the players were invading their professional field, and though perhaps unsaid, being paid handsomely for it. The BWA had been formed in October, 1908, with membership open to baseball writers from newspapers around the country. The object was to "promote uniformity in scoring methods, to act in conjunction with the leagues in rules revision, suggestions, and *to gain control over baseball press boxes, the conduct of which is a sore point among baseball men all over the country*" (italics added).[6] Joe S. Jackson, sportswriter from Detroit, was elected as first president. Membership included such distinguished writers as I.E. Sanborn from Chicago, Hugh Fullerton from New York and Tony Murnane in Boston.

In his letter to the National Commission in September, 1913, President Jackson wrote:

> Owing to this evil [i.e., articles contributed by the players], we, the newspaper men, are forced to do something to protect ourselves against a growing evil that threatens baseball reporters in a pecuniary way. [Ay, "there's the rub!"[7]] It also is making the reports of world series ridiculous, and must, in a way, hurt the series itself eventually. And it further belittles in the minds of the public, the trained baseball writer who labors all the year around as a competent critic, to be subordinated to a novice in the one biggest week of the baseball year. The commission will have the support and co-operation of this association in any move it may take to eradicate the evil that has been discussed.[8]

The National Commission's response supported the petition from the sportswriters. It ruled that "no players, eligible to compete in the world's series or any city series shall write, or pretend to write [addressing "ghost written" articles] an account of such series for any newspapers, nor shall any player allow the use of his name over an article purporting to be written by him. Violation of this order will result in the infliction of such penalty as the commission may determine."[9]

The National Commission even went so far as to imply the series would be canceled if players decided to test the ruling by continuing to write such articles for newspapers that presumably would include a byline with the player's name.[10] Presumably if the bylines appeared only after the first game was played, the commission, if indeed it decided to strictly enforce its decision, would either postpone or cancel the series unless the players agreed to discontinue the practice.

The players, to say the least, did not kindly look upon the commission's ruling. Dave Fultz, former Athletics outfielder and current president of the baseball players fraternity, issued a statement regarding to the ruling. "We do not pass upon the status of the player-author, as in our opinion that matter rests entirely with the player and the paper itself.... But, if our support should become necessary to enable one of our members to carry out a contract into which he has had a perfect right to enter and into which another has entered with him in good faith, we would back him up to the limit."[11] In a later statement, Fultz further elaborated upon the opinion of the player's fraternity: "We cannot believe that Mr. [Ban] Johnson made any such foolish statement [re: canceling the series]. In his position, at the head of a big business which relies for its stability upon the binding force of contracts, he could hardly afford to advocate the disregard of the contractual obligation wherever it suited a party's fancy. Nor would he wish to meet the large damage suits the players would be liable for in case they violated their contracts.... The public still has some rights, and big business is fast learning this fact."[12] Two of the players who apparently had agreed to author articles for newspapers were Athletics Eddie Collins and Frank Baker. In support of his players, and the fraternity as well, manager Connie Mack stated he would support his players if they decided to write newspaper articles during the series.[13]

The players' viewpoint was not unanimous. An editorial in the *Times* opined:

These men, whatever the grievances of their state — which in moments of irritation they call "slavery" — entered into it voluntarily and can escape from it whenever they choose. They are well, some say extravagantly, paid for their services, and their employers can fairly expect to have the exclusive use of their energies, mental as well as physical. Writing for the press is inevitably a distraction of the player's attention from his professional activities, and even when, as rumor whispers is sometimes the case, the star performer writes no more than his name at the end of

his supposed article, he yet may cause dissensions and controversies that his owners find troublesome.[14]

Of course, one of the owners who did not seem to find this "troublesome"
was Mack.[15]

The potential consequences of a players' lawsuit were significant. The issue
of calling off the series aside, the sanctity of the contract between the players
and newspapers, and one must not forget the likely core of the dispute, a significant amount of money, were also on the table. Using the previous year's
series as the basis for his argument, President Fultz pointed out that the amount
of money at issue here approximated $150,000 (or more precisely in his calcu-
lations, $147,572.28).[16] Here Fultz also cites the contract entered into by the
players and owners in the national agreement, in which it was stated that a
post-season series between the two league champions would be played. Therefore, the players had certain "vested rights." To call off the series would "deprive
a player of his vested rights, and naturally those who would call off the series
would be liable."[17]

"The National Commission could hardly be sued as a body, but there would
be nothing to prevent the players from bringing suits against the members of
the commission individually."[18] Fultz, as a representative of the fraternity, to
his credit did attempt to observe the controversy from the writers' viewpoint.
The practice was in some respects unfair to the writers.[19] But the players and
newspaper publishers also had valid contracts, entered into in good faith. If the
BWA and the National Commission wished to take issue with the practice, the
time to do so would have been before the signing of any such contracts, not
just prior to the beginning of the series. Certainly the situation was not unique
to 1913.

In the end, a compromise of sorts was reached. The National Commission
decided that it would not penalize any players if there were extenuating circumstances. Among these circumstances was that if the contract between the
player and the newspaper had been signed prior to September 27, the date of
the commission's ruling, the player would not be penalized. After the completion of the series, players who had written articles for the newspapers would
be called before the commission and would be asked to show their contracts.
Only agreements signed after September 27 would result in any (undefined)
penalties.[20] Ban Johnson said he had discussed the problem with manager Connie Mack, who assured him that second baseman Eddie Collins had signed his
agreement prior to September 27, and would therefore not be affected by the
ban.[21]

After the completion of the series, John McGraw went before the commission to discuss a proposed tour of the world he planned for both the Giants
and Chicago White Sox, and while doing so brought up the issue of players
serving as authors. McGraw admitted that members of his own club, includ-

ing himself, had been the primary abusers of the system of player-authors. "It is dishonest in a way, because few of the players write or dictate their stuff and some never see it. I have never written a line of my articles myself, though I have looked over them before they went into print. For a long time, I refused to allow the use of my name. Then, when I saw that everyone else was getting the money while posing as authors, I decided that I would be foolish to refuse it."[22]

The commission decided that it would withhold the monetary share of the series from the affected players until they submitted their respective contracts. Only those players who signed such contracts after September 27 would be fined. Affected players included McGraw, Mathewson, Marquard, Doyle and Meyers on the Giants, Collins and Baker from the Athletics, and non-series participants Hugh Jennings, Ty Cobb and Rabbit Maranville of the National League Boston club.[23] In the end, the commission decided not to punish any of the players, merely letting them off with a "don't do it again warning."[24] And so at last the games could be decided on the field.

Game One

Based on the decision empowered by the flip of a half-dollar coin, the series opened at the Polo Grounds on October 7, where once again the New York crowds had gone mad. McGraw's choice for opening game pitcher was Rube Marquard. Superstition would have suggested Mathewson for the important role of opening game pitcher, since he twice was the winning pitcher in first contests. Marquard, on the other hand, had won twice in the 1912 Series, and so became McGraw's choice. Mack started one of his "old" (both a figurative and literal designation) reliable aces, Chief Bender. The primary change McGraw carried out was in center field, where regular outfielder Fred Snodgrass was still bothered by the "charley-horse" he had developed near the end of the season. McGraw placed Tillie Shafer in Snodgrass' usual position, and placed Buck Herzog back in his regular position of third base. Shafer would lead off for the Giants. Second baseman Larry Doyle was also doubtful until game time as a result of a painful shoulder. Speculation was that if both Doyle and Snodgrass were unable to start, Eddie Grant would replace Doyle at second.[25] Mack's Athletics, in contrast, appeared in perfect condition.

Since ground rules differed somewhat in the National League as compared with those in the American League, the umpires, Bill Klem and Cy Rigler from the National League, with Tom Connolly and John "Rip" Egan representing the American League, were instructed by the National Commission to follow National League rules in New York and American League rules when playing in Philadelphia.[26] The differences, while seemingly minor, could potentially affect the outcome of a game. The infield fly rule in the National League permitted the runner to stand away from the base until the ball was caught or

Discussion of ground rules prior to Game One of the 1913 World's Series. Danny Murphy (left), Philadelphia team captain; Cy Rigler, left-field umpire; Bill Klem, home plate; Rip Egan, infield; Tom Connolly, right field; and John McGraw (Baseball Hall of Fame, Cooperstown, New York).

dropped; if dropped, the runner could continue to the next base. In the American League, base runners could not leave the base until the ball was caught or dropped. In the National League, a balk was called if the pitcher dropped the ball while in the act of pitching; in the American League, it was not.[27] Official scorers were Francis Richter from Philadelphia and J. Taylor Spink from St. Louis. In the event of a tie decision between the scorers, President Jackson of the BWA would break the tie.

The initial forecast called for possible rain, then was changed to simply an overcast day. Betting, while commonplace at such events, was not as heavy as observed in previous years; each team was a 10–9 favorite, the difference being the city in which the particular game was being played.[28] Only a single large bet was reported, a $1,000 wager at 2–1 on the Giants.[29] Reserved seats for the three games in New York were available only as a package, and ranged as high as $50–100 depending upon location.[30] Scalpers, of course, seemed to have plenty of tickets to sell. There were 8,000 reserved seats, with unreserved tickets available for sale at 8:00 A.M. the day of the game. Individual box seats purchased the day of the game were $25 in New York, while the price of bleacher seats was $1.[31]

The Athletics arrived in New York on October 6, and stayed at the Hotel Somerset, while the baseball writers holed up at the Hotel Imperial.[32] One hundred and fifty policemen were available for crowd control and player protection. Even the United States Congress, allegedly in session, was following the series. Republican House leader James Mann, just returning from a three-week vacation — the more things change, the more they seem to remain the same — was forced to adjourn Congress for the day as the chamber was 47 representatives short of a quorum. While waiting, however, Mann did find it necessary to announce that Home Run Baker had done so again, in the fifth inning off Marquard.[33]

At the site of the upcoming contest, a crowd growing to some 500 men and boys began arriving as early as midnight to buy tickets as soon as they went on sale. The first of these hearty souls, one John Harris, a chauffer living on West 49th Street, had taken his place in line at 4:00 P.M. the day before.[34] Minutes later, a second fan, Edward Pfeiffer from West 118th Street, took his place behind Harris. Much like the situation today when lines begin to form for tickets to events or grand openings, local merchants served sandwiches and hot coffee.

As the crowd gathered, the players entered the field about 1:00 P.M. through the gate located in deep center field. Typical of the informal atmosphere of the times, both newsmen as well as professional and amateur photographers joined the players on the field. "If you had a nickel for every picture that was taken, you could spend the winter at Palm Beach."[35] Even the players were caught up in the friendly atmosphere, albeit prior to the point at which the game was on the line. Manager John McGraw, certainly no proponent of player camaraderie with opponents, nevertheless went to the Athletics' bench where he shook hands with Eddie Collins and reserve outfielder Danny Murphy. "They seemed so friendly that you'd honestly believe they loved each other."[36] Frank Baker and Buck Herzog, teammates in the long ago in Maryland, shook hands for the photographers while the band played *There's a Girl in the Heart of Maryland.* Another cheer went up from the crowd as New York Mayor Ardolph Loges Kline, accompanied by an army major general, Thomas Barry, entered the field, shook hands with Christy Mathewson, and sat down in his box. McGraw was then asked to stand near home plate, where he was joined by Democratic Mayoral candidate Edward McCall, Commission Chairman Garry Herrmann and 19th century star Arthur Irwin, where McGraw was presented with a basket of flowers donated by Frank Chance and the Yankees.[37] While the photographers were snapping their pictures, one of them realized that the new Mrs. Marquard, more popularly known as vaudevillian actress and entertainer Blossom Seeley, was sitting nearby. The fascination with celebrity is not unique to current times, and so the twenty-two year-old Miss Seeley was also "subjected" to media attention. Though the Seeley and Marquard marriage would eventually dissolve, she remained a prominent actress for decades, and lived long enough to appear on the popular television show of the 1960's, *The Ed Sullivan Show.* Other celebrities in attendance almost read like a Who's Who in the sports, political and entertainment industries: Pennsylvania governor, and former professional ball player for "Cap" Anson's Chicago Colts, John Tener (who the following year would be elected president of the National League); Albert Spalding, traveling from his home in California; George Wright; Al Reach; George M. Cohan; Al Jolson; and Eddie Foy, among dozens of other notables for the times.[38] Finally after all preliminaries were completed, Manager McGraw and Athletics captain Danny Murphy met at the plate to cover the ground rules with the four umpires. Klem took his place behind the plate, with Egan in the infield. Rigler went to left field and Connolly to right.

The 1913 World's Series officially started at 2:00 P.M. on October 7, before an official paying crowd of 36,291, an increase of 500 patrons from the year

Polo Grounds, home of both the New York Giants and the New York Yankees in 1913, ready for the World Series. Ready for occupancy in June 1911, New York's first concrete and steel stadium replaced an earlier one that had burned. Located near Coogan's Bluff at West 159th Street in upper Manhattan, the Giants played there until the franchise moved to California in 1958. The structure served as home for the expansion New York Mets through 1963, after which it underwent demolition (Library of Congress, Bain Collection).

before. Marquard was on the mound for the Giants, Bender for Mack's Athletics in the bottom of the inning. John Brush Hempstead, son of Giants president Harry Hempstead and grandson of John Brush, a Civil War veteran and owner of the Giants until his death the previous November, had the honor of throwing out the ceremonial first-pitch. Klem threw the ball to Marquard and the teams were ready. Eddie Murphy led off for the American League champion, hitting a first pitch fly ball to right fielder Red Murray to start the game. Following a first-pitch strike, Rube Oldring followed with the first hit of the series, a single to right field just past the glove of second baseman Larry Doyle. Oldring became a little anxious after several tosses by Marquard to first, strayed too far from the bag, and was picked off base on a snap throw from Marquard to first baseman Fred Merkle. Oldring briefly argued with umpire Bill Klem that Marquard had balked, but the complaint was to no avail. Eddie Collins singled, which brought Frank Baker to the plate. Baker had earned his nickname "Home Run" in part as a result of the four-bagger he hit off Marquard back in the 1911 Series. Like Marquard, Baker was experienced in the postseason, and was not one to succumb to early pressure. However, this time Marquard had the better of him, as Baker hit a high fly that left fielder George Burns pulled in.

The day was overcast as Bender took the mound, the kind of weather that could make it difficult to pick up a fastball. A periodic drizzle made conditions even more difficult. Bender was no youngster, but he was still capable of a strong outing or two when given sufficient rest. And the gray skies were certainly to his benefit. Tillie Shafer, replacing the injured Snodgrass in centerfield, led off for the Giants. Shafer worked Bender to a full count, three and two, but sent an easy fly ball to rightfielder Eddie Murphy. Second batter Larry Doyle flied to Amos Strunk in left-center field. With two outs, shortstop Art Fletcher singled for the Giants' first hit. However, with George Burns at bat, Fletcher attempted to steal on Bender's first pitch. Wally Schang, Mack's starting rookie at that position, threw a perfect strike to Eddie Collins, covering the second base bag. The ball arrived before Fletcher had begun to slide. Collins easily tagged Fletcher out, and the first inning ended with no score.

Stuffy McInnis led off the second for the Mackmen, hitting a ground ball to Giant third baseman Buck Herzog, who threw McInnis out at first. Amos Strunk followed, and on four pitches became Marquard's first strikeout. Jack Barry hit a bounding ball to Fletcher at shortstop, who tossed to Merkle at first, and the Athletics were retired easily in order. In the bottom of the second, Burns, who had been at bat when Fletcher was caught stealing, led off against Bender. After waiting out a 3–1 count, Burns watched as the old right-hander tossed two straight strikes, catching Burns off guard, and providing Bender with his first strikeout. Herzog followed with another full count, and bounced a grounder to first where McInnis simply stepped on the bag. Red Murray hit a solid single to left field. Murray attempted to steal on Bender's first pitch to

Giants catcher Chief Meyers. But Meyers swung, hitting a weak fly ball that Oldring grabbed just beyond the infield. After two innings, the game was scoreless.

Marquard continued to look strong through the third inning. Rookie Wally Schang, batting for the first time in the postseason, hit a Marquard pitch off

Rube Marquard (1912) was called "the $11,000 lemon," reflecting the price McGraw paid for his contract and the pitcher's slow start in his career. But Marquard went on to win 201 games in an 18 year Hall of Fame career. He had 23 victories in 1913, giving him his third consecutive 20-victory season for the left-hander (Library of Congress, Bain Collection).

the handle of his bat, and lofted an easy fly ball to leftfielder Burns, bringing Bender to the plate. Bender was no slouch with the bat. He managed to hit six home runs in his career, including three in one season back in 1906. In the 1910 World's Series, he hit .333, with two hits in six at-bats. Bender hit a ground ball to Fletcher at short, who made a poor throw to Merkle at first, pulling him briefly from the bag. Bender, however, assuming the play would be an easy out, merely jogged to first, allowing Merkle time to recover and step on the bag for the out. Murphy followed with a line drive over the head of second baseman Doyle, putting an Athletic on first again. But once again, Marquard held his opponents, as Oldring hit a high bouncing grounder to shortstop. Fletcher grabbed the ball and stepped on second, forcing Murphy and ending the Athletics' half of the inning with no score.

The Giants drew first blood in their half of the third inning. Fred Merkle led off with a slow grounder to shortstop. Jack Barry briefly fumbled Merkle's hit, and despite recovering with a fast throw to first, the ball was beaten out by the hard-running Merkle. Merkle received a hit on the play. Marquard bunted the ball towards the right side of the infield. Collins grabbed the ball, throwing out Marquard, while Merkle took second base on the sacrifice. Shafer flied out for the second time, this time to Strunk in center-field, but too shallow to allow Merkle to advance. However, the left-handed hitting Doyle hit Bender's first pitch on a solid line to right, scoring Merkle who slid in ahead of Murphy's throw. Fletcher ended the inning with a fly out to right fielder Murphy. After three full innings, the Giants led, 1–0.

Marquard's effectiveness ended with the fourth inning. Leading off, Eddie Collins smashed Marquard's pitch into deep center field, where Shafer grabbed the ball just before it bounced into the hollyhocks growing by the fence. Collins ended up at third base with this, his second hit of the game. After fouling Marquard's first pitch, Frank Baker followed with a bouncing hit just off the glove of second baseman Larry Doyle, enabling Collins to score the tying run on the hit. As Christy Mathewson began to warm up out in right field, McInnis bunted the first pitch back to Marquard, who tossed the ball to Merkle, and Baker stood on second. Strunk smashed a hard grounder that Marquard grabbed before it passed through the pitcher's box and threw a strike to third base. Herzog tagged the sliding Baker for a close second out, providing hope for the yelling crowd that Marquard might work his way out of the jam. McGraw even signaled Mathewson to sit down. But Jack Barry bounced a pitch down the line at third base, the ball ending up at an advertising sign for whiskey on the left-field fence. Moments later Barry trotted into second base with a double, while Strunk held up at third. Schang, who had flied out leading off the previous inning, took ball one from Marquard, then hammered the next pitch into right-center field. Shafer, running towards the diamond at full speed, slightly misplayed the ball, stopped, and barely touched the ball as he turned to make the catch, the hit just beyond his reach. As the ball continued rolling, both Strunk and Barry scored, while Schang slid into third ahead of the throw. Arguably, Shafer could have made the catch on Schang's drive, which was called a hit.[39] The second triple of the inning had sent Philadelphia into a 3–1 lead. Bender ended the inning with a hard grounder back to the mound that Marquard grabbed and tossed to Merkle.

The Giants quickly had the chance to regain momentum. Burns bounced Bender's first pitch down the third-base line for a double, but was cut down at third when Herzog hit a pitch back to the pitcher and Bender threw to Baker for the tag. Murray struck out on three pitches, the last being an unexpected curve from Bender. Meyers ended the inning and short-lived rally with a fly to Oldring in left field.

The Athletics continued to hammer Marquard and build on their lead in the fifth inning. Murphy attempted to bunt his way on with the first pitch in the inning. He hit the ball a little too hard, and Marquard grabbed it, tossing to Merkle for the first out. Oldring followed with a slow grounder towards third. With a strong defensive play, Marquard hustled over, grabbed the slow bounder, and threw again to Merkle for the second out of the inning. Eddie Collins, already with two hits, including the fourth-inning triple, worked a 3–1 count before walking. This again brought the ever-dangerous Home Run Baker to the plate. One might wonder whether in those days of relatively few home runs if Marquard might have felt a sense of "deja vu." Baker, after all, had twice homered in the 1911 Series, one of which had been against Marquard, and with the single in his previous at-bat, was hitting .400 over the course of his World's Series appearances. Baker watched as Marquard's first pitch split the plate for a strike; Collins stole second on the pitch. Baker would not allow a second pitch to pass. On a high curve, the powerful left-handed hitting Baker pulled the pitch, smacking the ball into the right-field bleachers for his third home run against the Giants in postseason play. Marquard finished the inning with a short fly by McInnis to shortstop Fletcher. But the damage was done, and the Athletic lead was now 5–1.

The Giants once again attempted a comeback. Fred Merkle began the rally with a single to center field. Part-time outfielder Moose McCormick pinch-hit for Marquard and followed Merkle's single with one of his own past second base, Merkle stopping at second on the short hit. Tillie Shafer hit a slow ground ball to second that Collins easily handled, throwing the fast Shafer out at first, but allowing both Merkle and McCormick to advance to third and second, respectively. Larry Doyle grounded to shortstop Barry, whose poor throw to first allowed Merkle to score the Giants' second run of the game. Unlike Barry's earlier "bobble," he was given an error on the play. McCormick ended up on third base on the play, while Doyle remained at first. Another run scored when Fletcher poked an opposite-field single to right, and Doyle slid into third. This brought up George Burns, who already had doubled against Bender the previous inning. This time, however, Burns grounded to Baker at third base. Baker tossed to Collins at second, forcing Fletcher but allowing Doyle to score the third run of the inning for the Giants. With Burns at first, the tying run come to the plate with the name of Buck Herzog. However, the rally ended when Herzog popped the first pitch to Eddie Collins. The Athletics still led, but the Giants had narrowed the margin to a more manageable 5–4.

With Marquard out of the game via a pinch-hitter, Doc Crandall came in to pitch the sixth for the Giants. The right-handed Crandall had appeared in 35 games during the season, all but three in relief. Crandall stilled the Athletics' bats. Amos Strunk hit a fly ball to right-center field where Shafer made a fine running catch. Jack Barry followed with another fly, this time to left-center field where Shafer made the catch, barely moving from his position. Schang completed the top half of the inning with another outfield fly ball, this time to Burns in left field.

For two consecutive innings, the Giants had begun to hit Bender with some authority, though only in the previous inning had they managed to score. Though it appeared McGraw's men had acquired some momentum, Bender managed to settle down for his half of the sixth. Red Murray grounded out to Collins at second, while Meyers hit a similar grounder grabbed by Bender, who tossed the Giant catcher out at first. Merkle worked the count to three balls and two strikes, then swung ineffectually at the sixth pitch. Umpire Bill Klem behind the plate was distracted and missed the swing. Thinking the pitch was a ball, Klem sent Merkle to first. Needless to say, the Athletics protested, and Umpire Egan ruled that Merkle indeed had swung and missed, ending the inning. But more than simply a strikeout had taken place on the play. While turning to run to first, Merkle's spikes had caught, causing him to twist his ankle. Merkle would finish the game, but the ankle swelled and would have an impact on his future play.[40]

Crandall continued his short mastery of the Athletics in the seventh inning. Bender, leading off, struck out. Murphy grounded to Doyle at second base, who threw to Merkle for the second out. Rube Oldring finished the inning with a short fly over second, which Shafer grabbed in center field. The Giants, in their half of the seventh, attempted to again rally. Crandall was actually respectable as a hitter, hitting .306 in 49 at-bats during the season. His 15 hits included four doubles and a triple. In ten seasons, Doc compiled a lifetime hitting average of .285, including nine home runs. This time, however, Crandall merely grounded out to short, Barry to McInnis. Shafer started a rally with a single to center field. Doyle followed with a single to right field, and Shafer steamed into third. At this point in the game, with only a one-run lead, the Athletics had the choice of either playing for a double play and possibly allowing Shafer to score, or playing in position to cut Shafer off at home. They elected for the double play. The gamble paid off when Fletcher hit a sharp ground ball to Barry. Fielding the ball perfectly, Barry flipped the ball to Collins at second, who relayed the throw to McInnis at first. Once again Bender had stopped a Giant rally, this time with critical help from his defense.

For the third time, Crandall went to the box to face his American League opponents. Eddie Collins caught him flat-footed with a bunt single, his third hit of the game. Baker followed with Collins with his own third hit of the game, this time a single to left-center, Collins racing to third. McInnis slugged the third consecutive hit, a double that landed near the left-field line. Collins scored for the third time that day, and Baker slid into third. McGraw had seen enough. With the game nearly out of hand, Crandall was removed, and Jeff Tesreau, the 6'2" fastballer, entered the game. Strunk, the next batter, had apparently been given orders to bunt, the goal being to squeeze another run across the plate. Strunk, however, struck out on three pitches with what appeared to be Tesreau's spitballs. Moments later the Giants caught McInnis straying off second base on what may have started out as a hit-and-run with Jack Barry at-bat. Tesreau threw a pitch high to Meyers, who fired the ball to Doyle at second. At the same time Meyers was throwing to Doyle to catch McInnis off the bag, Baker made a break for home. Doyle's throw back to the plate caught Baker sliding in, and two were out.[41] McInnis remained at second. The inning ended when Barry hit a short pop-out to Doyle at second, but now the Athletics had a two run lead, 6–4.

George Burns led off for the Giants in the bottom of the inning, grounding to Baker at third, who threw to McInnis for the first out. Buck Herzog grounded to Collins for the second out. Red Murray kept the Giants alive with a ball that bounced off Baker's glove, beating out the late throw from shortstop Barry. Chief Meyers ended the inning with a fly to right-center, Strunk making another good running catch.

Tesreau returned to the slab in the ninth for the Giants. Schang bounced a pitch to third, where Herzog grabbed the ball with a leap, tossing out the runner at first. Bender grounded back to Tesreau, who threw to Merkle for the second out with time to spare since Bender again neglected to run out his hit. Murphy walked, becoming the first hitter to reach base since Tesreau replaced Crandall. However, the top of the inning ended when Eddie Murphy was caught trying to steal on a throw from Meyers to Doyle.

The Giants now were reduced to their final three outs. The question before Mack was whether he should remain with Bender, who had already thrown more than 100 pitches—not a particularly large number for a younger man. He had also allowed 11 hits by Giant batters, though the absence of any walks suggested Bender had retained his control. In the end, Mack's decision was to allow Bender to finish his game. Merkle grounded to Barry on the first pitch. Substitute catcher Larry McLean pinch-hit for Tesreau, but managed only a short fly to Jack Barry. Tillie Shafer ended what was an easy inning for Bender by becoming the fourth strikeout for Bender, two hours and six minutes after the official start. The Athletics left the field as 6–4 winners, and led in the series one game to none.

The primary difference between the two teams was Athletic power. Eddie

Collins and Frank Baker led the attack with three hits apiece, including a triple by Collins and home run by Baker. Collins scored three of the Athletics' six runs, while Baker drove in three. Wally Schang, a rookie appearing in his first World's Series, likewise contributed a triple, driving in two runs and helping drive Marquard from the game. Crandall was treated no better, giving up the sixth and final run by the Athletics. Bender, in turn, had also been hit hard at times, but only in one inning — the fifth when the Giants scored three times — did it appear he was significantly off his game.

Game One, October 7, 1913, at Polo Grounds[42]

Philadelphia Athletics	Ab	R	H	RBI	New York Giants	Ab	R	H	RBI
Murphy (RF)	4	0	1	0	Shafer (CF)	5	0	1	0
Oldring (LF)	4	0	1	0	Doyle (2b)	4	1	2	2
Collins (2b)	3	3	3	0	Fletcher (SS)	4	0	2	1
Baker (3b)	4	1	3	3	Burns (LF)	4	0	1	1
McInnis (1b)	3	0	1	1	Herzog (3b)	4	0	0	0
Strunk (CF)	4	1	0	0	Murray (RF)	4	0	2	0
Barry (SS)	4	1	1	0	Meyers (C)	4	0	0	0
Schang (C)	4	0	1	2	Merkle (1b)	4	2	2	0
Bender (P)	4	0	0	0	Marquard (P)	0	0	0	0
Totals	34	6	11	6	McCormick (PH)	1	1	1	0
					Crandall (P)	1	0	0	0
					Tesreau (P)	0	0	0	0
					McLean (PH)	1	0	0	0
					Totals	36	4	11	4

Philadelphia	0	0	0	3	2	0	0	1	0–6	11	1
New York	0	0	1	0	3	0	0	0	0–4	11	0

Philadelphia Athletics	IP	H	R	ER	BB	SO
Bender (W, 1–0)	9.0	11	4	3	0	4
New York Giants						
Marquard (L, 0–1)	5.0	8	5	5	1	1
Crandall	2.0	3	1	1	0	1
Tesreau	2.0	0	0	0	1	1

Error: Barry; 2B-Barry, McInnis, Burns; 3B-Collins, Schang; HR-Baker; SB-Collins; Time: 2:06; Att.: 36,291

CHAPTER SEVEN

Game Two

New York was not the only site where crowds followed the series. The area around city hall on Broad and Market streets in downtown Philadelphia were likewise packed with fans and/or motor cars, stretching to the theater district, watching the results as they were posted on an electric scoreboard. Baseball scoreboards could be observed up and down Chestnut Street, and wherever the scores were being posted, crowds were gathered. Trains brought fans back from New York, where hundreds had attended the game. Likewise, the Athletic players themselves who were brought home to Philadelphia following the victory could be observed working their way through the crowds at night. Home Run Baker, carrying his suitcase and a bat after disembarking from the North Philadelphia train station, was followed by dozens of fans who recognized one of the heroes of the first-game victory. Stuffy McInnis, walking with Baker, helped open a path through the crowd of admirers, who in its enthusiasm might injure the stars.[1]

The rain, which had largely held off through the first contest in New York, let loose in Philadelphia, leaving a damp field of play at Shibe Park for October 8. Athletic patrons who had purchased reserve seats, believing that such ducats would allow them the freedom of arriving at game time instead of having to sit hours in the damp conditions of the stadium, seemed to arrive en masse at game time. The result was a crush at the gates, and some patrons did not reach their seats until the second inning.[2] Some 5,000 fans were also waiting at the gate to purchase the 4,000 bleacher seats, which went on sale at $1 per ticket. Every ten feet was a policeman.

Prior to the game, Mathewson, Tesreau and Demaree each warmed up on the sidelines, while only Plank could be seen on the Athletics' side of the field. The Giants wore their blue-gray road uniforms. Not only were the Giants one game down as they prepared to face their American League opponents on their home turf, the "fates" themselves seemed to be rooting for Philadelphia. Fred Merkle's ankle, twisted the previous day, remained swollen despite the efforts of the Giant trainers to treat the injury the previous night. Fred Snodgrass was still less than 100 percent with a "charley-horse" that refused to respond to treatment, though he might be able to play in an emergency. And then, just prior to the end of practice before the start of the second game, catcher Chief Meyers split the thumb on his throwing hand as he reached for a pitch close to the ground, possibly breaking a finger. As Meyers walked off the field, clearly unable to play, McGraw "threw out his hands in a gesture that clearly indicated despair."[3]

Despite his injury, Snodgrass was tagged by McGraw to start at first base in place of Merkle. Shafer would remain in center field, and Herzog stayed at third base. In place of the injured Meyers, Larry McLean was inserted into the starting lineup. Mathewson would be the starting pitcher for the Giants—no surprise there, though with Tesreau and Demaree warming up alongside of Matty, confirmation of the starting pitcher took place only just prior to the beginning of the game. Plank was Mack's equally non-surprising opponent. The match-up was a repeat of the game that took place eight years earlier, when the equally youthful hurlers at that time faced off in the 1905 World's Series. Mathewson won that contest against Plank and the Athletics, pitching a 3–0 shutout in the opening game. The victory was one of three shutouts tossed by the tall right-hander in that series. He had been less successful in recent years, winning one of three decisions against these same Athletics in 1911, and neither of the two decisions the previous year against the Red Sox.

At 1:30 P.M., Walter Johnson, star pitcher for Washington, appeared at home plate, driving the Chalmers automobile he was receiving as most valuable player in the American League that season. After officially obtaining the key, he drove back off to a cheering crowd.[4] That crowd was officially listed as 20,563, a drop-off from previous post-season attendance, likely due in part to a combination of inclement weather, the ruling that patrons could not sit on the field, and the flat rooftops on the two-story houses outside the bleachers on Twentieth Street where fans could sit and watch the game either for free or at most a nominal fee to the owners. Among the attendees was Governor John Tener, staying at the downtown Bellevue-Stratford Hotel.[5]

At 2:00 P.M., the game began. Mack's only positional change from the previous day was inserting Jack Lapp as Plank's catcher, in place of Wally Schang. Otherwise the order of the lineup was the same. Tom Connolly was the umpire behind the plate for this second game of the series, Rigler on the bases. Third baseman Buck Herzog led off for the Giants instead of Tillie Shafer, worked the count to two balls and a strike, and then hit a short fly ball that second baseman Eddie Collins grabbed in right field. Larry Doyle followed Herzog, and after taking one ball, got his bat on a Plank curve and flied to Amos Strunk in center field. Art Fletcher batted third again, fouled off two pitches, and struck out on an outside fastball.

Mathewson proceeded to the slab, with McLean as his catcher in place of the injured Meyers. Eddie Murphy led off for the Athletics, and after working the count to two balls and two strikes, smacked the next pitch on a slow roll towards second baseman Larry Doyle. In his hurry to grab the ball, Doyle briefly

Eddie Murphy batting (1914). The 1913 season was the first as a regular outfielder for Murphy, who batted .295. In 1919, playing with the infamous Chicago White Sox, Murphy earned the nickname "Honest Eddie" since he was not involved in the fixing scandal (Library of Congress, Bain Collection).

fumbled it, allowing Murphy to reach base safely. Rube Oldring followed, and after fouling off one pitch and taking a called strike on the second, hit a single into left field. Murphy stopped at second, and the Athletics had two men on with nobody out. Eddie Collins, playing the inside baseball for which he was noted, bunted the first pitch up the first-base line. Snodgrass, sore leg and all, rushed in and threw a strike to Doyle covering his bag. Collins was out, but the sacrifice worked; men were now on second and third, and the always dangerous Home Run Baker came to bat. While it is unfair to put thoughts into the mind of another, Mathewson's history with Baker, and unquestionable awareness of the damage he had created the previous day, must have been in the pitcher's mind. Baker took the first pitch for a ball, then fouled off two more. Mathewson came back with a low pitch, Baker swung—and struck out. Stuffy McInnis, with one hit and an RBI the day before, had less power than Baker, but was still capable of inflicting damage. It nearly occurred as McInnis hit the pitch on a fly near the left-field line. Burns, however, made a good running grab to end the inning and prevent any significant damage.

Shibe Park, Game Two. Lefty Eddie Plank on the mound, with "the $100,000 infield" in position: Frank Baker at third, Jack Barry at shortstop, Eddie Collins at second (at extreme right edge above McInnis), and Stuffy McInnis on first (Library of Congress, Bain Collection).

Modern sportscasters from time to time report the myth which suggests when a player ends an inning with a strong defensive play, that player often seems to lead off the following half-inning. Whether the belief is generally true or not, it certainly appeared that way as Burns led off in the top half the second inning. In the movie version of such an event, the player would probably produce a game-winning hit. Not this time. Burns swung and missed the first two pitches, took one ball, and then proceeded to become Plank's second strikeout victim on a high fastball. Tillie Shafer, now listed as the fifth batter in the day's lineup, hit a fly near the right-field foul line that was hauled in by Eddie Murphy. Red Murray worked the count to two balls two strikes, then went after an out-of-reach high and outside pitch to become Plank's third strikeout. Twice the Giants had now gone down in order against Plank.

Amos Strunk was the first batter to face Matty in the bottom of the inning. Mathewson had barely escaped the previous inning without the Athletics scoring, but managed to settle down as he faced the lower half of Mack's lineup. Strunk took one ball and one strike, then topped the ball on a slow roller out to Doyle. Doyle handled the ball perfectly this time, tossing it to first baseman Snodgrass for the first out. Jack Barry hit the first pitch on a fly to left field, which was caught by Burns. Jack Lapp, appearing for the first time in the series, struck out on three pitches, Mathewson's second such victim.

Substitute catcher Larry McLean led off the Giants' half of the third inning. McLean had popped out to second the day before as a pinch-hitter. This time, McLean took one strike and hit a short fly ball to second baseman Barry for the first out. Snodgrass, Merkle's replacement at first, followed McLean in the eighth position in the batting lineup. After taking a ball and a strike, Snodgrass hit a sharp grounder over third base. On a normal day with healthy legs, Snodgrass could have reached second base, putting him in scoring position and, in retrospect, possibly changing the outcome of the game. But this was not a normal day given Snodgrass' injury, and he could merely limp to first base. Mathewson was now the batter. He was not a strong hitter, though in 1912, he did hit .264 in 110 at-bats. He hit .184 for the season just completed. This time, Mathewson smacked the ball into left-center field. Snodgrass was clearly hurting as he limped towards third base, barely beating the throw by Strunk, with Mathewson ending up at second on the throw. Had Snodgrass instead been on second, he would have scored on Mathewson's hit. McGraw replaced Snodgrass at third base with George "Hooks" Wiltse. Wiltse, a ten-year veteran pitcher for McGraw, had twice won more than twenty games in a season. On rare occasions, Wiltse had substituted in a positional role, including three times that season at first base. McGraw, thinking he had little choice in substitutes for Merkle, decided to replace Snodgrass with Wiltse.

The strategy did not pay off for McGraw, as Herzog bounced the pitch back to Plank while Wiltse started towards home. Rather than throwing the batter out at first, Plank threw home to prevent the run from scoring. Lapp ran Wiltse back towards third base and tagged the runner out. Mathewson ran to third on the play, while Herzog steamed into second. The Giants now had two outs, but two runners were in scoring position. Once again, however, Plank worked out of the jam. Doyle took five pitches for a full count, then ended the inning by hitting Plank's next pitch directly at Oldring in leftfield.

With Snodgrass out, McGraw sent Wiltse, one of the better fielding pitchers in the game, to play first base in the bottom of the inning. Plank led off the inning for the Athletics by hitting a bouncing grounder to Doyle at second. Doyle gloved it perfectly, throwing out Plank at first, Wiltse handling his first chance without difficulty. Murphy attempted to bunt his way on, but instead Mathewson grabbed the ball and tossed the ball to Wiltse for the second out of the inning. Rube Oldring smacked a hard grounder to third on Mathewson's first pitch. Confirming McGraw's faith in his defensive ability, Herzog gloved the ball, and with a perfect throw to Wiltse, the inning was over. After three innings, the teams were scoreless.

The fourth inning began with Art Fletcher hitting a hard grounder into the hole between shortstop and third. Shortstop Jack Barry fielded the ball perfectly and threw a strike to McInnis for the out. George Burns struck out on three consecutive pitches, Plank's fourth strikeout of the afternoon. Tillie Shafer hit a slow ground ball to Baker at third. Baker grabbed the ball, but his hurried throw was low, and the speedy Shafer was safe on the error. With Murray at bat for the Giants, Shafer tried to steal on the order of McGraw, coaching at first. Lapp's perfect throw to Collins cut him down and the Giants were finished for the inning.

Eddie Collins led off the bottom of the fourth for the Athletics with a high bouncing ball up the middle of the diamond. Mathewson grabbed the ball before it went past him and threw to Wiltse for the fourth consecutive play to Snodgrass' replacement. Baker ended the string when on a two-balls, one-strike count, he hit a hard grounder to Doyle at second. The hard-hit ball bounced off Doyle's glove into right field, and Baker was on first with a single. McInnis followed with a sacrifice hit, bunting the pitch just out of Mathewson's reach. Doyle grabbed the ball and tossed to Wiltse for the putout, and Baker reached second. Mathewson, pitching carefully to Strunk, worked the count to three balls and two strikes. After fouling off the next pitch, Strunk walked on a low pitch, putting runners on first and second. Jack Barry followed with a hard grounder over Mathewson's head, the ball heading towards center field. But Doyle grabbed the ball at second, stepped on the bag, and the inning was over without damage.

Red Murray started the Giants off in their half of the fifth inning. After taking one ball, he hit a high fly ball to left field, which Oldring caught for the first out. McLean came to the plate, and after one pitch smacked Plank's fastball on a line past third base for his first hit of the series. Wiltse came to bat for the first time. He fouled off the first two pitches, took two pitches for balls, then struck out swinging on an inside fastball. Mathewson followed Wiltse to the plate and walked on four consecutive pitches. With the Giants having men on first and second, it was Herzog's turn to attempt to break the scoreless tie. After working the count to two balls and one strike, Herzog hit a slow bouncer to Collins, who threw the Giant third baseman out at first; the Giants had missed another chance.

Lapp was the first batter in the Athletics' half of the fifth. His hard grounder to Doyle at second was picked up, and with Doyle's throw to Wiltse, the Athletic's catcher was the first out. Pitcher Eddie Plank came to the plate. After fouling off two of Mathewson's pitches, Plank smacked a hard grounder towards right field. Running hard, Doyle managed to put his glove on the ball, knocking it down but unable to make a play. Plank was on first with a single. Lead-off batter Eddie Murphy hit the first pitch a long way into left-center field. Left fielder George Burns made a fine running catch of a ball that might have been trouble. Oldring followed Murphy and hit a sharp grounder to shortstop. Fletcher handled the ball perfectly, and tossed to Doyle on the bag to force Plank and end the inning.

Doyle led off the sixth inning of the scoreless game. He hit Plank's second

pitch right back to the pitcher, who threw to McInnis for the putout. Art
Fletcher took a two-balls, one-strike count, and hit a high foul near the first-
base grandstand. McInnis caught the foul fly for the second out. George Burns
took one strike, then hit a fly ball to right fielder Murphy to end the easy inning
for Plank.

Collins started the bottom half of the inning for the Athletics. With one
strike on him, Collins bunted down the third-base line. The ball traveled a little farther than was intended, and Herzog made an attempt to catch it on the
fly. Herzog missed, the ball apparently falling just outside the foul line. At least
umpire Tom Connolly saw it that way, despite the loud opinions expressed by
thousands of amateur arbiters.[6] With two strikes on the Athletics' second baseman, Mathewson came back with a low pitch that Collins swung on and missed.
Baker came to bat and hit a hard grounder towards center field. Shortstop
Fletcher grabbed the ball with one hand while on the run, and threw a strike
to Wiltse for the second out. McInnis took the first two pitches for strikes, then
expecting a fastball, watched a slow changeup go by for the third strike as well
as the last out of the inning. The teams had now played six complete innings,
and the game was still scoreless.

Shafer led off the seventh for the Giants. On a two-ball, one-strike count,
he hit an easy fly ball to Strunk in centerfield. Red Murray fouled off Plank's
first two pitches, then hit another easy pop-up to shortstop, which Barry hauled
in. McLean, McGraw's powerfully built catcher, hit Plank's first pitch towards
the short left-field fence. The ball at first appeared to be a potential home run,
but leftfielder Oldring backed up to the barrier and caught the fly for the third
out of the Giants' half of the inning.

Strunk started the bottom of the inning by hitting Mathewson's first pitch
on a low line drive towards left field. Running hard towards the infield, Burns
grabbed the ball about a foot from the ground, robbing Strunk of a hit. Barry
followed Strunk and fouled off two pitches, took one pitch for a called ball,
then hit a hard grounder to third. Herzog grabbed the ball and threw to Wiltse
for the out. It was Lapp's turn at the plate. With two strikes, Lapp smacked a
pitch down the line at first, which was too hot for Wiltse to handle. Lapp was
on first with his first hit of the series. Plank ended the inning with a line drive
directly to Fletcher at shortstop. Seven innings were completed, with still no
score.

Hooks Wiltse led off the Giants' half of the eighth inning, his second
appearance at the plate; Wiltse had previously struck out against Plank in the
fifth. McInnis hit a weak grounder to Collins on the first pitch, who threw to
McInnis for the out. Mathewson hit Plank's first two pitches for foul strikes,
then took a pitch for a ball. Mathewson swung at Plank's fourth pitch and managed to hit a soft fly ball towards the right-field line. Playing relatively shallow,
right fielder Eddie Murphy ran towards the rapidly dropping hit, grabbed the
ball just before it hit the ground, and rolled over in the grass. At first it was not

clear whether Murphy had caught the ball on the fly or trapped the hit. But umpire Rip Egan, also following the ball's trajectory, ruled Murphy had indeed caught the ball on the fly. Mathewson's near-hit simply became the second out. Herzog smashed Plank's pitch on a hard drive towards right-center field, where Strunk also made a fine running catch. The Giants were robbed twice of hits by the Athletics' fine defensive play.

The bottom of the inning continued to demonstrate for the 20,500+ fans the strong defensive abilities of both teams. Red Murphy led off the bottom of the inning by taking two strikes, then lining Mathewson's third pitch for a hard grounder down the first-base line. Wiltse cut off the potential hit with an exemplary play, the likes of which would make a veteran proud, and stepped on the bag for the first out.[7] Oldring swung and missed Mathewson's outside pitch, then bounced the next pitch to Fletcher at shortstop, who tossed the ball to Wiltse for the second out. Eddie Collins appeared at the plate as the third batter for the inning. After taking two strikes, the Athletic second baseman lined a single past shortstop into left field. Baker followed with another hit on Mathewson's first pitch, again past Fletcher into left field, with Collins holding up at second. With the lead run in scoring position once again for the Athletics, Stuffy McInnis took one ball and one strike, then bounced the pitch down to Herzog at third. Herzog grabbed the grounder, stepped on the bag, and Mathewson had again worked his way out of the jam. "If only" is, of course, a meaningless phrase. But "if only" Wiltse had been unable to handle Murphy's potential hit to start the inning, the consecutive hits by Collins and Baker would have resulted in at least one run having scored. But Wiltse did make the play, and the Athletics did not score. Eight innings were completed, with still no runs.

Doyle opened the ninth inning for the Giants by taking one ball and one strike, then flying deep to Strunk in center field. Fletcher took Plank's first two pitches for balls, then singled past shortstop into left field. Appearing to weaken, Plank walked Burns on four consecutive pitches, putting Giants at first and second base, with the lead run in scoring position. Once again, however, Plank was able to hold the Giants. Tillie Shafer worked the count to two balls, one strike, then hit a short fly ball to Oldring. Murray ended the inning by hitting Plank's second pitch on a high fly to right field, which Murphy caught for an easy third out.

Philadelphia took its turn at bat for the bottom of the inning, well aware that one run would win the game for the home team, creating a two games to none lead in the series. Certainly they played like this would be their final at-bat. Amos Strunk hit Mathewson's second pitch over second for a single. Jack Barry attempted to sacrifice the potential winning run to second. After fouling off the first pitch, his bunt rolled just past Mathewson's right. Second baseman Larry Doyle grabbed the slow roller, and with little chance to make the out, nevertheless made a throw to Wiltse, which the first baseman could not reach, causing the ball to roll towards the stands. Barry went to second on the

Larry Doyle once said, "It's great to be young and a Giant." One of New York's favorites, "Laughing Larry" played 13 of his 14 seasons with McGraw, five times hitting over .300. He won the NL batting title in 1915, hitting .320. Photograph dated 1914 (Library of Congress, Bain Collection).

hit and error that followed, and Strunk headed towards third as Wiltse raced after the ball. Harry Davis, coaching at third for Mack, seemed unable to make up his mind on the play, twice sending Strunk towards home and twice calling Strunk back. By this time, Wiltse had recovered the ball, preventing a score.[8] Now the Athletics had the winning run on third base with nobody out, and no force possible. It was Jack Lapp's turn at bat, with a real chance to end the game. Lapp hit a slow grounder down the first-base line on which Wiltse made another fine defensive play, grabbing the ball, and throwing to McLean at home to tag a sliding Strunk. The throw from Wiltse was a little high, but McLean grabbed the throw and brought his glove down just soon enough to block Strunk's leg before it slid over the plate.[9] Barry went to third on the play, but there was one out. Now Mack had a decision to make. Plank had singled earlier in the game, but he was not a strong hitter. Mack could pinch-hit for his pitcher and potentially win the game, but it was equally possible that he would have to start an extra inning with a second-line pitcher. After initially calling Plank back to the bench, Mack changed his mind and elected to let Plank hit.

Plank also hit a ground ball to Wiltse at first, who threw to McLean standing at home. Barry held up, turned, and began heading back to third, while Lapp also headed toward third. McLean tossed the ball to Herzog as Barry was caught in the rundown. Herzog tossed to Mathewson, who tagged Barry for the out, Lapp ending up on third with Plank on second.[10] With two outs. Murphy ended the tension with a ground ball back to Mathewson, who threw to Wiltse for the final out. Nine innings had been played, and the game was still scoreless.

The game proceeded into extra innings, with both starting pitchers still on the slab. McLean led off the tenth inning, and on a two-ball, one-strike count, lined his second single into right field. Not the fastest of runners, McLean was replaced by pinch-runner Eddie Grant. Hooks Wiltse bunted Plank's first pitch towards first base. Plank grabbed the ball and touched the bag for the out; Grant reached second base on the sacrifice. Mathewson came to the plate with a chance to help his own cause, Grant being in scoring position. On a two-ball, two-strike count, the pitcher hit a line drive into left-center field for a hit. Grant came sliding in with the first run of the game. Herzog came to the plate and hit a sharp grounder to Collins at second. The normally smooth-fielding Collins hurried his throw to Barry, and instead of the out, the throw hit Mathewson in the head. The ball bounced into left field, Mathewson recovered and went to third while Herzog slid into second on the error. The Giants now had the lead, and with two runners in scoring position with only one out, were poised to add some insurance runs. Plank faced Doyle at the plate. His first-pitch curve went too far inside, hitting Doyle on the shoulder to load the bases. Fletcher took two pitches for balls, then hit a high bouncer that went over Baker's head into left field. Mathewson and Herzog scored the second and third runs of the inning, and Doyle slid into second. George Burns proceeded to foul off Plank's first two pitches, then took the third pitch for a ball. Plank's next pitch was high and outside, but Burns swung at the pitch and missed. Shafer took the first two pitches for balls, but ended the inning with a fly to right fielder Murphy as Plank walked slowly back to the team bench. The Giants now held a 3–0 lead as the game went into the bottom of the inning.

With McLean out of the game, McGraw sent Art Wilson in as catcher. Oldring led off for the Athletics and hit a hard ground ball down to third. Herzog grabbed the ball and threw to Wiltse for the first out. Collins worked Mathewson to a full count, three balls and two strikes, then watched a third strike go by on the inside corner. Collins was not pleased with the call but nevertheless headed back to the bench with the second out of the inning. This brought Frank Baker to the plate as the Athletics were down to their final out. Baker did his best, smacking a hard drive down the first-base line. Wiltse, playing in position behind the bag, managed to get his glove on the ball and knock it down. The ball bounced in the direction of second baseman Doyle, who was backing Wiltse up on the play. Doyle grabbed the ball and tossed it back to Wiltse on the bag for the final out, two hours and twenty-two minutes after the game's start.

In spite of two errors by Doyle — one in the first inning when Murphy eventually ended up at third base and the other in the ninth inning when his throwing error put Athletics on second and third — it was the Giant defense that made the difference. Despite being McGraw's third choice for the position, after Merkle and Snodgrass, Wiltse had several strong defensive plays at first base: Left fielder George Burns likewise made several fine catches to prevent possible runs from scoring. Mathewson had pitched well in spots, but the Athletics still managed eight hits, in addition to several hard-hit balls that could very well have been added to that total. And to his credit, Matthewson now had his fourth shutout in World's Series play, all against Athletics teams managed by Connie Mack. Sportswriters praised the thirty-five-year-old pitcher, whom they seemed to have consigned to an old age home for several seasons now.[11] Ironically, Mathewson might have been playing for Mack. During the "baseball wars" in the first years of the century, Mack had offered the then-unknown hurler $1,000 to join his Philadelphia team. The Giants, however, offered him $1,500 to remain with the team. Mathewson accepted, and had been with the Giants ever since.[12]

The Giants, meanwhile, managed seven hits against Plank, who was prevented from pitching his own shutout only because of the defensive play on the part of the Giants. Mack conceded that indeed Plank had pitched a wonderful game, "but was beaten by a more wonderful combination of the good breaks of the game and Mathewson's fine work in the box."[13] Writer Joe S. Jackson also pointed out an interesting sidelight to the game, specifically with respect to how Plank handled the Giant hitters.[14] Jackson noted that the last time the Giants had faced Plank in the postseason, the 1911 World's Series, outfielder Josh Devore struck out four times against the Athletics' left-hander. Largely because of the difficulties Devore had when batting against left-handers in general, Devore was released from the Giants. George Burns was his replacement in the outfield. Jackson observed that Burns was hitless in five appearances, walking once but striking out three times, "as many times as all his teammates put together."

Larry McLean, one of the defensive standouts for the Giants this day who was known for his battles with the bottle, became the subject of some ribbing on the part of certain writers.[15]

Temperance Hymn

O' brothers, I'll tell you of Larry McLean,
Brought up in Massachusetts, adjacent to Maine,
Brought up on a bottle, so I have heard tell,
The bottle that sends its adherents to Waco.[16]

O' brothers, take warning from Larry McLean,
And never, no never, touch water again.

He joined the Red Sox in nineteen o' one,
But soon they released the poor son of a gun.
He landed in Canada, strangely enough,
And punished a lot of Canadian stuff.

He came to Chicago in nineteen o' three,
The brands that we had did not satisfy he.

And so he got traded to St. Looey town,
For catcher O'Neill and Mordecai Brown.

But down in St. Looey he caused a big drought;
His thirsty companions just made him get out;
And then he was sentenced to far Port-a-land,
Where Pelkey procured that strong Burns-burning brand.[17]

In the midst of the season of nineteen o'six,
The Reds found themselves in their usual fix.
They sent for long Larry and kept the big guy,
Till Tinker decided the team should go dry.

Then back to St. Looey went Larry McLean,
The brewers, meanwhile, having caught up again.
But quickly he cleaned them, he drained them quite dry.
And got himself traded to Gotham, N.Y.

Now, in the world's series long Larry's a star;
He'll soon have sufficient to buy his own bar.
So, brothers, take warning from Larry McLean,
And never, no never, touch water again.

— Ring Lardner[18]

Game Two, October 8, 1913, at Shibe Park

New York Giants	Ab	R	H	RBI	Philadelphia Athletics	Ab	R	H	RBI
Herzog (3b)	5	1	0	0	Murphy (RF)	5	0	0	0
Doyle (2b)	4	0	0	0	Oldring (LF)	5	0	1	0
Fletcher (SS)	5	0	2	2	Collins (2b)	4	0	1	0
Burns (LF)	4	0	0	0	Baker (3b)	5	0	2	0
Shafer (CF)	5	0	0	0	McInnis (1b)	4	0	0	0
Murray (RF)	4	0	0	0	Strunk (CF)	3	0	1	0
McLean (C)	4	0	2	0	Barry (SS)	4	0	1	0
Grant (PR)	0	1	0	0	Lapp (C)	4	0	1	0
Wilson (C)	0	0	0	0	Plank (P)	4	0	1	0
Snodgrass (1b)	1	0	1	0	Totals	38	0	8	0
Wiltse (PR, 1b)	2	0	0	0					
Mathewson (P)	3	1	2	1					
Totals	37	3	7	3					

New York	0	0	0	0	0	0	0	0	0	3–3	7	2
Philadelphia	0	0	0	0	0	0	0	0	0	0–0	8	2

New York Giants	IP	H	R	ER	BB	SO
Mathewson (W, 1–0)	10.0	8	0	0	1	5

Philadelphia Athletics						
Plank (L, 0–1)	10.0	7	3	2	2	6

Error: Doyle (2), Collins, Baker; HBP-Doyle (Plank)
Time: 2:22; Att.: 20,563

CHAPTER EIGHT

Game Three

The teams returned to the Polo Grounds for the third game of the series. Speculation as to McGraw's choice of pitcher centered on either Jeff Tesreau or Al Demaree, with Tesreau the likely choice. Though the tall (6'2") right-hander was only in his second season for the Giants, he had experience in the previous year's postseason, winning one game but losing two, as well as in the opening game of the current series. Mack was more limited in his choices. Bender had some problems in the opener, while Plank, of course, had pitched ten innings the day before. Speculation centered on one of the youngsters, either Joe Bush or Bob Shawkey.[1] Bush had won fifteen games in the regular season, so the small (5'9") right-hander was the expected choice.

McGraw's club was still hampered by injuries. Snodgrass' leg continued to cause him problems. Merkle's swollen ankle was improved but still questionable. Catcher Chief Meyers, however, was through for the series. Two of his fingers had been placed in splints, and he would be unable to play until next season. The Giants were left with McLean and Wilson to handle the catching duties.[2]

Mack's choice the day of the game was indeed Bush. "This is the pitcher that Connie Mack has kept under cover for the last six weeks in order to use him in the world's series," was heard in the crowd.[3] Substitute catcher Ira Thomas, warming up Bush on the sidelines, stated that Bush was ready. "His fastball has a world of speed and a fine breaking curve."[4]

The crowd was the largest thus far for the series—36,896, an increase of some 600 patrons as compared with the previous Tuesday's match. Thousands more could not obtain tickets; consequently, speculators were having a field day. A $1 bleacher seat could be had for $20. As the buyer said, "I came 2,000 miles to see a world's series game, and I'm going to see it no matter what it costs. Out west where I come from, they used to hold folks up at the point of a pistol and take their money, but that system was very primitive compared with the way they get the money here in New York.[5] But what could the men do? Anything to oblige the ladies."[6]

The weather, which had been "iffy" each of the two previous days, continued in its damp, drizzly manner. Subjected to periodic rain all night, the

Frank "Home Run" Baker exhibiting his batting style prior to the start of Game Three in New York (Library of Congress, Bain Collection).

field on the morning of this third game was soggy at its best. Puddles were found throughout the infield, while the outfield grass was equally wet. The Giants' new groundskeeper, Henry Fabian, did his best, burning "many gallons of gasoline on the mire."[7] At least in the infield, his work was successful by the time the players came out for practice at 1:00 P.M. The ground was not perfect, but at least the puddles were gone. The outfield remained problematic, as the fielders slipped their way through practice. The band humorously participated in the festivities, playing "It Takes a Little Rain with Sunshine" as the players practiced.[8] Both Tesreau and Demaree warmed up in front of the Giants' bench, Bush and rookie Weldon Wyckoff in front of the Athletics' bench.

Manager Connie Mack remained in the clubhouse until a few minutes before the game. He entered the field from the clubhouse underneath the stands, and nearly did not arrive at all. An overzealous stadium guard did not recognize the tall, thin manager in a suit. The guard asked him where he was headed. "I want to get to the visitor's bench," Mack answered. The guard then asked, "Do you belong to the club?" Mack's reply, perhaps accurate, perhaps apocryphal given his reputation, was, "No, you blockhead. The club belongs to me!"[9] Nor was recognition of Bush unanimous. When his name was announced, a

Giant partisan was overheard asking, "Bush? Who is this Bush?" "He's the guy some of the minor leagues are named after" was the answer.[9]

Tesreau was McGraw's choice to start. With Meyers out, McLean was the primary alternative, a choice which was problematic. Tesreau was a spitballer, a pitch often difficult to catch by the best of backstops. Plus the weather was damp, conditions which would contribute to the challenge. McLean did not like the spitball, always having difficulty with that pitch. Or, as the writers were wont to point out, "He dislikes the spitball almost as much as he dislikes the taste of hops when he signs a contract.... He doesn't like to catch spitballs chiefly because he cannot and because, when a fellow cannot catch them they hurt and inflict serious damage to feet and shins, with both of which McLean is copiously supplied.... Pretend you are going to [pitch the spitball] but don't."[10]

At 2:00 P.M. the game was ready to begin. When the crowd saw Mathewson, hero of the previous day's game in Philadelphia, a loud cheer went up. Hooks Wiltse, whose defensive play was a major factor in the victory, was walking with Matty to the Giants bench. As the crowd cheered, Wiltse removed Matty's hat and waved to the crowd. Then Mathewson did the same with the pitcher-turned-first-baseman's cap.[11] Meanwhile, Tesreau had completed his warm-ups, and Philadelphia's Eddie Murphy walked to the batter's box.

Giants battery Christy Mathewson and Larry McLean warming up prior to Game Two in New York (Library of Congress, Bain Collection).

Perhaps as an omen for the home team, the sun appeared to be trying to break through the clouds. Merkle's ankle, while not healed, at least was flexible enough to permit McGraw to put him back in the lineup.

Tesreau's first pitch was a fastball down the center of the plate. After a ball, Murphy hit the third pitch hard on the ground to shortstop. Fletcher grabbed the bounder and threw to Merkle to get Mack's speedy lead-off hitter. Oldring was next. The first pitch to the left fielder was a strike, the second was fouled into the box seats behind the Giants' bench and grabbed by former heavyweight boxing champion "Gentleman" Jim Corbett.[12]

Oldring then lined Tesreau's third pitch over second base for the first hit of the game. Eddie Collins was next, hitting .571 so far in the series, with four hits. The first two pitches were taken for strikes. Collins did not allow another pitch to split the plate, smacking a hard liner into center field for his fifth hit. Oldring, running with the pitch, flew past second and slid headfirst into third. Much the same as had occurred in the previous two games of the series, the Giants found themselves in trouble in the opening inning. Both Marquard and Mathewson had managed to work their way out of their respective jams. Each time it was Baker who provided the respite for the Giant hurlers, the Athletics' third baseman having flied out against Marquard, while striking out against Mathewson. And it was now Baker who approached the plate to face Tesreau.

But Home Run Baker was too good a hitter to repeatedly miss such hitting opportunities. Marquard and Mathewson may have held him in those two instances, but the always dangerous Baker was still hitting .556 for the series, with five hits. Tesreau quickly had two strikes on the batter, and then the "fun" began. Baker smashed the next pitch on a line past Fletcher at shortstop into center field. Oldring trotted home with the first run, while the speed of the hit forced Collins to hold up at second base. McInnis' turn, and Mack quickly attempted a hit-and-run; the Athletics' first baseman swung and missed. McLean, however, dropped Tesreau's pitch, which appeared to be a spitball.[13] The two Mackmen had been on the move, however, resulting in a double steal as the runners advanced one base. With Collins on third and Baker on second, McInnis struck out. Again, however, McLean dropped Tesreau's spitball, forcing him to toss to Merkle for the strikeout. Amos Strunk hit a sharp grounder that Fletcher caught deep at short. Aware of Strunk's speed, the Giant shortstop hurried his throw, which sailed three feet over Merkle's head. Both Collins and Baker scored, while Strunk headed to second on the error. Jack Barry ended the inning with a first-pitch short fly ball to shortstop. Still, the damage had been done, and the Athletics had a fast three-run lead.

The Giants now took their turn at bat, facing young "Bullet Joe" with the well-respected fastball. Herzog worked the count full against the World's Series novice, then bounced a ball to shortstop. Barry handled the ball and threw to McInnis for the first out. Doyle took three pitches, two for balls, and finally hit a high bounder towards the pitcher. Bush was able to get his glove on the ball

**Eddie Collins getting a hit in Game Three, one of three base hits for the Athletics'
second baseman that day (Library of Congress, Bain Collection).**

sufficiently to knock it down, but could not recover in time, and the speedy
Doyle beat it out. With Doyle running from first, Art Fletcher attempted the
hit-and-run, but only managed to foul off the pitch. The young Bush, rattled
by the pressure, hit Fletcher on the arm with the next pitch, putting a second
runner on. George Burns, with one hit in eight at-bats thus far, took his turn
at the plate. After taking two balls and hitting a foul, Burns hit a solid line drive.
Unfortunately, it was directly at Collins, who caught the ball for the second out,
then tossed it to Barry at second before Doyle, almost to third base by the time
Collins made the catch, had a chance to return to the bag. The double play ended
the Giant rally.

Though the Giants did not score, Bush clearly was starting his first series
game with some difficulty. After sitting down on the bench next to Manager
Mack, Bush was the recipient of much-needed encouragement. "Words of
fatherly advice were given to the nervous boy.... He went back into the fray with
renewed confidence and an iron nerve, for he knew that he had a team behind
him that would play their hearts out to return him a victor."[14]

Wally Schang led off the Athletics' half of the second inning and proceeded
to strike out on a one-ball, two-strike pitch. Joe Bush, batting for the first time,
flied out to Murray in right field. So far, so good, as Tesreau appeared to

settle down. Eddie Murphy, on a two ball, two strike count, hit a hard grounder towards left field that Fletcher grabbed on the grass, but his throw was too late to catch Murphy running hard down to first. Wasting no time, Oldring followed with another single to right on Tesreau's first pitch, while Murphy raced into third base. With Collins now at bat, Oldring stole second base, putting both runners into scoring position. Collins took the first two pitches, one a ball, the other a strike, then smacked Tesreau's third pitch into center field for his sixth hit of the series. Both Murphy and Oldring scored the fourth and fifth runs for the surging Athletics. It was now Baker's turn. The third baseman was hitting .600 with his single in the previous inning. He came close to another, hitting a solid grounder over second base. Doyle made a fine stop and stepped on the bag for the force, ending the inning. The Athletics now had a five-run lead.

Bush clearly had settled down by the bottom of the inning. Tillie Shafer started the Giants' half with a slow roller to Collins following a first-pitch strike. The second baseman scooped it up and tossed it to McInnis for the out. Red Murray followed with an easy pop to second on Bush's fourth pitch that Collins again caught. McLean ended the inning with a foul pop that Schang had no trouble catching. It had taken Bush only eleven quick pitches to set the Giants down.

Tesreau regained his form for the third inning. McInnis led off and hit the first pitch to left where it was caught by Burns near the line. Strunk took three pitches for two balls and a strike, then hit another fly ball out to deep left-center field, where it was caught by Burns. Jack Barry, after taking the next three pitches for a ball and two strikes, swung at a curve from Tesreau. Barry hit a foul straight back that McLean settled under and caught for the third out.

Now it was New York's turn to try its hand again at hitting Bush's fastballs. Merkle led off. His ankle was still giving him problems, despite the attempts by the Giants' trainer to reduce the swelling. McGraw had initially preferred to start Wiltse, despite his being a weaker hitter; Merkle already had two hits from his first start in the series. But Merkle convinced McGraw his ankle was acceptable, and was in the starting lineup. This time, the plucky first baseman flied to right-center field on the first pitch, where Strunk, running over, waived Murphy off and grabbed the ball. Tesreau came to the plate for the first time and proceeded to strike out on three pitches. Herzog took one ball and one strike, swung and missed on an outside curveball, then ended the inning on a short fly ball to Collins at second. This time Bush put the Giants down, using only eight pitches.[15]

Tesreau came out for the fourth, facing Schang for the second time. Schang had struck out the first time, and repeated the "feat" again. On a count of one ball, two strikes, Schang swung and missed a high fastball, striking out for the second time. Bush came to bat and "blooped" the pitch into short center field. Though arguably the fly was Shafer's to catch, Burns came running in from leftfield, attempting to grab the ball. Though it appeared he might have been successful in doing so, the umpires ruled the ball had bounced. Bush was on first with a single. Murphy followed with an easy fly to Shafer in center, and Oldring ended the inning with a slow roller to second, which Doyle easily handled, throwing to Merkle for the out.

Doyle started off the Giants' half of the fourth inning, and with one ball and two strikes, hit an easy foul off third base, which Baker handled. Fletcher came to the plate. After taking two low pitches for balls, Fletcher ducked as the third pitch sailed over his head. After a second strike foul, the Giants' shortstop hit a hard grounder over second, which Collins was able to grab. Off-balance, he flipped the ball to Barry for the throw, but Fletcher beat the ball for a single. Continuing his difficult day at the plate, George Burns struck out on a two-ball, two-strike curveball. Schang whipped the pitch to McInnis, hoping to catch Fletcher off base. The play was close, but umpire Tom Connolly called Fletcher safe. Fletcher then stole second base with Tillie Shafer at bat. But with a runner in scoring position, Shafer grounded to second base, from where Collins threw him out. After four complete innings, the Athletics led, 5–0.

Eddie Collins led off the Athletics' half of the fifth. Collins at this point in the series was hitting a hot .667, six hits in nine at-bats. He nearly raised that average. On a one-ball, two-strike count, the second baseman smacked a line drive into short right field. Murray managed to run in for the catch. Baker followed with a high pop fly that Fletcher caught near the third-base foul line behind Herzog for the second out. McInnis finished the Athletics' half with a high fly to right-center field that Murray hauled in for the out, and Tesreau completed his third straight inning with a strong pitching performance. The question at this point for the home fans was whether their Giants could solve young Bush and put some runs on the scoreboard.

Red Murray started off the Giants' half with a full count, then walked on a pitch too high to hit. McGraw decided on the hit-and-run, and sent Murray off towards second on the pitch. However, McLean swung and missed. Schang threw down towards second with the intent of catching Murray, but the throw went wild and Murray continued into third base. Nobody was out. McLean hit the next pitch towards third, but the ball took a wild bounce and continued on into left field. Murray scored the Giants' first run of the game, and the Giants had a man on first. McLean was no speedster, so to increase the chances of scoring further, McGraw sent Claude Cooper in to run for the lumbering catcher. Cooper had batted .300, with three stolen bases, during the season in a utility role. Mack, taking no chances on Bush losing control of the game, had Carroll "Boardwalk" Brown begin to warm up.[16] It was not necessary. Merkle came to bat, but only managed a high fly ball to Murphy for the first out, bringing Tesreau to bat. On Bush's second pitch to his opposing pitcher, Cooper took off, safely reaching second on Schang's high throw. With another runner in scoring position, Tesreau only managed a weak grounder to Baker at third. Ignoring Cooper sliding into the bag, Baker threw to McInnis for the second out. Herzog likewise was unable to deliver, hitting a soft bounder in front of the plate that Schang picked up and threw to McInnis to end the inning. The score stood 5–1, but the Giants had lost an opportunity to pick up more.

The Giants' third-string catcher, Art Wilson, took over for McLean as Tesreau attempted to continue his performance from the previous three innings. Amos Strunk led off, and on a two-ball, two-strike count, lofted an easy fly to Burns. Jack Barry singled into right field, the first hit for the Athletics since early in the fourth. Schang came close to the first home run since Baker's in the opening game when he hit a drive into the right-field stands; at the last moment the ball went foul. The next pitch went the opposite direction. On an attempted hit-and-run, Schang hit a foul fly near the Athletics' bench, where it was caught by Wilson. Bush popped a soft fly towards center field, but not far enough to prevent Doyle from running out for the catch.

Doyle began the bottom of the sixth for the Giants. On a one-ball, two-strike count, he poked the pitch towards first. McInnis was able to get his glove on the ball, and ran to the bag for the putout. Fletcher watched three pitches go by for balls, followed by a strike. The fifth pitch was wide, and Fletcher was on with a walk. Burns was next. On a count of one ball, one strike, he hit a bouncer right back to Bush. The pitcher turned, fired to Barry to cut down Fletcher; Barry's throw to McInnis completed the double play, and the inning was over.

The Athletics once again managed to hit Tesreau hard in the seventh. Murphy took two balls and a strike, then hit a smash between Doyle and Merkle into right. Oldring hit a bouncer to Fletcher, who tossed it to Doyle for a force-out, but too late to catch Oldring hurrying to first. Eddie Collins managed two long fouls against Tesreau, then watched three straight balls. Rather than walking the Athletic second baseman, Tesreau came in with a pitch that Collins hammered over first base. As the ball bounced to the right-field wall, Collins steamed around second and slid into third with a triple, his second of the series and third hit of the game. Murray, with a thorough understanding of the directions in which such a ball may ricochet off the wall, was prepared to grab Collins' hit and perhaps catch the overconfident runner at some point. However, this time around the ball bounced off at an odd angle, and Murray could only watch as Collins continued past second.[17] Oldring scored the sixth run for the Athletics. Of course, even had Collins been cut down, the score would merely have stopped at 6–1. It was now Baker's turn. Baker continued the Athletic slugfest with a single past Doyle, and Collins came in with the seventh run. With the game quickly moving out of reach, McGraw pulled Tesreau and sent Otis "Doc" Crandall in to slow the onslaught. With McInnis at bat and Baker on first, Mack once again went to the hit-and-run, sending Baker towards second. But McInnis' hit towards second was grabbed on the fly by Doyle, who was running towards the bag in hopes of catching Baker. Doyle leaped and grabbed the potential hit, and stepped on second for the unassisted double play. Crandall had stopped the Athletics, but the score now stood at 7–1.

It required another catcher at another time to coin the phrase, "It isn't over until it's over." And for the Giants, and especially McGraw, the game was not over. Tillie Shafer led off. On Bush's third pitch he lined the ball over third, stopping at second with a double. Murray followed with a sharp line drive to left-center field. Oldring attempted a diving catch, but missed. Shafer scored and Murray was on first with the single. Bob Shawkey began to warm up for the Athletics, just in case, but it was not necessary. Wilson, making his first appearance at the plate, proceeded to strike out. Shafer, trying to steal on the third strike, was cut down by Schang's throw to Collins, a "strike him out, throw him out" double play. Merkle walked on five pitches and limped down to first. McGraw, sensing the game was nearly out of reach and not wishing Merkle to suffer further injury, sent Wiltse, who had been coaching for the Giants, in to run for his first baseman. Crandall hit a hard grounder directly at Collins, who threw to McInnis to end the inning. The Athletics' lead was now 7–2.

Crandall, one of McGraw's primary relief pitchers during the season, continued in the game as the Athletics prepared to bat in the eighth. Wiltse, having

Game Three home run by Philadelphia catcher Wally Schang, an eighth-inning blast into the right-field grandstand off Doc Crandall (Library of Congress, Bain Collection).

James "Doc" Crandall (ca. 1912). The nickname "Doc" described his role as "physician of the pitching staff." The name originated with writer Damon Runyon, who noted Crandall's role as one of the first relief pitchers (Library of Congress, Bain Collection).

run for Merkle, replaced the still-injured first baseman. The first batter to face Crandall in the eighth was Amos Strunk. Strunk bounced the pitch back to Crandall, who tossed it over to Wiltse for the first out. Now Wally Schang came to the plate. Despite his inexperience, Schang thus far was having a respectable series showing, playing adequate defense despite a few throws that left a little to be desired, while already contributing a triple and two RBIs for Mack. Crandall's first pitch to Schang was a strike. On the second pitch, Schang swung and cracked a long drive well into the deep corner of the right-field grandstand for his first series home run, and the second for the Athletics. The ball landed close to where Baker's first-game home run had descended.[18] Schang's teammates were jubilant as the catcher returned to the bench; Home Run Baker shook Schang's hand. "Bullet Joe" took his turn at the plate, holding what had become an 8–2 lead. Bush worked the count to three balls and two strikes, then struck out.

The Giants were down to their last two chances, facing a six-run deficit against a team that had thus far demonstrated pitching which could be rated as good to excellent. Some in the crowd had already given up and were heading to the exits. Herzog was the first batter for McGraw's Giants and hit a sharp line drive towards third. Baker reached and hauled in the drive for the first out. Larry Doyle hit an easy ground ball towards first base, where it was picked up by McInnis for a fast second out. "Disgusted" with his performance in the game, Doyle did not run out his grounder.[19] Fletcher took one pitch, then attempted to bunt his way on. Instead, the ball simply popped up, and Schang made the catch to end the Giants' half of the eighth.

The Athletics came to bat in what likely would be the last time for the afternoon, assuming Bush and the relief staff, if called upon, could hold a six-run lead. Right fielder Eddie Murphy was up first and hit a high fly to his counterpart Murray for the first out. Oldring fouled a pitch that Herzog caught for the second out. Eddie Collins, Mack's leading hitter with a .636 average and seven hits, hit a long fly to deep center field, which Shafer ran down and caught.

Now the Giants had one last try. Certainly, with the exception of the brief seventh inning rally, they were having no success against Bush's fastballs and curves. George Burns was first. After taking the first pitch for a ball, he hit a fly to right field, which Murphy caught easily. Shafer worked Bush for the hurler's fourth base on balls of the afternoon. Murray grounded to Barry at shortstop, who flipped the ball to Collins, forcing Shafer. Art Wilson came up as the Giants were down to their last out. Wilson had no more success than had his teammates in general for the afternoon, and fouled out to Baker to end the game. The Athletics, with an 8–2 victory on the Giants' home turf, two hours and twelve minutes after it began, now led the series two games to one.

Two factors accounted for what really was an easy victory: the pitching of Bush, and Athletic hitting prowess. Despite having thrown 122 pitches, Bush had held the Giants to five hits while allowing only one earned run. Three of the hits were barely so. And the youngster was not to turn twenty-one for another month. Defensively, his teammates, most notably members of "the $100,000 infield," had turned four double plays, and stopped the Giants during their sole significant rally in the seventh. Offensively, Eddie Collins for the second time in three days had three hits for the Mackmen, including his second triple. Schang hit the second home run of the series for the Mackmen.

In his defense, Jeff Tesreau was handicapped by the injury-prone defense behind him. This was particularly notable at catcher. Tesreau's regular backstop, Chief Meyers, was finished for the series. His replacement, Larry McLean, was adequate at best and near hopeless in handling Tesreau's spitter. Tesreau's spitball "was breaking beautifully in the early innings. McLean, however, seems to be afraid of this delivery, and seems to be afraid to call for it in places where Meyers would have taken a chance, and probably would have gotten his man." Jackson pointed out that in Tesreau's difficult first inning, the three Athletics who hit him — Oldring, Collins and Baker — all had two strikes before smacking their consecutive hits.[21] Meyers in those situations would probably have called for spitballs. McLean, however, signaled for fastballs, knowing his difficulty in handling the spitter. Each time, the Athletic hitter was ready for the pitch, and proceeded to produce a hit. Several additional times, McLean dropped pitches that were likely spitballs, as in the first when McInnis struck out. Doyle's error certainly was no help. In the end, the Athletics had scored three times in the inning, twice with two out, setting the tone for the rest of the game. One might add the second inning to Tesreau's problems. Both Athletic runs in that inning also came with two outs. While there is no certainty that with Meyers behind the plate the outcome might have been different, one can certainly make an argument for such.

Of course, one could as easily make the argument that even with an effective spitball, the outcome would have been similar. It was not like the Athletics were unfamiliar with the pitch. Charles Dryden, a member of the Baseball Writers of America and noted sportswriter, considered the American League to "consist of Ban Johnson, the spitball and the Wabash Railroad."[22] Dryden was equally known for his creation of such nicknames as "Peerless Leader" (Frank Chance), "Old Roman" (Charles Comiskey), and "the Hitless Wonders" (1906 White Sox).

The crowd of 36,896 produced a monetary take of $75,763.50 for the players. Since tickets were $1, $2, and $3, the question arose as to exactly where the 50 cents came from — a tip or short-change?[23] Among the ten thousand fans waiting at the gate was one David Jones from Scranton, Pennsylvania. David had arrived at the Polo Grounds at 3:00 A.M., waiting in line to obtain a ticket. Some hours later, Jones collapsed from exhaustion. Collected and revived by the police, Jones explained that this was the third consecutive game at which he arrived at such an early hour to wait in line — twice here in New York, and the day before in Philadelphia. Jones so impressed the fans that they held his position in line until he recovered.[24]

Writer/humorist Ring Lardner perhaps had the final say for the game, and perhaps the entire series. "It's pretty nice to be a member of the New York Giants. One is always sure of grabbing a share of the honor of winning the National League pennant and of the losers' end of the world series dough."[25]

Game Three, October 9, 1913, at Polo Grounds

Philadelphia Athletics

	Ab	R	H	RBI
Murphy (RF)	5	1	2	0
Oldring (LF)	5	3	2	0
Collins (2b)	5	2	3	3
Baker (3b)	4	1	2	2
McInnis (1b)	4	0	0	0
Strunk (CF)	4	0	0	0
Barry (SS)	4	0	1	0
Schang (C)	4	1	1	1
Bush (P)	4	0	1	0
Totals	39	8	12	6

New York Giants

	Ab	R	H	RBI
Herzog (3b)	4	0	0	0
Doyle (2b)	4	0	1	0
Fletcher (SS)	2	0	1	0
Burns (LF)	4	0	0	0
Shafer (CF)	3	1	1	0
Murray (RF)	3	1	1	1
McLean (C)	2	0	1	1
Cooper (PR)	0	0	0	0
Wilson (C)	2	0	0	0
Merkle (1b)	2	0	0	0
Wiltse (PR, 1b)	0	0	0	0
Tesreau (P)	2	0	0	0
Crandall (P)	1	0	0	0
Totals	29	2	5	2

Philadelphia	3	2	0	0	0	0	2	1	0–8	12	1	
New York	0	0	0	0	1	0	1	0	0–2	5	1	

Philadelphia Athletics	IP	H	R	ER	BB	SO
Bush (W, 1–0)	9.0	5	2	1	4	3

New York Giants	IP	H	R	ER	BB	SO
Tesreau (L, 0–1)	6.1	11	7	5	0	3
Crandall	2.2	1	1	1	0	1

Error: Schang, Fletcher; 2B-Shafer; 3B-Collins; HR-Schang; HBP-Fletcher (Bush); SB-Collins, Baker, Oldring, Fletcher, Murray, Cooper;
Time: 2:11; Att.: 36,896

CHAPTER NINE

Game Four

"Neither McGraw nor Mack lost any sleep last night wondering who to pitch today. The New York pitcher will not be Fromme; not at the start, anyway. Connie is going to say eeny-meeney-miney-mo just before gametime."[1] Ironic, given that McGraw was considered as having a strong, and perhaps the better, pitching staff. Certainly nobody expected Marquard and Tesreau to be hit as hard as they were. McGraw's complaint that the loss of Merkle and Meyers held little water as "young Bush, a newcomer in world series games, triumphed over the more experienced Tesreau the day before."[2, 3]

Ready or not, McGraw had some decisions to make. First and foremost, of course, was his choice of pitcher. Had Mathewson been the young 27-year-old of 1905, or even the 33-year-old of the two previous series, the choice might have been obvious. But a 35-year-old Mathewson had to be saved for Saturday in what McGraw hoped would be a series tied once again. Marquard? Well, Marquard had been hit hard the first game. This really left only Al Demaree as the remaining choice.

Hitting could hardly have been called timely for the Giants. Hoping to "prime" the batting order, McGraw sent Fred Snodgrass out to center field again, "charley horse" and all. Buck Herzog had gone hitless in thirteen at-bats, and despite having played a respectable defensive game, was clearly a liability. With Snodgrass in center, McGraw moved Tillie Shafer back to third base, benching Herzog, who was not happy with the decision. Merkle was returned to first base, his sprained ankle slowly healing. Four games, four different lineups. This lineup at least resembled that which had proven successful throughout the season for McGraw.

Mack had no such difficulty. His positional players remained the same. Why mess with success, especially with everyone healthy? In front of the Athletics' bench, Bob Shawkey, Boardwalk Brown and Chief Bender each warmed up, though "no one figured on the Indian."[4] Bender pitched best every four days, but with the outcome of the series quickly approaching, Bender convinced Manager Mack that he was ready to go; someone else, perhaps Plank, could face Mathewson for the fifth game. Certainly the cheer that went up as Bender shortly strode to the pitcher's box confirmed the popularity of Mack's decision.

247

Once again it was a capacity crowd that filled Shibe Park — the official total being 20,568. Additional hundreds watched from the rooftops across the street. The ruling by the National Commission that patrons could not be roped off on the field reduced the total numbers and consequently the monetary proportion allotted to the players. Today's game, the fourth, would be the last from which the players would earn their monetary share.

Tickets could be purchased from speculators along Broad Street, with tickets going as high as $15.[5] Four thousand $1 bleacher seats went on sale at 11:30 A.M., and quickly sold out. Speculating, scalping as it is now called, was illegal even then, and one of the persons picked up by the police for speculating was none other than Germany Schaefer of the Washington Senators. As Schaefer was led away by the police, someone shouted, "Say Germany, they can't arrest you for that." Schaefer's lamented reply, "I told them that, but they wouldn't believe me."[6] At the station, Germany argued that he was merely trying to dispose of the tickets at cost. The police captain appeared to be more concerned as to whether this really was the famous Schaefer. Schaefer regaled the officer with a funny story. The officer was convinced, Schaefer was released, and the game could go on.[7]

Bender strode out to the slab, and the game began precisely at 2:00 P.M. In addition to those at the Shibe Park, 15,000 Giants fans stood in Times Square, ready to follow events as they transpired.[8] Fred Snodgrass led off, and hit a weak fly to Baker at third. Doyle followed, hitting an equally easy fly ball to Strunk in center field. Art Fletcher hit the first pitch to shortstop Jack Barry. Barry scooped it up, tossed the grounder to McInnis, and the Giants were quickly retired.

Demaree came out to the pitcher's box just vacated by Bush. Hoping to stop the momentum of Mack's Athletics, Demaree quickly demonstrated this was not to be one of his better days. Often pitching sidearm, he simply had difficulty with controlling his pitches. The first batter, Eddie Murphy, hit Demaree's second pitch out to center field, where Snodgrass made the catch. This brought Oldring to the plate. Mack's leftfielder had produced the first hit in each of the previous three games, and continued the tradition for the fourth. On Demaree's first pitch, Oldring punched a solid hit to the right-field fence, and slid in with a triple. Eddie Collins was next, hitting .583 with seven hits. This time Collins bounced a hard grounder right to Merkle at first. Merkle rifled the ball to McLean at the plate, and the large catcher put the tag on a sliding Oldring. Collins was noted for his base-stealing prowess, and Demaree kept him close to the bag. Thinking Demaree was ready to pitch to the next batter, Frank Baker, Collins finally took off for second. Demaree, who had been standing hesitantly with the ball, threw to Merkle, hoping to catch Collins by then on his way to second. Merkle's throw was too late, hitting the bag, and the speedy Collins slid under the tag for the stolen base. The play went for naught, as Baker hit a foul off third base, which Shafer handled for the third out.

Bender had good speed on the ball during the first, and working carefully hoped to play with the corners of the plate.[9] George Burns led off, flying deep to Murphy in right field for the first out. Tillie Shafer was next, and with Bender keeping the ball high, the Giant third baseman struck out on a foul and two wild swings. Red Murray followed and was hit on the arm by the pitch. Voicing his complaint at Bender's "loss of control," Murray trotted to first. Catcher Larry McLean, who despite some defensive shortcomings demonstrated the previous day, could still hit, proving so by singling to right field. Murray reached third on the play. Fred Merkle, however, ended the Giant threat by fouling the second pitch to McInnis, who caught the ball near the Giants' bench.

Stuffy McInnis started off for the Mackmen in the home half of the inning with a Texas League "bloop" just over shortstop. Burns fell while chasing the hit. Instead, Snodgrass ran, or more precisely limped, towards the pop, but was unable to reach it, and McInnis was on with a "gift" single. Strunk sacrificed McInnis to second with a bunt that Demaree grabbed, tossing to first for the out. With Jack Barry now at the plate, Demaree tried to be "cute" with a changeup on the corner of the plate. Barry fouled the pitch over Merkle's head. Merkle ran after the ball and managed to get his glove on it and juggled it several times before dropping it. The play should not have been particularly difficult, as it was a soft fly between the base and the grandstand.[10] The normally reliable fielding first baseman simply seemed to have trouble determining which way to turn. Merkle received an error and Barry had another chance. He made the most of it, smacking a hard drive to left field. By the time Burns had retrieved the hit, Barry was on second and McInnis had scored. Barry argued with umpire Bill Klem that Merkle had interfered with him as he circled past first, but either the umpires did not see it or the interference was more in Barry's mind. Wally Schang took two quick strikes, then watched four balls go by and took first on the walk. With two runners on, Bender flied out to Burns in left on the second pitch, and Murphy flied to Snodgrass in center. The Athletics had wasted what might have been a significant scoring opportunity, but at least they now led, 1–0.

With the visiting crowd applauding, Demaree led off the third by hitting a long fly towards right field, which Murphy caught right on the foul line. Snodgrass attempted to bunt his way on, bad leg be darned, thinking that the Athletics might be caught napping. On a good day he might very well have done so. But Bender caught the grounder near third and threw the limping Snodgrass out. As he returned to the bench still limping, McGraw told him to just sit down and remain there.[11] Larry Doyle ended the top half of the inning with a high fly into center, which Strunk caught.

The Athletics took their turn in their half the third inning, now with a 1–0 lead. McGraw, meanwhile, made several defensive changes. Clearly Snodgrass was not able to contribute, and McGraw did not have the luxury of taking any further chances. He sent Tillie Shafer from third into Snodgrass' position in center and brought Buck Herzog from the bench to replace Shafer at third. Oldring led off and hit a simple grounder back to the pitcher, who tossed to Merkle for the first out. Eddie Collins worked the count full, finally hitting a long fly, which Burns raced to grab near the left-field foul line. Frank Baker took the first pitch for a ball, then grounded to Doyle for the second-to-first putout. Demaree had an easy inning, retiring the Mackmen in order.

Fletcher led off the fourth. The first pitch was called a strike by umpire Rip Egan behind the plate, a call with which Fletcher strongly disagreed. After a short argument, Fletcher was warned to resume his at-bat, which he reluctantly did. After a ball, Fletcher flied out on a pop into short right field, which Collins trotted out and took. Burns followed with a high infield pop on the first pitch that Baker handled without trouble. Tillie Shafer struck out on an inside fastball with a count of two balls, and two strikes, completing the inning.

Once again the Athletics tore into the opposing pitcher. McInnis took two strikes and a ball before grounding into an infield out on the next pitch, Doyle to Merkle. Then the fun began. Strunk smashed a hard shot towards third, which Herzog knocked down as he fell, but could not make a play as Strunk beat out a single. Barry took the first pitch for a ball, then lined a solid single into left-center field. Strunk raced into third base, beating the throw from Shafer to Herzog; Barry ran to second on the throw. The Athletics quickly had two runners in scoring position, with Schang coming to bat. Demaree had a two-ball, two-strike count on the Athletics' catcher when Schang bounced a ball towards second. Doyle had moved closer to the bag to watch Barry, and the ball proceeded through the infield and into center. Strunk and Barry both scored, Barry beating the throw. With that throw, Schang took second. McLean allowed Demaree's pitch to get past him, and Schang ran to third. Now it was Bender's turn. He hit a slow roller towards first. Merkle ran in for the play, but in his hurry to prevent the run, fumbled the ball. Schang scored the third run of the inning on the error, and Bender was safe at first. Murphy hit an easy fly in the infield, which Doyle caught for the second out. Oldring up. The left-fielder took the first two pitches for balls and hit the third on a line to center. Bender held up at second base. Collins attempted to cross the Giants up with a bunt; however, it went only a few feet in front of the plate, close enough for McLean to pounce on the ball and throw Collins out at first. The inning was over, but the Athletics now had a 4–0 lead.

Bender appeared to begin to tire in the fifth. The leadoff hitter for the Giants, Red Murray, walked on five pitches. McLean followed with a hard grounder past second, which Collins was almost able to reach. The ball bounced off his foot in to left field, and Murray took third. Hoping to maintain the rally, McGraw sent Claude Cooper into run for the lumbering catcher. McLean thus far in the game had the only two hits by the Giants, but his running was a liability. Merkle came up with two men on base, nobody out. Instead of waiting out Bender, Merkle took three wild swings at pitches and struck out. McGraw now sent Moose McCormick up to pinch-hit for Demaree. Moose came close to putting the Giants on the scoreboard, hitting a low line drive into left field. Oldring came on the run and just managed to grab the ball above the grass for a sensational run-saving catch. "To McCormick's credit it ought to be mentioned that he was just boldly larcenied out of a fine three-base drive.... When the ball was about to be nestled on the sward he [Oldring] plucked it in a way which was a great surprise to the ball as well as a stunning shock to Mr. McCormick. Harold thinks that there ought to be a law against that sort of thing."[12] Legal or not, McCormick was out while Murray held at third. Cooper then attempted a steal of second. Thinking it might be a double steal, Schang briefly hung on to the ball, and seeing that Murray remained at third, rifled the ball to Eddie Collins to cut down Cooper. The rally came to naught as the Giants failed to score.

Demaree was done for the afternoon. Hoping to hold the Athletics while his team might work another rally, McGraw returned Marquard to the pitcher's box. The Athletics had hit him hard three days earlier, with eight hits and five runs in five innings of work. But McGraw was running out of options at this point, and nothing was to be lost by providing one of his aces with a second chance. Mathewson could always go tomorrow. Art Wilson replaced McLean as catcher. The strategy at first appeared to work. Frank Baker, Marquard's frequent nemesis, led off, worked the count full, and struck out. McInnis took a ball, missed two strikes, and bounced the ball back to Marquard, who threw him out at first. Then trouble began once again. Amos Strunk walked on four straight pitches. Jack Barry pulled a pitch on a low drive into leftfield, which Burns attempted to grab just above the grass. He was able to get his glove on the ball but could not hold it, and Barry ended up on second with a double. Strunk, hesitating to see the outcome of Burns' effort, held up at third. Once again Schang appeared in a high-pressure situation, and once again the young catcher came through. He smashed another single to center, scoring both Strunk and Barry. Schang's RBI total for the day was now four. Bender hit the first pitch right back to Marquard, who threw to Merkle, and the Athletics were finished. But now the score stood at 6–0.

With the Giants finding themselves deeper in a hole, they came out for the sixth inning hoping to start some sort of rally. Bender had shown evidence for loss of effectiveness the previous inning, but still managed to hold the Giants without a score. In the sixth, he seemed to regain the form he showed earlier in the game. Herzog led off, took a called strike, then hit an easy grounder to Barry at short. A toss to first and Herzog was retired. Doyle repeatedly fouled Bender's pitches, then swung at and missed an inside curveball for the second out. Art Fletcher took the first two pitches for strikes, then hit an easy fly to Strunk in short center field.

Marquard took the slab for the Giants again in the bottom of the inning. Eddie Murphy took two strikes, including one on a call with which he strongly disagreed. After voicing his opinion, Murphy bounced Marquard's next pitch right to Doyle, who threw to Merkle for the out. Rube Oldring was next. While the batter was standing outside the box, Marquard threw a quick pitch over the plate. Marquard, Doyle and others argued with home plate umpire Rip Egan that the pitch should be called a strike. Egan disagreed, and the game resumed. Hearing complaints all day from both sides, Egan was having less than an ideal day. In the end, Oldring struck out on an outside pitch that Art Wilson had difficulty handling. The catcher recovered in time, throwing to Merkle for the second out. Eddie Collins swung and missed on Marquard's first two pitches, then hit the third on a short fly to Fletcher to end the inning.

The Giants came out for the seventh inning with only McLean's two singles to show for their offense. The inning started well. George Burns tried to evade an inside pitch from Bender. The bat managed to hit the ball, resulting in a slow grounder to Barry, which the shortstop could not field quickly enough to catch the speedy Burns. Shafer made the first out with an easy popup to Collins at second before Murray followed with a solid hit over Baker's head into left field. A fast retrieval held Burns at second. Art Wilson came to the plate, hitless so far in his only two plate appearances the day before. Wilson struck out, but on the third strike, Burns and Murray carried out a successful double steal, giving the Giants two runners in scoring position. Schang had nearly caught Burns at third with his throw, but Baker had difficulty handling the catcher's throw while avoiding Burns' oncoming spikes.[13] Merkle was now up, and he blasted the pitch to the front of the far left-field stands out of the reach of Oldring and Strunk, where on one bounced the ball went over the short fence into the bleachers. Though it had not entered on a fly, the hit was considered a home run, following the ground rules then in effect in Philadelphia. The Giants were now on the scoreboard and had cut the lead to 6–3. Marquard, however, could not maintain the rally as he hit a simple roller back to Bender, who threw him out. McGraw had considered using a pinch-hitter, and had Art Fromme warming up just in case. But with two out and the bases now empty, McGraw let Marquard hit.[14]

The Athletics took their turn in the bottom of the inning with their seemingly safe lead cut in half. Baker led off against Marquard, but once again this day the Giant left-hander had no problems with his adversary. Baker hit the second pitch for an easy popup to third, which Herzog caught. McInnis followed, took the first pitch for a strike, then hit a foul fly towards third which Herzog again caught without problems. Strunk bounced Marquard's third pitch right to Larry Doyle, and the second baseman threw to Merkle for a fast one-two-three inning.

Things were looking improved for the Giants as they came out for the top of the eighth inning. They had finally begun to hit Bender's pitchers, and Mack accommodated them by leaving him in the game. Buck Herzog led off. The Giant third baseman had thus far had a miserable offensive series, with no hits in ten at bats. This time, however, he hit Bender's first pitch on a line to left field, his first hit of the series, and the beginning of another Giant rally. Larry Doyle also swung at Bender's first pitch, hitting a sharp grounder to second. Collins fell down while he was fielding the ball, but still managed to hold on to it and throw it to Barry for a forceout. Art Fletcher smacked a shot right back at Bender, who threw his hands up simply to protect himself, knocking the ball down. Bender grabbed the ball off the ground, but made a wide throw to Barry covering second. Barry made a fine catch, forcing Doyle for the second out. Burns then pulled a sharp double right down the left-field line, scoring Fletcher from first with the Giants' fourth run of the game. Shafer followed with a drive down the opposite line in deep right, and Burns scored the Giants' fifth run while Shafer steamed into third with a triple. With the tying run now on third, Red Murray hit a sharp grounder right to Collins, who handled the play perfectly and threw to McInnis to end the Giant rally. New York had narrowed the score to 6–5.

Marquard came out for the bottom of the eighth, hoping to hold the Athletics long enough for the Giants to maintain their momentum. Jack Barry was the first to face Marquard, and he hit a long fly ball out to right field. Murray ran back, got under the ball and caught it. Schang was next, with two hits and four RBIs for the day. Schang worked the count full, then walked on an inside pitch. Now it was Chief Bender's turn to face Marquard. The question once again facing Mack was whether to pinch-hit or to allow Bender the chance to finish his game. At this point, the right-hander appeared to be tiring; nevertheless, Mack left him in. He attempted to bunt the first pitch, then flied to Murray for the second out. Eddie Murphy hit the first pitch on a grounder to Doyle, who scooped up the ball and stepped on second for a forceout. The score remained 6–5 as the Giants came out for their last chance at Bender.

McGraw sent Doc Crandall out to pinch-hit for the weak-hitting Art Wilson. He bounced the ball right to Collins, who tossed to McInnis for the first out. Merkle followed with a long fly to right, which Murphy ran down for the second out. With the Giants now down to their last out, McGraw send Eddie Grant to hit for Marquard. The utility infielder worked the count full, but then hit a high foul pop that Schang handled for the final out. After Schang made what was a relatively simple play, his teammates gathered around in a small celebration. The Giants had come close, but in the end went down 6–5 against Bender. The game took two hours and nine minutes.

It was a combination of events that led to the Giants' defeat. First, of course, was Bender's pitching. The first half of the game, relying primarily on his fastball, Bender limited the Giants to McLean's two singles. As Mack's pitcher began to tire, he started to rely more on his curveball. By the fifth inning, with the Giants starting to hit his offerings, the Athletics' defense stepped up to save the game. One example of this strong defense was Oldring's run-saving catch of Moose McCormick's low line drive. Had the ball fallen safely, at least one run would have scored, and had the ball rolled past the Athletic leftfielder, possibly more. In the seventh and eighth, the Giants finally did manage to batter Bender around. But when necessary, Bender came through, and pitching like the ace he was or at least one of Mack's aces if one includes Plank in the mix, held off the Giants when necessary.

While in a scale measuring earth-shaking events, the victory by the Athletics measured relatively low. This is not to say it lacked any impact in the thoughts of baseball fans. In Ontario, California, for example, in a trial involving the People vs. Duarte, in which the defendant was accused of serving liquor to a minor, the proceedings were interrupted mid-afternoon when councilman J.V. Caldwell, serving on the jury, was called to the phone. The judge, assuming this was important business, allowed Caldwell to leave. A laugh rang through the courtroom when the councilman, a native of Philadelphia, returned to the trial and announced that the Athletics had triumphed.[15]

Eddie Grant (1913) was quiet and highly educated. His private life was a series of tragedies, and he died a true hero in the war (Baseball Hall of Fame, Cooperstown, New York).

Likewise, even halls of higher education took notice of the series. At Columbia University, located not far from the Polo Grounds, professor Franklin Giddings was describing to his students in Kent Hall the ethnic origins of the English people. He had just finished a discussion of the practical effectiveness of contributions of the English to current events. Giddings proceeded to look at his watch, and continued his lecture with, "It was to have happened at 2:00. I know of no reason why it should have been postponed." The students became giddy. "Men and women, youths and girls, looked out the window and there rose visions of Shibe Park, of the men of the

Doc Crandall pinch-hitting for Art Wilson in the ninth inning of Game Four. Facing Chief Bender on the mound, Crandall grounded out (Library of Congress, Bain Collection).

Giant team fighting to tie the score of the series, of the groups downtown standing by the thousands before the scoreboards. Practical effectiveness? They thought of Mathewson and Marquard." But then Professor Giddings brought the students back to reality. "No, I know nothing to have postponed it, the blowing up of the Gamboa dike that will let in the water of the Panama Canal." The disappointment was audible.[16] It seems that same hour represented the official opening of the canal.

World shaking or not, some did take the contest seriously. In San Francisco, one Edward Lynch was passing some men busily baling hay on the street when someone asked whether anyone had any information about the game. Lynch's reply was interpreted as disparaging the meaning of the game. One of the baleman disagreed, giving the opinion that this was indeed the most important event of the day. When Lynch laughed, he was struck on the head with a baling hook. He was taken to the hospital in serious condition.[17]

And finally, in a sense of rubbing salt on a wound, the National Commission notified Giants shortstop Art Fletcher that he was fined $50 for his arguing of a call with umpire Tom Connolly in the ninth inning of the previous day's game after teammate Tillie Fletcher was called out in a close play.[18]

Game Four, October 10, 1913, at Shibe Park

	New York Giants					Philadelphia Athletics			
	Ab	*R*	*H*	*RBI*		*Ab*	*R*	*H*	*RBI*
Snodgrass (CF)	2	0	0	0	Murphy (RF)	5	0	0	0
Herzog (3b)	2	0	1	0	Oldring (LF)	4	0	2	0
Doyle (2b)	4	0	0	0	Collins (2b)	4	0	0	0
Fletcher (SS)	4	1	0	0	Baker (3b)	4	0	0	0
Burns (LF)	4	2	2	1	McInnis (1b)	4	1	1	0
Shafer (3b,CF)	4	0	1	1	Strunk (CF)	2	2	1	0
Murray (RF)	2	1	1	0	Barry (SS)	4	2	3	1
McLean (C)	2	0	2	0	Schang (C)	2	1	2	4
Cooper (PR)	0	0	0	0	Bender (P)	4	0	0	1
Wilson (C)	1	0	0	0	Totals	33	6	9	6
Crandall (PH)	1	0	0	0					
Merkle (1b)	4	1	1	3					
Demaree (P)	1	0	0	0					
McCormick (PH)	1	0	0	0					
Marquard (P)	1	0	0	0					
Grant (PH)	1	0	0	0					
Totals	34	5	8	5					

New York	0	0	0	0	0	0	3	2	0–5	8	2
Philadelphia	0	1	0	3	2	0	0	0	x–6	9	0

New York Giants	*IP*	*H*	*R*	*ER*	*BB*	*SO*
Demaree (L, 0–1)	4.0	7	4	2	1	0
Marquard	4.0	2	2	2	2	2
Philadelphia Athletics						
Bender (W, 2–0)	9.0	8	5	5	1	5

Error: Merkle (2); 2B: Burns, Barry (2); 3B: Shafer, Oldring; HR: Merkle; HBP: Murray (Bender); SB: Burns, Murray, Collins
Time: 2:09; Att.: 20,568

CHAPTER TEN

Game Five

Hundreds of fans greeted the Giant players as they returned to New York following their defeat in the fourth game of the series. The demonstration was more subdued than the previous return after their victory the previous Wednesday. Nevertheless, the faithful remained certain that McGraw and his players could yet pull out the series.[1]

McGraw's choice of pitcher was obvious. The Athletics had already faced McGraw's best: Marquard, Mathewson, Tesreau and Demaree, and only Mathewson had shown any long-term effectiveness. Besides, Marquard had pitched four innings the day before (and given up two runs). So Saturday's fifth game was a do-or-die situation for McGraw.

Mack had more flexibility in his choice. His decision of Bender the day before had paid off, and now he held a three-games-to-one lead, needing only to win once in the next three to clinch the series. And as of 1913, no team had yet come back from such a deficit in a seven-game series. Sportswriters were guessing the choice would be either Bob Shawkey or Boardwalk Brown.[2] Eddie Plank was an option, but was seemingly not needed for Saturday's game. The thinking was that if "Mathewson is good tomorrow, he is likely to beat anybody. If he is not right and the Athletics strike a hitting streak, anybody may beat him. That is the way Mack will figure it."[3]

As they had been for most of the series, the skies were overcast and rain was a constant threat. Nevertheless, when Mathewson came through the center-field gate and walked towards the Giants' bench, the crowd of 36,632, many of them women, gave him a continuous cheer, one which lasted until he walked to the box to start the game. Meanwhile, on the Athletics' side of the field, Brown, Plank and Joe Bush all warmed up until Mack made his choice. Once he was certain the Giants would pitch Mathewson, Mack decided it would be the "elderly" Plank. Mack's choice meant the Athletics would go all-out this day to finish the series, and to do so he would go with his best. Certainly Plank's performance in the second game, during which he allowed seven hits until losing in the 10th inning, was nothing for which to hide his head. Meanwhile, Bill Klem took his place behind the plate where he would call balls and strikes. Rip Egan would umpire the infield, with Rigler in left and Connolly in right field.

Mack decided on the same lineup that had been successful through most of the series, including Schang in place of Lapp to catch Plank. McGraw decided Snodgrass was still too lame to start, so Herzog remained at third and Shafer in center. Art Fletcher also learned in a letter from the National Commission that his fine for the "insulting" remarks he addressed to umpire Tom Connolly near the end of the third game on Thursday would be $100, not the originally stated $50. The letter referred to "his insulting an umpire in coarse terms and by uncouth actions."[3]

The Athletics quickly jumped on Mathewson in the top half of the first. Eddie Murphy led off, and on Mathewson's first pitch bounced the ball towards left field. Fletcher was able to knock the ball down, but was too late to throw out the runner. Rube Oldring attempted to sacrifice Murphy to second, but bunted the first pitch foul. The second pitch was bunted towards Mathewson, who picked the ball up and fired to Art Fletcher for a force at second. Eddie Collins lined a single to right, Oldring racing around to third. With the runner in scoring position, Frank Baker hit Mathewson's first pitch on a line to left field, where George Burns made a fine running catch. His throw to the plate in an attempt to catch Oldring was in time but high, and McLean had difficulty holding the ball. Burns was credited with an error, Oldring was safe, and Collins went to second on the throw. McInnis bounced the pitch to Herzog at third. Herzog briefly ran Collins back towards second, then tossed to Doyle, who tagged Collins out. The inning was over, but the Athletics were leading, 1–0.

Umpire Bill Klem had some observations for Plank regarding the pitching motion he had used in the first inning. McGraw had voiced a complaint that the way in which the Athletics' pitcher was raising his foot during his pitching motion constituted a balk.[4] Klem went to the mound and asked Plank to demonstrate his pitching motion by pitching to Schang. Apparently Klem was satisfied with whatever he saw; he went back to his position behind the plate and then all were ready to proceed.[5] Buck Herzog led off the Giants' half of the inning and only managed a fly to Eddie Murphy in right field. Larry Doyle followed with a high bounce that went over Plank's head. Jack Barry, however, made a running stab to grab the ball and threw on a line to McInnis for an out. Art Fletcher worked the count full, and after fouling off two pitches, hit Plank's next pitch far out to left field. Oldring caught the ball at the fence; Fletcher barely missed a tying homer. Instead, the Athletics led 1–0 after the first inning.

The Athletics' second began with center fielder Amos Strunk. Strunk hit Mathewson's curve directly towards Doyle, who tossed to Merkle for the first out. Barry hit a high fly ball into right field, which Murphy caught for the second out. Schang took the first two pitches for strikes, and followed with a hard grounder off Mathewson's glove for a single. Plank, however, ended the inning with a pop fly to Herzog at third.

George Burns led off the Giants' half of the inning with a hard grounder towards third that Baker picked off. Baker's throw to McInnis was wide, but McInnis held on for the out. Tillie Shafer worked the count full, then hit a high foul fly, which McInnis caught on the run near the grandstand. Murray ended the Giants' half of the inning with a bouncer right back to Plank, who threw to McInnis for the out.

The third inning started with the Athletics' Eddie Murphy hitting a single into left field, his second for the day in two appearances. Oldring then set in motion the play that would clinch the game for Mack. Oldring smacked a hard grounder to second baseman Doyle, a possible double-play ball. Doyle ran in for the ball, fumbled it, and everybody was safe — Murphy on second, and now Oldring on first. Eddie Collins moved the runners up with a sacrifice bunt on Mathewson's next pitch. Athletics were now on second and third. Baker bounced a bunt some sixty feet towards first. Merkle picked up the ball and looked towards Murphy coming in from third. Knowing he would be caught at home, Murphy turned and started back to third. Merkle in the interim was about to tag Baker, running up the line towards first. Thinking quickly, Baker stopped, turned and ran back towards home with Merkle on his heels. Murphy, noting Merkle was busy with Baker, decided to race towards home again. Merkle threw to McLean, but his throw was late and Murphy scored. What about Baker? Doyle had failed to cover first on the play, and so when Baker passed Merkle on the way towards first base, there was nobody covering to whom McLean could throw. Baker was safe, and Oldring went to third. The Athletics now led 2–0. McInnis hit a long sacrifice fly to left field, and Oldring scored the third run for the Athletics. Amos Strunk ended the circus with a ground ball to Doyle. The Athletics were ahead, 3–0.

The Giants went quietly in their half of the third. Larry McLean led off with a fly to short left field, which Oldring handled easily. Fred Merkle, whose careless play in part led to the Athletics' two runs in the top of the inning, lined the ball directly to Collins for the second out. Mathewson hit a ground ball to Barry at short. Barry had trouble handling the ball, but recovered in time to throw Mathewson out at first.

Mathewson had pitched well the first third of the game; it was primarily his defense that had let him down. The question remained as to whether Matty could hold the Athletics long enough for his teammates to recover and provide some offensive support. Jack Barry led off the visitors' half of the fourth with a hard grounder to short. Fletcher scooped it up, tossed to Merkle: one out. Wally Schang hit a short fly ball into right field that Murray caught on the run for the second out. Plank hit a short fly just beyond second base, which Fletcher managed to grab with a long running stretch.

The Giants now took their turn in their half of the fourth. Buck Herzog led off by being called out on strikes. Larry Doyle bounced to first for an easy play by McInnis. Art Fletcher hit an easy fly to Strunk in center field, and the Giants were quickly retired. Plank had retired the first twelve Giants he had faced in this crucial game.

In a game moving quickly, the Athletics came out for their half of the fifth inning. Eddie Murphy grounded to second and was put out, Doyle to Merkle. On one pitch, Oldring likewise grounded to Doyle, who flipped to Merkle for the second out. Eddie Collins, again swinging on the first pitch, hit a fly ball to Shafer in center, and the Athletics once again went down in rapid fashion.

The Giants finally began to show some offense in their half of the fifth inning. George Burns lined a shot directly at McInnis, which the Athletic first baseman caught on the fly. That made thirteen retired in a row. Shafer finally broke the string with a walk. McGraw signaled for the hit-and-run, and Shafer took off for second with the pitch. Murray, however, merely hit a short infield pop fly. Plank, Barry and Baker were all in position to make the catch. Plank barely had to move as he settled under the ball for the catch, even called for the ball, but collided with Baker coming over from third. The collision resulted in Plank dropping the fly for an error. The catch would have resulted in a double play since Shafer by then was nearly to second base. Instead, Shafer was now at second and Murray safe on first. Still, the Giants were hitless. Larry McLean finally managed the Giants' first hit with a single to left-center field. Shafer came home with the Giants' first run, as Murray held up at second base. But Fred Merkle, having another bad day, grounded to Collins at second. Collins flipped to Barry, who threw to McInnis for a double play. Plank was out of the inning and the Giants had only managed a single run.

Mathewson walked out to the box for the sixth, now behind "only" 3–1. Frank Baker led off with a single on the first pitch, his second hit of the game and ninth in the series, raising his average to .474. McInnis sacrificed, McLean throwing him out while Baker advanced to second on the play. Strunk bounced a pitch to Doyle at second and was thrown out. Baker advanced to third on the groundout. But the inning ended without a score as Barry grounded to short. Fletcher's throw to Merkle was low, but Merkle dug it out.

Mathewson led off the Giants' half of the sixth. After taking three pitches for balls, the pitcher managed the Giants' second hit of the game as he lined Plank's pitch over Collins' head. But Herzog quickly killed the possible rally with a ground ball to Barry. Barry flipped to Collins for the force, and Collins whipped the ball to first. The throw nearly went wild, but McInnis managed to grab it to complete the double play. Doyle ended any possibility of a threat with a long drive to right, which at first had home run potential, but Murphy grabbed the ball at the wall. Little did they know at the time that this was the last gasp for the Giants in the series.

Now the seventh, Philadelphia at bat. Wally Schang was first up, took two pitches for balls, then fouled off the next two pitches. Mathewson threw his fadeaway, and the Athletic catcher was out on strikes. Plank up. He hit a slow grounder to Doyle, who easily threw him out at first. Murphy walked, Mathewson's first base on balls for the game and only his second for the series. Oldring ended the inning with a pop foul that McLean caught near the Giants' bench.

Art Fletcher led off the bottom of the inning with a high fly ball to center that Strunk caught for the first out. Burns grounded the next pitch to Barry at shortstop; Barry to McInnis, two out. Shafer followed with a nearly identical grounder to short, which Barry picked up and threw to McInnis for a fast half-inning.

Collins led off the top of the eighth, hitting Mathewson's third pitch to Doyle for an easy play. Frank Baker, facing Mathewson for what would be his last time, grounded the ball back to the pitcher. Mathewson to Merkle and two were out. McInnis hit a slow ground ball out to short, which Fletcher grabbed and fired to first — a fine play for the third out of the inning.

The Giants now took their turn in the bottom of the eighth with time running out for a rally. Murray tried first, but merely hit a ground ball to third, which Baker handled, throwing to McInnis for the first out. Five outs to go for Plank. Larry McLean, the one Giant who seemed to be having a respectable series on offense unless one includes Mathewson and his .600 batting average hit a fly to left that Oldring took for the second out. Four outs to go for Plank. Merkle ended the inning with a first-pitch ground ball to short. Barry to McInnis and the Giants were down to their last three outs.

The Athletics came out for their half of the ninth. Strunk led off by hitting a Mathewson fastball on a high fly to Shafer in center. Barry hit a sharp grounder to Herzog. The Giant third baseman briefly had trouble finding the "handle" but Herzog recovered quickly enough to throw Barry out. Schang ended the inning by striking out for the second time of the day. As Mathewson finished striking out the final batter, he turned and walked to the clubhouse in deep centerfield, knowing he had done his best.[6]

The Giants were now down to their last chance, both in the game and in the series. McGraw sent Doc Crandall to pinch-hit for Mathewson. He could only manage a weak grounder to second. Collins to McInnis, the first baseman's 45th putout of the series without an error, and the Giants had one out. Herzog hit Plank's first pitch on a pop just beyond shortstop. Barry ran out and made a fine catch. One out to go. Larry Doyle hit a high fly to right field. Eddie Murphy settled under the easy fly and caught it for the final out, one hour and thirty-nine minutes after the start. The Athletics had won the game, 3–1, and the series, four games to one, Mack's third such championship in four years.

As the game ended, the Athletics ran onto the field in celebration. Fans, even though this was New York, crowded the Athletics, cheering and pounding Plank on the back. At some point, Plank was raised onto the shoulders of some of the crowd and carried aloft. McGraw worked his way to the visitors, shaking hands and congratulating Mack, and doing the same with Plank.[7] Connie Mack, in turn, thanked McGraw, and invited the Giants' manager over to the box seats where he introduced him to Mrs. Mack.[8]

Mathewson had pitched well, allowing only six hits among his 89 pitches. One might have an argued that he deserved to win; only his support, both defensive and offensive, had let him down. In the two complete games he threw, Mathewson had an ERA of 0.95, allowing only two earned runs and two walks, while striking out seven. A poor throw by Burns in the first inning failed to catch Oldring at the plate for the Athletics' first run. Merkle's poor play in the third was central to the Athletics' other two runs.

One could make the same argument for Plank on the winning side. He too pitched two complete games, winning one and losing one, with two earned runs allowed and an ERA of 0.95, identical to Mathewson. Plank also struck out seven. The thirty-eight-year-old Plank had fooled the Giants repeatedly with a fastball mixed in with a sharp-breaking curve. Only in the fifth inning, when the Giants scored their sole run, did Plank have any problems. He became stronger as the game proceeded, retiring the final eleven batters in a row. In each of the sixth, eighth and ninth innings, Plank required only eight pitches to retire the side.

The players' share for the series came to $135,163.80, with 60 percent going to the victorious Athletics. Each of the players on the winning team received $3,244, while each Giant received $2,162. The crowd capacity of Shibe Park was smaller than that in Boston, so the total share was some $11,900 less than that of the previous year.[9] Only three players on the Giants' squad did not appear in the series: utility men Jim Thorpe, Grover Hartley, and pitcher Art Fromme. Mack, on the other hand, stuck with the same starting lineup for each game with the exception of Jack Lapp instead of Wally Schang catching in the second game. He went with only three different pitchers. Players who did not appear for the Athletics were utility men Jimmy Walsh, Tom Daley, Bill Orr, Danny Murphy, Ira Thomas, Harry Davis, and Doc Lavan, and pitchers Boardwalk Brown, Duke Houck, Bob Shawkey, Weldon Wyckoff, Herb Pennock and the ill Jack Coombs. While there was concern as the series started that the absence of Coombs could be critical, in the end it made no difference.

McGraw praised two participants in particular as the outstanding players of the series: his own Christy Mathewson and Athletics second sacker Eddie Collins. "I cannot say enough in praise of Mathewson. He has the greatest heart of any ballplayer I never knew, and by heart I mean courage.... To show that he is a great money player, he not only supplied all of the good pitching I got in the series, but he also led the club in batting, banging the ball for an average of .600. I regret to see him growing old. I don't believe that there will ever be another like him for ability, brains and courage."[10]

For Collins, McGraw was equally effusive. "I want to go on record as saying that Collins is the greatest ballplayer in the world. He showed it in this series. Ty Cobb may mean more in the box office because of his ability as a drawing card, but Collins wins more games for a club, which is more important in my mind.... Collins is not playing for individual glory."[11]

Writer Hugh Fullerton, with faint praise for McGraw, simply considered the Giants "outclassed," with the Athletics as the greatest team in baseball.

Just one thing was proved by the world's series of 1913, ninth of the lot that the National Commission has staged, which was ended today. That is, that in the National League, as in the American, there is no pitching staff that can stand up to the offensive strength of Connie Mack's teams.... It has been clearly proved that the Athletics, if in the National League, could win its title just as surely as they have won that in the American in three of the last four seasons. They outclassed New York offensively and defensively. That did not surprise. But their boxmen proved more effective than those of the Giants. And that was an awakening.... After watching the Giants in three successive world series, two of these with the Athletics, it may be said, without any show of partisanship, that they do not class with the American League champions.[12]

Of McGraw, Fullerton had to say, "McGraw is 40 percent of his team. Without him as its leader, it probably could not win a National League championship. With him driving it, and getting the full value of its mechanical power, it cops."[13]

Other writers expressed similar sentiments. It is long recognized that there is a significant difference between a season-long marathon, 154 games during the era of Mack and McGraw, and a short series of seven to nine games. "The Giants can do the 154 game route with deadly strength and wear down their adversaries, but fail in the short distance. Others again, like the Chicago White Sox, can concentrate tremendous energy into a short series, but do not last when forced to go the Marathon route. The Athletics alone can handle either order with perfect ease and success, making them, therefore, the best short and long distance people living."[14] "The Giants played Bush-league ball of an inferior pattern."[15] Phelon also expressed praise for first baseman Stuffy McInnis, exemplary both at bat and on defense, as well as rookie catcher Wally Schang, who replaced Jack Lapp in four of the five games. Larry McLean likewise came in for praise when describing his hitting. But McLean, unlike Schang, had difficulty handling some of the pitches — particularly Tesreau's spitballs — and was too slow afoot once he did reach base. Art Wilson was an adequate replacement on defense, but could not hit. In the end, "a crippled team, unable to play good ball, was easily whipped by a strong team which didn't have to play its very best brand of ball."[16]

Praise was not lacking either for Connie Mack. In perhaps a prescient statement, "Today's victory gives Connie Mack three world's series in four years and adds considerably to the dimensions of his present niche in the *baseball hall of fame*" (italics added).[17]

Only six players remained from the teams that had first met in the 1905 World's Series, which pitted McGraw and Mack against each other for the first time: Wiltse and Mathewson for the Giants, and pitchers Plank and Bender, and position players Eddie Murphy and Harry Davis for the Athletics. Despite their "advancing age," each of the pitchers played significant roles in the series that just concluded. Wiltse's impact was at first base rather than on the mound. Murphy batted .227 for the Athletics, with five hits in twenty-two at-bats. Davis did not make an appearance.

Game Five, October 11, 1913, at Polo Grounds

Philadelphia Athletics	Ab	R	H	RBI
Murphy (RF)	3	1	2	0
Oldring (LF)	4	2	0	0
Collins (2b)	3	0	1	0
Baker (3b)	3	0	2	2
McInnis (1b)	2	0	0	1
Strunk (CF)	4	0	0	0
Barry (SS)	4	0	0	0
Schang (C)	4	0	1	0
Plank (P)	3	0	0	0
Totals	30	3	6	3

New York Giants	Ab	R	H	RBI
Herzog (3b)	4	0	0	0
Doyle (2b)	4	0	0	0
Fletcher (SS)	3	0	0	0
Burns (LF)	3	0	0	0
Shafer (CF)	2	1	0	0
Murray (RF)	3	0	0	0
McLean (C)	3	0	1	1
Merkle (1b)	3	0	0	0
Mathewson (P)	2	0	1	0
Crandall (PH)	1	0	0	0
Totals	28	1	2	1

Philadelphia	1	0	2	0	0	0	0	0	0–3	6	1	
New York	0	0	0	0	1	0	0	0	0–1	2	2	

Philadelphia Athletics	IP	H	R	ER	BB	SO
Plank (W, 1–1)	9.0	2	1	0	1	1

New York Giants	IP	H	R	ER	BB	SO
Mathewson (L, 1–1)	9.0	6	3	2	1	2

Error: Plank, Doyle, Burns; SF: Baker, McInnis
Time: 1:39; Att.: 36,632

Epilogue

So what became of those men who faced each other in the 1913 Series, the third and last between two of the greatest managers and tacticians in baseball history? The teams disbanded for the winter and the players went home with more than two to three thousand dollars in their respective pockets, a tidy sum for those days. The managers, Connie Mack and John McGraw, began to prepare for the season that would follow. Shafer retired. Plank thought about it, changed his mind, and returned for four more seasons. Schang, Bush and Shawkey and others were at the beginning of what would be long and successful careers, though primarily with teams other than those for which they had initially competed. To partially paraphrase Larry Doyle, "It was a great time to be young — as a Giant or not."

New York Giants

Larry McLean, catcher and batting star for the Giants in the series, would come to a tragic end. He remained with the club for two more years, though he never again approached a full-time role. And he never quite came to terms with the bottle, which ultimately led to his demise. He was suspended by McGraw in June 1915 for "breaking training," a polite way of stating he was a drunk. McLean did not take the suspension well, and in St. Louis on June 12 attacked McGraw in the Buckingham Hotel where the club was staying. After wrecking the lobby and flooring two opponents, the massive McLean escaped out the door; he was finished with the Giants.[1] In March 1921 McLean, by then ballooning to some 250 pounds, was shot during a bar fight in Boston while climbing over the counter to attack the bartender. Apparently the manager, one John Conner, had refused to sell him cigarettes.[2] The night before, a drunken McLean had chased another bartender out the door.

George Burns continued as the starting left fielder for the Giants through 1921. Considered the "Polo Grounds model of well-behaved dependability," Burns was also noted for his ability to master the difficult "sun field" in the stadium.[3] Five times he led the league in walks, twice in stolen bases. In 1914, he was credited with 62 steals. Shifted to center field in 1921 when the Giants obtained Emil Meusel, he became expendable when McGraw became determined to obtain Heinie Groh from the Reds. In 1921, he was traded by McGraw to Cincinnati for Groh. Ironically, McGraw had traded Groh to Cincinnati back in 1912 in exchange for Art Fromme. Burns' last season in the majors was with Philadelphia in 1925, when he still managed a batting average of .292. In 1927, he was still playing professionally as a player-manager with Williamsport in the New York–Pennsylvania League, followed by similar positions with Springfield in the Eastern League and San Antonio in a league in Texas. Returning to the Giants as a coach in 1937, where he continued for several years, Burns finally retired to a job in a tannery in Gloversville, New York. His lifetime batting average in the majors was .287. Burns was among the select group who had more than 2,000 lifetime hits, finishing with 2,077. Burns died in 1966.

Claude Cooper moved to the Federal League the following season, and played with Brooklyn during the two years of the league's status as a major league. After briefly joining the Philadelphia National League team, he retired after the 1917 season. A World War I veteran, Cooper died in 1974 from the effects of emphysema.

The 1913 season was the final campaign for Doc Crandall with the Giants. The following year, he signed with St. Louis of the Federal League, with whom he won 21 games in 1915. After a brief appearance with Oakland in the Pacific Coast League, he joined the Los Angeles Angels of the same minor league; in 1918, he hit five home runs with the Angels. A brief stint with Boston in the National League, also in 1918, was his final year in the majors. Returning to California, Crandall spent 13 seasons with the Los Angeles Angels, winning 224 games against 147 losses and compiling a lifetime ERA of 2.92. In 1928, he pitched briefly with Sacramento before returning to the Angels for a last season. He died in 1951, following a series of strokes.[4]

Al Demaree played one more season with the Giants, winning 10 and losing 17 during the 1914 season. Traded to the Phillies for Hans Lobart the following year, Demaree won 14 and 19 games during his two years with that club. Returning to New York for the 1918 season, he won eight games in the short season. He retired in 1919 with Boston in the National League. Heading out to the Pacific Coast League, Demaree pitched several seasons with Seattle, followed by a stint managing the Portland Beavers. One day after taking on the post of manager, he pitched a complete-game victory against Oakland. After retiring from baseball, Demaree spent 25 years as a syndicated cartoonist. He died in Los Angeles in 1962.

"Laughing" Larry Doyle, he of the "It's great to be young and a Giant," played with McGraw from 1907 to 1920, when he was released to manage Toronto in the International League.[5] Tagged "Laughing Larry" for his laugh and sense of humor, he spent nearly his entire career with the Giants. His roommate for much of this period was Christy Mathewson, a man he looked upon with awe when he first joined the Giants. In addition to his being the recipient of the Chalmers Award in 1912 as the league's most valuable player, the team captain won the batting title in 1915 with an average of .320. In August 1916 Doyle was traded to the Cubs for controversial infielder Heinie Zimmerman. Doyle played through the 1917 season with Chicago, returning to New York in January 1918 following a complex three-way trade between the Cubs, Braves and Giants.[6] He compiled a lifetime average of .290, with 1,887 hits. Doyle was living in retirement in New York state by 1942, when he contracted tuberculosis. Fortunately the Trudeau Sanitarium was located in the town, and he remained there until the disease was controlled. The sanitarium complex closed in 1954; Doyle remained in the town until his death in 1974.

Whether the phrase "It's great to be young..." was actually said by Doyle in 1911, or was apocryphal, is unclear. Certainly the image of a youthful Doyle leaning back on the Giants' bench and looking up at a sunlit sky while uttering the statement on life is compelling enough.[7] At the least, one can envision him thinking it.

Art Fletcher remained with the Giants for twelve years, into the 1920 season. The smooth-fielding shortstop was a mainstay on McGraw's teams from 1909 until he was traded to the Phillies in June 1920 in the deal that brought Dave Bancroft to the Giants. In several of those years, he was voted the top fielding shortstop in the league, leading the circuit in assists in 1915 and from 1917 through 1919. Though batting was not considered his strong point, Fletcher's final average was .272, with more than 1,500 hits. In 1923, Fletcher retired and in turn was hired to manage the Phillies, a post he held for a difficult four years while owner William Baker sold out from under Fletcher any players he might have found useful. In 1926, manager Miller Huggins hired him as a coach, his job for nineteen years until forced to retire because of a heart attack. It had been reported that when Huggins died during the 1929 season, Fletcher was offered the job as Yankee manager. However, his experience with the Phillies had apparently soured him on the job.

The baseball writers as well as Fletcher's wife supported his decision, believing that with his "aggressiveness and worrisome nature" he could never have withstood the pressure in New York and the stress of managing some of the Yankee players. "I just turned down the best job in baseball," he reportedly told his wife after a conference with owner Jake Ruppert. "I'm glad," was her reported reply.[8] In ensuing years, he appeared to have turned down numerous other offers to manage various teams.

During those Yankee years, Fletcher was "considered a master strategist," particularly adept at stealing the signs from opposing teams. He had apprenticed in this art when playing under McGraw, and honed his talent when managing the Phillies. One example was the success the team had when facing Burleigh Grimes, one of the toughest pitchers in his time. Grimes threw a spitball, and threw it well. Only the Phillies seemed to hit Grimes when on the mound. Later Fletcher described his secret. Grimes would bring his glove and ball to his face before every pitch, whether a spitball or not. Fletcher noticed that when Grimes was prepared to throw the wet one, he would spit on the ball, causing the bill on his cap to bounce slightly. That was the tipoff.[9]

During these nineteen years back in New York, he became what is considered the highest-paid coach in history, earning a reported $10,000 per year from the Yankees.[10] Fletcher died of another heart attack while sitting in his car with his wife at a light in Los Angeles where they had come for a visit.[11]

Eddie Grant became the answer to a tragic trivia question: Who was the only major leaguer killed in action during the First World War? The regular third baseman with the Philadelphia Phillies, the team with which he started, and again with Cincinnati, the team for which he played prior to joining the Giants in 1913, Grant served primarily a utility role with McGraw. Grant was unusual for his time in many respects. Sportswriters sometimes referred to the Harvard-educated player as "Attorney Grant" and "Harvard Eddie."[12] A quiet man, he preferred the opera over the more baldy forms of entertainment frequented by his teammates. Grant had more than his share of tragedy before joining the Giants. As the 1910 season was ending, Grant walked into a Philadelphia drug store and was introduced to a tall, lovely young woman named Irene Soest. The two fell in love, and by that Christmas were engaged. Completing a story that sounded almost fictional, they were married February 28, 1911, in the chapel where Irene had taught Sunday school. That November, the newlyweds traveled to Boston for the Harvard-Yale football game, and to see the city where Grant planned to set up a practice. But the morning of the game, Irene woke with chest pains, dying in Grant's arms. It was a tragedy about which Grant rarely spoke.[13]

Grant played through the 1915 season with the Giants, compiling a lifetime batting average of .249, retiring at the age of 32. He spent 1916 working on his law practice and helping as a minor league coach for the Giants. With the entry of the United States into the European war in April 1917, Grant was among the first to enlist. As a college-educated man, Grant quickly rose in ranks to captain, serving with the 77th Division from New York, known as the "Statue of Liberty" Division. On October 5, 1918, Grant and the rest of Company H were ordered to participate in the rescue of the "Lost Battalion," part of the 307th and 308th Infantry, which were surrounded by the Germans during the Argonne offensive. The troops were led by Grant's friend Charles Whittlesey. Because of heavy losses, Grant took command of his relief battalion. On October 5, while trying to help his fallen lieutenant, Grant was killed when a shell exploded near him. Ironically, the attack was called off several minutes later when the colonel decided, "My men deserve a better break than being sent to slaughter."

On Memorial Day in 1921, the Giants dedicated a monument to Grant in deep center field that contained a plaque reading "Soldier, Scholar, Athlete." The monument stood until the Polo Grounds were demolished some 40 years later, at which time the monument disappeared. Its whereabouts today is unknown.

Charles "Buck" Herzog played with four clubs during a thirteen-year National League career. He joined Cincinnati after the 1913 season with New York, managing that club for three years. He returned to New York for a season in the trade that sent Mathewson to the Reds as manager. Herzog signed a three-year contract with McGraw, reportedly at a salary of $10,000 per season. But in September 1917 Herzog was suspended by Giant president Harry Hempstead for refusing to accompany the team on a road trip. The following year, Herzog was with the Braves. After a one-and-a-half year sojourn with Boston, he joined the Cubs in 1919 and became field captain until retiring in 1920. Known primarily for his fielding, Herzog had a lifetime batting average of .259. He stole 312 bases during his career. Regarded as one of the most aggressive of the Giant players, McGraw once said of him, "I hate his guts, but I want him on my club."[14] Herzog and Tiger outfielder Ty Cobb, about as aggressive as they came, once came to blows in Ft. Worth, Texas, as a result of Cobb allegedly spiking Herzog intentionally on a play. At the time, the Giants and Tigers were accompanying each other during spring training travels. The men met in a hotel room, where they carried out what could only be described as a brawl. After retiring as a player, Herzog had one more job in professional baseball — managing the Newark Bears of the International League in 1924. But in March, prior to the start of the season, he was asked to resign. No reason was ever released. Destitute and ill in his final days, Herzog received aid from baseball commissioner Ford Frick and former baseball club owner Larry MacPhail when they learned of his plight. Herzog died of tuberculosis in Baltimore in 1953. Although flowers were sent from several baseball organizations, only seventeen people attended the funeral.[15]

Arthur "Tillie" Shafer turned down a significant raise from the Giants, retiring after four seasons with a respectable .273 lifetime batting average. In southern California, where he lived out his life, Shafer developed a successful real estate firm as well as a partnership in a produce operation while maintaining his interest in sports by becoming a top amateur golfer. Among his achievements on the links was a victory in the Los Angeles Country Club championship for 1926, as well as qualifying for the state amateur six times. In 1929, Shafer qualified for the National Amateur at Pebble Beach.[16] A veteran of World War I, Shafer succumbed to prostate cancer in 1962.

Harry "Moose" McCormick became a baseball immortal of sorts primarily for something he did not do. When Al Bridwell singled McCormick home with the winning run against the Cubs in a hot 1908 pennant race, Fred Merkle, then on first base, headed for the clubhouse instead of touching second. Johnny Evers of the Cubs obtained "the" ball, or at least "a" ball, and touched second. The game was later ruled a tie, the Cubs and Giants tied for the pennant, and the Cubs won a one-game replay. The play became forever known as Merkle's boner.

Prior to playing professional baseball, McCormick was a teammate of Christy Mathewson at Bucknell College, joining the Giants in 1904 after a year at Jersey City. McCormick played with the Giants in 1908, 1909, 1912 and 1913, compiling a lifetime average of .285, primarily as a reliable pinch-hitter and part-time outfielder. Though hardly known for his speed, McCormick did manage to steal 13 bases in the pennant-winning year of 1913, and 22 bases lifetime. After retiring, McCormick worked for the Hess Steel Company in Baltimore until he enlisted in the army during World War I. He became a member of the 42nd Infantry Division, the Rainbow Division, a name given to the men by the Chief of Staff, Major Douglas MacArthur, because it comprised a "rainbow" of National Guard units from 26 states. During the conflict, one in which the division participated in some of the bloodiest action seen by American troops, McCormick rose to the rank of captain.[17]

Following the war, McCormick briefly served as manager in Chattanooga (1914–1915), then as graduate manager of athletics and baseball and basketball coach at Bucknell from 1922–1925. In 1926, he was hired to become baseball coach at the United States Military Academy at West Point, a position he held until 1937, when he retired to work as an insurance broker. In May 1941 he re-enlisted to become chief of physical education and training for the Army Air Force at Mitchell Field on Long Island, where he served until the end of the war. He returned to Bucknell, where he worked until retiring in 1958. McCormick died on July 9, 1962.

Mention the name Fred Merkle, and to anyone who knows baseball, his name is followed most likely by the word "boner." The specifics of the event are described above. What is not often mentioned is how unfair the pejorative label actually was. No question Merkle should have touched the second-base bag on the play. But this was a common behavior in days when fans invariably ran onto the field as the game ended — and often before. Sometimes those fans were not particularly friendly. To his credit, McGraw never blamed Merkle for the play and always regarded the first baseman as a "shrewd and aggressive player."[18] Merkle became involved in a second disputed play during the 1912 World's Series, when in the final game, Merkle and catcher Chief Meyers allowed a foul fly by Sox outfielder Tris Speaker to fall between them. Speaker came back to hit a single to start a game-winning rally.

Merkle's home run in the 1913 Series was not unusual for him. He hit 60 lifetime homers, including 12 in the 1911 season, no small feat during the dead-ball era. He was considered strong on defense, and a smart, aggressive runner on the bases, stealing 272 bases in his career. His lifetime average was .273, with a career-high of .309 in 1912. In August 1916 he was traded for catcher Lew McCarty across the river in Brooklyn, where he played for portions of two seasons before ending up in Chicago with the Cubs. In 1920, he went to Rochester in the International League, returning to the majors briefly with the Yankees in 1925 and 1926 as a part-time player and pitching coach. He later became a partner in a Florida firm that manufactured artificial fishing bait. Merkle spent most of his later years trying to avoid the limelight, though he did participate in baseball clinics for boys. He also became an avid bridge player in later years. In seemingly good health, Merkle died of a heart attack in his sleep on March 2, 1956. Ironically, "Circus Solly" Hofman, the Cub player who is credited with realizing Merkle's mistake, and who yelled to Evers to tag the second-base bag, died a week later.[19]

John "Chief" Meyers had the opportunity to play in only one game in the 1913 Series, going hitless in four at-bats. But his value to the team could be seen in the 1912 Series, when he cut down a record 12 runners attempting to steal. His presence in 1913 at the least might have resulted in a much-closer series. Meyers played seven seasons with the Giants, leaving in February 1916 when picked up on waivers by Brooklyn.

He was released on waivers by Brooklyn in August 1917, and signed by Boston, where he finished his career. In the eight years through the 1916 season, Meyers led all catchers in hitting with an average of .297.[20] His lifetime average was .291. He retired the following year. After baseball, Meyers served for 25 years as chief of police for the Indian Service of Southern California. He died July 25, 1971, just shy of his 91st birthday.

John Joseph "Red" Murray continued with the Giants until 1915, when he was traded to the Cubs midway through the season. One of the few college players in his time, Murray had been signed by the Cardinals in 1906 while attending and playing baseball for Notre Dame. Murray was McGraw's regular right fielder for much of his career, which lasted from 1906 through 1917. In 1916, Murray became involved in the lawsuit filed between the Federal League and major league baseball. Nearly signed by the Federal League, Murray became a free agent when the suit was dismissed by circuit court Judge Kenesaw Landis, part of the decision leading to the compromise that resulted in dissolution of the league.[21] The Giants re-signed Murray in 1917 as a replacement for outfielder Dave Robertson, who had enlisted in the army.[22] Murray enlisted in the navy the following year. Murray's lifetime average was .270, and stole 321 bases. After retirement, he served as city recreation director in Elmira, New York, from 1939 until he retired in 1958. Murray died December 4, 1958.

Like Merkle, Fred Snodgrass is remembered primarily for a mistake, in his case the error that resulted from dropping a fly ball hit by Clyde Engel of the Red Sox in the 1912 World's Series. And like Merkle, the mistake overshadowed a successful career. A self-described "quick tempered kid," he was signed by McGraw off the campus of St. Vincent's College in 1908 for a salary of $150 per month.[23] He played eight seasons in the outfield for the Giants, finishing up after his release from the Giants in August 1915 with a season and a half with the Boston Braves. In his first game with Boston, Snodgrass doubled in the winning run against Pittsburgh.

Snodgrass' lifetime average was .275; he is also credited with having stolen

215 bases. His last year in professional baseball was with Vernon in the Pacific Coast League in 1917. After baseball, Snodgrass owned an appliance store in Oxnard, California, for 25 years, and served as a banker, rancher, and even for a short time as mayor of the city. Snodgrass died April 5, 1974, at age 86.

George "Hooks" Wiltse, regular-season pitcher and substitute first baseman (and pinch-runner) during the series, played twelve seasons in the majors, all but the last one with McGraw's Giants. Twice, in 1908 and 1909, he won more than 20 games, his total including a 1908 no-hitter in ten innings against Philadelphia. His service with the Giants at the time was a record for a left-handed pitcher with one team.[24] In December 1914 Wiltse was released from the Giants and hired as manager of Jersey City of the International League. His tenure there lasted only until June 1915 when he was released. Shortly afterwards, he joined the Brooklyn team of the Federal League, playing first base as well as pitcher. Wiltse later managed at Reading of the New York State League and the Buffalo Bisons of the International League (1919–1924). In 1925, Wiltse resigned as Bison manager, the result of an argument with the owners who, in Wiltse's opinion, would not sign the types of players he had in mind.[25] Shortly afterwards, Wiltse was hired as pitching coach by the Yankees. Wiltse died in 1959.

Art Wilson played 14 seasons in the majors, six with McGraw's Giants. With New York, he played primarily a utility role, only twice appearing in more than sixty games in a season. In January 1914 Wilson jumped the Giants to sign with the Chicago Whales, managed by Joe Tinker, in the new Federal league. That season, the only one during which Wilson was the regular catcher for a major league club, he batted .291 with ten home runs. At the same time Wilson was signed by the Federal League Whalers, he was also used as a lure for pitcher Jeff Tesreau from the Giants. Tesreau, however, remained with New York.[26] In 1916, Wilson was sold to Pittsburgh. In July of that year, however, Wilson was traded back to Chicago, this time to the Cubs, for Frank Schulte. Wilson was traded to the Boston Braves with Larry Doyle; he remained with the Braves through 1920. While with the Braves, Wilson's most notable achievement was to catch a baseball thrown by pilot Rogers Humphreys during a spring training game at the Braves' park in Miami, Florida.

> Wilson and Humphreys [who met while Wilson played with Bloomington in the Three I League] thought out the stunt about the same time. The flyer wanted to try it and Art agreed to stop the game whenever the aviator chose to attempt the feat.... Flying at something under 200 feet, Humphreys started his bombardment. The first two balls went wide.... The players were rather timid at attempting the catch, for a ball dropped from such a height feels like a ton or more when it lands. Wilson was game, however, and when Humphreys circled the park for a third time he was waiting out in the center of the diamond waiting for a catch.... Wilson, with his big catching mit, managed to hold it when it came down.[27]

He finished his major league career in 1921, briefly appearing with Cleveland, from which he was released to Columbus of the American Association in

June. Wilson's lifetime average was .261. Wilson also briefly managed Pittsfield in the Eastern League. He died alone in a hotel room in Chicago in 1960.

The 6'2" Jeff Tesreau had a relatively short career with the Giants, one lasting from 1912 to 1918. He appeared in three World Series—1912, 1913 and 1917—with a series record of one win, three losses. Known particularly for a wicked spitball, Tesreau's lifetime pitching record for McGraw was 115–72, with a lifetime ERA of 2.43. His first season with the Giants, 1912, during which he won 17 games, included a no-hitter thrown against Philadelphia. Tesreau retired in 1918 to become baseball coach at Dartmouth College, a position he held for 27 years. With Tesreau as coach, Dartmouth won the Eastern Intercollegiate League title several times.[28] In September 1946 while preparing to leave on a fishing trip, Tesreau suffered a stroke, causing him to fall into the Reservoir Pond in Hanover, New Hampshire. Though saved from drowning, he died the next day at age 57.

Rube Marquard overcame the sobriquet with which he had initially been labeled, the "$11,000 lemon," with a Hall of Fame career. He started off the pennant-winning year of 1912 with 19 consecutive victories on his way to a total of 26. This represented the third consecutive year, and the last, in which he was a twenty-game winner. Saddled with the nickname "Rube," Marquard was actually born in Cleveland, Ohio. He later recalled that the name originated with a news story in the *Indianapolis Star,* which described his victory that opened the 1908 American Association season. The paper was comparing "Smokey" Joe Wood, pitching for Kansas City, with their own eighteen-year-old fire-baller. "The right-hander for Kansas City looks like he is going to develop into a great pitcher. They call him Smokey Joe Wood. But we have a left-hander with Indianapolis who looks like he is going places, too. He resembles one of the great left-handed pitchers of all times: Rube Waddell."[29]

Marquard spent eight seasons with the Giants, winning a total of 103 games. In 1915, he no-hit the Brooklyn Robins in a game that took one hour and sixteen minutes to play. By then, he appeared to be wearing down despite claiming he was having no arm trouble. That season, however, the Giants, with what had been considered a strong team during spring training, never could put a complete story together and finished last. McGraw, not always the calmest of individuals in the best of times, rode the players hard out of frustration. Marquard in particular, at twenty-six already a veteran, objected to the riding. By midyear he had had enough, and requested a trade. As Marquard recalled the conversation, he first asked McGraw to trade him if he was so bad. "He could still lick any club in the league." "Who would take you?" was McGraw's reply. "Lick any club in the league. Heck, you couldn't even lick a postage stamp." "Give me a chance to trade myself then. What would you sell me for?" McGraw replied, "$7,500." So Marquard made a phone call to Wilbert Robinson, former Dodger coach and former friend of McGraw's before they separated due to an argument. Uncle Robbie jumped at the chance, and Marquard was on his way across the river to Brooklyn.[30]

Marquard played six years with Brooklyn, winning 56 games, and was instrumental in helping the Robins win two pennants: in 1916, when he won 13 games with an ERA of 1.58, and in 1920, with 10 victories. Much of this period, Marquard was married to actress Blossom Seeley, though the marriage that originated in scandal (Seeley being already married when they became lovers) eventually broke up over differences of opinions on her career. During the 1920 World Series, Marquard was arrested for scalping series tickets, and was fined $1 by the court. Because of Rube's notoriety and the embarrassment to the club, owner Charles Ebbets said that Marquard would never pitch for Brooklyn again; he made good on his threat.[31] In December 1920 Marquard was traded to Cincinnati for pitcher Dutch Reuther. He had an outstanding season with the Reds, winning 17 games. However, in February 1922 Marquard and infielder Larry Kopf were traded to the Braves for pitcher John Scott. Marquard was not considered to be a "sensation" pitching in Boston, but it was felt that "he'll win occasionally, and that helps."[32] He did not help much, as the Braves finished in the cellar with a record of 53–100. Marquard did manage to win 11 games. The following season was not significantly better. Marquard again won 11 games, and the Braves improved to 54–100, one-half game out of the basement. By 1925, Marquard was nearly finished. He pitched primarily in relief, though did manage the occasional strong outing in a starting role. On April 26, he pitched eight innings of shutout ball against a hard-hitting Robins team. Such outings were few, however, and Marquard retired at the end of the season. In 1926, Marquard managed Providence in the Eastern League, and later Jacksonville in the Southeastern League. In later years, he was a scout and coach for the Atlanta Crackers, as well as being employed at several racetracks. In 1971, Marquard was inducted into the National Baseball Hall of Fame. Marquard died at the age of 93 in 1980.

Few baseball historians would disagree with anyone stating that Christy Mathewson was one of the greatest pitchers to ever wear a major league uniform. His 25 victories in 1913 marked the twelfth time in thirteen seasons he reached that mark, including four seasons in which he won at least 30 games. Three of those 30-victory seasons were in succession, from 1903–1905. In 1914, he again entered the 20-victory column, winning 24 and losing 13. This was his last such spectacular year, however, as the strain on his arm and advancing age finally took their toll.

Mathewson was always one of manager McGraw's favorites. Though no sentimentalist, McGraw would send Mathewson to another team only if an opportunity arose that would allow the pitcher to remain in the game after retiring from the mound. The opportunity presented itself in 1916, when Cincinnati was in need of a manager. In July, the Giants and Reds swung a deal in which Mathewson, infielder Bill McKechnie and future Hall of Famer Edd

Roush went to the Reds for manager Buck Herzog and outfielder Wade Killifer; the trade was made in part because Mathewson wanted the chance to manage at Cincinnati. Mathewson's contract was through the 1918 season. The Cincinnati ballclub was in the midst of some hard times, either finishing in or near the cellar the previous three seasons, and would do so again in 1916. Mathewson was the seventh manager in recent years to attempt to turn the fortunes of the club around, a daunting task. "The baseball world was shocked yesterday by the news that Christy Mathewson, one of the game's greatest exponents, had signed to manage the Cincinnati Reds at the age of 37 years, the very prime of life. Mathewson is the seventh prominent baseballist to succumb to this disease in a space of twelve years."[33] A tremendous ovation greeted Matty when he brought out the lineup at his debut on July 21, or at least as loud as 2,500 fans could cheer. It did little good fortune-wise, as the Reds still lost to the Phillies that day.[34] On September 4 of that year, two old workhorses met for the final time, as Mathewson and Mordecai "Three Finger" Brown of the Cubs were opposing pitchers in the second game of a doubleheader. Heavily publicized, the matchup would be the last for each in what had been called "the most sentimental hurling duel ever staged."[35] Each was at one time among the greatest in the game, but that was years before. Prior to the game, the pitchers received bouquets of American Beauty roses. The game was hardly a pitching duel, as the Cubs managed eight runs and fifteen hits off Mathewson, and the Reds had ten runs and nineteen hits off Brown. The victory was Matty's 373rd, the last of his long career. For the crowd, the presence of the two toeing the pitching slab once again was sufficient.

> For the sentimental public the Labor Day game on the north side was the close of a baseball period. It was Brown of the old Cubs and Mathewson of the old Giants. The only thing remaining of the Cubs was the name and Brown. Mathewson was in a Cincinnati uniform. All either pitcher had of his old skill was control, and yet, for the sentimental, it was a great game, something in lavender, which had to be viewed in a perspective of years.... Brown and Mathewson in the old days when the Cubs and Giants fought for pennants were safe custodians of the peculiar public happiness which depends upon baseball scores, and, miserable a jade as popularity is, they have held the affections of the people they thus peculiarly served.[36]

Neither Brown nor Mathewson appeared on the field again as a player — in all respects a proper ending to fairy-tale careers.

By 1918, the Reds had improved to the point where they finished third in the war-shortened season. By that time, Mathewson had enlisted in the army and was serving in a chemical warfare branch, reaching the rank of captain. During a training exercise, Mathewson was accidentally exposed to poison gas, severely damaging his lungs. Whether this was a direct cause of his later illness is difficult to ascertain, but shortly afterwards he developed tuberculosis. In these pre-antibiotic days, the only treatment consisted of rest and exposure to fresh air, and Mathewson spent several years at the tuberculosis sanatorium at

Saranac Lake, New York. He initially returned as coach for McGraw's Giants, but poor health forced him to retire in 1920. A brief recovery allowed him to return to baseball as president and part-owner of the Boston Braves. In 1924, he suffered a relapse. On October 7, 1925, the eve of the World Series, Mathewson died. Mathewson was considered an inspiration to American youth for his clean living as well as his athletic prowess. "He had sterling qualities of character. He was a thorough sportsman, being always a modest winner and a good loser. But, more than that, he commended himself to the public through many years as a man in whom self-control, correct habits and personal integrity were conspicuous, though he was engaged in a calling where they are often painfully lacking."[37]

His 373 victories still represent a National League record, albeit one tied with Matty's contemporary, Grover Cleveland Alexander. He pitched 79 lifetime shutouts, and retired with an ERA of 2.13. His 267 strikeouts in 1903 was a league record for decades. In 1905, he pitched three shutouts against the Athletics in the World's Series, probably the greatest performance ever for a pitcher in a post-season role.

John McGraw continued to manage the Giants for another two decades after the 1913 Series. The stars of 1913, however, began to age. The 1914 team, while still demonstrating strong pitching on the part of Mathewson (24 wins) and Tesreau (26 wins), was overtaken by the "Miracle Braves" and finished second. In 1915, the bottom dropped out for the Giants as they finished in the cellar (69–83). The turnaround began in 1916. The Giants won 27 of their last 31 games, including a still-record 26 wins in a row. But the team started in fourth place and finished the streak in fourth. Still, the team had improved to 86–66. By 1917, the Giants were among the favorites for the pennant, based largely on their streak at the end of the previous season and not the "big name" players currently on the squad.

The 1917 Giants won six of their first seven games with players such as Ferdie Schupp, Slim Sallee, and Heinie Zimmerman, and veterans such as Herzog and Fletcher. The team won the pennant easily, finishing ahead of the second-place Phillies by 10 games. They faced a strong White Sox team in the series, largely the same squad that in two years would be ignominiously known as the "Black Sox." Red Faber won three times, Eddie Collins was once again a nemesis for McGraw, and the Sox took the series in six games. McGraw had now lost four consecutive post-season series: 1911–1913 and 1917. In 1919, McGraw became a partial owner of the team following its purchase by Charles Stoneham.

Rebuilding with the likes of Frankie Frisch, George "Highpockets" Kelly, Ross Youngs and Irish Meusel, brother to Bob Meusel of the Yankees, McGraw again won the pennant in 1921. This time he faced the Yankees, the American League tenants of the Polo Grounds. Victorious in the best-of-nine series, McGraw finally broke his post-season losing streak in a series that took eight games. The Giants won again in 1922, once again beating the Yankees in the World Series. In 1923, the Yankees vacated the Polo Grounds, which they had shared with the Giants, and moved into their own new stadium in the Bronx just across the river. The teams met in October in their third consecutive World Series matchup, but this time the Yankees, led by Babe Ruth, were the victors. The Giants did win two games in the 1923 Series, courtesy of home runs by Casey Stengel. McGraw worked his magic once more in 1924, this time losing to the Washington Senators and Walter Johnson in seven games. This marked the tenth time, and last, McGraw's Giants played in the post-season series.

The 1932 season represented the beginning of the third decade for McGraw as the Giants' manager, as well as his forty-third year in professional baseball if one includes his seasons as a player. The stress of managing an underachieving team contributed to McGraw's health problems, aggravated by the chronic sinusitis he continually suffered and not helped by food poisoning. By 1932, the quickly aging McGraw also began suffering prostate problems, and had difficulty urinating, the first signs of the cancer which he did not yet realize he had developed.[38] The spring started out damp and cold, which only contributed to his discomfort. The team lost five of its first six games, including an opening day blowout by the Philadelphia Phillies. Increasingly, the team was guided by his assistant, Dave Bancroft. By June 1 McGraw had had enough. Again feeling miserable, McGraw tried to provide a pep talk for his team prior to a home game, once again against the Phillies, before going back to his apartment. The talk did little good, as once again the Giants were defeated. This left their record at 17–23, and the team in the cellar.

McGraw finally made the decision that it was time for him to retire. The question came down to his successor. Choices included Bancroft, who had frequently spelled him in that position but who also had previously failed at Boston, and Frankie Frisch. McGraw had personal problems with Frisch in the past, although he was not one to let his personal feelings stand in the way of a decision that might be best for the team. Unfortunately for McGraw, Frisch was now with the Cardinals, whose owner, Branch Rickey, would not be willing to deal.[39] That left McGraw's third choice: first baseman Bill Terry. As he had with many of his players, McGraw had exchanged harsh words with Terry, including an argument over the year's salary. But again, this was a man McGraw respected. So on Thursday, June 2, a rainy day which had resulted in postponement of the game, McGraw put the question to Terry. The first baseman was stunned, but accepted contingent on one thing: he was to be his own man, not a front man for McGraw. McGraw agreed, and thirty years as manager came to an end. McGraw only reappeared in his office briefly in the following months—to remove the pictures of the two players he had respected the most, Ross Youngs and Christy Mathewson. As Terry later recalled, "One day, coming back from a trip, I noticed that the pictures of Matty and Ross Youngs that had been on the wall of his office were missing, and when I saw him [McGraw] again I kidded him about being there in my absence.... He had them hung over his desk. I think he wanted them where he could always see them."[40] McGraw returned to the diamond once more when he was picked to manage the National League team in what became the first all-star game, held in Chicago on July 6. His job consisted of naming the lineup. Terry made the decisions during the game. The cancer was discovered a year later, far too late to treat given the state of medicine for the time. McGraw died at the age of sixty on February 25, 1934. In 1937, he officially joined the immortals upon his induction into the National Baseball Hall of Fame.

Philadelphia Athletics

Amos Strunk played 10 seasons with the Athletics, most of the last six as the starting center fielder. While not a spectacular hitter, he did play a strong defense, the role for which he was best known. One writer even went so far as to consider Strunk "the greatest defensive outfielder that the game has ever produced. In the matter of fielding his position on the defense, the Ty Cobbs of today and the Curt Welches [primarily with Toledo and Philadelphia of the 1880s American Association] of other days never even approximated the same class displayed by Amos. It is impossible to even conceive of anything in human form performing more sensational and unerring feats than Amos shows consistently day in and day out ... he has no weaknesses to either side, in front or back there, by the palings."[41]

Still, even on offense his speed allowed him to play a critical role in Mack's lineup. Strunk was "best known as the key man in Connie Mack's famed double squeeze play. With Mr. Strunk on second base and a team-mate on third, the batter, usually Collins or Barry, would bunt. The man on third would zoom home, followed closely by Mr. Strunk ... never breaking stride as he rounded third." "It was a combination of speed and timing," was the only response made by Strunk.[42] Often injury-prone, Strunk rarely played a full season. His top hitting year was 1916, with an average of .316. But by 1917, Connie Mack, ever in need of an infusion of cash, continued the "fire sale" he had begun following the debacle in the 1914 World Series. In December 1917 Mack dealt Strunk along with Joe Bush and Wally Schang to the Boston Red Sox for several second-rate players plus $60,000. At least for Strunk the deal worked out well. Strunk bounced back and forth between Philadelphia and other teams for the rest of his playing career. In June 1919 Mack worked out a deal with Red Sox owner Harry Frazee once again, and Strunk along with Jack Barry, whom Mack had traded earlier, returned to Philadelphia. There was some suggestion this was in response to pressure from other club owners, worried that receipts in Philadelphia (and also Washington) were so reduced that other clubs were also affected.[43] Strunk only lasted until the following season, when he was claimed on waivers by the Chicago White Sox. Strunk finished his major league career back in Philadelphia in 1924, batting a mere .143 for Mack, then retiring after 17 seasons with a lifetime batting average of .284. After briefly serving as a player-manager for Shamokin of the New York–Pennsylvania League in 1925, he retired permanently from professional sports. Strunk went into the insurance business after baseball, working fifty years until just before his death in 1979.

Rube Oldring was awarded a new car following the 1913 season, a Cadillac no less, for being voted the most popular player by the fans. He followed his championship year with an equally successful 1914 season, batting .277 as Mack and his Athletics won their fourth pennant in five years. Unlike 1910, 1911 and 1913, however, the Athletics lost — nay were swept — by a surprising Boston Braves team. Oldring's poor showing in the 1914 post-season was one of the contributing factors in the Athletics' defeat, hitting a mere .067 (one single in fifteen at-bats). Oldring did provide an unusual explanation for his problems, described in more detail elsewhere.[44] An announcement had been placed in the local newspaper that Oldring and a local woman, Hannah Ann Thomas of Quinton, New Jersey, were engaged to be married. Another woman, Helen Oldring, saw the announcement, and filed papers claiming she was Oldring's common-law wife. Oldring did admit that at one time he had lived with this other woman, but was not married to her. The matter was eventually settled, Oldring did legally marry Miss Thomas, and they apparently lived happily for some 47 years. A personal note on the part of this author: Hannah Thomas was a clerk at the time for the Snellenberg Department Store in Philadelphia.[45] Also employed there as a clerk about the same time was Max Adler, the author's grandfather.

For a variety of reasons, most having to do with "red ink," Mack began to break up his team after the 1914 season, selling and trading during the next several years the players who had been so successful in maintaining a dynasty. Oldring's turn came in 1916, when, after playing ten seasons in Philadelphia, he announced his retirement in June. Shortly afterwards, Mack gave him his release, allowing him to work out a deal with any other club. Though his initial intention was to retire to his 51-acre property, Eldridge Farm near Bridgeton, New Jersey, in July 1916 Oldring signed with the New York Yankees. He made a noteworthy start that July against the Tigers, producing three hits and a spectacular outfield catch.[46] On July 27, his grand slam home run helped beat the White Sox. Oldring played 43 games that season with the Yankees, hitting a less-than-spectacular .234, and was released by the Yankees before the end of the season. In March 1918 Oldring returned to the Athletics for one last season, hitting .233 in 49 games for Mack. His career average finished at .270.

During the next ten years, Oldring played and/or managed at a number of minor league towns, starting with the Suffolk Nuts of the Virginia League. His debut was auspicious, given their record of 49–58, good enough for fifth place in the six-team league. Oldring was replaced by "Gabby" Street after the season. In 1922, he joined the Richmond Colts of the Virginia League, replacing both initial manager Ray Ryan and replacement John Keller in May of that year.[47] The team was in the cellar when Oldring took over, and finished there. Oldring was more successful the following year, managing the Wilson (NC) Tobacconists to the Virginia League pennant. In 1926, he returned to Richmond as manager and left fielder, leading the Colts to the Virginia League pennant, and then, other than briefly coaching a high school team in Shiloh, retired for good. Oldring spent most of his post-baseball career as a farmer in New Jersey as well working for the Philip J. Ritter Company in Bridgeton, evaluating crops for processing and canning; he also bowled and played softball for the company teams. In 1948, Oldring ran unsuccessfully for sheriff of Cumberland County. Among other characteristics of the campaign was his being accompanied by a pet pig on his travels. Oldring died at age 77 in 1961.

Jack Barry played eleven years in the major leagues, eight with Mack, who considered him the greatest shortstop there ever was.[48] Mack's viewpoint was also echoed by sportswriters, including, among others, Hugh Fullerton, a scribe for New York and Chicago papers. Even as Barry approached the end of his relatively short career with the Red Sox, Fullerton still considered Barry, by then a second baseman, to be "the brains of the infield, and the kingpin of the entire team."[49] His teaming with Eddie Collins in the middle of "the $100,000 infield" proved to be a wise maneuver on the part of Mack, as the two not only became friends, but developed their own methodology in dealing with opposing runners. One example is how they dealt with the double steal, a common practice of the times when runners were at the corners. Collins' arm was weaker than Barry's. When runners were moving, Collins would cut in front of second and Barry would cover the bag. If the runner on third took off, Collins would grab the throw from the catcher and throw home. If the runner on third remained there, he would allow Barry to catch the throw.[50]

As with most of the better-paid Athletic players, Barry's days with the team were numbered following the 1914 World Series. In June 1915, shortly after Mack sold Bob Shawkey to the Yankees, rumors began that Barry would be the next to go.[51] Several days later, the rumors proved true, as Barry went to the Red Sox for a disclosed price of $8,000.[52] Reportedly, a number of teams had been interested, but Boston was Barry's preference since he was from the Boston area. Red Sox owner Joseph Lannin announced that Barry would be moved from shortstop to second base, where he would remain for the rest of his career. This left McInnis as the sole survivor of Philadelphia's famed infield. Never a strong hitter, Barry's average during the two seasons as a full-time player with the Red Sox did not rise above .214. With Barry at second, and serving as team captain as well the Red Sox won consecutive pennants in 1915, when they beat the Phillies in the series, and 1916, when they defeated Brooklyn. An injury prevented him from participating in the 1916 Series.

In 1916, Lannin sold the Red Sox to Harry Frazee for a reported $500,000.

Following the season, manager Bill Carrigan resigned, and Frazee named Barry as his replacement. In his sole season in that position, Barry led the Red Sox to a second-place finish with a record of 90–62, nine games behind Chicago. During the season, Barry enlisted in the naval reserve at the Boston Navy Yard, volunteering for service after the season.[53] Barry's naval service consisted of managing the Charlestown (MA) Navy Yard baseball team, and he was discharged in 1918. Barry had an offer to return to the Athletics, but decided instead to retire. His lifetime batting average was .243, his defensive skills and "smarts" being his most notable attributes on the diamond. After a brief "career" as an automobile dealer, Barry was hired as full-time coach of the Holy Cross baseball team in 1921, a position he kept through 1960. His coaching record with the college was 616-150-6, never losing more than eight games in a season, and only failing to finish above .500 twice in the thirty-nine years. In 1952, the American Association of College Baseball Coaches named him coach of the year in leading the team to the College World Series championship. In 2007, the man called the "Knute Rockne of college baseball" was honored by his selection into the National College Baseball Hall of Fame. Barry died from lung cancer in 1961 at age 74.

Jack Lapp played eight seasons with Mack, primarily in a platooning role. His sole season as a full-time catcher was 1915, batting .272. Still, Lapp was considered excellent on defense, "on fly balls without a superior in the American League."[54] He also participated in four World Series with the Athletics: 1910, 1911, 1913, and 1914. Mack "gave Lapp as a gift" to the White Sox in June 1916 with the only stipulation being that the Sox continue his present contract. Mack's reasoning was that he had a number of young catchers who could serve as Lapp's replacement.[55] Lapp's primary competition with the Sox was future Hall of Famer Ray Schalk, and he never really had a strong chance to break into the lineup. He batted .208 in 40 games for the season, and was released to Columbus of the American Association the following March. Lapp's lifetime average was .263. In 1920, Lapp died at age 35 of pneumonia, which had developed from a case of influenza.

John Franklin Baker entered baseball lore with two home runs in the 1911 Series against two future Hall of Famers: Christy Mathewson and Rube Marquard. Even newspapers of the period joined the act.[56] The 1913 season was one of four in succession — 1911–1914 — in which Baker led the league in home runs. In three of those seasons, 1911–1913, he also produced over 100 RBIs, leading the league with 130 in 1912, and 117 in 1913. All were impressive numbers for the period. As already noted, he hit .450 in the World's Series of 1913, including a home run once again off Marquard. Baker was also considered one of the best defensive third basemen of the time, anchoring that position in "the $100,000 infield" and leading the league in fielding percentage in 1911 and 1912.

Baker fell off during the 1914 Series, as did most of the team, slumping to .250 in eight at-bats. The following season, Baker and Mack began a dispute over the salary provided by his multi-year contract that still had a year to run. "I'll come back if Connie asks me," was Baker's statement. Mack's reply was that Baker was already under contract.[57] Neither Mack nor Baker would compromise, the result being that Baker held out the entire season. He still kept in "baseball shape," initially playing for the Upland team of the independent Delaware County League. The owner of the team, John Crozer, was a wealthy farmer, reportedly paying Baker $10,000 to manage and play for the team.[58] Mack was not pleased. "I want to say that I never want to see Baker again.... I have no time to deal for a man who is unfair in his dealings.... A man who breaks his word once is likely to do it again. I don't want Baker in my club."[59]

Baker did wish to return to major league baseball, and the end result was that in February 1916 after a four-hour conference at the Ruppert brewery, Mack sold Baker to the Yankees for $25,000. The Yankees then signed Baker to a three-year contract at $8,000 per annum.[60] Baker played the remainder of his major league career six seasons, in New York, joining a squad that developed into the original Murderer's Row, which actually referred to the first six batters in the 1918 Yankee lineup. In 1919, his last full season, Baker hit 10 home runs. When his first wife died from scarlet fever following the 1919 season, Baker announced his retirement so he could tend to his children and maintain his business interests. After missing the 1920 season, Baker was initially unsure of any return for the 1921 season. The severe illness of his daughter was also weighing on his mind. But after a conference with Yankee manager Miller Huggins and the improvement in the health of his daughter, Baker returned in 1921. Age and injuries limited Baker's playing time his last two seasons, and Baker announced his permanent retirement in February 1923. His lifetime batting average was .307. In six World Series, four with the Athletics and two with New York (1921, 1922), Baker batted .363. Even this number is misleading, since his average for the four series in which he played for Mack was .378. His 18 RBIs were at one time the record for the post-season. Tall and solid at 6 feet, 175 pounds, Baker swung a 52-ounce bat.

Other than briefly managing the Easton Farmers of the Eastern Shore League near his farm in Trappe, Maryland (among his players being a young Jimmie Foxx), Baker retired to become a "gentleman" farmer while raising four children with his second wife. He was selected to be a member of the National Baseball Hall of Fame by the Veteran's Committee in 1955. In his later years, Baker managed several farms, raised and trained hunting dogs, and was a supporter of youth baseball. In both 1950 and 1951, he participated in old-timers games at Yankee Stadium, a field that had not existed in his time. Baker died at age 77 in 1963.

John Phalen "Stuffy" McInnis was the youngest member of Connie Mack's $100,000 infield, and the last to remain with the team after Mack began to break it up. The 5'9½" first baseman was also one of the smallest to ever play the position. Originally a shortstop when he broke into the majors in 1909, he was positioned increasingly at first base until 1912, when this became his permanent position. Not a power hitter, his highest total of home runs was four in 1913, McInnis nevertheless was a man who consistently got his bat on the ball. He rarely walked. At the same time, he was one of the more difficult men in the lineup to strike out, showing a total of 189 for his 19-year career. Three times he whiffed fewer than 10 times in seasons in which he had more than 500 at-bats. Twelve times his season average was over .300, finishing with 2,405 hits and a lifetime average of .307. On defense he could be extraordinary. In 1921 with the Red Sox, he made one error in 1,651 chances, a fielding average of .9993, with a league record of 1,300 consecutive chances without an error. Lifetime, he committed only 160 errors in 21,200 chances, a fielding percentage of .993. Among the innovations McInnis developed as a first baseman were the "knee reach, a leg split to reach the throw while keeping his foot on the bag — common today, but unusual in McInnis' time, catching throws with one hand, and using a claw-type mit."[61]

With the breakup of his pennant-winning team, Mack's Athletics proceeded to the league cellar, creating a vicious curve: fans stayed away because the team had become so pathetic, and with fewer fans it became more difficult to sign or maintain quality players. After three straight seasons in the cellar, McInnis' turn came in January 1918, two months after Strunk, Bush and Schang went to Boston, and what in reality was probably part of the same trade, with additional players to be named later.[62] In February, Larry Gardner, Tilly Walker and Hick Cady were named as the additional players.[63] The Red Sox were both American League and World Series champions that year, in no small part due to the players obtained from the Athletics.

McInnis played four years with the Red Sox, hitting around .300 in each of them. In December 1921 McInnis was traded to Cleveland for first baseman George Burns, outfielder Elmer Smith and infielder Joe Harris. Both Smith and McInnis objected, however, Smith because he did not wish to move from a pennant winner to a second-division club, and McInnis because he had a no-trade contract.[64] But as was common in that period, the players really had little choice — McInnis finally agreed to the trade and Smith went to Boston. (Perhaps ironically, Smith joined the pennant-winning Yankees in July, part of the trade in which the Yankees also acquired Joe Dugan.) McInnis played only that one season in Cleveland, batting .305, and was picked up on waivers by the Boston Braves in February 1923.

Once again McInnis came through, playing a strong defense, while batting .315 and .291 for the two seasons with the Boston Nationals. The following spring of 1925, McInnis held out for a salary increase, something the Braves management did not support, and in truth could not afford. In April, Braves vice president Emil Fuchs gave him his unconditional release. McInnis was not out of baseball for very long, signing with the Pittsburgh Pirates at the end of May. By September, he was the third-leading hitter in the league, albeit in a part-time role; he finished at .368, a major factor in the Pirates' pennant-winning season. One of four veterans of World Series play on the Pirates that year, McInnis' steady play was significant in the Pirates coming from a 3–1 game deficit to defeat the Washington Senators.

McInnis played one more season with Pittsburgh, mostly in a part-time role. In September 1926 he was given his release, leaving under a cloud. A vote had been taken among the players some weeks earlier to the effect that vice president and former manager Fred Clarke should be asked to resign. McInnis had revealed the vote to the newspaper writers, with the result being that his services were no longer required. Only a month later, he signed a two-year contract to manage and play for the Philadelphia Phillies, the sixth man in nine years to attempt a miracle in that city. Although the Phillies started strong with some decent hitting and pitching, no miracles were in order, and the team once again finished in the cellar. At the end of the season, McInnis was replaced by Burt Shotton.

McInnis spent his last years in baseball, first as a manager of the Salem Witches in the New England League (1928), then as baseball coach at several colleges, the last at Harvard (1949–1954). He died in 1960 at age 69.

Wally Schang went on to become one of the most respected catchers of his day, not only for the Athletics, but also for the Yankees — arguably their greatest player at that position until Bill Dickey came along. Only Ray Schalk of the White Sox came close. His potential became obvious as the 1913 season progressed, finishing with an average of .266 with three home runs, plus another in the series (and a .357 batting average in that classic). The Chalmers Award, presented by Chalmers Automotive, a Detroit automobile company, was presented to the most valuable player in each league, and went to Walter Johnson that year (who received 54 votes). Schang finished eighth in the voting, receiving eight tallies. His World Series share of the money on top of a minimal ($1,000) salary for the season also allowed Schang to marry a Philadelphia woman, Marie Aubrey. Though the marriage would end in divorce in 1928, she and Wally did have one daughter, Joan.

Schang led American League catchers in hitting the following year, the last in a string of pennants for Mack in that era. Hampered by a broken thumb, Schang still managed to hit .287, with three home runs and 45 RBIs. Schang survived the breakup of the Athletics until the end of the 1917 season, after which he, Joe Bush and Amos Strunk were traded to the Red Sox for pitcher Vean Gregg, catcher Chet "Pinch" Thomas and outfielder Merlin Kopp, as well as an infusion of $60,000 for the Athletics.[65] Gregg would go 9–14 in his one season for Mack, Thomas never played for the Athletics, and Kopp never hit higher than .240 for Mack. Schang went on to produce two .300+ seasons in the next three years for the Sox. In 1918, Schang hit only .244 in 88 games, but once again he had an outstanding series, hitting .444 (.545 on-base percentage), as well as producing several outstanding defensive plays, as the Sox defeated the Chicago Cubs in six games.

Despite having another outstanding year in 1920, Schang once again found himself traded — again to a pennant winner. In December 1920 Schang, pitchers Waite Hoyt, a future Hall of Famer, and Harry Harper, and infielder Mike McNally went to the Yankees in exchange for catcher "Muddy" Ruel and three part-timers. While the trade at the time was considered "even Steven," Huggins was particularly pleased with two of the acquisitions: the 21-year-old schoolboy Hoyt, and the veteran Schang.[66] "Behind the plate, Huggins will have one of the greatest backstops in the game in Schang. He is a catcher whose value is not dependent on his mechanical ability alone, but on his handling of pitchers."[67]

Schang played five seasons with New York, including three more World Series contests, hitting .316 and .319 his first two years there, and still managing an average of .292 in 1924. But Schang was 35 years old by then, and the fall off in his play showed it. In February 1926 Schang was traded to the St. Louis Browns. At the age of 37, Schang was still capable of putting together one last outstanding year, hitting .330 while playing part-time. He continued with the Browns for three more seasons, hitting .318 in 97 games in 1927. In 1929, at age 40, Schang returned to the Athletics for one last season. He served mostly as a coach, but did manage to participate in 45 games, hitting .174. In November, Mack gave him his unconditional release. Within weeks, Schang and another veteran, Joe Dugan, were signed by the Tigers. After hitting only .184 in 30 games, Schang was released again at the end of June, signing with Chattanooga of the Southern Association the following month. He batted .247 as a substitute. Over the next several years, Schang moved from team to team in the minor leagues, playing in Shreveport of the Texas League (1932), batting .214; player/manager at Joplin of the Western Association (1934), batting .257; and Muskogee in the same league (1935). Now 46 years old, Schang still was determined to remain in baseball. He had also remarried in 1929 to a young woman, 20-year-old Dorothy Batty of Dixon, Missouri. After the marriage, Schang and his bride had purchased her parents' farm. But Schang had no desire to return to farming, a challenge in the best of times, let alone the years of the Depression. In 1936, he signed as a coach with the Cleveland Indians, helping to develop future stars such as Bob Feller, who was also his roommate for a time. In 1939, Schang became the manager of the minor league Ottawa Senators in the Canadian-American League. Both catchers became injured over the course of the season, so Schang filled in as a substitute, playing in 40 games at age 50. Three doubleheaders were included in his string. His playing career came to a permanent finish in 1942, when as manager of the Owensboro Oilers of the Kitty League, he batted seven times, reaching base in five of those appearances.

Schang spent his last years back on the farm in Dixon, often being observed around town. Never seriously considered for the Hall of Fame, Schang died in 1965 at age 75.

One could present the case that Eddie Collins was the greatest player on the field in the series, and few would argue with the opinion. At only 5'9", 175 pounds, too small to be a power hitter, Collins was considered one of the best at "simply" putting the bat on the ball, never striking out more than 37 times in a season. He produced a lifetime total of 3,315 base hits, nearly 1,500 bases on balls, a batting average of .333, and an on-base percentage of .424. As a base-runner, he was considered more "brainy" than merely fast. Collins was a firm supporter of the belief that one stole off the pitcher, not the catcher. He studiously followed the moves and mannerisms of those on the slab, the result being that he stole 741 bases lifetime. Records are incomplete, but it appears he was successful approximately 75 percent of the time.

During the 1913 Series, Collins was one of the leading hitters on the Athletics, his .421 average being second only to Baker's .450. He scored five runs, tying Collins with Oldring for the highest in that category. His three stolen bases was the highest. The following season Collins was the recipient of the Chalmers Award, the honor presented on behalf of Chalmers Automotive for the league's most valuable player. He batted .344, second in the league behind Cobb, and led the league in both on-base percentage (.452) and runs scored (122), the third consecutive season leading that category. His slump in that year's World Series contest against the Braves, when he managed to hit only .214, was one of many factors which resulted in the Athletics losing in four straight games.

Collins was among the first to depart when Mack began to disperse the team after the season. A fan could shake his head at the irony, given not only Collins' loyalty to Mack and the team — Collins had reportedly been offered a three-year contract worth $75,000 if he jumped to the Federal League — but also the fact that Collins' wife, Mabel Doane, was a close friend of Connie Mack's wife.[68] In addition to the increasing cost it would require to keep Collins with the Athletics, there were rumors as early as July of dissension on the team. Collins could also be cocky on the field, an attitude that upset some of his less-educated teammates. An anti–Collins faction developed, with catcher Ira Thomas as the alleged leader. Among the complaints voiced by the pro–Thomas faction was that in a series of articles Collins had written for a magazine, he had let known a little too much inside information.[69] There may also have been an element of jealousy. Both Collins and Thomas were reportedly confidants of Mack, yet it was Thomas who was named captain in 1914. The problem had become so advanced that certain players, possibly including Oldring and Lapp, would only follow orders from Collins and ignore Thomas.[70] Mack had no choice but to remove any possible troublemakers. On December 8, it was announced that Collins' contract had been purchased by the Chicago White Sox for a reported $50,000. Collins was then signed by the Sox to a five-year contract, at $10,000 per year (with some reports at double that). Despite rumors that Collins would also be named manager, he was not, although he did become team captain. Thomas barely saw playing time in his last two seasons with the team.

With the addition of other quality players, most notably Shoeless Joe Jackson from Cleveland and Claude Williams from Detroit, the White Sox put together a competitive team that won pennants in 1917 and 1919. After two consecutive .300+ seasons, Collins "slumped" to .289 in 1917, but recovered his hitting eye in the series against the Giants. The defining moment of the series occurred in the fourth inning of the sixth game, and Collins was at the center of the play. In what was called the "break of the game," Collins was on third base, Joe Jackson on first, and nobody was out. Happy Felsch hit a grounder back to pitcher Rube Benton. Benton grabbed the ball and stayed there watching Collins midway between third and home, motioning to Jackson and Felsch to keep moving. The play was described by the media.

> Not until Benton was nearly on top of him did Collins make a move, then he raced back toward third, with Rube after him. Benton tossed the ball to [third baseman Heinie] Zimmerman and Collins doubled in his tracks with the great Zim in hot pursuit toward the plate. [Catcher] Rariden meanwhile was thirty or forty feet from the home station and nobody behind him. Zimmerman chased Collins so far it was too late to hand the ball to Rariden who had to step out of the way and let Collins past. In desperation Zim tore after Collins, who beat him the rest of the way to the plate easily, scoring the first run.[71]

Collins' run proved to be the game, and ultimately the series, winner. Unfortunately, it was Zimmerman who was excoriated by the crowd as well as history. To its credit, the *Daily Tribune* and other papers did place the blame where it belonged, on Rariden or first baseman Walter Holke for not covering the plate. Zimmerman's alleged comment about the play, almost certainly apocryphal, was "Who the hell was I supposed to throw the ball to, Klem?"[72]

Collins' average in the war year of 1918 dropped to .276 in 97 games. Even though Collins was 31 years old and married with two children, he enlisted in the Marines in August. After training at Paris Island, South Carolina, Collins was assigned to the quartermaster's department, and was posted near his Lansdowne home at the Philadelphia Navy Yard, where he spent most of his time in the service.

From the beginning of the season, the 1919 White Sox were torn by dissension, with Collins and his supporters on one side, and Chick Gandil and his supporters on the other. Gandil had long had a strong dislike for Collins, dating to years before when Gandil played for Washington and had his nose broken by Collins' aggressive play. The situation was aggravated by the penny-pinching ways of Sox owner Charles Comiskey. The story is well known. Despite the dissension, the Sox were American League champions and overwhelming favorites to defeat the National League champion Cincinnati Reds. Eight players on the Sox participated in a scheme to "throw" the series. Whether each of the men actually received any money from the gamblers is unclear. In the end, the series was thrown, and the eight participants were banned from organized baseball for life. The team went into a decades-long decline.

Collins was named as manager midway during the 1924 season, but the talent simply was not there and the team finished no higher than fifth in the two full seasons under his leadership. In November 1926 Collins was replaced by catcher Ray Schalk and at the same time was released as a player. The firing came as a surprise to Collins, a man admired by the Chicago media. "Chicago has lost as fine a sportsman as ever wore a baseball uniform. Collins is more than a brilliant second baseman and conscientious manager; he is a gentleman with a fighting heart."[73]

Collins rejoined Mack and the Athletics on December 23, playing four more years in utility and coaching roles. He retired as a player in 1930, serving as a coach through the 1932 season. In 1934, he joined the Boston Red Sox as a vice president and general manager, positions he held until declining health in the late 1940s forced his resignation as general manager. Collins was among the first players inducted into the National Baseball Hall of Fame in 1939. He died in 1951 from a stroke at age 63.

John Edward "Eddie" Murphy, the "Pride of White Mills [PA]," batted .295 in his first full year with the Athletics, one of only three seasons in which he played in more than 100 games. In two of those seasons, 1913 and 1914, he scored over 100 runs. During the pennant-winning season of 1914, his batting average was .272; in the series that year, he hit .188 with no RBIs. In July of the following year, Murphy's contract was purchased by the White Sox, where he joined Eddie Collins, who had been his teammate on the pennant-winning teams in Philadelphia. Though less than one year since the completion of the 1914 Series, this left only eight men on the Athletics from those teams. Murphy quickly hit his stride with the new team, and finished with an average of .315 in his last season playing a full-time role in the outfield. With the Sox, Murphy's role was primarily that of a pinch-hitter, with occasional time in the outfield. He was quite effective in this role, as the White Sox won pennants in both 1917 and 1919.[74] Defensively, Murphy was too much of a liability to be out there fulltime.[75]

Murphy was one of the "honest ones" from the 1919 team that threw the series that year. Though only appearing in 30 games, primarily as a pinch-hitter, he hit a career high of .486, with 17 hits in his 35 at-bats. In the series he went hitless. In recognition of his honesty, White Sox owner Charles Comiskey provided a $1,500 bonus in 1920 to Murphy and the other honest players, the sum representing the difference between the winning and losing shares.[76] "As one of the honest ballplayers of the Chicago White Sox team of 1919, I feel that you were deprived of the winner's share in the world's series receipts through no fault of yours."[77]

Eddie Collins, at least, considered Murphy as "the greatest pinch hitter he ever saw."[78] But that alone could not save Murphy from filling a needed roster spot, and he was released in June 1921. Murphy was quickly signed by Cleveland, but without making any appearances for that club, Murphy was sent to

Columbus of the American Association on June 10. He played in that city through the 1925 season, when he was traded to Rochester. His last year in the majors was a short stint with Pittsburgh in 1926. In the ensuing years until his retirement in 1930, Murphy played with minor league teams in Jersey City (1927–1928) and Montreal (1928). During World War II, Murphy worked with the USO. He was a supervisor of the WPA in Lackawanna County, Pennsylvania, where he spent his last years. Murphy died from prostate cancer in 1969 at age 77.

Leslie Ambrose "Bullet Joe" Bush was only a 20-year-old rookie when he appeared in the 1913 Series. He ensured his role on Mack's staff with a 17-win season the following year. In the 1914 Series Bush made one appearance, losing the third game in 11 innings in as good a pitching performance as any for the Athletics. With the breakup of the team by Mack, the Athletics plummeted into the cellar during 1915. Bush could do no more than a 5–15 record. As the Athletic fortunes dropped even further in 1916, Bush produced a record of 15–24 for a team that went 36–117; over 40 percent of the Athletic victories were therefore attributed to Bush. The Athletics were considered to have minimal prospects from the "get-go," and managed to support that early evaluation over the course of the season.[79] Bush even managed to twirl a no-hitter on August 26 against Cleveland. Nevertheless, even though Mack was arguably desperate for quality players, in December 1916 Bush, Amos Strunk and Wally Schang were traded to the Boston Red Sox for Vean Gregg, Chet Thomas and Merlin Kopp, plus a cash payment of $60,000 for Mack.

Bush contributed 15 victories to the Red Sox's pennant drive for 1918, adding a save in the series victory against Chicago. In 1919, however, he injured his arm in spring training, and was lost to the team for the season. Bush and the Sox management did not view his inability to pitch in the same manner — Bush arguing his arm was effectively useless, and management believing otherwise.[80] A winter's rest was sufficient to restore his arm, and Bush went on to produce 15- and 16-victory seasons the next two years. Development of a fork-ball provided an additional pitch, relieving some of the stress on his arm.[81]

In a surprise move, owner Harry Frazee sprung another "blockbuster" deal with the Yankees in December 1921, sending Bush, pitcher Sam Jones and shortstop Everett Scott to the Yankees in exchange for shortstop Roger Peckinpaugh and pitchers Rip Collins, Jack Quinn and Bill Piercy. The trade gave the Yankees what was considered at the time to be "the best staff of moundsmen in its history."[82]

Bush spent three productive years in New York, winning 26 games his first season in 1922, and finishing fourth in the voting for most valuable player. He contributed one victory to the Yankee series championship in 1923, while losing one game when the Giants' Casey Stengel hit a home run that proved to be a game winner. The 1924 season proved erratic for Bush, even with 17 victories. The result was that in December, he went to the St. Louis Browns in a deal in which Urban Shocker joined the Yankees. Bush contributed 14 victories to the Browns for the 1925 season. In February 1926 Bush was traded again, this time to Washington for pitchers Tom Zachary and Win Ballou. Bush managed only one victory for Washington, a May 13 four-hitter against his former Browns team. Repeatedly pounded, his ERA approaching 7.00, Bush was released on June 24. A week later, he signed with Pittsburgh, managing to produce six victories, including a two-hit September shutout of the Phillies, over the remainder of the season for the National League contenders. The Pirates were pennant winners in 1927, but Bush could only contribute a single early victory, and on June 15, once again received his release. There were no hard feelings on the part of the realistic veteran: "Two great teams I've been on are the Yankees and the Pirates; they are wonderful ballclubs, too, but that's not what I mean. I'm talking about the ace-high birds who will play with you and fight for you from the drop of a hat.... I'm out now. But I'm for these Pittsburgh boys till they close the parks. I hope they win by eighteen games."[83] Bush was not out long, signing with McGraw before the end of the month. His first outing was a 4–1 victory over Boston. But that was all Bush could do, and on July 19, he once again was released. Briefly joining the Toledo Mud Hens, Bush contributed four victories, but in what was almost becoming routine, the club released him at season's end. Bush came back for one more try the following year, as in December his original manager, Connie Mack, re-signed him for one more try in the big leagues. He contributed two victories, and in November was released for the final time in the majors, sharing that distinction with Tris Speaker and Ty Cobb that day.[84] He retired with a lifetime record of 196–184. Bush could also wield an acceptable bat. Sometimes used as a pinch-hitter, Bush retired with 313 base hits and a lifetime batting average of .253. Bush died at age 81 in 1974.

Eddie Plank was already a seven-time twenty-game winner when the 1913 season started. Though he managed a record of "only" 18–10, a drop from 26 wins the year before, it still represented the second-highest total from the Athletics' staff. Given his age of thirty-eight years, it was still quite the achievement. His two-hit performance in the final game of the series represented his second, and final, victory in the post-season classic.

By 1914, Plank finally began showing evidence of his "advanced age." His 15–7 record was his lowest victory total in six years, and the second lowest in his career until that point. His 2.87 ERA was his highest since 1902. In the series, however, he appeared to regain his old form, losing a 1–0 gem to the Braves in the ninth inning. His final World Series record was 2–5, belying the quality of pitching he actually exhibited. His opponents in three of his series included the likes of Mathewson, McGinnity and Marquard — no shame in that Giant trifecta. A better indication of Plank's performance than his won-loss record is seen in his post-season ERA of 1.32 and 3:1 strikeout-walk ratio.

Rumors persisted through the 1914 season that Plank and other prominent players were listening to agents representing the "upstart" Federal League.[85] In

Plank's case, the rumors were true, as he signed a contract with the St. Louis Terriers a month after the World Series. Mack wished Plank the best, though he still expressed his bitterness. "I was through with him. He was after the money and was quite willing to go to the Federals. He was a wonderful pitcher, and he is a good one yet."[86] Plank had reportedly earned $5,000 in the 1914 season. Several days after Plank joined the new league, teammate Chief Bender likewise jumped from the Athletics.

Plank won 21 games his one season in the new league, the eighth time in his career he reached that level, and led the league with an ERA of 2.01. At the completion of the season, Plank considered himself to be a free agent. Meanwhile, the league itself had disappeared, and with the negotiations between the former Federal League and the rest of organized baseball completed, Terriers owner Phil Ball was now the new owner of the American League St. Louis Browns. Ball considered Plank to be his "property" via the reserve clause. Plank appealed to the National Commission. On February 7, 1916, the National Commission ruled it would respect the reserve clauses of Federal League contracts. The ten-year rule would not apply to Plank since he had left the Athletics in 1914 before waivers had been obtained. "His [Plank] transfer to the St. Louis club is a matter of record and his salary for 1916 is a matter of negotiation between him and that club."[87]

Plank spent his last two seasons in the majors with St. Louis, producing a record of 16–15 for a fifth-place club in 1916, and slumping badly to a 5–6 record in his final season of 1917. His ERA that final season was still an impressive 1.79 for a seventh-place team. On August 6, Plank lost an eleven-inning 1–0 heart-breaker to Walter Johnson and the Washington Senators, and a week later announced his retirement from baseball. Despite some wavering, he stuck to his decision even after being involved in a January, 1918 trade to the Yankees.

Plank spent his last years back on his Gettysburg farm and working at an automobile dealership in the town. He would also serve as a tour guide at the famous battlefield on occasion. On February 22, 1926, Plank suffered a stroke, dying two days later. Only fifty years old, Plank was buried not many miles from his most famous World Series opponent, Christy Mathewson. Dr. Henry Hanson, president of Gettysburg College, which Plank had attended for a time (though never was graduated), eulogized the man's qualities of

"gentlemanly characteristics and moral, upright life, both on and off the baseball diamond."[88]

As a pitcher, Plank was most noted for a powerful side-arm fastball and effective breaking pitch. He was slow and deliberate on the mound, sometimes accused of almost going into a trance while standing near the slab and watching the batter. His strikeout total of 2,246 was a result of catching the batter off-stride as much as the result of speed. Plank's lifetime record was 326–194, the win total being the highest in the twentieth century until surpassed by Walter Johnson. In 1946, Plank was elected to the Baseball Hall of Fame.

Charles Albert "Chief" Bender was the right-handed ace of Mack's 1913 squad, the counterpart to Eddie Plank. Tall and husky (6'2", 185 pounds), Bender was noted for both a potent fastball and sharp curve as well as a changeup which kept batters off-stride. Further confusing the hitter, he could throw these pitches overhand, side-arm and even using an underhand "submarine" style. His 21-victory season in 1913 was one of two such in his career, but his consistency year after year resulted in a career total of 212 wins against 127 losses. His 13 saves in 1913 also led the league in that (later reconstructed) category.

Bender was particularly successful in the postseason. The only pitcher besides Plank to appear with Mack's 1905, 1910–1911 and 1913–1914 pennant winners, Bender pitched in ten games during those five series, winning six of his ten decisions, and producing an ERA of 2.44. His shutout in the 1905 Series against the Giants was the only Athletic victory in that match-up.

The then-thirty-year-old right-hander had one of his best seasons with Mack in 1914, finishing 17–3 with an ERA of 2.26. His victory total included 14 in a row, ending on September 12 when the New York Yankees' catcher Ed Sweeney hit a ninth-inning home run to break up a pitching duel between Bender and Ray Keating. In the series that year against the Braves, Bender appeared in only the first game. After retiring the Braves in the first inning, Bender was hit hard and was removed in the sixth after allowing six earned runs. Bender later complained he was suffering from stomach trouble during the game. Others had a different view. Second baseman Johnny Evers of the Braves suggested that arm trouble was the problem, since it was generally known that "Bender has had to have his arm treated with electricity after every game he pitched during the season, and for several days afterwards to put life into it."[89] Whatever the reason, Mack was clearly disappointed with his star pitcher.

Whether Bender really was through was arguable. But Mack had lost money during the season, and the loser's share of the series money allowed the team merely to break even financially. On October 31, Mack waived his three primary starters from recent years—Bender, Plank and Coombs—and presumably their combined salary of $17,000.[90] Claimed on waivers by both Boston and Cincinnati, Bender nevertheless jumped to the Baltimore Terrapins of the Federal League for 1915. He could only manage a weak 4–16 record, while Bender's ERA ballooned to almost 4.00. On August 30, he was released by the Terrapins.

Bender's arm still merited interest within baseball, and reportedly both the Giants and Phillies had interest in his joining their respective staffs. In February 1916 Bender signed with Philadelphia. That season he managed seven victories for the reigning league champions. In the winter following the season, however, Bender encountered significant legal troubles when he was accused of leaving the scene of a hit-and-run death in Philadelphia. The victim, one James Curran, had been crossing the busy thoroughfare of Broad Street when he was hit and killed. The driver reportedly turned down a side street and left. However, a policeman happened to observe the license number, and the car was traced to Bender.[91] Three days later, the Phillies gave Bender his release. On February 27, a coroner's jury exonerated Bender of any negligence and the pitcher was subsequently re-signed by the team. Despite winning eight games for the Phillies, Bender was waived after the season and was hired for a job at a Philadelphia shipyard. Claimed by the Yankees, Bender reportedly told the team he could not report until July. The Yankees released him, and for practical purposes, Bender's major league pitching career was over.[92]

Bender spent the next few seasons managing a variety of minor league teams. In 1919, while negotiating with Cincinnati Reds manager Pat Moran for a position on the team, he was offered a job in May as player/manager for the Richmond Colts, newly established in the Class B Virginia League.[93] He led the team to the second-half league pennant both as a manager and as the league's dominant pitcher with a record of 29–2 and 295 strikeouts. During subsequent years, he pitched and/or managed at New Haven of the Eastern League, for whom he won 25 games in 1920, Reading and Baltimore in the International League, Johnstown (PA) in the Mid-Atlantic League, and as baseball coach at the Naval Academy in Maryland.

During 1925, Bender made one last appearance on a big league mound while serving as pitching and first-base coach for the White Sox. On July 21 during the first game of a doubleheader against the Red Sox, Bender took the mound during the ninth inning. The first batter, Ira Flagstead, was walked. After Bender retired the next two batters, outfielder Roy Carlyle hit a home run. First baseman Phil Todt then fouled out to end the inning. Bender walked off the mound to cheers. In that same game, catcher Ray Schalk of the White Sox established what was then the lifetime record for games caught.[94] "I can still pitch as good as ⅔ of the men in the American League," Bender said, "and I hope to be able to take a regular turn in the box soon."[95] Bender did return to the roster soon enough to pitch three innings in an exhibition against Battle Creek several days later as well as against Saginaw at the end of August. But in reality his big league pitching days were over, and he was released from his coaching duties to return to the Naval Academy after the season.

This was not the end of his career in baseball, however. Once again during the 1930s and 1940s, he managed a variety of teams in variety of places, including a team in the House of David League, Wilmington of the Inter-state League, Newport News of the Virginia League and Savannah in the South Atlantic League.

Despite his disappointment with Bender because of the pitcher's performance in the 1914 World Series, Connie Mack always had a soft spot in his heart for the hurler. In 1939, Bender was signed by the Athletics as a scout, and several years later was brought in as a coach for the club by Mack, a position he maintained until his death. Signed by Mack originally for an $1,800 bonus, Bender rarely earned much more than that despite being the pitcher that Mack often said was the one man he would call on if a victory was needed.[96] In 1953, Bender was voted into the Baseball Hall of Fame. He died in May the following year from a combination of cancer and heart disease at age 71.

Cornelius McGillicuddy — Connie Mack — was synonymous with baseball for more than two generations of fans. For over a decade after his death, the name remained in the public eye as the eponymous title of the stadium in Philadelphia where he was found for more than forty years. He built and dismantled two dynasties: 1910–1914 and 1929–1931. And even though the other team in Philadelphia, the Phillies, rarely provided much competition on the field, Mack faced significant challenges throughout his tenure in maintaining a fan base sufficient to turn any sort of profit. In the end, once age forced his resignation, his sons felt they had no choice but to sell the team, knowing the franchise would likely have to move. It is a toss-up whether it was age, or a broken heart, which led to his death.

But that was over four decades after the 1913 Series, when at fifty he was still a comparatively young man. In 1914, the Athletics once again won the American League pennant handily, finishing 8½ games in front of second-place Boston, 19 games in front of third-place Washington. On paper, the Athletics were far superior to the "Miracle Braves' they faced in the series. But, of course, it bears repeating that the game is played on the field, not on paper. And on the field the Athletics were clearly outclassed. Mack blamed the new Federal League and the interest his players allegedly had shown in jumping. One could make an argument otherwise. Except for the first game, lost by a score of 7–1, the Athletics were simply out-pitched. Their combined batting average for the series was an anemic .172; of the 22 hits by the team, two were by the pitchers. Two of the pitchers whom Mack sold or traded off after the season, Plank and Bender, joined the new league. Bender clearly had his best years behind him, and while Plank still had some wins remaining in his forty-year-old arm, even his days on the diamond were numbered. The reality was that Mack simply could not afford to maintain an expensive, but aging squad. One might argue that Mack went too far, consigning the Athletics to years of being cellar-dwellers. But attempting to keep the team afloat would be a problem throughout its years in Philadelphia. The solution was to trade or sell off players: Eddie Collins went to the White Sox for $50,000; Home Run Baker went to the Yankees for $25,000. And so it went until every player of note was gone. Attendance reflected the abysmal nature of the team, falling from a high of 675,000 patrons in 1909, to just over 146,000 in 1915 when the Athletics won 43 games and lost 109. The team finally hit bottom in 1916 and 1919 when they won only 36 games; Mack finished in the cellar seven consecutive years during this period.

Ever on the lookout for talent, Mack rebuilt the team during the 1920s, signing or otherwise acquiring a team worthy of inclusion in the Hall of Fame: Jimmie Foxx, Lefty Grove, Al Simmons and Mickey Cochrane among many others. By 1929, he had returned to the top, winning three consecutive pennants and two World Series. During the 1929 postseason, Mack pulled a surprise when he opened the series against Chicago with veteran pitcher Howard Ehmke. Most had expected one of Mack's front-line pitchers to start: George Earnshaw or Grove. But Ehmke had told Mack that he had at least one more quality game in his arm, so the manager had Ehmke scout the Cubs for weeks before the end of the series to learn their strengths and weaknesses. Ehmke did so, and pitched a superb 3–1 victory to open the series. Attendance during the pennant-winning year of 1929 was a respectable 839,176. But attendance fell to barely 297,000 within four years, and with a depression on, Mack could not afford his high-priced stars. Once again he held a sale, sending Earnshaw to the White Sox for $25,000 and Foxx, Grove, Rube Walberg and others to the Red Sox for $275,000 plus players. In total, the team was sold off for approximately $500,000. By 1935, the Athletics were again last, and would finish in the basement ten more times before Mack retired.

Amid family disagreements which resulted from transferring of stock from the Shibe family to Connie and his sons, Mack announced his resignation as manager on October 18, 1950, turning the team over to former player and current coach Jimmy Dykes, and ending the leadership he had provided since the Athletics joined the American League in 1901. He remained as honorary chairman of the board, but in reality had little say in the team. Athletic teams under Mack had won a record 3,582 games and lost 3,814. Mack's complete managerial record was 3,731–3,948. Under Mack, the Athletics won pennants nine times: 1902, 1905, 1910, 1911, 1913, 1914, 1929, 1930 and 1931, They were world champions five times: 1910, 1911, 1913, 1929 and 1930. There was no post-season series in 1902. On November 4, 1954, the Macks sold the team to Arnold Johnson, a vending machine magnate from Chicago. Aware of the financial challenges that faced the team, Mack prophesized, "I'd die if the Athletics are ever moved out of Philadelphia."[97] When shortly afterwards Johnson announced the team would transfer to Kansas City, the news broke Mack's heart.

In October 1955 Mack fell out of bed at his home, suffering a broken hip. He underwent surgery to repair the damage, spending three weeks in the hospital. Unable to walk, Mack also could not to take part in the winter pilgrimage south which he had carried out most years since 1888. On February 8, 1956, his ninety-three-year-old heart finally gave out. The "Grand Old Man," "Mr. Baseball," "The Tall Tactician" were among the names by which he became known. He was the last manager to appear in the dugout wearing a suit, not a uniform. Among the behaviors remembered was his positioning of players by waving a scorecard. A gentleman to the last, he rarely lost his temper or expressed any emotion at all in front of the team. If he needed to discipline a player, he did so privately to avoid embarrassment. "He was a nice guy, and he finished first."[98]

Among the many tributes to Mack published upon death was one written by Grantland Rice, arguably one of the greatest sports writers of the twentieth century. The tribute was originally presented in 1946 at a retirement dinner for longtime football coach Amos Alonzo Stagg.[99] Amidst amusing remarks reflecting the advanced ages of both Stagg and Mack, Rice's poetic presentation represented the bittersweet memories found in the hearts of sports fans in general, memories which evoked both the long spent youth for each of the two honored individuals as well as their own youth found in the distant past. More romanticized than actually "romantic," the era of baseball epitomized by Connie Mack still evokes in the twenty-first century a more innocent period for professional baseball.

A more detailed account of how the Mack family acquired the Philadelphia Athletics, as well as Shibe Park, can be found in a variety of sources.[100, 101, 102] Unofficially, Shibe Park was renamed Connie Mack Stadium prior to the 1941 season when a friend of Mack's, Harry McDevitt, placed a sign with that name over the inscription of Shibe Park. To the fans, however, and to their credit also the Mack family, the stadium retained the name of Shibe. Following Mack's death, the park was officially renamed Connie Mack Stadium. By that time, only the Phillies remained in the city.

The quality of play by the Athletics briefly revived in the post-war years, breaking the .500 mark in 1947, and reaching a high of .545 (84–70) in 1948. By 1954, they once again settled into the familiar territory of the cellar (51–103), the eighth time in thirteen seasons. Attendance likewise plummeted, from a high of 945,076 in 1948, and steadily dropping to a low of 304,666 in 1954. Loss of receipts was also reflected in the coffers of visiting clubs, which also pressured the Macks for changes. The Mack sons decided they had no choice but to sell; Chicagoan Arnold Johnson made an offer exceeding $3.3 million, and in November 1954 the sale was completed. The franchise was moved to Kansas City, site of a Yankee farm club, and over a half-century of Philadelphia Athletic history in the American League came to an end.

The New York site of the Giants franchise survived only another three years. Despite fielding a competitive team, the Giants had been world champions after sweeping Cleveland in the 1954 Series, it was clear that attendance, barely passing the 600,000 mark by 1957, was not sufficient to support the team if it continued in the aging Polo Grounds. Owner Charles Stoneham, who had purchased the team in 1919, was persuaded to join the Dodgers' Walter O'Malley in moving to California. The 1957 season was their last in New York, and the franchise which had played in that city since the previous century joined the move west.

Appendix:
World's Series Team Totals

New York Giants: Batting/Fielding Totals

	G	AB	R	H	2B	3B	HR	RBI	BB	SO	SB	BA	PO	A	E
Fred Merkle	4	13	3	3	0	0	1	3	1	2	0	.231	38	1	2
Larry Doyle	5	20	1	3	0	0	0	2	0	1	0	.250	13	19	3
Art Fletcher	5	18	1	5	0	0	0	4	1	1	1	.278	8	10	1
Buck Herzog	5	19	1	1	0	0	0	0	0	1	0	.053	6	7	0
Red Murray	5	16	2	4	0	0	0	1	2	2	2	.250	9	0	0
Tillie Shafer	5	19	2	3	1	1	0	1	2	3	0	.158	8	0	0
George Burns	5	19	2	3	2	0	0	1	1	5	1	.158	14	0	1
Larry McLean	5	12	0	6	0	0	0	2	0	0	0	.500	13	3	0
Chief Meyers	1	4	0	0	0	0	0	0	0	0	0	.000	4	2	0
Art Wilson	3	3	0	0	0	0	0	0	0	2	0	.000	4	1	0
Fred Snodgrass	2	3	0	1	0	0	0	0	0	0	0	.333	3	1	0
Moose McCormick	2	2	1	1	0	0	0	0	0	0	0	.500	-	-	-
Eddie Grant	2	1	1	0	0	0	0	0	0	0	0	.000	0	0	0
Claude Cooper	2	0	0	0	0	0	0	0	0	0	1	-	-	-	-
Chr. Mathewson	2	5	1	3	0	0	0	1	1	0	0	.600	0	5	0
Doc Crandall	4	4	0	0	0	0	0	0	0	0	0	.000	0	2	0
Jeff Tesreau	2	2	0	0	0	0	0	0	0	1	0	.000	0	1	0
Rube Marquard	2	1	0	0	0	0	0	0	0	0	0	.000	0	8	0
Al Demaree	1	1	0	0	0	0	0	0	0	0	0	.000	0	2	0
Hooks Wiltse	2	2	0	0	0	0	0	0	0	1	0	.000	15	3	0

New York Giants: Pitching Totals

	G	IP	H	R	ER	BB	SO	W	L	ERA
Chr. Mathewson	2	19	14	3	2	2	7	1	1	0.95
Rube Marquard	2	9	10	7	7	3	3	0	1	7.00
Jeff Tesreau	2	8	11	7	6	1	4	0	1	6.48
Doc Crandall	2	4	4	2	2	0	2	0	0	3.86
Al Demaree	1	4	7	4	2	1	0	0	1	4.50

Philadelphia Athletics: Batting/Fielding Totals

	G	AB	R	H	2B	3B	HR	RBI	BB	SO	SB	BA	PO	A	E
Stuffy McInnis	5	17	1	2	1	0	0	2	0	2	0	.118	45	0	0
Eddie Collins	5	19	5	8	0	2	0	3	1	2	3	.421	16	18	1
Jack Barry	5	20	3	6	3	0	0	2	0	0	0	.300	9	16	1
Frank Baker	5	20	2	9	0	0	1	7	0	2	1	.450	6	6	1
Eddie Murphy	5	22	2	5	0	0	0	0	2	0	0	.227	14	0	0
Amos Strunk	5	17	3	2	0	0	0	0	2	2	0	.118	14	0	0
Rube Oldring	5	22	5	6	0	1	0	0	0	1	1	.273	10	0	0
Wally Schang	4	14	2	5	0	1	1	6	2	4	0	.357	16	3	1
Jack Lapp	1	4	0	1	0	0	0	0	0	1	0	.250	7	1	0
Chief Bender	2	8	0	0	0	0	0	0	0	1	0	.000	0	5	0
Eddie Plank	2	7	0	1	0	0	0	1	0	0	0	.143	1	3	1
Joe Bush	1	4	0	1	0	0	0	0	0	1	0	.250	0	1	0

Philadelphia Athletics: Pitching Totals

	G	IP	H	R	ER	BB	SO	W	L	ERA
Eddie Plank	2	19	9	4	2	3	7	1	1	0.95
Chief Bender	2	18	19	9	8	1	9	2	0	4.00
Joe Bush	1	9	5	2	1	4	3	1	0	1.00

(Source: Richard Cohen and David Neft, *The World Series.* New York: Macmillan, 1986.)

Chapter Notes

Introduction

1. While the post-season terminology today simply refers to the "World Series," newspaper writers of the time used both "World" and "World's."

2. John Thorn, Phil Birnbaum and Bill Deane, eds., *Total Baseball*, 8th edition (Toronto, Ontario: Sport Media Publishing, Inc., 2004).

Chapter One

1. Connie Mack, *My 66 Years in the Big Leagues* (Philadelphia: John C. Winston Co., 1950), p. 3. Some aspects of Mack's life, as well as possible quotes in his autobiography, may have been idealized.

2. Ibid.

3. Ibid.

4. Mike Roer, *Orator O'Rourke: The Life of a Baseball Radical* (Jefferson, NC: McFarland, 2005), p. 205.

5. *Washington Post*, September 9, 1886, p. 4.

6. *New York Times*, September 12, 1886, p. 5.

7. *Washington Post*, September 12, 1886, p. 2.

8. Ibid., October 10, 1886, p. 2.

9. *Chicago Daily*, January 22, 1891, p. 6.

10. Ibid., February 15, 1891, p. 6.

11. *Chicago Daily Tribune*, June 3, 1893, p. 7.

12. *Washington Post*, July 12, 1896, p. 4.

13. Ibid., September 4, 1894, p. 6.

14. Ibid., November 10, 1896, p. 8.

15. Mack, *My 66 Years*, p. 28.

16. Doug Skipper, in *Deadball Stars of the American League*, ed. David Jones (Dulles, VA: Potomac Books, 2006), p. 583.

17. *Washington Post*, December 6, 1901, p. 8.

18. *Los Angeles Times*, June 20, 1902, p. 4.

19. *Washington Post*, October 19, 1902, p. 15.

20. Ibid.

21. *Chicago Daily Tribune*, July 11, 1902, p. 6.

22. Mack, *My 66 Years*, p. 31. Another apocryphal quote?

23. Bruce Kuklick, *To Everything a Season* (Princeton, NJ: Princeton University Press, 1991), p. 18.

24. Ibid.

25. Alan Levy, *Rube Waddell* (Jefferson, NC: McFarland, 2000), p. 133.

26. Ibid., p. 167.

27. *Washington Post*, October 1, 1905, p. SP1.

28. *New York Times*, October 10, 1905, p. 4.

29. Ibid.

30. *Chicago Daily Tribune*, October 11, 1905, p. 10.

31. Ibid.

32. *Chicago Daily Tribune*, October 13, 1905, p. 6.

33. Levy, *Rube Waddell*, p. 184.

34. Ibid., p. 188.

35. Ibid., p. 208.

36. *Washington Post*, March 31, 1907, p. D4.

37. Levy, *Rube Waddell*, p. 211.

38. *Washington Post*, April 30, 1907, p. 8.

39. J. Edward Grille, *Washington Post*, April 28, 1907, p. S2.

40. Levy, *Rube Waddell*, p. 223.

41. Ibid., p. 230.

42. *Washington Post*, February 8, 1908, p. 8.

43. Ibid., February 9, 1908, p. S2.

44. Ibid., October 6, 1908, p. 8.

45. Arthur Allen, *Vaccine* (New York: W.W. Norton, 2007), p. 74.

46. *Washington Post*, April 30, 1909, p. 8.

47. Ibid., August 16, 1909, p. 4.

48. Ibid., August 27, 1909, p. 8.

49. Ibid., August 28, 1909, p. 4.

50. J. Edward Grillo, *Washington Post*, February 18, 1910, p. 8.

51. J. Edward Grillo, *Washington Post*, April 16, 1910, p. 8.

52. *Washington Post*, April 18, 1910, p. 8.

53. Ibid., October 20, 1910, p. 6.

54. *Chicago Daily Tribune*, October 22, 1910, p. 20.

55. Ibid.

56. John J. Evers, *Washington Post*, October 24, 1910, p. 2.

57. *New York Times*, March 6, 1911, p. 8.

58. *Chicago Daily Tribune*, April 20, 1911, p. 22.

59. Ty Cobb, *Chicago Daily Tribune*, October 17, 1911, p. 9.

60. Rube Marquard, *New York Times*, October 17, 1911, p. 1.

61. *Chicago Daily Tribune*, October 19, 1911, p. 10.

62. William Kashatus, *Money Pitcher: Chief Bender and the Tragedy of Indian Assimilation* (University Park: The Pennsylvania State University, 2006), p. 101.

63. Ibid., p. 102.

64. *Washington Post*, March 31, 1912, p. S4.

65. *New York Times*, April 25, 1912, p. 11.

66. Hugh Fullerton, *Los Angeles Times*, July 2, 1912, p. III2.

67. Joe Jackson, *Washington Post*, July 30, 1912, p. 8.

68. *New York Times*, September 1, 1912, p. S1.

69. Hugh Fullerton, *Chicago Daily Tribune*, September 11, 1912, p. 11.

70. *Washington Post*, September 7, 1912, p. 9.

Chapter Two

1. Grantland Rice, *Los Angeles Times*, February 26, 1934, p. 10.

2. Charles Alexander, *John McGraw* (New York: Viking Penguin, 1988), p. 12.

3. Michael McGraw, *The McGrath Family of Truxton, New York* (2002), p. 83–85. Online at http://home.austin.rr.com/mfmcgraw/McGraths%20of%20Truxton%2001.pdf. According to Michael McGraw, a descendent of the family, John McGraw's mother died in August 1883, one month after giving birth to his sister, named Helen (Nellie). McGraw also differs from Alexander in stating that three children, not four, died during the epidemic. Much of the early information about John William McGraw is drawn from this source.

4. Alexander, *John McGraw*, p. 14.

5. Ibid., p. 16.

6. Graham, *McGraw of the Giants* (New York: G.P. Putnam's Sons, 1944), p. 9.

7. Alexander, *John McGraw*, p. 20.

8. Ibid., p. 21.

9. John J. McGraw, *My Thirty Years in Baseball* (New York: Boni and Liveright, 1923), p. 175. Quoted in Alexander, p. 21.

10. *Washington Post*, July 12, 1893, p. 6.

11. Ibid., July 13, 1892, p. 6.

12. Alexander, *John McGraw*, p. 34.

13. *Washington Post*, August 17, 1893, p. 6.

14. Ibid., April 23, 1894, p. 6.

15. *New York Times*, April 26, 1894, p. 3.

16. Alexander, *John McGraw*, p. 40.

17. *Chicago Daily Tribune*, September 26, 1894, p. 11.

18. Jack Smiles, *EE-Yah: The Life and Times of Hughie Jennings, Baseball Hall of Famer* (Jefferson, NC: McFarland, 2005).

19. *Washington Post*, October 5, 1894, p. 6.

20. Ibid., April 7, 1895, p. 9.

21. Ibid.

22. Ibid., March 15, 1896, p. 8.

23. *Washington Post*, February 4, 1897, p. 8.

24. Ibid., March 7, 1897, p. 9.

25. Alexander, *John McGraw*, p. 54.

26. *Chicago Daily Tribune*, September 13, 1897, p. 4.

27. *Washington Post*, September 17, 1897, p. 8.

28. *Los Angeles Times*, October 12, 1897, p. 2.

29. *Washington Post*, March 3, 1898, p. 8.

30. Alexander, *John McGraw*, p. 58.

31. Ibid., p. 59.

32. *Chicago Daily Tribune*, September 24, 1898, p. 4.

33. *Washington Post*, March 12, 1899, p. 8.

34. Alexander, *John McGraw*, p. 65.

35. *Washington Post*, August 27, 1899, p. 23.

36. Alexander, *John McGraw*, p. 68.

37. *New York Times*, March 1, 1900, p. 8.

38. Ibid., March 10, 1900, p. 10.

39. Alexander, *John McGraw*, p. 70.

40. *Chicago Daily Tribune*, May 18, 1901, p. 6.

41. *Washington Post*, June 20, 1901, p. 8.

42. Ibid., March 22, 1902, p. 8.

43. Alexander, *John McGraw*, p. 87.

44. *Chicago Daily Tribune*, May 2, 1902, p. 13.

45. Ibid., July 8, 1902, p. 6.

46. Alexander, *John McGraw*, p. 91.

47. Ibid., p. 92.

48. Cait Murphy, *Crazy '08* (New York: HarperCollins, 2007), p. 25.

49. Ibid.

50. *New York Times*, July 24, 1902, p. 6.

51. *Chicago Daily Tribune*, April 15, 1904, p. 8.

52. Alexander, *John McGraw*, p. 107.

53. *New York Times*, June 1, 1904, p. 7.

54. *Los Angeles Times*, June 26, 1904, p. B3.

55. *Washington Post*, August 8, 1904, p. 8.

56. Ibid., July 21, 1904, p. 8.

57. *Chicago Daily Tribune*, July 31, 1904, p. B2.

58. Murphy, *Crazy '08*, p. 31.

59. Benton Stark, *The Year They Called Off the World Series* (Garden City Park, NY: Avery Publishing Group, 1991), p. 139.

60. Quoted in Stark, p. 174.

61. Alexander, *John McGraw*, p. 112.

62. Ibid., p. 113.

63. *Washington Post*, June 6, 1905, p. 9.

64. *New York Times*, June 2, 1905, p. 4.

65. Murphy, *Crazy '08*, p. 28.

66. Alexander, *John McGraw*, p. 115.

67. *New York Times*, October 8, 1905, p. 11.

68. *Ibid.*, October 10, 1905, p. 4.

69. *Washington Post*, October 16, 1905, p. 8.

70. Alexander, *John McGraw*, p. 119.

71. *New York Times*, March 4, 1906, p. 11.

72. *Ibid.*, March 21, 1906, p. 10.

73. *Ibid.*, April 27, 1906, p. 12.

74. *Ibid.*, May 18, 1906, p. 1.

75. *Ibid.*, May 20, 1906, p. 3.

76. *Washington Post*, May 15, 1907, p. 9.

77. J. Ed Grillo, *Washington Post*, May 26, 1907, p. S3.

78. The origin of the term "pinch-hitter" may have been a play on the phrase "in a pinch," as suggested by Alexander, p. 111–112, in reference to utilityman Sammy Strang of the Giants. Peter Morris quotes a writer for the *New York Telegram*, 1909, with the phrase, again in reference to Strang. Morris, *A Game of Inches*, p. 312.

79. W.J. Lampton. *New York Times*, April 23, 1908, p. 7.

80. *Chicago Daily Tribune*, April 30, 1908, p. 8.

81. *Washington Post*, May 1, 1908, p. 8.

82. *Chicago Daily Tribune*, May 3, 1908, p. B1.

83. *New York Times*, May 3, 1908, p. S1.

84. *Chicago Daily Tribune*, September 6, 1908, p. B1.

85. I.E. Sanborn, *Chicago Daily Tribune*, September 5, 1908, p. 10.

86. *Washington Post*, September 24, 1908, p. 8.

87. Ronald Mayer, *Christy Mathewson. A Game-by-Game Profile of a Legendary Pitcher* (Jefferson, NC: McFarland, 1993), p. 167–168.

88. Alexander, *John McGraw*, p. 139.

89. *New York Times*, April 16, 1909, p. 7.

90. J. Ed Grillo, *New York Times*, June 17, 1909, p. 8.

91. Alexander, *John McGraw*, p. 145. Alexander suggests most of the fines were actually mailed to Raymond's wife without the pitcher's knowledge.

92. *Ibid.*, p. 148.

93. The actual quote from English writer George Borrow reads, "Youth will be served, every dog has its day, and mine has been a fine one."

94. *Washington Post*, March 10, 1911, p. 8.

95. *New York Times*, March 14, 1911, p. 9.

96. *The Sporting Life*, September 2, 1911, p. 15. Quoted in Alexander, *John McGraw*, p. 154.

97. *Washington Post*, October 12, 1911, p. 8.

98. *Ibid.*, October 13, 1911, p. 8.

99. *Los Angeles Times*, October 15, 1911, p. VII3.

100. Joe Jackson, *Washington Post*, October 14, 1911, p. 1.

101. Rex Beach, *New York Times*, October 15, 1911, p. 1.

102. Richard Marquard, *New York Times*, October 15, 1911, p. 3.

103. Christy Mathewson, *Washington Post*, October 15, 1911, p. S1.

104. Rube Marquard, *Washington Post*, October 17, 1911, p. 1.

105. Lawrence Ritter, *The Glory of Their Times* (New York: Collier Books, 1966), p. 173.

106. Christy Mathewson, *Washington Post*, October 17, 1911, p. 2.

107. *New York Times*, October 18, 1911, p. 1.

108. *Ibid.*

109. *New York Times*, March 23, 1912, p. 9.

110. *Ibid.*, April 16, 1912, p. 14.

111. *New York Times*, August 19, 1912, p. 7.

112. Mayer, *Christy Mathewson*, p. 237–238.

113. Hugh S. Fullerton, *New York Times*, October 6, 1912, p. S2. Also quoted in part by Mayer, p. 238.

114. Hugh S. Fullerton, *New York Times*, October 7, 1912, p. 12.

115. *Washington Post*, October 6, 1912, p. S2.

116. Mayer, *Christy Mathewson*, p. 239.

117. *Los Angeles Times*, October 7, 1912, p. III3.

118. Jeff Tesreau, *Washington Post*, October 9, 1912, p. 2.

119. *New York Times*, October 11, 1912, p. 1.

120. John J. McGraw, *New York Times*, October 11, 1912, p. 2.

121. Hugh Fullerton, *New York Times*, October 17, 1912, p. 21.

122. *New York Times*, October 17, 1912, p. 1.

123. Jeff Tesreau, *Washington Post*, October 17, 1912, p. 2.

Chapter Three

1. William A. Phelon, "Who Will Win the 1913 Pennants?" *Baseball Magazine*, May, 1913, p. 32.

2. *Chicago Daily Tribune*, April 11, 1913, p. 15.

3. C. Paul Rogers III, in *Deadball Stars of the American League*. ed. David Jones (Dulles, VA: Potomac Books, Inc., 2006), p. 614. Norman Macht, biographer of Connie Mack, believes it may have been Mack who signed Coombs.

4. *Washington Post*, April 29, 1913, p. 8. The legal limit for the mound height at this

time was no more than fifteen inches above the
level of the playing field. This rule did not preclude a home team from stretching such a limit
to its advantage.

5. *New York Times*, May 2, 1913, p. 9.
6. Ibid., May 3, 1913, p. 12.
7. Ibid., May 4, 1913, p. S1.
8. John Leidy, in *Deadball Stars of the
American League*. ed. David Jones (Dulles, VA:
Potomac Books, Inc., 2006), p. 722–723. Leidy
is the grandson of Ray Fisher.
9. *Philadelphia Inquirer*, May 9, 1913, p. 10.
10. Ibid., May 10, 1913, p. 12.
11. Hugh Fullerton, *Chicago Daily Tribune*,
September 18, 1906, p. 6.
12. Paul Mittermeyer, in *Deadball Stars of
the American League*. ed. David Jones (Dulles,
VA: Potomac Books, Inc., 2006), p. 610–614.
13. *Philadelphia Inquirer*, May 12, 1913, p.
S4.
14. *Washington Post*, May 17, 1913, p. 8.
15. Ibid., May 25, 1913, p. S4.
16. Ibid., p. S1.
17. *Sporting Life*, February 24, 1912. File,
Baseball Hall of Fame and Museum.
18. Jim Nasium, *Philadelphia Inquirer*, June
4, 1913, p. 14.
19. Alphonse and Gaston were two French
characters in a comic strip written by Frederick Burr Opper, which ran during the first
decades of the twentieth century. Alphonse and
Gaston were paragons of extreme politeness,
often using the phrase, "After you, my dear
Gaston," followed by, "After you, my dear
Alphonse." The theme was adapted by baseball for situations in which two fielders
would watch an easy fly ball land between
them.
20. Don Geiszler, in *Deadball Stars of the
American League*. ed. David Jones (Dulles, VA:
Potomac Books, Inc., 2006), p. 632.
21. File, National Baseball Hall of Fame;
October 18, 1913 (unnamed source).
22. Undated file, National Baseball Hall of
Fame.
23. Jim Nasium, *Philadelphia Inquirer*, June
17, 1913, p. 10.
24. Stanley Milliken. *Washington Post*, June
26, 1913, p. 8.
25. *New York Times*, July 2, 1913, p. 7.
26. *Philadelphia Inquirer*, July 6, 1913,
p. S1.
27. Sam Weller, *Chicago Daily Tribune*, July
20, 1913, p. C1. Larry Chappell produced little
long-term impact on major league diamonds,
playing five seasons with Chicago, Cleveland
and Boston. His triple this day was his only
one for the season, and one of two in his career.
He was associated with two noteworthy events:
In 1915, he was part of the trade that brought

Shoeless Joe Jackson from Cleveland to Chicago. More significantly, Chappell was one of
six major leaguers to die in the uniform of the
United States during World War I, succumb-
ing to influenza in November 1918, two days
before the armistice.
28. *Philadelphia Inquirer*, July 22, 1913, p.
10.
29. Jim Nasium *Philadelphia Inquirer*, July
26, 1913, p. 10. The phrase "Running for
Sweeney" originated with horse racing, and
meant the fix was on.
30. Ibid., July 27, 1913, p. S1.
31. Ibid., July 30, 1913, p. 10.
32. Ibid. Gehenna was the Greek mythical
reference to hell.
33. Ibid., July 31, 1913, p. 10.
34. Ibid., August 1, 1913, p. 12.
35. Ibid., August 15, 1913, p. 10.
36. I.E. Sanborn, *Chicago Daily Tribune*,
August 23, 1913, p. 13.
37. Jack Warhop would pitch eight seasons
for the Yankees, compiling a lifetime record of
69–93 between 1908 and 1915. Warhop might
have been forgotten except for an item of
trivia: On May 6, 1915, Babe Ruth hit the first
of his 714 major league home runs off Warhop.
Three weeks later, Ruth hit his second lifetime
home run, again off Warhop.
38. *Philadelphia Inquirer*, August 31, 1913,
p. S1.
39. Jim Nasium, *Philadelphia Inquirer*, September 2, 1913, p. 11. The bleachers in 1913 were
378 feet from home plate. Since according to
the report the ball might have continued
beyond the back of the bleachers had it not
been stopped by a fan, the hit probably traveled some 425 feet, not a prodigious clout by
modern standards, but still substantial for the
times. A lower grandstand was present at the
time; the upper deck was added a decade later.
This author frequently sat in the lower deck of
the left-field bleachers during the 1960s in what
by then was named Connie Mack Stadium. If
memory serves, there were some 25 rows from
the field to the back wall.
40. *Philadelphia Inquirer*, September 3,
1913, p. 12. "Slow Joe" Doyle was a former New
York Highlanders and Cincinnati Reds pitcher
known for his slow approach to the game. He
was also observed napping on the tarpaulin
from time to time on a hot day. Apollo Belvi-
dere is a 5th Century B.C.E. Greek marble
statue by the sculptor Calamis, depicting a god
holding a bow.
41. Ibid., September 14, 1913, p. S1.
42. Jim Nasium, *Philadelphia Inquirer*, September 21, 1913, p. S1.
43. *Philadelphia Inquirer*, October 2, 1913,
p. 12.

Chapter Four

1. William Phelon, "Who Will Win the 1913 Pennants?" *Baseball Magazine* No. 7 (May 1913), p. 12–24.

2. *Washington Post*, August 25, 1912, p. S4.

3. *New York Times*, September 27, 1912, p. 11.

4. Ibid.

5. *New York Times*, February 1, 1913, p. 1. (Mathewson, or his ghost writer, reported Thorpe's 1910 pitching record as 10–10 [*Washington Post*, February 3, 1913, p. 10]).

6. Don Jensen, in *Deadball Stars of the National League*, ed. Tom Simon (Washington, D.C.: Brassey's, 2004), p. 81.

7. Christy Mathewson, *Washington Post*, February 10, 1913, p. 8.

8. Sean Lahman, in *Deadball Stars of the National League*, ed. Tom Simon. (Washington, D.C.: Brassey's, 2004), p. 258. The April 12 game was against Brooklyn, not Chicago, as stated in the Lahman biography. *Total Baseball* also lists that date for Groh's debut. Boxscores for that game, however, show Bob Becker as a pinch-hitter, not Groh. The game was called in the eighth inning by Klem because of darkness. Was the story true? Groh does not refer to it in his own story in Ritter's *The Glory of Their Times*. And 5'7, while certainly not large, was hardly rare for the time.

9. *New York Times*, February 5, 1913, p. 9.

10. Ibid., March 12, 1913, p. 9.

11. Ibid., April 11, 1913, p. 10.

12. Ibid.

13. Ibid., April 15, 1913, p. 9.

14. Ibid.

15. Ibid., April 23, 1913, p. 9. Reference is to Stanislaus Zbyszco, Polish wrestler of the period who later defeated Strangler Lewis for a world title.

16. Ibid., April 25, 1913, p. 9.

17. Ibid.

18. Ibid., April 26, 1913, p. 12.

19. Ibid.

20. Ibid., April 27, p. S1.

21. Ronald Mayer, *Christy Mathewson* (Jefferson, NC: McFarland, 1993), p. 245.

22. *New York Times*, May 1, 1913, p. 9.

23. R.J. Lesch, in *Deadball Stars of the National League*, ed. Tom Simon (Washington, D.C.: Brassey's, 2004), p. 47.

24. *New York Times*, August 13, 1911, p. C5. Also sited by Lesch, p. 48. Dating back thousands of years, the swastika was a common decoration even found in the flooring of synagogues from the first millennium C.E. In modern times, obviously pre–World War II, it was a common theme in Native American and other religious traditions, representing in the view of some the four seasons. At least one minor league team used it for a logo. The infantry patch for the American 45th Infantry Division during World War I included a swastika as well.

25. Lesch, p. 48.

26. *New York Times*, March 10, 1914, p. 10.

27. Ibid., May 17, 1913, p. 9. In response to a question printed in the April 10, 1913, *Sporting News*, p. 7, O'Toole also reportedly received $2,500 of the selling price when Pittsburgh purchased his contract from St. Paul.

28. *Los Angeles Times*, August 26, 1956, p. A10.

29. *New York Times*, May 23, 1913, p. 16. The act (S.R. 1791) was originally introduced to the New York legislature by state senator Martin Saxe on May 23, 1907, amending the 1895 law addressing civil and religious rights, prohibiting for the use of unauthorized pictures for entertainment purposes without consent.

30. Ibid., May 30, 1913, p. 5.

31. Quoted by Peter Gordon, in *Deadball Stars of the National League*, ed. Tom Simon (Washington, D.C.: Brassey's, 2004), p. 75.

32. Ibid.

33. *New York Times*, June 14, 1913, p. 12.

34. Mayer, *Christy Mathewson*, p. 4.

35. The uneducated "country hick" stereotype of the major league ballplayer of the time was mostly mythical. While there were certainly a proportion that might be placed in the category — Shoeless Joe Jackson coming to mind — approximately one-quarter of major league players had a college education. By comparison, the population as a whole included some 5 percent with a college education. John Dreifort. *Baseball History From Outside the Lines* (Lincoln: University of Nebraska Press, 2001), p. 41. Also quoted by Murphy, p. 45.

36. *New York Times*, June 24, 1913, p. 8.

37. *Sporting News*, July 3, 1913, p. 4. Quoted by Alexander, *John McGraw*, p. 169. The original quote apparently was in the *New York Globe*.

38. Ibid.

39. *New York Times*, July 1, 1913, p. 1.

40. Ibid., July 6, 1913, p. S1.

41. Ibid., July 10, 1913, p. 8.

42. Ibid.

43. Ibid.

44. Ibid., July 12, 1913, p. 5.

45. Ibid.

46. Ibid., July 17, 1913, p. 8.

47. *Detroit Free* Press, May 7, 2007, p. 7B. The phrase "walk-off home run" did not exist in 1913, of course. So when was it added to the baseball lexicon? According to the *New Dickson Baseball Dictionary*, as well as an even more authoritative source, announcer Ernie Harwell, pitcher Dennis Eckersley may have coined the

phrase in 1988. The first use reportedly was on July 30, 1988, by the Gannett News Service.

48. Ibid., August 23, 1913, p. 5.

49. Byron, nicknamed the "Singing Umpire," was noted for renditions such as "You'll have to learn before you're older, you can't get a hit with the bat on your shoulder." Mike Shatzkin, *The Ballplayers* (New York: William Morrow, 1990), p. 144.

50. *New York Times*, August 26, 1913, p. 7.

51. Ibid., August 28, 1913, p. 7.

52. Ibid.

53. Ibid.

54. Ibid., September 6, 1913, p. 8.

55. Eason in his brief major league career pitched a 2–0 no-hitter for Brooklyn against St. Louis on July 20, 1906. On June 29, 1905, Eason was Brooklyn's starting pitcher in a game won easily by the Giants, 11–1. Nothing noteworthy there, except the substitute right fielder for the Giants late in the game was Archie "Moonlight" Graham.

56. Ibid., September 9, 1913, p. 8.

57. Ibid.

58. *Chicago Defender*, September 13, 1013, p. 7.

59. *New York Times*, September 21, 1913, p. S3.

Chapter Five

1. W.J. Lampton. *New York Times*, October 2, 1913, p. 10.

2. The term "dipsey-doodle" was coined by Mordecai Brown. In Cindy Thomson and Scott Brown, *Three Finger: The Mordecai Brown Story* (Lincoln: University of Nebraska Press, 2006).

3. Irwin M. Howe, *Los Angeles Times*, October 2, 1913, p. III3.

4. Ibid., September 29, 1913, p. III3.

5. Hugh S. Fullerton, *New York Times*, September 27, 1913, p. 10.

6. Ibid.

7. Irwin M. Howe, *Los Angeles Times*, September 29, 1913, p. III3.

8. Hugh S. Fullerton, *New York Times*, September 27, 1913, p. 10.

9. Ibid.

10. Ibid.

11. Ibid.

12. Hugh S. Fullerton, *New York Times*, September 28, 1913, p. S1.

13. Irwin M. Howe, *Los Angeles Times*, September 29, 1913, p. III3.

14. Hugh S. Fullerton, *New York Times*, September 28, 1913, p. S1.

15. Ibid.

16. Ibid.

17. Ibid.

18. Ibid.

19. Ibid.

20. Hugh S. Fullerton, *New York Times*, September 28, 1913, p. S2.

21. Hugh S. Fullerton, *New York Times*, September 29, 1913, p. 10.

22. Irwin M. Howe, *Los Angeles Times*, September 29, 1913, p. III3.

23. Hugh S. Fullerton, *New York Times*, September 29, 1913, p. 10.

24. Ibid.

25. *Washington Post*, September 29, 1913, p. 6.

26. Stanley Milliken, *Washington Post*, November 7, 1913, p. 8.

27. Hugh S. Fullerton, *New York Times*, September 30, 1913, p. 14.

28. Ibid.

29. Irwin M. Howe, *New York Times*, October 2, 1913, p. 12.

30. *New York Times*, October 31, 1913, p. 12.

31. Hugh S. Fullerton, *New York Times*, October 1, 1913, p. 10.

32. Ibid.

33. Ibid.

34. Ibid.

35. I.E. Sanborn, *Chicago Daily Tribune*, October 7, 1913, p. 25.

36. Hugh S. Fullerton, *New York Times*, October 3, 1913, p. 12.

37. Ibid.

38. Charles Alexander, *John McGraw*, p. 165.

39. Hugh S. Fullerton, *New York Times*, October 3, 1913, p. 12.

40. Ibid.

41. Ibid.

42. Curt Smith, *Storied Stadiums* (New York: Carroll & Graf, 2001).

43. *Washington Post*, September 27, 1913, p. 8.

44. Hugh S. Fullerton, *New York Times*, October 3, 1913, p. 12.

45. Irwin M. Howe, *New York Times*, September 25, 1913, p. 11.

46. Hugh S. Fullerton, *New York Times*, October 2, 1913, p. 12.

47. Ibid.

48. Smith, *Storied Stadiums*.

49. Hugh S. Fullerton, *New York Times*, October 2, 1913, p. 12.

50. Ibid.

51. Peter Morris, *A Game of Inches.* (Chicago: Ivan R. Dee, 2006), p. 38.

52. *Washington Post*, October 3, 1913, p. 8.

53. Harry Williams, *Los Angeles Times*, October 4, 1913, p. III3.

54. *Washington Post*, October 3, 1913, p. 8.

55. Irwin M. Howe, *New York Times*, September 30, 1913, p. 14.
56. Hugh S. Fullerton, *New York Times*, October 5, 1913, p. S2.
57. Ibid.
58. Hugh S. Fullerton, *New York Times*, October 5, 1913, p. S2.
59. Ibid.
60. Ibid.
61. Ibid.
62. Ibid.
63. Irwin M. Howe, *Los Angeles Times*, September 30, 1913, p. III3.
64. Hugh S. Fullerton, *New York Times*, October 5, 1913, p. S2.
65. Irwin M. Howe, *Los Angeles Times*, September 30, 1913, p. III3.
66. *Washington Post*, October 3, 1913, p. 8.
67. Harry A. Williams, *Los Angeles Times*, October 4, 1913, p. III3.

Chapter Six

1. John J. Evers, *Washington Post*, October 20, 1910, p. 8.
2. *New York Times*, October 16, 1910, p. C5.
3. Jeff Tesereau [sic], *Washington Post*, October 10, 1912, p. 2.
4. John McGraw, *New York Times*, October 15, 1912, p. 7.
5. *New York Times*, September 25, 1913, p. 11.
6. *Washington Post*, October 15, 1908, p. 9.
7. (With due respect to) William Shakespeare, *Hamlet*, Act 3, Scene 1, c. 1603.
8. *New York Times*, September 25, 1913, p. 11.
9. Ibid.
10. *Los Angeles Times*, October 1, 1913, p. III1.
11. Ibid.
12. *New York Times*, October 1, 1913, p. 10.
13. Ibid.
14. *New York Times*, October 3, 1913, p. 10.
15. Ibid.
16. *New York Times*, October 2, 1913, p. 12.
17. Ibid.
18. Ibid.
19. Ibid.
20. *Los Angeles Times*, October 7, 1913.
21. Ibid.
22. Joe S. Jackson, *Washington Post*, October 13, 1913, p. 8.
23. Ibid.
24. *New York Times*, October 14, 1913, p. 11.
25. I.E. Sanborn, *Chicago Daily Tribune*, October 7, 1913, p. 25.
26. *Los Angeles Times*, October 7, 1913, p. III1.
27. Ibid.
28. Ibid.
29. *Washington Post*, October 6, 1913, p. 5.
30. *Los Angeles Times*, October 7, 1913, p. III1.
31. *Chicago Daily Tribune*, September 26, 1913, p. 13.
32. *New York Times*, October 6, 1913, p. 8.
33. *Chicago Daily Tribune*, October 8, 1913, p. 7.
34. *New York Times*, October 7, 1913, p. 1.
35. *New York Times*, October 8, 1913, p. 1.
36. Ibid.
37. Ibid.
38. Ibid.
39. *Los Angeles Times*, October 8, 1913, p. III1.
40. *New York Times*, October 8, 1913, p. 1.
41. Ibid., p.3.
42. Source for all game box scores was www.baseball-almanac.com.

Chapter Seven

1. *New York Times*, October 8, 1913, p. 5.
2. *Chicago Daily Tribune*, October 9, 1913, p. 25.
3. I.E. Sanborn, *Chicago Daily Tribune*, October 9,1913, p. 23.
4. *Los Angeles Times*, October 9, 1913, p. III2.
5. Ibid.
6. I.E. Sanborn, *Chicago Daily Tribune*, October 9, 1913, p. 25.
7. Ibid.
8. *New York Times*, October 9, 1913, p. 1.
9. I.E. Sanborn, *Chicago Daily Tribune*, October 9, 1913, p. 25.
10. Ibid.
11. Harry A. Williams, *Los Angeles Times*, October 9, 1913, p. III3.
12. *Washington Post*, October 9, 1913, p. 8.
13. Ibid. p. 2.
14. Joe S. Jackson, *Washington Post*, October 9, 1913, p. 8.
15. *New York Times*, March 27, 1910, p. S1.
16. Reference was to a court case decided in Waco, Texas, in which the court ruled being intoxicated was a mitigating circumstance in a murder. (*Abe Little v. State*, 42 Tex. Crim. 551, 1901).
17. Probably a reference to heavyweight fighter Arthur Pelkey. Pelkey's bout with Andy Morris in May 1913 was stopped by referee Tommy Burns. Shortly afterwards, Burns became Pelkey's manager.
18. Ring Lardner, *Chicago Daily Tribune*, October 10, 1913, p. 23.

Chapter Eight

1. Joe S. Jackson, *Washington Post*, October 9, 1913, p. 8.
2. I.E. Sanborn, *Chicago Daily Tribune*, October 10, 1913, p. 25.
3. *Los Angeles Times*, October 10, 1913, p. III4.
4. Ibid.
5. *New York Times*, October 10, 1913, p. 3.
6. Ibid.
7. Ibid.
8. Ibid.
9. Ibid.
10. Hugh S. Fullerton, *New York Times*, October 10, 1913, p. 3.
11. *New York Times*, October 10, 1913, p.3.
12. Ibid.
13. Ibid.
14. *New York Times*, October 10, 1913, p. 1.
15. *New York Times*, October 10,1913, p. 3.
16. Ibid.
17. *New York Times*, October 10, 1913, p. 1.
18. I.E. Sanborn, *Chicago Daily Tribune*, October 10, 1913, p. 25.
19. *New York Times*, October 10, 1913, p. 3.
20. Joe S. Jackson, *Washington Post*, October 10, 1913, p. 1.
21. Ibid.
22. Hugh S. Fullerton, *New York Times*, October 10, 1913, p. 3.
23. *New York Times*, October 10, 1913, p. 1.
24. *Chicago Daily Tribune*, October 10, 1913, p. 23.
25. Ring Lardner, *Chicago Daily Tribune*, October 11, 1913, p. 22.

Chapter Nine

1. Ring Lardner, *Chicago Daily Tribune*, October 11, 1913, p. 22.
2. *Washington Post*, October 10, 1913, p. 2.
3. Ibid. p. 6.
4. *New York Times*, October 11, 1913, p. 3.
5. Ibid. p. 1.
6. Ibid.
7. Ibid.
8. Ibid. p. 4.
9. *Los Angeles Times*, October 11, 1913, p. III4.
10. I.E. Sanborn, *Chicago Daily Tribune*, October 11, 1913, p. 21.
11. *New York Times*, October 11, 1913, p. 3.
12. *New York Times*, October 11, 1913, p. 1.
13. *Los Angeles Times*, October 11, 1913, p. III4.
14. *New York Times*, October 11, 1913, p. 3.
15. *Los Angeles Times*, October 11, 1913, p. II8.

16. *New York Times*, October 11, 1913, p. 4.
17. *Los Angeles Times*, October 11, 1913, p. I2.
18. *Washington Post*, October 11,1913, p. 8.

Chapter Ten

1. *Washington Post*, October 11, 1913, p. 8.
2. Ibid.
3. *New York Times*, October 12, 1913, p. 1.
4. *Los Angeles Times*, October 12, 1913, p. VII9.
5. *New York Times*, October 12, 1913, p. S2.
6. Ibid.
7. I.E. Sanborn, *Chicago Daily Tribune*, October 12, 1913, p. B1.
8. John J. McGraw, *New York Times*, October 12, 1913, p. S1.
9. *New York Times*, October 12, 1913, p. S2.
10. John J. McGraw, *New York Times*, October 12, 1913, p. S1.
11. Ibid.
12. Hugh Fullerton, *Washington Post*, October 12, 1913, p. S1.
13. Ibid.
14. Wm. A. Phelon. "Why the Giants Lost" *Baseball Magazine* (December, 1913), p. 14.
15. Ibid.
16. Ibid.
17. Grantland Rice, *Boston Traveler and Evening Herald*, October 11, 1913, p. 1.

Epilogue

1. *Washington Post*, June 12, 1915, p. 8.
2. *Los Angeles Times*, March 21, 1921, p. III2.
3. *New York Times*, August 16, 1966, p. 39.
4. *Los Angeles Times*, August 18, 1951, p. A1.
5. *New York Times*, March 2, 1974, p. 34.
6. Ibid. January 6, 1918, p. 20.
7. Robert E. Gallman, *Journal of Economic History* Vol. 53 (December 1993), p. 924.
8. Arthur Daley, *New York Times*, February 8, 1950, p. 42
9. Ibid.
10. *New York Times*, February 7, 1950, p. 27
11. *Chicago Daily Tribune*, February 7, 1950, p. B1.
12. Kevin Coyne, "Ultimate Sacrifice," *Smithsonian* (October 1974), pp. 72–81.
13. Ibid.
14. *New York Times*, September 6, 1953, p. 50.
15. *Washington Post*, September 8, 1953, p. 20.

16. *Los Angeles Times*, January 11, 1962, p. C4.
17. *New York Times*, July 10, 1962, p. 33.
18. Ibid., March 3, 1956, p. 20.
19. *Washington Post and Times Herald*, March 12, 1956, p. 14.
20. *New York Times*, July 28, 1971, p. 38.
21. Ibid., February 8, 1916, p. 12.
22. *Chicago Daily Tribune*, July 17, 1917, p. 9.
23. *New York Times*, April 6, 1974, p. 34.
24. Ibid., May 9, 1915, p. 16.
25. Ibid., January 31, 1925, p. 10.
26. Harry Williams, *Los Angeles Times*, February 25, 1914, p. III1.
27. *Chicago Daily Tribune*, April 2, 1918, p. 13.
28. *New York Times*, September 25, 1946, p. 26.
29. Lawrence Ritter, *The Glory of Their Times* (New York: Collier Books, 1966).
30. Ibid.
31. Thomas Rogers, *New York Times*, June 3, 1980, p. D17.
32. Irving Vaughan, *Chicago Daily Tribune*, March 23, 1922, p. 15.
33. Ring Lardner, *Chicago Daily Tribune*, July 22, 1916, p. 9.
34. *New York Times*, July 22, 1916, p. 6.
35. Lee Allen, *The Cincinnati Reds: An Informal History* (New York: Putnam, 1948). Quoted in Cindy Thomson and Scott Brown, *Three Finger: The Mordecai Brown Story* (Lincoln: University of Nebraska Press, 2006).
36. *Chicago Daily Tribune*, September 6, 1916, p. 6.
37. *New York Times*, October 9, 1925, p. 22.
38. Alexander, *John McGraw*, p. 307.
39. Ibid.
40. Frank Graham, *McGraw of the Giants* (New York: G.P. Putnam's Sons, 1944), p. 265.
41. Quote from John McMurray in *Deadball Stars of the American League*, ed. David Jones (Dulles, VA: Potomac Books, 2006), p. 627.
42. *Philadelphia Inquirer*, July 26, 1979 (Player file, National Baseball Hall of Fame).
43. *New York Times*, June 27, 1919, p. 22.
44. Bill Bishop in *Deadball Stars of the American League*, ed. David Jones (Dulles, VA: Potomac Books, 2006), p. 619.
45. Undated news clipping from player's file, National Baseball Hall of Fame.
46. *New York Times*, July 16, 1916, p. E7.
47. W. Harrison Daniel and Scott Mayer, *Baseball and Richmond* (Jefferson, NC: McFarland, 2003).
48. *Boston Herald American*, April 25, 1975 (Player file, National Baseball Hall of Fame).
49. Hugh Fullerton, *New York Times*, September 29, 1916, p. 10.

50. Norman Macht in *Deadball Stars of the American League*, ed. David Jones (Dulles, VA: Potomac Books, 2006), p. 625.
51. *New York Times*, June 30, 1915, p. 12.
52. Ibid., July 3, 1915, p. 8.
53. *Los Angeles Times*, July 29, 1917, p. VII1.
54. *Sporting Life*, February 24, 1912 (Player file, National Baseball Hall of Fame).
55. *Washington Post*, January 8, 1916, p. 8.
56. *Los Angeles Times*, September 4, 1912, p. III2.
57. *New York Times*, April 15, 1915, p. 10.
58. *Los Angeles Times*, April 28, 1915, p. III2.
59. Ibid.
60. *New York Times*, February 16, 1916, p. 12.
61. Aaron Davis and C. Paul Rogers III, in *Deadball Stars of the American League*, ed. David Jones (Dulles, VA: Potomac Books, 2006), p. 629.
62. *Chicago Daily Tribune*, January 11, 1918, p. 11.
63. *Washington Post*, March 1, 1918, p. 10.
64. Ibid., December 22, 1921, p. 15.
65. *Chicago Daily Tribune*, December 15, 1917, p. 15.
66. *New York Times*, December 16, 1920, p. 26.
67. *Washington Post*, February 9, 1921, p. 11.
68. *Chicago Daily Tribune*, December 9, 1914, p. 18.
69. *Los Angeles Times*, December 10, 1914, p. III1.
70. Ibid., December 18, 1914, p. III3.
71. *Chicago Daily Tribune*, October 16, 1917, p. 16.
72. Richard Smiley, "I'm a Faster Man than You are, Heinie Zim," *National Pastime* 26 (2006), p. 97.
73. *Chicago Daily Tribune*, November 13, 1926, p. 8.
74. *Washington Post*, September 4, 1917, p. 8.
75. James Crusinberry, *Chicago Daily Tribune*, July 18, 1918, p. 9.
76. Ibid., October 5, 1920, p. 19.
77. Ibid.
78. Eddie Collins, *Los Angeles Times*, June 19, 1927, p. B2.
79. *Washington Post*, April 9, 1916, p. S1.
80. *Chicago Daily Tribune*, August 15, 1919, p. 19.
81. *Washington Post*, November 5, 1921, p. 17.
82. *New York Times*, December 21, 1921, p. 26.
83. John Kieran, *New York Times*, June 18, 1927, p. 13.
84. *New York Times*, November 4, 1928, p. 161.

85. I.E. Sanborn, *Chicago Daily Tribune*, November 24, 1914, p. 16.

86. James Crusinberry, *Chicago Daily Tribune*, December 3, 1914, p. 11.

87. *New York Times*, February 8, 1916, p. 12.

88. Ibid., February 28, 1926, p. S3.

89. John J. Evers, *New York Times*, October 10, 1914, p. 8.

90. *Los Angeles Times*, November 28, 1914, p. I.

91. *New York Times*, February 19, 1917, p. 6.

92. Ibid., June 2, 1918, p. 28.

93. Daniel and Mayer, *Baseball and Richmond*.

94. *New York Times*, July 22, 1925, p. 15.

95. *Washington Post*, July 22, 1925, p. 13.

96. Arch Ward, *Chicago Daily Tribune*, May 25, 1954, p. C1.

97. *Washington Post and Times Herald*, February 9, 1956, p. 49.

98. *New York Times*, February 10, 1956, p. 20.

99. Grantland Rice, *Los Angeles Times*, February 10, 1956, p. C1.

100. Doug Skipper in *Deadball Stars of the American League*, ed. David Jones (Dulles, VA: Potomac Books, 2006), p. 583.

101. Kuklick, *To Everything a Season*.

102. Norman Macht, *Connie Mack and the Early Years of Baseball* (Lincoln: University of Nebraska Press, 2007).

Bibliography

Books

Alexander, Charles. *John McGraw*. New York: Viking Penguin, 1988.

Allen, Arthur. *Vaccine*. New York: W.W. Norton, 2007.

Bogen, Gil. *Johnny Kling*. Jefferson, NC: McFarland, 2006.

Cohen, Richard, and David Neft. *The World Series*. New York: Macmillan, 1986.

Daniel, W. Harrison, and Scott Mayer. *Baseball and Richmond*. Jefferson, NC: McFarland, 2003.

Fleitz, David. *Ghosts in the Gallery at Cooperstown*. Jefferson, NC: McFarland, 2004.

Gagnon, Cappy. *Notre Dame Baseball Greats, From Anson to Yaz*. Charleston, SC: Arcadia Publishing, 2004.

Gay, Timothy. *Tris Speaker: The Rough-and-Tumble Life of a Baseball Legend*. Lincoln: University of Nebraska Press, 2005.

Graham, Frank. *McGraw of the Giants*. New York: G.P. Putnam's Sons, 1944.

Johnson, Lloyd, and Miles Wolff (eds.). *The Encyclopedia of Minor League Baseball*. 2nd ed. Durham, NC: Baseball America, 1997.

Jones, David (ed.). *Deadball Stars of the American League*. Dulles, VA: Potomac Books, 2006.

Kashatus, William. *Money Pitcher: Chief Bender and the Tragedy of Indian Assimilation*. University Park: Pennsylvania State University Press, 2006.

Koszarek, Ed. *The Players League*. Jefferson, NC: McFarland, 2006.

Kuklick, Bruce. *To Every Thing a Season*. Princeton, NJ: Princeton University Press, 1991.

Lee, Bill. *The Baseball Necrology*. Jefferson, NC: McFarland, 2003.

Levy, Alan. *Rube Waddell*. Jefferson, NC: McFarland, 2000.

Lowry, Philip. *Green Cathedrals*. New York: Addison Wesley, 1992.

Macht, Norman. *Connie Mack and the Early Years of Baseball*. Lincoln: University of Nebraska Press, 2007.

Mack, Connie. *My 66 Years in the Big Leagues*. Philadelphia: John C. Winston, 1950.

Masur, Louis. *Autumn Glory: Baseball's First World Series*. New York: Hill and Wang, 2003.

Mayer, Ronald A. *Christy Mathewson: A Game-by-Game Profile of a Legendary Pitcher*. Jefferson, NC: McFarland, 1993.

Montville, Leigh. *The Big Bam: The Life and Times of Babe Ruth*. New York: Broadway Books, 2006.

Morris, Peter. *A Game of Inches*. Chicago: Ivan R. Dee, 2006.

Murphy, Cait. *Crazy '08*. New York: HarperCollins, 2007.

Neft, David, and Richard Cohen. *The World Series: Complete Play-by-Play of Every Game, 1903–1989*. New York: St. Martin's Press, 1990.

Ritter, Lawrence. *The Glory of Their Times*. New York: Collier Books, 1966.

Roer, Mike. *Orator O'Rourke: The Life of a Baseball Radical*. Jefferson, NC: McFarland, 2005.

Schoor, Gene. *The History of the World Series*. New York: Morrow, 1990.

Shatzkin, Mike (ed.). *The Ballplayers.* New York: Morrow, 1990.

Simon, Tom (ed.). *Deadball Stars of the National league.* Washington, D.C.: Brassey's, 2004.

Smiles, Jack. *"EE-Yah," The Life and Times of Hughie Jennings, Baseball Hall of Famer.* Jefferson, NC: McFarland, 2005.

Smith, Curt. *Storied Stadiums.* New York: Carroll & Graf, 2001.

Stark, Benton. *The Year They Called Off the World Series.* Garden City Park, NY: Avery Publishing, 1991.

Thomson, Cindy, and Scott Brown. *Three Finger: The Mordecai Brown Story.* Lincoln: University of Nebraska Press, 2006.

Thorn, John, et al. *Total Baseball. The Ultimate Baseball Encyclopedia.* 8th ed. Toronto, Ontario: Sports Media Publishing, 2004.

Newspapers and Periodicals

Baseball Magazine
Boston Traveler and Evening Herald
Chicago Daily Tribune
Chicago Defender
Journal of Economic History
Los Angeles Times
National Pastime
New York Times
Philadelphia Inquirer
Reach Official American League Guide: 1914
Smithsonian
Spalding's Official Baseball Guide: 1914
Sporting News
Washington Post
Washington Post and Times Herald

Websites

www.baseball-almanac.com
www.baseball-reference.com
www.thedeadballera.com
www.ancestry.com

Photographs

National Baseball Hall of Fame Library and Museum (BHOF)
Bain Collection, Library of Congress (LOC)

Index

Numbers in **bold italics** indicate pages with photographs.

Acosta, Merito 147
Agnew, Sam 101
Ainsmith, Eddie 115, 136
Alexander, Grover Cleveland "Pete" 66, 81, 92, 154, 157, 158, 163, 171, 173, 174, 276
Alexander, Walt 126
"Alphonse and Gaston" 108
"American All-Stars": trip to Cuba 41
American League 9
Ames, Leon "Red" 15, 35, 59, 62, 63, 65, 66–68, 70, 72, 74, 76, 78, 81, 82, 84, 85, 149, 152, 153, 157, 158, 160, 164, 176, 182, 185, 186; signed by McGraw 156; traded to Cincinnati 161
Austin, Jimmy 102, 109, 134

Baker, Frank "Home Run" 24, 25, 27, 29, 32, 37, 38, 83, 84, 92, **94**, 95, 98, 100, 103, 105–108, 117, 118, **192**, 218, **225**, **235**, 294; death 282; hitting star of season 147; home runs off Marquard and Mathewson in 1911 series 33, **34**; homer off Marquard, 1913 series 213; led league in home runs 281; purchased from Reading 23; sold to Yankees 282
Balenti, Mike 109, 127, 128, 135
Bancroft, Dave 267, 277
Barnie, Bill 42, 43
Barry, Jack 24, 25, 28–33, 38, 92, **94**, 97, 99, 100, 103, 105, 110, 147, **192**, **225**, 278; death of 281; return from injury 134; signed out of Holy Cross 23; traded to Red Sox 280
Baseball Writers Association, controversy with 208–211
Baumgardner, George 127
Bedient, Hugh 89, 90, 92, 95
Bender, Albert "Chief" 15–17, 19–22, **26**, 27–32, 36, 37, 92, **94**, 95, 98, 101, 103,

106, 107, 109, 114, 115, 117, 120, 122, 123, 125, 127, 129, 132, 134–136, 139, 140, 142, **255**, 291–293; accused of "hit and run" 292, 293; coach with Mack 293; death of 294; debut 14; first game in 1913 series 211–221; fourth game in 1913 series 247–256; leading team in victories 147; 1905 series 63, 64
Benton, John "Rube" 168
"Black Sox" scandal 100, 287, 288
Blanding, Fred 128, 130
Boardman, Charley 146
Bodie, Frank "Ping" 113, 123, 129, 130, 133, 134, 139, 140
Boehling, Joe 116, 136
Bohen, Pat 146
Boston Red Sox: 1912 World's Series 87–91
Bowerman, Frank 63, 67
"Bowl of Gehenna" 126
Brennan, Ad: fight with McGraw 171–**173**
Brennan, Bill (umpire) **162**, 187, 188
Bresnahan, Roger 16, 53, 56, 57, 59, 60, 63–67, 156, 161, 175, 176, 181; traded to Cincinnati 74
Brickley, George 146
Bridwell, Al 68, 72, 74, 76, 157, 159, 269; traded to Cincinnati 79
Brotherhood of Professional Baseball Players (Players League) 7
Brouthers, Dan "Big Dan" 44–46
Brown, Carroll "Boardwalk" 36, **94**, 95, **96**, 97, 98, 101, 103, 104, 106–108, 113–115, 118, 121, 122–124, 126, 127, 129, 133–136, 138, 139, 142, 147, 257
Brown, Mordecai "Three Finger" 28–30, 60, 67, 70–73, 86, 168, 177, 186; final match with Mathewson 275
Brush, John (owner of Giants) 60, 61, 73
Burns, George **85**, 152–154, 158, 163,

166–168, 175, 178–182, 185, 187, 189, 190, 265; death of 266

Bush, "Bullet" Joe *94*, 95, 98, 99, 103, 107, 109, 115, 117, 122–124, 126–129, 132, 135, 141, 143, 144, 265, 283, 284; death of 290; game three, 1913 series 237–244; traded to Red Sox 278, 289; traded to Yankees 289

Cady, Nick 118

Caldwell, Ray 135, 147

Carey, Max 179, 184, 189, 190

Carrigan, William "Red," "Rough" 114, 119, 138, 145, 281

Century Boat Club 101

Chadwick, Henry: death of 69

Chance, Frank 28, 30, 36, 66, 72, 73, 95, 96, 99, 124, 157, 213, 245; passing on Schang 112

Chapman, Ray 121, 130, 132, 141, 142

Chappell, Larry 123, 124, 129

Chase, Hal 96, 98, 100, 123, 134, 140

Chesbro, Jack 61

Cicotte, Eddie 122, 124, 129, *131*, 134, 139, 140

Clarke, Fred 71, 166, 181

Coakley, Andy 15, 16, 102; in 1905 series 63, 64

Cobb, Ty 20, 24, 37, 81, 103, *104*, 107, 108, 112, 113, 121, 122, 125, 132, 133, 168, 211, 269, 278; alleged fight with Nap Rucker 169

Cohan, George 5

Collins, Eddie 22, 24, 25, 28–33, 36–38, 82, 92, 93, *94*, 97, 99–101, 107, 108, *192*, *225*, *238*, 276, 278, 280, 285, 287, 294; death of 288; early life playing under name of Eddie Sullivan 102; leading hitter on team147; McGraw: "greatest player in world" 262; traded to White Sox 286

Collins, Jimmy 49

Collins, Ray 92, 95, 114, 120, 139

Columbia Park (Philadelphia) 10, 16; demolition of 23

Comiskey, Charles 29, 30, 245, 287, 288

Commercial Motion Picture Company 161

Connolly, Tom (umpire) *212*

Coombs, Jack *18*, 22, 25, 26, 28–33, 35, 36, 38, 82, 83, 92, 143, 147, 292; typhoid fever 93–95

Cooper, Claude 150, 152, 185, 266

Cottrell, Ensign 108

Crandall, Otis "Doc" 68, 70, 73, 78, 79,

81, 152, 156, 160, 163, *164*, 166, 170, 171, 174, 179, 182, 184, 186, 187, *243, 255*; death of 266; in 1913 series 241, 242

Cravath, Clifford "Gavy" (or "Gavvy") 92, 157, 158, 163, 172

Crawford, Sam 14, 20, 103, 108, 121, 122, 125, 145

Cree, William "Birdie" 96, 97, 106, 117

Cross, Lave 11, 16, 17, 22

Cruthers, Press 146

Dahlen, Bill 16, 58, 59, 64, 67, 155, 188, 189

Daley, Tom 94, 97, 107, 122, 137, 143, 146

Dauss, George "Hooks" 107, 121, 126, 133, 144

Davis, Harry 11, *12,* 20, 22, 27, 28, 30–33, 35, 54, 82, 83, *94*, 117, 142, 143

Delahanty, Ed 14

Demaree, Al 87, 149, *150*, 152–155, 157–161, 163, 167, 170, 171, 174–179, 181, 182, 184, 185, 187–189, 191; death of 266; fourth game, 1913 series 247–251

Devlin, Art 59, 64, 71, 73, 76, *77*, 79, 166

Devore, Josh 78, 88, 89, 152, 177; traded to Cincinnati 161

Dineen, Bill 56; umpire 117

"dirty" baseball, accusations of 43–45

Donlin, "Turkey Mike" 16, 53, 54, 61–64, 66, 68, 69, 73, 160; marriage to Mabel Hite 74

Dooin, Charley "Red" (manager of Phillies) 171, 172, 187

Doyle, Larry 35, 68, 73, 74, 76, 80, 81, 88, 89, 151, 153, 156, 162, 166, 167, 170–172, 174, 176, 184–186, 188–190, 192, *230*, 265, 266, 272; death of 267

Drucke, Louis 76–78

Dubuc, Jean 108, 121, 125, 132, 144

Duffy, Hugh 49

Dygert, Jimmy 17, 21, 22, 25, 26; sold to Baltimore 29

East Aurora Roycroft club 111–112

Egan, John "Rip" (umpire) *212*

Eisenhower, Pres. Dwight 5

Emslie, Bob (umpire) 44, 69, 71, 72

Engel, Joe 106, 137

Engle, Clyde 120, 139

Evans, Billy umpire 126

Evers, John 28, 30, 71, 72, 80, 157, 159, 165, 175, 176, 181, 185, 190, 269, 292

Falkenberg, Cy 103, 110, 112, 120, 128, 141

Feller, Bob 285

Ferguson, Charles 101, 136
Fisher, Ray 106, 117, 135, 147; coach at University of Michigan 101; role in 1919 World Series 100
Fletcher, Art 32, 33, 78, 79, 81, 82, 89, 151, 153, 160, 163, 165, 167, 170, 174, 175, 179–182, 185, 188–191, 276; death of 268; fined by National Commission 255, 258; signed by McGraw 166; Yankee coach 267
Flick, Elmer 11
Ford, Russ 97, 106, 117, 118
Foxx, Jimmie 282, 294, 295
Frazee, Harry: purchase of Boston Red Sox 280, 289
Frisch, Frankie 276, 277
Fritz, Harry 146
Fromme, Art 158, 163, 165–167, 170, 174, 177, 179, *180*, 181, 184, 186, 188–190, 192; traded to Giants 161
Fultz, Dave (president of baseball players fraternity) 209, 210, 287

Gaffney, John (manager Washington Nationals) 6, 7
Gandil, Arnold "Chick" 92, 98, 106, 115, 137, 138, 146
Gardner, Larry 91, 120, 139, 283
Gedeon, Joe 105
Gilhooley, Frank 135
Gilmore, Frank 6, 7
Goddard, Mary 40
Gowdy, Hank 79
Graham, Archibald "Moonlight" 65
Graney, Jack 112, 120, 121, 128, 130, 141
Grant, Eddie 159, 182, 187, 192, *254*; killed during war 268
Griffith, Clark 14, 58, 84
Grimes, Burleigh 267
Groh, Henry "Heinie" 164, 167, 176, 182, 191, 266; "bottle bat" 151; traded to Cincinnati 161
Groom, Bob 92, 106, 138

Hall, Charley 9 5, 138
Hall, Marc 122, 132
Hamilton, Billy 49
Hamilton, Earl "Lefty" 127, 128
Hanlon, Ned (manager Baltimore Orioles) 9, 43–45, 47, 49, 60; manager of Brooklyn 51; manager of Pittsburg [*sic*] 8
Hartley, Grover *164*, 165, 173, 189
Hartzell, Roy 107
Henriksen, Olaf 90, 102

Herrmann, Garry (owner of Cincinnati Reds) 213; member of National Commission 57
Herzog, Charles "Buck" 32, 33, 68, 73, 79, *80*, 151, 153, 155, 158, 159, 162, 167, 172–174, 180, 181, 184, 185, 188, 275, 276; death of 269
"Hey Barney" affair 62
Heydler, John 75
Hofman, Art 28, 72; death of 271
Hogan, William 6
Hooper, Harry 88, 89, 91, 92, 113, 114, 118–120
Houck, Byron 37, *94*, 95, 97, 98, *99*, 101, 103, 106, 107, 109, 113, 114, 116–118, 120, 122, 123, 129, 130, 138, 140, 142–144, 146, 147
Hoyt, Waite 285
Huggins, Miller 161, *162*, 191; manager of Yankees 267, 282, 285
Hughes, Tom 97, 106

injunction against Mack's players 11

Jackson, "Shoeless" Joe 22, 28, 37, 101, *110*, 113, 121, 128, 132, 287
James, Bill 162
Janvrin, Hal 93
Jennings, Hugh 24, 27, 44, 47, 50, 51, 54, 211
Johnson, Ban 13, 53, 54, 56–58, 61; founding of American League 9
Johnson, Walter 27, 36, 92, 97, 106, 107, 115, 137, 140, 223, 277; "One monumental whack" 136
Jones, Sam, and part ownership of Athletics 10

Kahler, George 111, 120, 121, 128
Keating, Ray 96, 98, 100, 106, 118
Keeler, "Wee Willie" 14, 44–46, 48–51, 57, 76; final season 78
Kelley, Joe 44–46, 48, 50, 51, 57, 61
Kelly, George "Highpockets" 276
Kenney, Bert (manager of Olean, NY, team) 40
Kerr, Dickie 100
Klem, Bill 35, 62, 72, 151, 154, 159, 160, *212*
Kling, Johnny 29, 30, 73, 177
Kuhn, Bowie 101

Lajoie, Nap 56, 113, 121, 128, 130, 141; signing by Mack 11
Lake, Joe 108

Lancaster, Burt: appearance in *Field of Dreams* 65
Land, Grover 110
Landis, Kenesaw Mountain 101
Lannin, Joseph (owner of Boston Red Sox) 280
Lapp, Jack 26, 33, 34, 84, 93, **94**, 98, 101, 102, *105*, 108, 115, 118, 120, 125, 126, 132, 138, 141, 143, 145, 286; death of 281; early career 106
Lathan, Arlie 43
Lavan, Johnny "Doc" 134, 146
Lawson, Alfred 41
Leonard, Hubert "Dutch" 119, 120, 145, 146
Leverenz, Walt 109, 134, 144
Lewis, George "Duffy" 88, 91, 92, 113, 114, 118, 139
Lincoln, Abraham 5
Livingston, Patrick "Paddy" 26, 106
Luderus, Fred 155, 157, 163, 187; "with a pair of shoulders like Zbyszco..." 154
Lynch, Thomas (president of National League) 177, 187

MacArthur, Douglas 270
Mack, Connie (Cornelius McGillicuddy) *21*, *37*, 54, 81–84, 92, **94**, 101, 265, 278, 279, 281–283, 288–293; Athletic dynasties 294; death of 295; family and early life 5–7; first American League championship 14; investment in Players League 7; manager Milwaukee Creams/Brewers 9; manager/part owner Philadelphia Athletics 9–11; marriage to Margaret Hogan 6; 1910 series championship vs. Cubs 28–30; 1911 series championship vs. Giants 32–35; player/manager with Pittsburg [*sic*] 8, 9; sale of Athletics 295; sell-off of players 294; tributes 295, 296; with Washington Nationals 6, 7
Mack, Earle (son) 8
Mack, Roy (son) 8
Mack, Tom (Connie's brother) 93
Magee, Sherry 92
Maine, USS, explosion in Havana harbor 50
Mann, James 213
Maranville, Walter "Rabbit" 187, 211
Marlin, Texas 76, 151; choice as Giants training site 68
Marquard, Richard "Rube" 32–34, 73–76, 81, 151, 159, 161–163, 165, 167, 170, 171, 173, 176, 178, 180–182, 184–191, *216*, 281, 289; controversy over Frank Baker home run 83, 84; death of 274; first game in

1913 series 211–221; labeled as $11,000 lemon 78; origin of name 273; reliever in fourth game 1913 series 251–256; sold to Brooklyn 274
Mathewson, Christy 57–61, 66–69, 73–75, 78, 85, 87, 149, 153, 156, 158, 161, 164, 165, 167, 169–172, 175–179, 181, 183–192, *236*, 266, 269, 275, 277, 281, 289, 291; controversy with Marquard 83, 84; death of 276; early career 168; exposed to poison gas during war 275; fifth game 1913 series 257–264; in 1911 series 81–83; in second game, 1913 series 223–233; 1911 season 79–81; 1911 World's Series 32–35; pitching in 1905 series 63, 64; pitching in 1912 World's Series 87–91; three shutouts in 1905 World's Series 15–17; traded to Cincinnati 274
Mathewson, Henry 65, 66
Mattick, Wally 113
McAvoy, Wickey 146
McConnell, George 117
McCormick, Harry "Moose" 61, 71, 72, 74, 76, 89, 154, 155, 159, 163, 171, 174, 184, 269; death of 270; teammate of Mathewson at Bucknell 160
McGann, Dan 62, 64, 65, 67–69
McGillicuddy, Margaret Hogan (wife of Joe) 6, 8
McGillicuddy, Mary McKillop (mother of Joe) 5, 24
McGillicuddy, Michael (father of Joe) 5
McGinnity, Joe "Iron Man" 15, 17, 51–54, 57, 60–63, 66, 68–70, 72, 289; release from Giants 73, 74
McGrath (McGraw) (father) 39
McGraw, Blanche Sindall (second wife) 55
McGraw, Ellen Comerfort (mother) 39; death 40
McGraw, John Joseph 13, 14, 32, 34–36, 147, *162*, *212*, 265, 267, 269, 270, 271, 273, 276; fight with Ad Brennan 171–173; ill health and death 277, 278; marriage to Blanche Sindall *55*; 1905 World's Series 16–17; 1911 league championship season 78–81; 1912 league championship season 85–87; 1912 World's Series 87–91; pre-professional career 39–40; refusal to play 1904 World's Series 60–62; retired as manager 277; signed to manage New York Giants 56, 57; vs. Athletics in 1905 series 63–65; vs. Mack in 1911 series

81–84; with Baltimore Orioles 42–56;
with Cedar Rapids Canaries 42
McGraw, Minnie Doyle (first wife) 48;
death 52
McInnis, John "Stuffy" 12, 30, 32, 35, 37,
92, 38, *94*, 97, 100, 101, 103, 106, 107,
192, *225*, 282; death of 284; obtained
from New England League 23; traded to
Red Sox 283
McKean, "Big Ed" 41
McKechnie, Bill 96, 99, 274
McLean, "Long Larry" 182, *183*, 184, 185,
188, *236*; shot to death 265
McMahon, John "Sadie" 45–48, 152
Meriden (Connecticut State League) 6
Merkle, Fred 35, 68, 78–81, 85, 86, 90,
150–152, 155, 159, 163, 168, 171, 174–178,
180, 185–187, 190–192, 269; death of 271;
early life 166, 167; injured in 1913 series
opener 219; Merkle "boner" 70–72
Meusel, Bob 276
Meusel, Irish 276
Meyers, John "Chief" 32, 33, 74, 81, 83,
88, 89, 154, 165, 167, 172, 174, 175, 178,
181, 186–188, 192, *195*, 270; death of 271;
injury prior to second game, 1913 series
223
Milan, Clyde 98, 115, *116*, 136–138
Mitchell, Bill 110
Mitchell, Roy 124, 142
Moeller, Danny 115, 136
Moriarity, George 108, 126
Mullane, Tony 43, 45
Mullin, George 104, 107, 115
Murderer's Row (original) 282
Murphy, Danny 12, 16, 18, 23, 26, 27–29,
31, 36, 45, 64, *94*, 100, 109, 114, 117, 122,
123, 126, *212*
Murphy, Eddie 33, 93, *94*, 97, 101, 102,
103, 107, 108, 115, 118, 147, *192*, *224*, 288;
death of 289
Murray, John "Red" 74, 76, 81, 82, 88, 90,
152, 161, 165, 167, 170, 173–177, 179–181,
186–189; death of 271

National Commission to oversee major
leagues 57
New England League 168
New York-Pennsylvania League 40
Nichols, Charles "Kid" 49, 50, 59

O'Brien, Thomas "Buck" 88, 95, 123
O'Day, Hank 16, 163; and Merkle's "boner"
71, 72

Oldring, Reuben "Rube" 22, 27–29, 35,
37, 83, *94*, 95, 97, 98, 101, 103, 104, 107,
108, *201*, 286; death of 280; released 279
O'Loughlin, "Silk" 20, 88, 101, 102, 113
$100,000 (One Hundred Thousand Dollar)
infield 30, 192, 200
O'Rourke, "Orator" Jim 61
Orr, Billy *94*, 132, 143

Paskert, George "Dode" 92
Pathé Frères Motion Picture Company 161
Peckinpaugh, Roger 107
Peffer, Monte 146
Pennock, Herb 36, 93, 98, 103, 138, 140,
142, *143*, 144–146
Pfiester, Jack 28, 71, 73
Philadelphia Athletics: clinching of 1913
pennant 144–145
Plank, Eddie 14–16, 20–22, 24, 26–28, 32,
33, 37, 92, 93, *94*, 97, 98, 100, 102, 103,
104, 106–108, 110, 111, 114–118, 120,
124–128, 130, 132, 134, 138–140, 147, 168,
225, 265, 290; death of 291; Federal
League 291; fifth game 1913 series
257–264; first 20 victory season 13; in
1905 series 63, 64; in second game, 1913
series 222–233; signed by Mack 11
players' share from 1913 series 262
Polo Grounds *214*, 276, 277; loss of New
York Giants 296
Powers, Mike "Doc" 11, 17, 63, 105; death
of 23
Pulliam, Harry 59, 62, 63, 69; president of
National League 57; suicide of 75

Quigley, Ernie umpire 184

Rariden, Bill 152
Rath, Morris 122–124
Raymond, Arthur "Bugs" 76, 78, 161;
problems with liquor 74, 75; release and
death of 80, 87; suspended by McGraw
77
Redford, Robert (as Roy Hobbs, character
in *The Natural*) 100
Richter, Francis (official scorer) 212
Rickey, Branch 277; debut as manager 142
Rigler, Charley (umpire) 156, 175, 185,
190, *212*
Rixey, Eppa 171, 173
Robinson, Wilbert 43–45, 47, 50, 53, 86,
88, 273; tutelage of Marquard 79
Robison, Frank and Stanley (brothers) 53;
owners of St. Louis Browns 51